Cryptoeconomics

The book offers a succinct overview of the technical components of blockchain networks, also known as distributed digital ledger networks. Written from an academic perspective, it surveys ongoing research challenges as well as existing literature. Several chapters illustrate how the mathematical tools of game theory and algorithmic mechanism design can be applied to the analysis, design, and improvement of blockchain network protocols. Using an engineering perspective, insights are provided into how the economic interests of different types of participants shape the behaviors of blockchain systems. Readers are thus provided with a paradigm for developing blockchain consensus protocols and distributed economic mechanisms that regulate the interactions of system participants, thus leading to desired cooperative behaviors in the form of system equilibria. This book will be a vital resource for students and scholars of this budding field.

Dr. Jing Li is a Blockchain Security Engineer at CertiK. She received a PhD in Electrical and Computer Engineering from the University of Houston in 2022, and a BS and MS in Computer Science from North China Electric Power University, Beijing, China, in 2014 and 2018, respectively. Her research interests include security and incentive in blockchain systems, game theory, and applied cryptography.

Dr. Dusit Niyato is a professor and IEEE fellow at the School of Computer Science and Engineering at Nanyang Technological University, Singapore. He received a PhD in Electrical and Computer Engineering from the University of Manitoba, Canada, in 2008. His research interests include the Internet of Things (IoT), machine learning, and incentive mechanism design.

Dr. Zhu Han is the John and Rebecca Moores Professor in the Department of Electrical and Computer Engineering at the University of Houston. A winner of the 2021 IEEE Kiyo Tomiyasu Award, he has been an IEEE fellow since 2014 and an AAAS fellow since 2020. Since 2017, his published research ranks among the top 1 percent most cited in the field, according to Web of Science.

Cryptoeconomics

Economic Mechanisms Behind Blockchains

JING LI
University of Houston

DUSIT NIYATO
Nanyang Technological University, Singapore

ZHU HAN
University of Houston

CAMBRIDGE
UNIVERSITY PRESS

Shaftesbury Road, Cambridge CB2 8EA, United Kingdom

One Liberty Plaza, 20th Floor, New York, NY 10006, USA

477 Williamstown Road, Port Melbourne, VIC 3207, Australia

314–321, 3rd Floor, Plot 3, Splendor Forum, Jasola District Centre, New Delhi – 110025, India

103 Penang Road, #05–06/07, Visioncrest Commercial, Singapore 238467

Cambridge University Press is part of Cambridge University Press & Assessment, a department of the University of Cambridge.

We share the University's mission to contribute to society through the pursuit of education, learning and research at the highest international levels of excellence.

www.cambridge.org
Information on this title: www.cambridge.org/9781316515785
DOI: 10.1017/9781009026611

First published 2023

A catalogue record for this publication is available from the British Library

Library of Congress Cataloging-in-Publication Data

Names: Li, Jing, 1992- author. | Niyato, Dusit, author. | Han, Zhu, 1974- author.
Title: Cryptoeconomics : economic mechanisms behind blockchains / Jing Li, Dusit Niyato, and Zhu Han.
Description: Cambridge, United Kingdom : Cambridge University Press, [2023] | Includes bibliographical references and index.
Identifiers: LCCN 2023027695 (print) | LCCN 2023027696 (ebook) | ISBN 9781316515785 (hardback) | ISBN 9781009026611 (epub)
Subjects: LCSH: Cryptocurrencies. | Blockchains (Databases)–Economic aspects.
Classification: LCC HG1710.3 .L52 2023 (print) | LCC HG1710.3 (ebook) | DDC 332.4–dc23/eng/20230719
LC record available at https://lccn.loc.gov/2023027695
LC ebook record available at https://lccn.loc.gov/2023027696

ISBN 978-1-316-51578-5 Hardback

To our future – Jing Li

To my parents – Dusit Niyato

To those who can get benefits from Web3.0 – Zhu Han

Contents

1   Introduction

As the core technology of the Bitcoin project [1], blockchain attracts various researchers from all walks of life. Most previous research preferred to construe the blockchain as a decentralized ledger, focusing on the technology components. In the past decade, there has been a surge in research activities that focus on the behaviors driven by economic principles regarding a decentralized digital ledger from different scales. Historically, the blockchain protocols were first implemented heuristically within the engineering community, and the theoretical analysis of these protocols appeared at a later time.

For this reason, there still exist a number of gaps between the engineering practices and the theoretical proofs or analyses of those protocols in terms of security, decentralization, efficiency, and other related performance indices. These theoretical gaps lead to the need of the following.

1. Reaching the consensus regarding the scope of challenges and problems faced by the protocol or mechanism design of blockchain networks, and then finding a viable paradigm of protocol modeling and design that guarantees secure operation of the target blockchain networks.
2. Investigating the interaction between a blockchain protocol and its peripheral systems or networks which overlay or underlay upon the blockchain network; furthermore, provision of the theoretical analysis with respect to different performance indices for a distributed ledger system including security, scalability, and service efficiency.
3. Providing a theoretical insight into the emerging applications of blockchain technologies in a plethora of areas, and, more importantly, supplementing a series of mathematical tools that are able quantitatively to analyze the dynamics of these blockchain-based approaches, especially from a (behavioral) economics perspective.

With the aforementioned major goals in mind, this book aims to categorize the building technologies of blockchains in a stack of protocols and mechanisms that defines the interaction among nodes in the ledger networks and service-related entities or stakeholders. Such an approach of behavior abstraction emphasizes the fundamental characteristics of agent rationality in distributed systems, and then creates a paradigm of ledger protocol design based on the mathematical tools of game theory, algorithmic mechanism design, optimization theory, and contract or portfolio theory. The proposed paradigm helps to transform the interpretation of blockchain technologies, from its technical basis of computer networking and cryptography (e.g., those focusing on data communication and security) to the new perspective of a financial–social-economic network. By doing so, we are able theoretically to deal with different parties or agents involved in the blockchain networks, for example, adversaries for security modeling and rational entities for performance evaluation, with a layered but consistent framework of analysis. Such a framework of study also leads to the following main objectives of this book.

- The book provides a succinct overview of the technical components of the blockchain networks (equivalently, distributed digital ledger networks). Based on these building blocks, we dedicate seven chapters to how the mathematical tools of game theory and algorithmic mechanism design can be applied to the analysis, design, and improvement of the blockchain network protocols. In particular, from an engineering perspective of economic theory, we provide an in-depth insight into how the economic interests of different types of participants in the blockchain system shape the way of their behaviors. Consequently, by properly designing the distributed economic mechanism that regulates the interactions of the system participant, we provide a paradigm for designing the blockchain consensus protocols, which lead the blockchain network as a whole to the desired joint behaviors in the form of system equilibria.
- In addition to the economic theoretic analysis of the consensus protocols in blockchain networks, we extend our study to the more complex economic systems that are either embedded into a blockchain network, or use the blockchain network as a component subsystem. With such extended studies, we not only provide a generic and consistent framework of ecosystem analysis from the perspective of economic theory (more precisely, microeconomics theory), but also supply the readers with an extended mathematical toolbox for blockchain system analysis and design. Such an approach, in particular, emphasizes the expressiveness and power of game-theoretical analyses. We provide a series of case studies to illustrate the incorporated approaches that emphasize the importance of both theoretical analysis and engineering implementation.
- The book also provides an extensive overview of both the prevalent blockchain networks and the emerging blockchain applications in the form of a series of case studies. These case studies help the readers to understand how the blockchain network protocols evolve as the target performance indices changes at the designing stage of the protocol, and, with different economic preference, how a particular set of blockchain protocols can be adapted to meet the requirement of service provision in different scenarios.

We believe that the proposed book is useful to a variety of readers, particularly those from the computer science and computer networking fields, as well as those with an economics background. The materials from this book can be used to guide the development of more efficient, scalable, and robust blockchain protocols as well as the deployment of the blockchain applications in related domains. The target audience for this book is the researchers, engineers, and undergraduate and graduate students who are looking for a source to learn the technical framework of blockchain networks, and those who need theoretical guidance in mechanism design of distributed blockchain networks and other systems alike.

1.1 Two Camps: Computer Science Problem and Incentive Mechanism Problem

The advent of blockchain technology benefits a wide range of areas, including finance, business, transportation, and entertainment. Blockchain is the technology that was first proposed in the Bitcoin project, followed by extensive research and application. Owing to the sophistication and diversity of the blockchain system, the interpretation of blockchain is manifested into two camps [2].

1. Blockchain is a solution to computer science problems. The first camp mainly focuses on (a) consensus analysis, (b) cryptography application, and (c) distributed system design.
2. Blockchain is a solution to incentive mechanism design problems. The second camp primarily focuses on (a) economics analysis and (b) game theory and equilibrium.

In earlier research of blockchain, the first camp had made enormous contributions to the technical components. It is worth noting that blockchain is not a single new technology but a combination of multiple technologies. The springing up and brisk developing of computer and network technologies directly promoted the blockchain evolution.

The concept of blockchain was first outlined in 1991 [3]. Stuart Haber and W. Scott Stornetta presented the fundamental notion of blockchain, a chain of hashed records, to address the time-stamping problem, the embryonic form of data structure in the blockchain, while not defining the name "blockchain." Then, in 1997, Adam Back created Hashcash [4], a Proof of Work (PoW) mechanism for email antispam and anti-DoS (denial of service) that has since formed the foundation for most cryptocurrency projects. A brief history of blockchain is shown in Fig. 1.1.

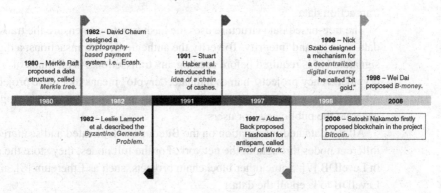

Figure 1.1 Origins of blockchain.

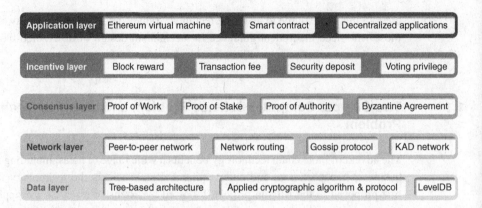

Figure 1.2 Five layers of blockchain technology.

Until the advent of Bitcoin in January 2009, the blockchain had its first real-world application. According to bitcoin's white paper [1], "Bitcoin: A peer-to-peer electronic currency system," Satoshi Nakamoto adopted cryptography and Proof of Work (PoW) in the Bitcoin network to ensure data security and consistency and introduced incentive mechanisms to allow transactions to be completed without the involvement of a third party, ushering in a new era of decentralization.

To better understand the second camp, we first give a rough description of blockchain technical components from the first camp perspective. As a collection of technologies, blockchain is composed of a set of interdependent and interrelated components. To facilitate the description, we adopt the recognized five-layer architecture (shown in Fig. 1.2), and explain the components and layers in the following.

- **Data layer:** The data structure of most conventional blockchains is described as a linked chain of blocks in which transactions are organized in a sequential manner. In addition to Bitcoin, various PoW-based blockchain projects also use chain structure to manage the blocks. Each block of Bitcoin includes a Merkle hash tree [5], which is a tree-based data structure of transaction hashes. The root hash of tree is obtained by calculating the leaf nodes, which refer to the hashes of transaction data.

  The tree-based data structure uses the hash function to ensure the transaction data security and integrity. To verify the authenticity of transactions, a digital signature [6] is required before sending any transaction. As all kinds of cryptocurrency projects' names indicate, "crypto" means that these projects must rely on cryptography for security. Bitcoin uses an elliptical-curve cryptography to generate the public keys for users.

  All the data and information on the Bitcoin are duplicated and scattered in different nodes throughout the network. For the full nodes, they store the metadata in LevelDB [7]. Some other blockchain projects, such as Ethereum [8], also utilize LevelDB to keep all the data.

- **Network layer:** The network layer refers to the network model, network routing protocols, as well as some other communication protocols. The public blockchain is built upon a peer-to-peer (P2P) network, in which each node joins by connecting to some other nodes. A P2P network consists of a group of computers or clients that communicate with each other. The term "peer" means that every node is treated equally in the network. There is no centralized party with nodes. The peer nodes serve both as providers of resources and as consumers of services. The distributed and decentralized P2P network is the foundation of blockchain.

The network layer functions are almost carried out by the P2P network. In addition to mining and transferring value, some blockchain nodes also have the same functions as P2P nodes. To participate in the network, all nodes must have the routing function [9], which helps them to share information with each other. The most often used unstructured P2P network protocol is the gossip protocol [10]. After a miner generates a block, the others will broadcast the result and block via a gossip protocol. Bitcoin changed the way it distributed gossip messages in 2015 to improve privacy. It currently employs a technique known as "diffusion" [11]. Another well-known communication protocol is called the Kademlia (KAD) protocol [12]. The KAD network refers to a P2P network that implements the KAD protocol. As a more efficient protocol, some blockchain projects adopt the KAD network as their network layer to enable the blocks and transactions transmission optimization [13].

- **Consensus layer:** The consensus layer specifies the rules for nodes to reach an agreement on blockchain's state. The popular consensus protocols include the Proof of Work (PoW) in Bitcoin and the Proof of Stake (PoS) in Ethereum. To illustrate the consensus layer, we discuss the PoW algorithm here as it is the most common algorithm for permissionless blockchains, used by Bitcoin [1]. Taking PoW as an example, the protocol determines who is eligible to create a new block, the time slot between two contiguous blocks, and stipulates all nodes to work on the longest chain. Different consensus algorithms employ various principles to determine the rules for nodes based on their actual needs. Ethereum is now experiencing the transition from PoW to PoS since PoW is energy intensive and costly [14]. Unlike PoW's elite hardware requirements, PoS only needs participants to stake some cryptocurrencies to the main chain. The creator of each block is selected randomly, similar to the miners of PoW, and is responsible for finalizing transactions and working on the longest chain [15]. Some other protocols can be referred to Proof of Authority [16] and Byzantine Agreement [17].

- **Incentive layer:** The incentives layer establishes an incentive system using the blockchain's cryptocurrency. In the initial design of Bitcoin, the incentives refer to block reward and transaction fee, incentivizing the miners to work on the longest chain and encouraging the other participants to finalize the blockchain's ledger. From the Bitcoin project it is clear that any permissionless blockchain system requires an incentive strategy to keep it running. Miners should be appropriately compensated for their effort, and incentives should push them to act honestly. As the nexus to bind the different technologies to form the blockchain, incentives are apparently less discussed by the first camp whereas they have been emphasized and characterized by the second camp. Ethereum proposed the concept of the security deposit in their Casper protocol [18], which will be one of the most essential incentive components in Ethereum 2.0. According to the latest update of staking deposit requirements on the Ethereum website, everyone needs to stake some ethers to the network before joining the Ethereum [19]. Moreover, anyone who wants to become a full validator must stake 32 ethers. Another crucial incentive is the voting privilege, which is less used in PoW-based blockchain but indispensable to PoS-based blockchain. The reason is that PoS protocols rely on voting mechanisms to reach consensus [20]. Incentives are the focus of this book. We further illustrate the details in Chapters 3 and 4.

- **Application layer:** The application layer includes Ethereum Virtual Machine, smart contracts, decentralized apps (Dapps), and so on. The Ethereum Virtual Machine is a software framework that allows developers to construct Ethereum-based decentralized applications (Dapps). All Ethereum accounts' data and smart contracts codes are stored on this virtual machine [21]. Similar to the Ethereum accounts (also known as the externally owned account), smart contracts are also a type of account (contract account). The smart contract is a collection of codes with a unique address or account, which can be created by any developers and can operate automatically on Ethereum [22]. The Dapps that interface with the blockchain network make up the most important part of the application layer. These Dapps interoperate with the blockchain network via application programming interfaces (APIs). Unlike the traditional apps (centralized apps), the Dapps run on a decentralized network environment and often require the users to interact with the developer's smart contract to get the download permits. Applications can send instructions to all the underlying layers, which enables all layers to cooperate with each other to perform more advanced functions.

The first camp is much bigger than the second camp. One main reason is that many techniques of blockchain have existed for decades. The researchers in computer science have an abundance of reference literature and research experiences due to years of accumulation. Although the blockchain has remained the focus of both the industry and academia for almost a decade, most of the available literature on blockchains is still at a stage of targeting the audiences who are mainly interested in obtaining the hands-on experience of blockchain implementation. There are only a handful of books for researchers, engineers, and graduate or undergraduate students to understand theoretically the dynamics in economic incentives of blockchain networks from a comprehensive and in-depth perspective. For this reason, there is an urgent need to develop a comprehensive reference to provide a systematic treatment of the following.

1. How blockchain incentives can be modeled, designed, and analyzed.
2. What the impact of the incentives on protocols design will be.
3. How it can be further improved or incorporated into various emerging distributed applications, and with what techniques.

In Section 1.2, we introduce the second camp, which formulates a new concept called "Cryptoeconomics." This nomenclature represents the fact that cryptoeconomics is an area of interdisciplinary research, which requires researchers to possess a variety of research backgrounds, including (but not limited to) cryptography and economic mechanism design, etc.

1.2   Cryptoeconomics Camp

Compared with the abundant research of camp one, scant attention has been paid to the incentive mechanism design for distributed systems. A sophisticated blockchain system requires multi-dimensional design, not only from the computer science perspective but also from the mechanism design perspective.

The computer science content determines the existence of a blockchain framework. Simultaneously, the incentive mechanism improves the system performance by regulating participants' behaviors and coordinating all operations through the costs and benefits. Researchers have gradually realized that computer science and economic incentives are inextricable inside a blockchain system as the technologies evolve. In order to develop blockchain technology in an all-around way, none of the parts can be studied independently.

1.2.1   Definitions and Explanations

Ethereum founder Vlad Zamfir first defined cryptoeconomics as "A formal discipline that studies protocols that govern the production, distribution, and consumption of goods and services in a decentralized digital economy" [23]. The other versions of definition are listed as follows: "Cryptoeconomics is the application of incentive mechanism design to information security problems" [2]. Zamfir identified that cryptoeconomics has played a crucial role in distributed systems, that is, to encourage more entries and to incentivize the desired behaviors. Vitalik Buterin expounded on the concept as "Cryptoeconomics is about building systems that have certain desired properties, use cryptography to prove properties about messages that happened in the past, use economic incentives defined inside the system to encourage desired properties to hold into the future" [24]. Josh Stark proposed that "Cryptoeconomics is the practical science of using economic mechanisms to build distributed systems, where the financial incentives guarantee essential properties of that system and where the economic mechanisms are guaranteed by cryptography" [25]. He presented the most detailed explanation regarding the keywords of this definition as follows.

- Practical science: Bitcoin, PoW, Ethereum, PoS, State Channels, Plasma, Sharding, etc., are the applications of cryptoeconomics. Any incentive mechanism involved a blockchain system is designed upon the science of cryptoeconomics.
- Using economic mechanisms to build distributed systems: Cryptoeconomics has most in common with mechanism design. Mechanism design is also called "reverse game theory." An applicable economic mechanism for distributed system requires the abilities of making rules of participation, realizing microincentives, designing the scalable incentives, and being easy to execute in a leaderless environment.

- The important properties of that protocol are guaranteed by financial incentives: A consensus protocol functioning smoothly requires there are proper financial incentives compensating participants' costs due to working on the issued tasks. Without participants' efforts on accomplishing tasks, there will be no security guarantee in a leaderless system. Hence, the insecure system will be deemed as having no market value.
- The economic mechanisms are guaranteed by cryptography: Cryptography and cryptographic protocols are the underlying fundamentals of a blockchain network which provide secure and trusted platforms and protect all mechanisms from potential attacks. Economic incentives refer to the monetary subsidies and attributed privileges for the participants who accomplish tasks as required. Cryptography can provide protection from abuse and interruption, thus ensuring the mechanisms will operate normally.

We conclude the interpretation of cryptoeconomics concept in two ways.

- It provides the theoretical interpretation, from the perspective of untrusted economic networks, of the consensus protocols assisted by cryptographical functionalities in decentralized blockchain networks regarding the activities of the entities in the network and the dynamics of the network as a whole.
- It extends the analytical framework based on the economic networking point of view to modeling, designing, and analyzing the participant interactions in any ecosystem that is extended from or build upon blockchain networks.

Therefore, on one hand, the behavioral analysis from the economic perspective of the blockchain networks answers a series of fundamental questions regarding cryptography and distributed system security. Such an analytical approach plays a vital role in designing appropriate protocols in digital ledger networks, especially for those built upon massive P2p networks without an explicit governance infrastructure. On the other hand, from the engineering perspective, a well-functioning, scalable cryptoeconomic network is able to serve as an efficient platform for decision arbitration and allocation of the resources ranging from physical utilities (e.g., hardware) to financial assets, and, more broadly, various conceptual resources including data, trust, and social attention (e.g., votes). As a result, the convergence of computer networking, cryptography, and economic theory sheds light on better characterization of the decentralized or self-organized systems particularly relying upon the advance of the blockchain technologies, as depicted in Fig. 1.3. This, in return, requires a comprehensive study of the technical building blocks, such as consensus protocols, incentive mechanisms, cryptographic and networking functionalities, and all the related primitives from an interdisciplinary perspective.

Despite the similarities between cryptoeconomics and incentive mechanisms, the differences are certainly worth studying. Cryptoeconomics provides more of an alternative framework for analyzing decentralized projects with incentives. The second

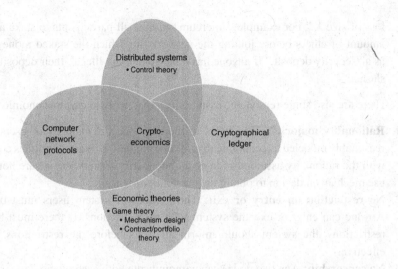

Figure 1.3 Cryptoeconomics as an interdisciplinary analytical framework.

camp proposed a collection of primitives under the cryptoeconomics framework, providing another angle of interpretation regarding the existing cryptoeconomics applications. We will introduce the details in the following section.

1.2.2 Concepts, Assumptions, and Models

For better analyzing the efficiency and equilibrium of cryptoeconomic outcomes, Vitalik Buterin proposed some crucial concepts that can be referred to as the following [24].

1. **Cryptoeconomics resource:** This is the incentives that a system can distribute to the participants, and the computation power that the participants can contribute to the system. For example, tokens for block generation, or the hash power of individual computer.
2. **Cryptoeconomics security margin:** This is an amount of money X such that a user can prove "either a given guarantee G is satisfied, or those at fault for violating G are poorer than they otherwise would have been by at least X." In brief, a cryptoeconomics security margin indicates the fraction of all cryptoeconomics resources that an attacker would need to take over the whole network. For example, if a blockchain network can resist a 51% attack, then we would say that the security margin is 0.5, and the guarantee G is "no double-spending." It means that if an attacker wants to launch a double-spending attack, he or she must have at least one half of the total hashing power (i.e., cryptoeconomics resource).
3. **Cryptoeconomics proof:** This is a message signed by an actor that can be interpreted as "I certify that either P is true. Otherwise, I have to suffer an economic

loss of size X." For example, Ethereum requires all participants to stake a certain amount of ethers before joining the network, for which the staked money serves as a "security deposit." If anyone has done something illegal, their deposit will be slashed.

There are also some reasonable assumptions that apply to cryptoeconomics [26].

1. **Rationality majority:** This refers to the case that the majority of users can be reasonably modeled as economically rational entities. This assumption is consistent with the rationality assumption in economic theory. Otherwise, we are not able to use mechanism design to obtain the economic incentives.
2. **No restriction on entry or exit:** The number of system users must be large. Anyone can enter or exit the system with no restrictions. If there must be some restrictions, the system should inform all users before the restrictions become effective.
3. **No censorship:** Any two nodes can communicate with each other.
4. **Anonymous:** The anonymous users cannot have their real identities revealed. The core natures of blockchain should not be compromised.

These assumptions are the basis for designing cryptoeconomics applications. Security models differ from the assumptions since various applications may have different security models and margins [24]. However, all the cryptoeconomics applications should follow the same assumptions mentioned.

1. **Uncoordinated choice model:** A model that assumes that all participants in a protocol do not coordinate with each other and have separate incentives, and are all smaller than size X.
2. **Coordinated choice model:** A model that assumes that all actors in a protocol are controlled by the same agent.
3. **Bribing attacker model:** An attack is capable of making payments to participants conditional of them taking certain actions.
   - Budget: The amount that the briber must be willing to pay in order to execute a particular strategy
   - Cost: The amount that the briber actually does pay if the strategy succeeds.
4. **Fault attribution:** This is a process by which an incentive mechanism infers which strategies were taken by the players in the network and is a nascent field of study that addresses realistic issues faced by any open or public distributed system.
   - It helps us penalize players who did not play the strategy intended by the mechanism.
   - It makes easy to have robust coalitional dominant strategy equilibrium.

These components consist of the cryptoeconomics analysis framework. So what is the outcome criterion of cryptoeconomics research? According to Ethereum Foundation's talk [27], a good outcome should meet the following requirements.

1. Easier exchange: The incentive must have good liquidity and be liquidated very quickly.

2. Trustless trades: The trades can be processed without a third party.
3. Liquidity for small markets: The liquidity of outcomes should not be limited or impacted by market size.

A key conclusion of the talk is that if the mechanism cannot help the system know your customers (KYC) better and always leads to the rich getting richer, then a bad outcome would always exist. Unfortunately, a considerable amount of research using game theory and economics theory cannot achieve fairness as expected.

A better mechanism should be as simple as possible, therefore reducing the dependency on parameter selection. Moreover, the mechanism must be feasible and easy to implement in a distributed and decentralized system.

As blockchain technology evolves, more and more researchers have been making strides in academic research and commercial applications, demonstrating that cryptoeconomics promises to provide sufficient stability, persistence, and robustness. The success of cryptoeconomics applications corroborates Buterin's point and enriches the related conceptual architecture.

1.2.3 Case Studies: Bitcoin and Schelling Coins

Bitcoin is acknowledged as the first P2P digital currency payment system due to its underlying technology, which refers to a decentralized and distributed database comprising various components. As the first application of cryptoeconomics system, we can say the following.

1. Bitcoin uses PoW consensus to resist Sybil attack.
2. Bitcoin uses block rewards and transaction fees to compensate miners for their effort, and to incentivize them to work on the longest chain.
3. Most of Bitcoin's users are honest and rational.
4. Bitcoin has no access restriction. Anyone can enter or exit the network at any time.
5. Any two Bitcoin users can communicate with each other relatively quickly.
6. Users in Bitcoin network are anonymous, and there is no way to restore users' real identities.

Therefore, as a decentralized system that is embedded with an incentive mechanism, Bitcoin is the canonical example of a cryptoeconomics application. The cryptoeconomics resource of Bitcoin refers to the hashing power which is required by PoW. Bitcoin is apparently grounded on the cryptoeconomics assumptions, as discussed in Section 1.2.2. Using the concepts and security models, Table 1.1 describes the interpretations of a Bitcoin project under the cryptoeconomics analysis framework [24].

Another canonical example of cryptoeconomics is Schelling Coin. Schelling Coins are a decentralized oracle construction. The underlying mechanism relies on a game-theoretic concept known as Schelling points, which was proposed by Thomas Schelling in his paper [28]. The way it works is as follows. Suppose two strangers are in different rooms and have not communicated beforehand. They need to pick up the same number from a set of numbers: **10000 34592 45183 40569 857**. If successful, both of them will

Table 1.1 A new interpretation of Bitcoin.

Model	Parameters	Security margin
Honest majority	Honest users are more than or equal to 2/3 of total users	0.5
Uncoordinated majority	The coordinated users account for less than 1/2 of total users	0.25
Coordinated majority	The coordinated users account for up to 100 percent of total users	0
Bribing attacker	Budget >(block reward + tx_fees)*number_of_blocks.	0

get rewards. Otherwise, they will be punished. In theory, each number has the same probability of being selected. However, in practice, the probability of selecting **10000** is far greater than the others. The reason is that **10000** looks much more special than the others. The uniqueness results in a natural convergence point.

A similar working process happens in Schelling Coin [29].

1. During an even-numbered block, all users can submit a hash of the ETH or USD price together with their Ethereum address.
2. During the following block, users can submit the value whose hash they provided in the previous block.
3. Define the "correctly submitted values" as all values N where H(N+ADDR) was submitted in the first block and N was submitted in the second block, both messages were signed or sent by the account with address ADDR.
4. Sort the correctly submitted values.
5. Every user who submitted a correct value between the 25 percent and 75 percent gains a reward of N tokens.

Similar to the case of Schelling points, everyone tries to offer a correct answer while they consider that all the others will also prefer to give the correct answers. Because the correct answer is desired the most by the system, providing a correct answer means a higher probability of obtaining the reward. Thus, we can have the following conclusions.

1. Under the uncoordinated choice model, if there is no bribing attack, it is easy to tell the same truth, but difficult to tell the same lie.
2. If there exists a bribe attack, the Schelling Coin game will be corrupted.

In addition to these two cases, some other well-known cryptoeconomics instances have been widely explored. Most of the projects focus on the efficiency issue. The main reason for this is that the scalability problem has inhibited the prospects of blockchain development. This chapter introduces two of the most representative ones.

1. **Arbitrum:** Ethereum is the worldwide second-most-valuable cryptocurrency by market value, but its exponential growth has been limited by network congestion

and costly fees. Arbitrum technology is one of the potential solutions to Ethereum's recent transaction cost problem, and is proposed by Offchain Labs [30]. Arbitrum intends to lower transaction costs and congestion by transferring as much processing and data storage as possible away from Ethereum's primary network (layer 1). Layer 2 scaling solutions are used to store data outside of Ethereum's blockchain. This is because it is constructed on top of layer 1 (the core Ethereum network) and so maintains Ethereum's security. Layer 2 projects such as Arbitrum are believed to be critical solutions for Ethereum's scaling problem at the present. The Ethereum network will be updated in the coming years and beyond to minimize costs and congestion. These improvements, particularly Eth 2.0, will aid Ethereum's scaling and cost reduction.

2. **Keepers:** Keepers, proposed by ChainLink, is a decentralized network that allows developers and researchers reliably to automate smart contract triggers, reducing the latency, increasing the process efficiency, and reserving the computation resources. Instead of competing with each other, nodes in Keepers are incentivized to perform all registered jobs. The advantages of joining the network include: (1) providing developers with hyperreliable, decentralized smart contract automation, (2) offering expandable computation, allowing developers to build more advanced Dapps at lower costs, and (3) achieving flexibility and programmability [31]. DeFi protocols like bZx [32] and xToken [33] have integrated Keepers to enhance functionality and improve the user experience without compromising security or transparency.

1.2.4   Summary: Economics, Cryptoeconomics, and Cryptography

When Vitalik first coined the concept of "Cryptoeconomics," the concept had been debated, and some microeconomists argued that it should be a subfield of economics. Furthermore, terms with similar forms are liable to be confused, such as cryptoassets and cryptocurrency. According to Vitalik Buterin's definition, cryptoeconomics bridges the cryptography and economic incentives together, focusing on the strategic interactions of different entities not only inside but also beyond the blockchain network. It follows that cryptoeconomics is not just "economics applied to digital assets like cryptocurrencies and tokens." Cryptocurrencies and cryptoassets are the new objects for economic study and analysis, and these markets have particular features and qualities. Figure 1.4 presents a brief illustration regarding the relations between cryptography, economics, and cryptoeconomics. Based on all the introductions in previous sections, we can conclude the following.

1. Cryptoeconomics is not a subfield of economics, but rather an area of applied cryptography that takes economics incentives and economics theory into account.
2. Cryptoeconomics can compete with cryptography by lowering the interactive computation.
3. Cryptoeconomics design should be distributed and decentralized, and can be applied on top of the trustless platform, where most of the economic mechanism designs are not.

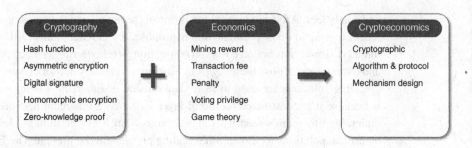

Figure 1.4 Cryptography, economics, and cryptoeconomics.

Moreover, the practical implementation of cryptoeconomics differs from classical economics [23]. That is, the equilibrium and experiments are easier to achieve and conduct; this will be seen in Part III. However, the centralized software development and deployment make practice difficult, which further affects the accuracy in evaluating the cryptoeconomics implementation. We further discuss the detailed impact in Chapter 10.

This section has identified the definitions and the corresponding explanations. Finally, we can summarize that cryptoeconomics is used for incentivizing the rational participants' entries and desired behaviors in a distributed system.

1.3   Why Cryptoeconomics Matters

As we discussed previously, Bitcoin is the first, as well as the most significant, instance of cryptoeconomics. The integration of cryptography and mechanism design sparks a revolutionary shift from a traditional P2P network to a blockchain network.

Although cryptography is robust when assuring the security and privacy of a system, the cost of development and deployment is increasingly expensive because of unpredictable attacks and risks. According to Vlad's talk in [2], cryptoeconomics can benefit the following issues.

1. The disincentivization of Byzantine faults: Bitcoin uses the PoW consensus and incentive mechanism to solve the Byzantine General Problem.
2. The "individual rationality" of deciding whether to run a node on a blockchain protocol: How does the incentive mechanism maximize the users' utilities when running their nodes on blockchain?
3. The economic barriers to Sybil attacks: A proper economic incentive mechanism is able to resist Sybil attacks without PoW.

Building systems that have specific desired properties require the coordination of cryptography and mechanism design. To be more specific, this book explains the importance of cryptoeconomics by introducing the project of Bitcoin. As a fundamental of cryptoeconomics, the incentive mechanism is applied in every step to secure the distributed system, including the **transaction confirmation**, **mining**, and **longest-chain generation.**

A Bitcoin network refers to a chain of blocks known as the shared public ledger, which records all the confirmed transactions. The data structure and chronological order of transactions, blocks, and the chain are enforced by cryptographic approaches. The incentives should be noted, motivating trustless and anonymous participants to accomplish these tasks correctly, from confirming the transactions to establishing the whole chain. A transaction recording the involved traders' account balances and terms will be broadcast to the Bitcoin network, protected by signatures, and thus immutable from being tampering by any malicious party. A general confirmation takes at least 10 minutes, completed by a participant called a miner, and through a process called mining. The validation and confirmation of transactions rely on the miner's effort. To compensate for miners' labor and get a quicker confirmation, each participant will set a customized service fee for its transaction in units of satoshi per byte. For this reason, miners will prioritize the transactions with higher fees.

Confirming and adding a transaction into a block are also known as the mining process. Only the miner winning the hash puzzle contest in PoW is entitled to append its mined block to the blockchain, relying on the miner's intensive computational resource. Note that PoW is a form of zero-knowledge proof that requires a participant to demonstrate its validity by exerting a certain amount of computation effort. This consensus protocol is the core of a blockchain system, established through cryptographic rules and for the purpose of being secure from double-spending. Similarly, a miner can exert all the energy on mining and winning PoW only because of the monetary incentive. That is the reason for the birth of BTC (the cryptocurrency issued by Bitcoin), compensating for the miners' computation cost on mining and ensuring the robustness of the Bitcoin ecosystem.

The PoW consensus cannot guarantee that only one miner wins in each round. Then the fork occurs when two winners finish mining simultaneously. The solution is called the longest-chain rule, which means only the chain of blocks that cost the greatest effort to build can be accepted as the valid version of the blockchain, preserving the consistency and neutrality of the whole network and safeguarding the efforts and benefits for a majority of miners. All recorded transactions will be deemed invalid for the blocks on forks and be shifted to unconfirmed, where the underlying efforts get no rewarded. To prevent its effort from being in vain, a rational miner will consciously comply with the rule.

By issuing tokens and offering fees, the Bitcoin network incentivizes trustless participants to operate as required. It compensates miners' work on the longest chain, coordinating all parties to defend against the Sybil attack and preserving the system's security and stability. Bitcoin uses cryptoeconomics to solve two problems: The security problem is how to resist the Sybil attack; and the incentive problem is how to motivate the unknown participants to participate correctly. Vitalik concluded the use of cryptography and incentives as follows [34].

1. Blockchain technology uses cryptography to secure the protocols and preserve the users' privacy.
   - Hashing: PoW; encoding wallet addresses; verify the integrity of data of transactions and balance of accounts on the network.
   - Elliptical curve cryptography: the Elliptic Curve Digital Signature Algorithm can ensure the transaction authenticity and integrity.
   - Erasure code: Blocks are encoded using erasure codes, so that any block of the chain can be efficiently restored from a small number of coded pieces.
   - Zero-knowledge proof, homomorphic encryption.
2. An incentive is used to motivate or drive one to do something or behave in a desired way.
   - Rewards: Increase actors' token balances if they do something good, for example, block reward and transaction fee.
   - Penalties: Reduce actors' token balances if illegal behavior occurs, for example, security deposit.
   - Privileges: Incentivize participants by giving them decision-making right, for example, voting weight.

As the foundational instance of a cryptoeconomics system, Bitcoin has clearly corroborated Josh's definition that (a) the important properties of that protocol are guaranteed by financial incentives, and (b) The economic mechanisms are guaranteed by cryptography.

Based on the explanations and analysis of cryptoeconomics, we can conclude the scenarios in which cryptoeconomics can be applied, as follows.

1. Security of lower-layer interactions: Any channel between a pair of participants, for example, state channel and payment channel.
2. Light clients: How should we design a fast and feasible incentive mechanism for a group of participants and deploy it in a decentralized system?
3. Decentralized applications: Encourage the users' participation and activity.
4. DoS resistance of off-chain protocols: Guarantee the security of on-chain assets and motivate the efforts of off-chain users.
5. Blockchain-based peer to peer markets: Incentivize the participants from the different chains to interact in a desired way.

This book intends to answer these questions based on a review of the literature, which serves as a trigger for further research.

1.4   Organization of the Book

The goal of this book is to provide a comprehensive overview of cryptoeconomics, introducing technical components including cryptography and mechanism design. Considering the surge in research focus on the computer science content of blockchain technology, this book places emphasis on the algorithmic mechanism design and mathematical tools of game theory in or beyond a blockchain network.[1]

In particular, this book analyzes how the economic interests of heterogeneous participants shape the way of strategic behaviors and presents an in-depth insight into how rational interactions among various parties determine the decision-making of system from an engineering perspective.

Consequently, we plan to present a mechanism paradigm for assisting the blockchain consensus protocols by properly designing the economic mechanism upon a distributed system, which enables the blockchain network to function with the desired properties in the form of system equilibria.

The main objectives of this book are three-fold.

1. The first objective is to provide the readers with a generalist background and a succinct overview of the distributed ledger networks and the blockchain technology that the ledgers are constructed upon. By transforming the interpretation of the blockchain networks from a computer networking perspective to the perspective of financial–social-economic networks, we establish the formal connection between the blockchain technologies and the research domain of cryptoeconomics.
2. The second objective is to present the state-of-the-art paradigm, based on a series of economic theoretical tools such as game theory, blockchain protocol modeling, and analysis and design. This will be achieved through classification of a variety of problems in protocol analysis and design with respect to the domain to which different mathematical tools belong.
3. The third objective is to provide the audience with a comprehensive overview of the development of the blockchain network protocols and their emerging applications in a plethora of domains, including the Internet of Things (IoT), smart cities, healthcare, self-governance, etc.

By organizing the overview into a series of case studies, this book extends the aforementioned paradigm of system analysis and design from the scope of blockchain protocol design to a broader scope of modeling and analyzing the ecosystems that are either embedded into the blockchain networks or use blockchain as a subsystem. In order to achieve the above objectives, the book is composed of four parts, as described below.

- **Introduction**

   This chapter leads the contents of this book by resolving the inconsistency in the literature regarding the definition of "cryptoeconomics." It provides an intuitive description on how the concept of "cryptoeconomics" came into shape through engineering practice. By providing a succinct overview of the technical component

---

[1] Some text from Chapters 5–9 is reused with permission from the papers "A survey on consensus mechanisms and mining strategy management in blockchain networks, cloud/fog computing resource management and pricing for blockchain networks, contract-theoretic pricing for security deposits in sharded blockchain with Internet of Things (IoT)" and "Cloud/edge computing service management in blockchain networks: Multi-leader multi-follower game-based ADMM for pricing."

of blockchain networks and reviewing them from a social-economic network point of view, this chapter lays the foundation for the technical discussion of the following chapters.

- **Part I: Cryptoeconomics Basics**

  Before presenting the framework of blockchain network modeling and design, this part presents a roadmap of how a cryptographical problem or a problem of distributed system analysis can be cast into the context of social-economic network analysis. In particular, a series of issues including incentivized decentralization, incentivized security (i.e., rational cryptography), and mechanism design for distributed consensus are introduced. This part will help the readers to be well prepared with the necessary knowledge on cryptography, networking protocols, and mathematical tools in economic theory for the later discussion on protocol and system analysis and design in the rest of this book.

- **Part II: Consensus Protocol Design in Blockchain Networks**

  This part of the book provides a technical overview on the procedures, constraints, and goals of consensus protocol design in blockchain networks. In particular, an interdisciplinary point of view from both cryptographical design and distributed system design is highlighted. The inherent differences from typical distributed consensus protocols of the blockchain network protocols are reviewed. Following the quantitative description of a cryptoeconomics system, the specific goals, constraints, and challenges in protocol design from a social-economic networking perspective are discussed. This part helps the readers to learn the necessary theoretical toolbox for establishing a social-economic network-based analytical framework for blockchain networks and protocols.

- **Part III: Mechanism Design in Blockchain Networks and Beyond**

  With the scope of the study on blockchain networks and their difference from existing systems precisely identified, this part of the book focuses on the process of modeling, analyzing, and designing the blockchain networks from a social-economic network perspective. In particular, a prototypical framework for blockchain network modeling is presented, particularly by employing the mathematical toolboxes including game theory, auction theory, contract theory, and those which can be frequently found in microeconomics studies. A diversity of practical problems regarding the design, deployment, and maintenance of blockchain networks are discussed. For each problem, regarding its specific operational goals, system performance indices, resource constraints, and deployment requirement, different mathematical models are applied to either address the issues in a componential level of the blockchain network, or formulate the blockchain network from a unified macroscopic perspective.

- **Part IV: Open Questions of Cryptoeconomics**

  With the theoretical paradigm of blockchain network modeling and analysis presented in Part III, this part of the book extends the scope of the study to the various applications of the blockchain networks, and in subsequence, the impact by the social-economic network property of the blockchains on the design, deployment and maintenance of these applications. By reviewing the development of the blockchain networks and the applications built upon or interconnected with blockchains, this part also provides an insight into the prospects, challenges, and open issues in the future course of technological evolution of blockchains.

To summarize, the key features of this book are as follows.

1. A generic and unified framework of protocol analysis and design for blockchain networks, especially from the economic theory-based point of view.
2. Comprehensive treatment of the state-of-the-art analytical techniques, especially in the domain of game theory and mechanism design, for the purpose of modeling the dynamics of blockchains as well as a variety of ecosystems that are either used by, or extended from, the blockchain networks.
3. Coverage of a wide range of emerging applications of blockchains, and the related techniques for modeling, analyzing, and designing them.
4. An in-depth insight into the key research issues and open problems in the course of blockchain analysis and design to guide future research activities.

Part I

Cryptoeconomics Basics

2 Cryptography Basics

In Chapter 1, we introduced the fundamentals of blockchain technology and the definitions of cryptoeconomics. Through the cooperation of different technologies, blockchain achieves security and enables decentralization among the participants across a distributed network.

As interdisciplinary research, cryptoeconomics provides a different perspective on blockchain technology, which integrates cryptography and economics to construct reliable and decentralized peer-to-peer (P2P) networks that persist over time despite attempts to tamper them. The cryptography that underpins these systems ensures that P2P communication inside the networks is secure, and the economic incentives are used to motivate all participants to contribute to the network's development over time. Therefore, a deep understanding of cryptography and economic incentives is crucial for cryptoeconomics research. Cryptography guarantees secure operations of all mechanisms, including the incentive mechanisms. Take the core consensus of Bitcoin, that is, Proof of Work (PoW), as an example. Hash functions are used for verifying transactions and mining competition. Asymmetric encryption can generate digital signatures for users, ensuring the authenticity and integrity of their transactions.

Starting from this chapter, we explain the cryptography primitives highly associated with cryptoeconomics. Section 2.1 introduces the security basics, including the critical definitions of security and privacy in the blockchain. Section 2.2 presents the necessary cryptography primitives, and Section 2.3 illustrates an application of cryptography in blockchain.

2.1 Security Basics

Since a blockchain system is built upon a typical P2P network, any common attack that occurs in the network may also exist in the blockchain. An attack is a threat that is carried out and, if successful, leads to severe consequences. Security concerns may change depending on the types of blockchain. Different blockchain networks always vary in the levels of access control. A blockchain network can be labeled as either public, consortium, or private, indicating who is permitted to join and operate the network and how users gain access.

A public blockchain allows users to freely enter and quit the network. Uncensored people validate transactions and reach consensus under the rationality majority assumption. The most well-known example of a public blockchain is Bitcoin, which achieves consensus using PoW. Users on the Bitcoin network, known as "miners," attempt to solve a challenging hash problem in order to gain the opportunity to produce blocks and receive a monetary reward. Aside from the use of asymmetric cryptography and hash functions, a public blockchain network has minimal identities and access restrictions.

A private blockchain is more centralized in comparison with a public blockchain. Private blockchain users are not, in general, anonymous. Only confirmed identities are permitted to access the network. Users in this permissioned network are compelled to abide by the system's regulations. Otherwise, because their identities are known, they will face punishment in the real world. As a result, private blockchains need stronger authentication and access restrictions.

The consortium blockchain is a hybrid of public and private chains that incorporates features from both. It is not as centralized as a private blockchain, but it does need identity authentication before entering the network. A consortium blockchain is most beneficial when multiple companies operate in the same industry and need a single platform to transfer transactions and make decisions. Quorum [35] and Corda [36] are two instances of consortium blockchains. For the consortium blockchains, the requirements of authentications and access controls depend on the actual needs of business.

Before introducing the hacks and frauds in blockchain network, we first discuss the common cyber-attack categories [37].

1. **Active attacks** can involve some modification of the data stream or the creation of a false stream, and can be subdivided into the following categories: replay, masquerade, modification of messages, and denial of service.

   (a) In the replay attack, the attacker's primary goal is to save a copy of the data that was originally present on that network and subsequently resend the data multiple times or utilize this data for other personal purposes. When data is damaged or leaked, it becomes insecure and dangerous for users and the system.

   (b) A masquerade takes place when one entity pretends to be a different entity.

   (c) Modification of messages means that the attackers may modify (partially or totally), delay, or reorder the data to produce an unauthorized effect.

   (d) The denial of service attacks generally have a specific target. They inhibit regular communication from taking place. For example, an entity may silence all messages addressed to a specific destination. Another type of service denial is the interruption of a whole network, either by deactivating it or by flooding it with messages to decrease performance.

2. **Passive attacks** aim to learn or use information from the system while having no effect on system resources. Passive attacks are similar to eavesdropping or monitoring transmissions. Therefore, passive attacks are challenging to detect. Major types of passive attacks are the release of message contents and traffic analysis. All the information transferred through the network may contain confidential data. A passive attack monitors the contents of this sensitive data. The most effective way to prevent passive attacks is encryption.

3. Based on the origin of the attack, we have another two types of attack: **insider attacks** and **outsider attacks** [38].

   (a) Insider attacks are carried out by malevolent users who have been granted authorized (i.e., insiders) access to the system. Insiders with authorized access have a considerable advantage over external attackers since they are familiar with network architecture and system protocols. Furthermore, because many firms focus on protecting against outsiders, there may be less security against insider assaults.

   (b) Outsider attacks mean that the attackers are from outside the system, and know only the system design but none of the keys.

While blockchain technology creates a tamper-proof ledger of transactions, it is not impervious to hacks or fraud. Those with malicious intent can exploit known vulnerabilities in blockchain technology and have been successful in a number of attacks over the years. Listed below are a few examples [39].

1. **Phishing attacks:** Phishing is a fraud designed to filch a user's credential. Fraudsters send emails (containing the bogus URLs) to the crypto wallet owners that appear to be from a reputable source. The disclosure of user credentials and other sensitive information may lead to losses for both the individual and the blockchain network.

2. **Routing attacks:** Blockchains rely on massive amounts of data being sent in real time. Data can be intercepted as it travels to internet service providers by hackers. Routing attacks are often undetected by blockchain participants, so everything appears normal. However, criminals have extracted sensitive data or currency behind the scenes.

3. **Sybil attacks:** In the Sybil attacks, hackers establish and utilize a large number of fake network identities to overwhelm the network and bring it down.

4. **The 51% attacks:** Mining necessitates a significant amount of computational power, particularly for large-scale public blockchains. However, if a miner or a group of miners could pool enough resources, they might control more than half of the mining power on a blockchain network. Having more than 50 percent of the power indicates that the attacker can control the ledger and launch the double-spending attack.

Information security mainly focuses on securing information from unauthorized access, use, disclosure, interruption, alteration, or destruction in order to preserve confidentiality, integrity, and availability [40].

1. **Confidentiality** means maintaining permitted constraints on information access and disclosure, including preserving personal privacy and proprietary information.

2. **Integrity** means preventing unauthorized information alteration or deletion, as well as assuring information nonrepudiation and authenticity.

3. **Availability** means information must be available and accessible when needed.

Apart from the principles that we have discussed above, the following concepts are associated with information security [41].

1. **Nonrepudiation:** This feature ensures that no one can deny taking a particular action, such as sending, validating, or receiving a message. For example, any transaction on the public blockchain must be signed before transmission. The digital signature can ensure that no one can forge this transaction without the transaction owners' private keys, and the owners cannot deny that a valid-signed transaction is not from themselves.
2. **Authenticity:** This property means that the messages are from the sources that they claim to be from. It involves the proofs of identities.
3. **Accountability:** This means that the messages and actions on the Internet are traceable. If a fault device or lost data package exists, then the fault sources can be located.

The field of information security has grown and evolved significantly in recent years. The CIA triad (i.e., confidentiality, integrity, and availability) is always the fundamental principle to secure a network or system. The most effective way to ensure this triad is cryptography, which has been widely applied for achieving information security in communications, databases, and the emerging blockchain networks.

2.2   Cryptography Primitives

The goal of cryptography is to ensure that only the intended party has access to the information. The sender encrypts a message to make it unreadable, while the recipient decrypts it to make it understandable. From ancient times to the present, the military has always made the most frequent use of codes because protecting their own secrets and cracking the enemy's secrets is essential for victory. Ancient China had rich military practices and developed military theories, including standardized and systematic methods of confidential communication and identity authentication. The ancient military book *Liu Tao* (1128 BC–1015 BC) describes how the monarch communicated confidentially with his generals during the war. However, by today's standards, most of the classical cryptographic schemes are considered too weak to secure the modern system. These techniques include the following.

1. *The Caesar substitution cipher.*
2. *Monoalphabetic substitution.*
3. *Polyalphabetic substitution (the Vigenere cipher).*
4. *Transposition ciphers.*

Modern cryptography is built upon mathematics, which plays an important role in encryption, public key, authentication, and digital signatures. The basic math concepts include counting techniques, permutations, plotting a curve, raising a number to a power, modular arithmetic, and congruence [42]. This book briefly introduces the cryptographic algorithms and protocols that are most frequently used in blockchain. Here are some key terms and concepts in a modern cryptography system [43].

1. Plaintext: This is the original message or data that is fed into the algorithm as input.
2. Encryption algorithm: The encryption algorithm performs various substitutions and transformations on the plaintext.
3. Secret key: The secret key is also input to the encryption algorithm. The exact substitutions and transformations performed by the algorithm depend on the key.
4. Ciphertext: This is the scrambled message produced as output. It depends on the plaintext and the secret key. For a given message, two different keys will produce two different ciphertexts.
5. Decryption algorithm: This is essentially the encryption algorithm run in reverse. It takes the ciphertext and the secret key and produces the original plaintext.

There are several ways to encrypt data. Each one has both advantages and disadvantages. Often, any cryptographic method will be not used alone, but in conjunction with other methods for the purpose of creating a more secure system. In this chapter, we first introduce two different ways of performing cryptographic algorithms, namely, symmetric encryption and asymmetric encryption.

2.2.1   Symmetric Encryption

In a symmetric encryption algorithm, users adopt the same cryptographic keys for both plaintext encryption and ciphertext decryption. In practice, the symmetric encryption always has a smaller key size, and thus it is much more efficient than the asymmetric encryption. It can also reduce the key-generation time since the private key and public key are identical. One of the fundamental disadvantages of symmetric encryption over asymmetric encryption is that both parties must have access to the secret or private key. Considering the pros and cons of symmetric encryption, it is often used in securing the session keys. There are two typical kinds of symmetric encryption algorithms.

1. **Stream cipher:** A stream cipher processes the input elements continuously, producing output one element at a time. The generator's output, known as a keystream, is merged with the plaintext stream one byte at a time using the bitwise exclusive-OR (XOR) operation. This algorithm is no longer widely employed.
2. **Block cipher:** A block cipher processes the plaintext input in fixed-size blocks and 128 bits are encrypted at a time. Longer plaintext quantities are processed as a series of fixed-size blocks by the algorithm. The common block cipher algorithms are as follow [44].
   (a) Data Encryption Standard (DES): This is a block cipher algorithm that takes plaintext in blocks of 64 bits and converts them to ciphertext using keys of 48 bits. The key creation process includes 16 rounds of encryption, with each round using a new key. It is an early data encryption standard proposed by the United States National Bureau of Standards (NBS; now the National Institute of

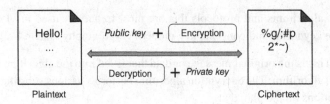

Figure 2.1 Asymmetric encryption.

Standards and Technology, NIST). As a consequence of widespread approval by standards organizations across the world, the DES has become the international standard for data security.

(b) Advanced Encryption Standard (AES): DES was considered insecure owing to its small 56-bit key size. The block size of AES is 128 bits and the key length is also increased to 128, 192, or 256 bits. The AES algorithm works in a substitution and permutation way. Solid-state drives (SSDs), hard-disk drives (HDDs), WiFi in local area networks (LANs), cloud computing storage, and website TSL or SSL certificates, which are used to encrypt internet browser connections and transactions, all employ AES encryption.

2.2.2   Asymmetric Cryptography

Asymmetric cryptography, also known as public-key encryption, was first publicly proposed by Diffie and Hellman in 1976. The biggest difference between asymmetric encryption and symmetric encryption is the separate encrypt or decrypt keys (public key and private key); see Fig. 2.1. The usage of two keys has significant implications for security, key distribution, and authentication.

A public blockchain is built upon a collection of cryptographic protocols and algorithms. This chapter aims to cover all the essential parts. The first asymmetric cryptographic protocol that needs to be introduced is Diffie–Hellman (DH) Key Exchange [45]. Although the DH protocol is not explicitly used in blockchain, it exists almost everywhere in the network. The only purpose of the DH protocol is to enable two parties to securely exchange their secret keys in the insecure Internet.

2.2.2.1   Diffie–Hellman Key Exchange

The DH protocol is not used for encryption or decryption, but is used for protecting the underlying session channel. The protocol design is based on the discrete logarithm (DL) problem. The DL problem is defined as follows [46]: For a given cyclic group G and its generator g, and an element a of G, it is difficult to compute the a for the given g^a. The general description of key exchange is listed as follows.

1. At the initialization stage, the system first selects a cyclic group G and the generator g, which are known to all the others (including the attackers).

2. Alice picks an element a on group G and sends g^a to Bob, in which a is private and g^a is public.
3. Bob picks an element b on group G and sends g^b to Alice, in which b is private and g^b is public.
4. With the secret key a, Alice computes: $(g^b)^a = g^{ab}$.
5. With the secret key b, Bob computes: $(g^a)^a = g^{ab}$.
6. As a result, Alice and Bob can obtain a secret session key g^{ab} without knowing each other's secret key.

For the attacker, anyone can know the group G and the generator g, as well as the public message g^a and g^b transmitted between Alice and Bob. According to the DL problem, it is difficult to work out a and b on the group G. Furthermore, there is no way to compute g^{ab} with g^a and g^b. Consequently, we can conclude that Alice and Bob are able to securely communicate with each other in an insecure network.

2.2.2.2 RSA Algorithm

The RSA algorithm is named after its inventors: Ron Rivest, Adi Shamir, and Leonard Adleman [47]. The mathematical design is based on the factoring problem, namely, the difficulty of factoring the product of two large prime numbers [48]. RSA can be used for both encryption and digital signatures. As one of oldest asymmetric cryptosystems, it has been widely applied to various scenarios for secure data transmission. RSA has been used until now because of its outstanding advantages.

1. Benefiting from its underlying mathematical design, RSA has survived various attacks, demonstrating security for data transmission.
2. RSA is easy and efficient to implement.
3. Distributing public keys to users is easy.

However, RSA also has some obvious drawbacks since it significantly relies on the large prime numbers. The disadvantages of RSA are listed as follows.

1. RSA requires large prime numbers, so the algorithm introduces high latency during data processing and transmission.
2. There must be a trusted third party to help verify the public keys.
3. It is difficult to generate the proper large prime numbers.

Suppose that Alice tries to communicate with Bob in an insecure network. Both of them obtain a key pair from the system. Alice encrypts a message by using Bob's public key. Bob receives the encrypted message and decrypts it by using his private key. We first introduce the key-generation algorithm.

1. Select two large prime numbers, p and q, and compute their product $n = pq$. The larger the prime number, the more difficult the algorithm.
2. The length of n is the length of secret key. The key length should be 1048 bits or 2048 bits in practice.

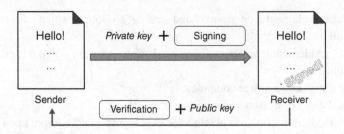

Figure 2.2 How does a digital signature work?

3. Compute $\phi = (p - 1)(q - 1)$, and select an integer e, where $1 < e < \phi$ and $gcd(e, \phi) = 1$.
4. Compute d, where $ed \equiv 1 \mod \phi$.

Thus, the public key is (n, e) and the private key is (n, d), where d, p, q, and ϕ are all private and cannot be revealed to public. After Bob gets his key pairs, Alice can encrypt message M as follows.

1. Obtain Bob's public key (n, e).
2. Compute the ciphertext $C = M^e \mod n$.
3. Send the ciphertext C to Bob.

Then Bob can decrypt the ciphertext C by simply computing $M = C^d \mod n$. As we mentioned before, RSA can be used for both encryption and for a digital signature. The signature scheme is the reverse process of encryption, see Fig. 2.2. If Alice wants to sign a message M, she will do the following.

1. Compute the message digest $H(M)$ using a hash function.
2. Sign the message using her private key and get the signature: $s = H(M)^d \mod n$.
3. Send the signature s and message M to Bob.

After receiving signed message, Bob will verify the signature as follows.

1. Reveal the signed message using Alice's public key (n, e): $H'(M) = s^e \mod n$.
2. Compute the message digest $H(M)$ using the same hash function.
3. If $H'(M) = H(M)$, the signature is valid.

In practice, the message M can be encrypted using an RSA encryption algorithm before transmission. The combination of encryption and digital signature can guarantee the integrity, confidentiality, and nonrepudiation of the data.

2.2.2.3 Elliptic-Curve Cryptography (ECC)

Before the prevalence of elliptic-curve cryptography (ECC), all public-key encryption algorithms were based on RSA and DH. ECC is a public-key cryptography based on the algebraic structure of elliptic curves over finite fields that can also implement the

Table 2.1 NIST-approved ESCDA security parameters.

Bit length of n	Maximum cofactor (h)
160–223	2^{10}
224–255	2^{14}
256–383	2^{16}
384–511	2^{24}
≥ 512	2^{32}

encryption and digital signatures functions. We can use the different underlying elliptic curves to realize the ECC algorithm. Different curves give varying levels of security, key length, and encryption or decryption efficiency.

The elliptic curve over a finite field GF(p) means that all the elements on this curve must be limited to integer coordinates within the square matrix of size $p \times p$. One of the most commonly used curve functions is as follows:

$$y^3 = x^3 + ax + b \quad (a, b \in \text{GF}(p), 4a^3 + 27b^2 \neq 0).$$

The private keys in the ECC are integers within the field and must be encoded to hexadecimal, which can be randomly selected on the curve. The public keys in the ECC are points (x and y coordinates) over a certain ECC curve. Typically, there are some standard and approved curves, the corresponding field size (which defines the key length, e.g., 256-bit), and security strength (usually the field size divided by 2, or less), performance (operations per second) and many other parameters.

The elliptic curve digital signal algorithm (ECDSA) is a digital signature scheme based on the ECC. Table 2.1 shows the NIST-approved ECDSA security parameters [49]. Digital signatures are a crucial component of blockchains for transaction confirmation and identity authentication. Users must prove to others the authenticity of their identity and prevent it from being falsified by attackers. From the system's point of view, a transaction or block can only be finalized when it has a certain number of valid signatures. Take Bitcoin as an example, Bitcoin uses secp256k1 as the underlying curve of ECDSA; secp256k1 refers to a specific shape with a unique set of parameters, which is defined in Standards for Efficient Cryptography (SEC) [50]. The curve function is

$$y^2 \equiv x^3 + 7 (\text{mod} p).$$

According to [49], we can observe that secp256k1 is not mentioned. It was seldom used before the birth of Bitcoin. The underlying structure of the majority of common curves is random, while secp256k1 uses a nonrandom structure. Compared with the random structure, a nonrandom structure can increase the computation efficiency. As a consequence, it can be up to 30 percent quicker than other curves in the best case [51]. Furthermore, the deterministic feature of secp256k1 can reduce the possibility that a developer added backdoor or introduced vulnerabilities into curve. ECDSA consists of three algorithms: key generation, signing and verification [52].

1. **Key generation**
   (a) Select a random integer a on the elliptic curve as the private key.
   (b) Compute the public key $Q = (x_Q, y_Q) = aP$, where P is a base point on the secp256k1 curve [50].
   (c) Send Q to the specific user. In Bitcoin, the hashed public key is used as the user's public address.

2. **Signing**
   (a) Select a different random integer $r \in [1, n-1]$ before signing each message, where n denotes the order of P.
   (b) Compute $R = (x_R, y_R) = rP$.
   (c) Compute the signature $s = r^{-1}(H(M) + ax_R)$ with the message digest $H(M)$.
   (d) Send the signature pair (x_R, s) to the recipient.

3. **Verification**
   (a) Compute $u_1 = s^{-1}H(M)$ and $u_2 = s^{-1}x_R$.
   (b) Compute $V = (x_V, y_V) = u_1 P + u_2 Q$ with the base point P and public key Q.
   (c) Check if $x_v = x_R$ is satisfied. Otherwise, the signature is invalid.

ECDSA can produce a unique public key from a randomly selected private key (unsigned 256-bit integer [51]), which is a one-way computation that makes it impossible to reveal the underlying private key of any public key. Then, using a hash function, this public key will be converted to the user's wallet address. We present the principles of hash functions in Section 2.2.3.

As the key algorithms in asymmetric cryptosystems, both ECC and RSA are able to ensure data confidentiality, integrity, and authenticity. However, which one is more efficient and secure? The advantages and disadvantages of ECC compared with RSA are given as follows.

1. **Advantages of ECC**
   (a) ECC can offer the same security level as RSA by using a much smaller key size.
   (b) ECC has a much more shorter key-generation time than RSA. ECC key-generation time grows linearly with the key size, while RSA grows exponentially [53].

2. **Disadvantages of ECC**
   (a) The ECC algorithm is more complex and more difficult to implement than RSA.
   (b) ECC needs a longer time to verify the signature than RSA [53].

Considering the drawbacks of ECDSA, Ethereum will no longer use it in its future design. Thousands of validators from various committees will be required to provide thousands of signatures in a short period of time. Every node cannot verify every signature in such a short time. For example, if each block has 64 committees, each with as many as 2048 validators, and each block will require 131,072 (64×2048) signatures to be calculated and confirmed (12 seconds). Ethereum intends to employ BLS (Boneh–Lynn–Shacham) [54] signatures to achieve more efficient signature verification in consensus.

2.2.3 Hash Function

The hash function is a one-way function; as this implies, the hash function cannot be reversed by any method, that is, there is no way to restore the input from the output hash. The function can turns any arbitrary-length input into a fixed-length output, in which the possibility of two different inputs with the same output is extremely low. The hashed output serves as a message digest, which is often used for guaranteeing data integrity together with a digital signature. Generally, the hash function $h(\cdot)$ has the following properties [43].

1. **Compression:** h can map any arbitrary-length input to an fixed-size output.
2. **Ease of computation:** $h(x)$ is easy to compute with any input x.
3. **Avalanche effect:** Any changes of input will result in a significant change in output.
4. **Preimage resistance:** For any given output $h(x)$, it is computationally infeasible to find the input x.
5. **Second preimage resistance:** For any give output $h(x)$ and its input x, it is computationally feasible to find a second input $x' \neq x$ that $h(x) = h(x')$.
6. **Collision resistance:** It is computationally infeasible to find any two inputs $x! = x'$, such that $h(x) = h(x')$.
7. **Puzzle friendliness:** For every possible N-bit output value y, if k is chosen from a distribution with high min-entropy, then it is infeasible to find x such that $h(k||x) = y$ in time significantly less than 2^N [55].

In blockchain, the hash functions play an important role in connecting blocks and ensuring the integrity of the data contained within each block. Any change to the block data might induce inconsistency, causing the blockchain to become invalid. The key properties of hash function can guarantee the users to have unique and unchangeable public address in an efficient way. The commonly used cryptographic hash functions are listed as follows.

1. **Message Digest Algorithm 5 (MD5):** This algorithm was a widely used hash function that outputs a 128-bit hash value. However, it has been broken as a result of not complying with the collision resistance requirement.
2. **Secure Hashing Algorithm (SHA):** This refers to a family of cryptographic hash functions published by NIST, including the following.
   (a) *SHA-0*: The output is 128 bits, and it is no long in use.
   (b) *SHA-1*: The output is 160 bits, and it has not been considered secure since 2005 [56].
   (c) *SHA-2*: This family consists of several hash algorithms, for example, SHA-256 and SHA-512. The numbers after "SHA" indicate the different sizes of output. Both of them are still in use.
   (d) *SHA-3*: This is the latest generation of SHA family and it was published by NIST in 2015. This generation consists of four famous hash algorithms: SHA3-224, SHA3-256, SHA3-384, and SHA3-512.

Through the cryptographic algorithms and hash functions, the blockchain ledger contains only the valid transactions and blocks, which can efficiently secure the whole network. In particular, Bitcoin adopts the SHA-256 as its underlying hash algorithm. Implementing a cryptographic hash function is advantageous in preventing fraudulent transactions, double-spending in blockchain, and other issues. In this case, how do the hash algorithms work in blockchain? What are the uses of hash functions in blockchain? Typically, hashes are used in two major parts within a blockchain: data structure and mining.

2.2.3.1   Data Structure

The hash function serves as the basis of the data structure for decentralized ledger technology to preserve the data integrity for blockchain. This "ledger" is composed of a collection of sequential blocks. The hash function links these blocks together and makes it impossible for attackers to tamper with any contents of the blockchain. To grasp the uses of hash function in data structure, it is of great importance to comprehend the basic data structures in blockchain. Two representative data structures of blockchain include the following.

1. **Linked list:** This refers to a linear collection of data elements, which contains a pointer that points to the next element. Blockchain is a linked list, where each block is the "data element" and the block hash is the "pointer." The hash value of each block is calculated through the contents inside the block and the previous block's hash value. The hash value is used to link a block to the preceding block; see Fig. 2.3. According to the avalanche effect of the hash function, modifying any blocks will cause inconsistencies in all subsequent blocks' hashes, which ensures that the whole linked list is tamper-resistant.
2. **Merkle tree:** The Merkle tree enables the P2P blockchain network to quickly verify blockchain transactions and transfer massive volumes of transactions from one node to the others. As the identifier of a Merkle tree, the root hash is stored in the block header, together with some other information:

    (a) version number,
    (b) hash of the previous block,
    (c) hash of the Merkle tree,
    (d) timestamp,
    (e) nonce,
    (f) the hash puzzle target.

    A root hash contains all transaction data within a block. From Fig. 2.3, we can see that each transaction has its own hash, and all the leaf nodes refer to the transaction data, while nonleaf nodes denote the hash value of two adjacent transactions. By using the hash function, the Merkle tree can guarantee that it is impossible to modify any transactions inside the block and to find any other trees with the same hash value. The tree root hash will also be used as one of the inputs for calculating the block hash. Consequently, by keeping the root hash within a block and ensuring the integrity of the transactions within the block, the block header's integrity is also safeguarded.

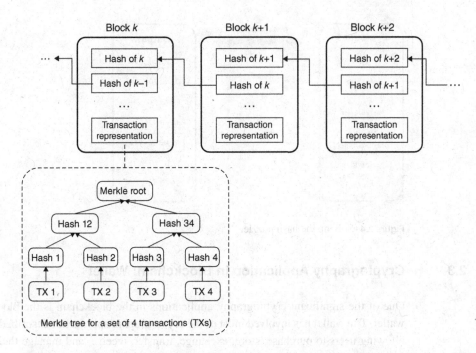

Figure 2.3 Illustration of a chain of blocks, where the transactions in a single block is represented by a Merkle root. Reprinted with permission from the paper "A survey on consensus mechanisms and mining strategy management in blockchain networks" published in *IEEE Access*.

2.2.3.2   Mining

The process of minting new Bitcoins by solving a hash puzzle is known as bitcoin mining. Solving the hash puzzle is fundamentally a difficult mathematical task for all miners. The hash puzzle is the heart of Bitcoin mining and PoW, which requires all the miners to find a hash value that satisfies the difficulty requirement. Specifically, the network will set up a hash target before each block generation. Miners will try to calculate the hash of a block by changing the nonce value repeatedly until the hash value yielded is less than the target; see Fig. 2.4.

The miner can only iterate the nonce by repeatedly adding 1 to the previous nonce. The other contents of the input have been predetermined. Only the output that satisfies a certain requirement can be accepted as the winner. Once a miner has won the puzzle game, the miner is able to create a new block and append it to the chain.

In blockchain, hash functions are commonly employed to ensure the integrity and immutability of data recorded on the distributed ledger. Because the ledger is stored decentralized and distributed, with each node keeping its own copy, ledger immutability is essential. Otherwise, nodes might alter their copies of the ledger to benefit themselves, causing the network's consensus to be broken.

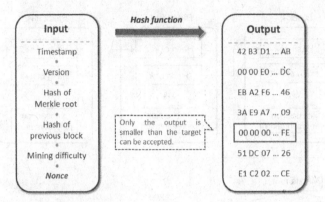

Figure 2.4 Solving the hash puzzle.

2.3   Cryptography Application in Blockchain: Wallet

One of the significant cryptography applications in the blockchain is the blockchain wallet. The wallet has involved most of the cryptographic approaches described above, allowing users to purchase, store, exchange, transfer, receive, and manage their cryptocurrencies and other cryptoassets. All processes can be executed securely because of cryptographic protection.

Similar to the traditional bank account, every wallet has its unique identity, called the wallet address, which enables the wallet user to track all transactions associated with the address. When it comes to transferring money, users may make a request for a certain quantity of bitcoin or other cryptoassets to another person, and the system will produce a unique address that can be given to a third party. Users can also exchange Bitcoin for other cryptoassets and vice versa, known as swapping.

2.3.1   Cryptography in Blockchain Wallet

Essentially, the digital wallet is a piece of software. Anyone who uses the wallet must first install it on a personal device and then start the initialization to obtain the wallet address. A blockchain wallet allows users to generate multiple addresses. The key and address generation is described as follows.

1. Use a random number to generate a private key first.
2. The wallet picks some points on a certain elliptic curve and takes the private key as the input of an ECDSA cryptographic algorithm. The output is the public key.
3. The wallet calculates the public key by using the SHA-256 hash function.
4. The wallet hashes the public key and obtains the wallet address.

We can observe that the wallet address is calculated with a public key and private key from Fig. 2.5. Anyone can send cryptocurrencies using the public address. As mentioned above, a hash function is used to convert the input into a given output

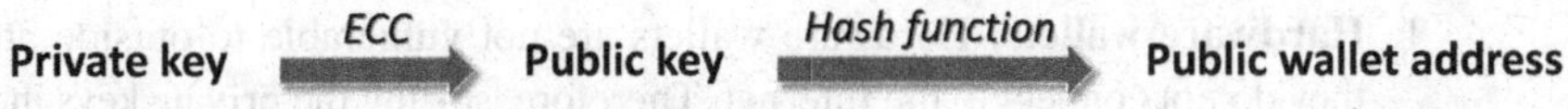

Private key **ECC** ⟶ **Public key** *Hash function* ⟶ **Public wallet address**

Figure 2.5 How to generate the public wallet address.

unknown to the public but associated with the public address. Even though the private key is associated with the public key and the wallet address, it is unable to be revealed since hash is resistant to "reverse-engineering."

In addition to the public address, the underlying key pairs also enable the encryption and digital signature for data security and state finalization. The owner of the wallet will use their private key to sign a transaction before sending it to the blockchain network. Once the transaction is broadcast to the public, the other nodes will use the public key which is associated with the private key to validate the transactions and finalize the network state.

2.3.2   Blockchain Wallet Security

Security is the most important concern for wallet users, since a hacked wallet will result in huge financial losses. Blockchain wallet provides a variety of ways to secure the accounts. Some safeguards include encrypting the wallet with a strong password, using two-factor authentication for exchanges, and storing large amounts of money in a hardware wallet. The password of the wallet is the only way for users to access the cryptoworld.

1. The wallet address is the only identity of the wallet user.
2. Anyone with the password can access to the wallet.
3. No one can access the wallet without the password.
4. If a user deletes the wallet application without saving the password, the user loses access to the wallet.

Most current wallets are created using a 12-word mnemonic seed that may be used to recover the wallet if it is lost or corrupted. These words should be carefully preserved in a secure location, as they can be used to steal the user's cryptocurrencies if they are discovered.

A mnemonic seed is a random string (12 or 24) of English words that serves as a password substitute. The seed can be used to recover the wallet, if a user loses access to their phone or device. Users' mnemonic seeds, like passwords, are not stored by any wallet company. The wallets may be retrieved even if the company goes out of business since these seeds follow an industry standard. The most common way to back up a seed phrase is to write it down on a piece of paper.

In addition to the security measures introduced above, there are a few optional methods that are not considered necessary but can help to protect users' wallets from malicious attacks.

1. **Hardware wallets:** Hardware wallets are not vulnerable to outside attacks since they do not connect to the Internet. Therefore, storing the private keys in a hardware wallet is the most reliable option for keeping the keys secure.
2. **Secure internet:** When trading cryptocurrencies and cryptoassets, utilize a secure internet connection rather than public Wi-Fi networks can avoid the majority of potential hacks. A VPN (virtual provate netweok) is able to conceal and protect surfing activities by changing the IP (internet protocol) address and location.
3. **Diversify investments:** Users can diversify the cryptocurrency investments in multiple wallets. Since there is no limitation for wallet creation, using one wallet for daily transactions and keeping the rest in a separate wallet will protect the portfolio and mitigate the loss of any breach to the cryptoaccount.
4. **Phishing:** Phishing scams contain fraudulent URLs that may lead to the leakage of a user's sensitive information. Users must be careful while trading the cryptocurrencies.

2.4   Summary

This chapter first introduces the basics of information security, including the CIA triad and other crucial concepts. In order to achieve the security goal, cryptography is considered the most effective tool. Then, the fundamental cryptography primitives that are associated with blockchain networks are outlined, depicting how cryptography can resist attacks and ensure security in the blockchain networks. Finally, taking the crypto wallet as an example, this chapter illustrates how the different cryptographic algorithms and protocols safeguard the security of users' assets in detail. The cryptoworld is constantly evolving. More and more traditional industries and businesses are undergoing a shift from centralization to decentralization, which further promotes the development of blockchain-related research. This chapter aims to help scholars interested in blockchain get a quick overview of the underlying cryptographic algorithms and protocols.

3 Economic Incentive

In traditional centralized governance systems, a centralized party frequently facilitates ownership transfers, possession transfers, property rights protection, and contract enforcement. The centralized administrative party is responsible for assuring correctness and security [57]. Before the Bitcoin was created, there there was a great deal of research focusing on the problem of how to achieve a uniform agreement on the system state among nontrusting parties. The most outstanding advantage of Bitcoin is the use of incentives to build up a fully public distributed system in an efficient way, where security and correctness can be achieved through consensus and incentives. Subsequently, other public blockchain projects also utilize the incentive mechanism to support the network and promote the circulation of cryptocurrencies since all of these projects share the same honest-majority assumption.

The central issue of cryptoeconomics is the use of incentives to construct a secure distributed system. Generally, the incentives can be divided into two main categories: transaction fees and blockchain rewards. However, as the research on cryptoeconomics progresses, the incentive has developed new branches: penalty and privilege. This chapter introduces two mainstream incentives in Sections 3.1 and 3.2.

3.1 Uses of Incentives: Transaction Fee and Block Reward

Blockchain is also known as the Distributed Ledger Technology, which serves as a decentralized and distributed ledger and is responsible for recording the transactions. The transactions can be initiated by any party in the system. In general, the term "transaction" refers to the records of the senders' data, and these are organized in a tree data structure inside a single block. Figure 3.1 shows a typical life cycle of a transaction. These blocks are sequentially connected before and after in a chronological manner through the cryptographic algorithm, eventually forming a chain called "blockchain," which makes it difficult to tamper with a single transaction record and a single block. Before being confirmed and finalized by the blockchain, a transaction must experience the following steps.

1. Generation: A transaction sender first accesses his or her wallet client, gets the receiver's address, and fills in the transfer amount. The transaction is signed using the sender's private key. Then the transaction is broadcast to the blockchain network.

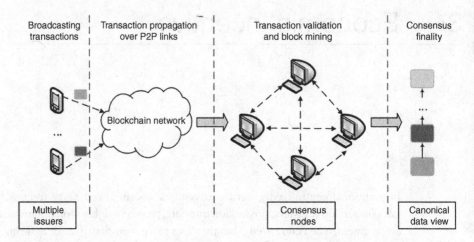

Broadcasting transactions | Transaction propagation over P2P links | Transaction validation and block mining | Consensus finality

Blockchain network

Multiple issuers | Consensus nodes | Canonical data view

Figure 3.1 The life cycle of a transaction. Reprinted with permission from the paper "A survey on consensus mechanisms and mining strategy management in blockchain networks" published in *IEEE Access*.

2. Propagation: The transactions are propagated by the peer nodes using various P2P communication protocols, for example, gossip protocol.
3. Validation: We should note that "transaction validation" in the general case is different from "transaction confirmation." These transactions will be kept in a memory pool until they are ready to be validated. The memory pool is viewed as a temporary waiting area for all the transactions before being confirmed by a block, which allow the transaction data to be shared and synchronized with all the peer nodes. The peer nodes verify the validity of unconfirmed transactions, that is, checking if the signatures and the target account address are correct, if the sender's account has enough money, and if a double-spending exists. If any of the conditions is not satisfied, then the transaction will be declined.
4. Packaging: The nodes (or miners) select transactions from the memory pool and pack them into a block. Different miners can choose the same transactions. At this time, these packed transactions are still not confirmed. To append its own block to the acknowledged public chain, the miner must first solve a hash-based mathematical puzzle, where the process is also known as mining. Once the miner successfully solves this mathematical problem, it is entitled to broadcast this block throughout the blockchain network.
5. Block verification: Like the unconfirmed transactions, the newly generated block also needs to be verified. Other nodes can verify the validity of the block by checking the hash result which is attached in the block. If the block is valid, then it will be appended to the blockchain and the new blockchain will be synchronized with all the nodes, where the process is referred to as "reach a consensus."
6. Confirmation: After the block has been added to the chain, the transactions are also confirmed over the blockchain. That means the transactions are now officially

recorded and confirmed by the nodes in the blockchain network. As such, the transactions can be performed, and never be tampered with.

The incentive mechanism in blockchain can be identified as two types: (1) transaction fee and (2) block reward. We introduce the incentives in details in the following.

3.1.1   Transaction Fee

After introducing the complete life cycle of a transaction, we dive into the details of a transaction so that we can have a better understanding about the transaction fee and block reward. In the following subsections, we illustrate the transactions of Bitcoin and Ethereum.

3.1.1.1   Bitcoin Transaction Fee

What does a typical Bitcoin transaction contain? The transactions on the Bitcoin network are mainly about transferring money. Some other alt-coin projects are similar to the Bitcoin network, and their transaction contents are almost the same. Therefore, this type of transaction usually contains the sender's signature, the receiver' address, the transfer amount, and the transaction fee.

Figure 3.2 shows the variation in trends of Bitcoin price and average transaction fee of Bitcoin in the past year. We can observe that the average transaction fee price increases significantly during the first few months and flattens in the following months of this year. The average Bitcoin transaction fee has fluctuated between $10 and $1.

Through Fig. 3.2, we can observe how the price fluctuates over time. Each block of the blockchain has a limited amount of storage capacity, and the miners select only the transactions with the higher fees to get more profits. If more transactions are waiting in the pool, the senders must pay a higher fee to get their transactions confirmed in time. The transaction fees are almost influenced by the transactions amount. These fees can compensate the miners' effort on mining and incentivize them to support the blockchain network. As a result, transaction fees promote a more reliable and more cost-efficient network.

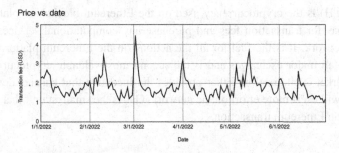

Figure 3.2 The Bitcoin transaction fee fluctuates over time. Data source: www.blockchain .com/charts/fees-usd-per-transaction.

from	Transaction sender's address.
to	Transaction receiver's address.
msg.value	It contains the amount of wei sent in the transaction.
msg.data	It contains the message sent in the transaction.
Gas limit	The maximum amount of gas (or energy) that the sender is willing to spend on a particular transaction.
Gas price	It is denoted in Gwei.
nonce	The transaction numbers sent by a sender.
Transaction hash	A unique hash that denotes the transaction id.
Signature	It is generated by sender's private key.

Figure 3.3 Transaction content.

That explains the one of functions of transaction fee: *Incentivize the miner to confirm the transaction*. The other function is to *eliminate the waste of miners' computation resources*. The Bitcoin network was invented as the first P2P payment system, thus it is mainly responsible for transferring cryptocurrencies and recording the payments. However, the other blockchain projects can be used to store any type of information. For example, it is not the same case for Ethereum; we discuss the transaction fee on Ethereum in the following.

3.1.1.2 Ethereum Transaction Fee

An Ethereum transaction refers to an action initiated by an externally owned account, in other words an account managed by an individual, not a smart contract [58]. For example, if there is a direct transfer of funds or assets between the two accounts, then the state-changing action must be recorded in a transaction. The major transaction contents in Ethereum are listed in Fig. 3.3.

Ether (ETH) is the cryptocurrency used on the Ethereum blockchain platform. It is used to pay for transaction fees and purchase any computational services on the Ethereum network. It is the fuel for all the actions on the Ethereum platform. Ether is traded on all major exchanges and is the second most-valuable cryptocurrency in terms of market capitalization. Ether provides the incentive that ensures developers and miners will exert more effort on the network. Gas is the smallest unit that must be included in an Ethereum transaction.

Gas

Gas refers to the unit that measures the amount of computational effort required to execute specific operations on the Ethereum network [59]. Like the mechanism behind the transaction fees on Bitcoin, Ethereum transactions also consume the miners' computation resources. Thus the fees on Ethereum can compensate for the gap between the mining reward and actual resource expenditure. Gas was developed to provide a practical distinction between the ETH cryptocurrency's actual market price and the computational expenses of running Ethereum's virtual machine [59]. Gas costs help make the Ethereum network safe because they prevent a hacker from launching a DoS attack on the network since he or she must pay for each fundamental action.

Gas fees are paid in the Ethereum currency, Ether (ETH). The minimum denomination of gas is Wei, in which Gwei is equal to 10^{-18} ETH. The other denominations include Kwei, Mwei, and so on. Since the Wei is too small and not commonly used, Gwei is often used instead. However, in Solidity, if we do not indicate the denomination, the compiler takes it as Wei by default.

$$1\ Ether = 10^9\ Gwei = 10^{18}\ Wei. \tag{3.1}$$

Also, when sending the cryptocurrency to other accounts, Solidity provides various kinds of denominations: Ether, Finney, Gwei, and Wei. In the following, we show how the other denominations stand in the hierarchy of Wei.

1. Kwei (Babbage) = 10^3 Wei
2. Mwei (Lovelace) = 10^6 Wei
3. Gwei (Shannon) = 10^9 Wei
4. Microether (Szabo) = 10^{12} Wei
5. Milliether (Finney) = 10^{15} Wei
6. Ether = 10^{18} Wei

Suppose that Alice is going to send one Ether to Bob through her wallet app. How can they know the exact transaction fee? The transaction fee calculation function is as follows:

$$Transaction\ fee = Gas\ limit \times Gas\ price. \tag{3.2}$$

If the gas limit is 21,000 units, and the gas price is 200 Gwei. Then the total fee would be $21,000 \times 200 = 4,20,0000$ Gwei. As a result, Alice must attach 1.0042 ETH to the transaction and send them to Bob. Bod will receive 1 ETH and miner will get 0.0042 ETH. The Ethereum transaction-fee mechanism has been upgraded through the London Upgrade [60] since August 5, 2021. The benefits of this improvement include improved transaction cost estimation, faster transaction inclusion, and balancing ETH issuance by burning a percentage of transaction fees [59].

After the London network upgrade, every block has a base fee and tip fee, which is described in equation (3.3). As the base fee of the transaction fee is burnt, users are required to add a tip in their transactions. The tip can further compensate miners for processing users' transactions:

$$Transaction\ fee = Gas\ limit \times (Base\ fee + Tip). \tag{3.3}$$

Therefore, if Alice would like to send 1 ETH to Bob after 2021, she may include a tip of 10 Gwei, so the total transaction fee will be: $21,000 \times (100 + 10) = 2,310,000$

Table 3.1 Gas costs of the common operations on Ethereum.

Name	Description	Gas cost
STOP	Halts execution	0
ADD	Addition	3
SUB	Subtraction	3
MUL	Multiplication	5
DIV	Division	5
MOD	Modulo remainder	5

Gwei. Therefore, 1 ETH will be given to Bob, the tip 0.00021 ETH will be given to miner, the remaining base fee will be burned. Moreover, Alice can also set a maximum transaction fee; if the fee is not used up, the remaining fee would be returned. Next, we will introduce the gas price and gas limit.

Gas Price and Limit

We briefly outlined the basics of gas in the previous section. Fundamentally, only the miner takes both the block reward and the fees, and all the other nodes just execute the transaction without incentives. In fact, incentive for transaction execution and propagation is also significant but less studied, we will discuss this research gap in a later section.

Unlike Bitcoin, Ethereum enables developers to develop decentralized apps and deploy smart contracts, diversifying the functions of the blockchain platform. Any operation of transaction requires computation resources to execute on the blockchain. The Ethereum protocol defines how many gas units each basic operation consumes. Table 3.1 shows the gas costs that are determined by the Ethereum protocol. Take a look at the recommended transaction fee price [61]. At this moment, the standard gas price is 162 Gwei and the transaction will be mined in less than five minutes. If a user pays 196 Gwei, the transaction will be mined in less than two minutes. Thus, faster operations will need higher fees.

Most of the famous Ether wallet apps are able to set the gas price automatically for the transaction senders to the recommended value. If the transaction is not time sensitive, the sender can adjust the price manually to a lower value. Suppose that a transaction has three operations: an addition that cost 3 gas, a multiplication that cost 5 gas, and a subtraction that costs 3 gas according to the protocol standard. Thus, the total amount of gas the transaction needs is 11. Therefore, if the price of gas is 50 Gwei (50 billion Wei), the transaction fee is 50 Gwei multiplied by 11 = 55 Gwei.

Each transaction sets a limit called the gas limit to the maximum number of computation steps a code execution can use. This is the maximum number of units of gas a user wants to pay for a transaction. The gas limit is essential since it is challenging to estimate in advance how much gas a transaction would actually need. It is also considered as a security mechanism that can prevent high fees from being incorrectly charged due to the unpredictable errors on Ethereum. A standard ETH transfer requires a gas limit of 21,000 units of gas. However, to take the smart contract as an example, it generally contains multiple operations, which surely require more computation resources. In order to compensate for Ethereum's computation overhead, the transaction that is used for executing the smart contract must be granted a higher gas limit. Assume that the gas limit is only set to 10,000, then the smart contract cannot be executed as it needs 20,000 units of gas. Therefore, all the states will be reverted to the initial states.

However, if the gas limit is set to 21,000, the transaction consumes 20,000 gas units. Any gas not used in a transaction will be returned to the user. Therefore, we may infer that the gas price, not the gas limit, truly dictates the value paid for transaction fees. Note that Ethereum has a block gas limit rather than a block size like Bitcoin.

All the verified transactions are ready to be confirmed by the block miner. Every new block represents the latest update to account balances. A block simply refers to a set of related Bitcoin transactions that took place within the same period. New blocks are created after further mining occurs, or a transaction occurs where Bitcoin is exchanged. Bitcoin blocks containing all the most recent transactions are added to the blockchain every 10 minutes. That means, in theory, a transaction will receive its first confirmation within 10 minutes of the request being sent. Unless you are sending more than $1,000,000 worth of cryptocurrency, it is unlikely that the transaction sender needs more than six confirmations for the transaction to be processed, so typically, it should not take more than one hour for the transaction to be fully confirmed.

3.1.2   Block Reward

The transactions, when submitted, are picked up by the blockchain network and is inserted into a "pool of unconfirmed transactions." The transaction pool is a collection of all the transactions on that network that have not been confirmed yet. Miners on the network select transactions from this pool and add them to their "block." Transactions also contain metadata information which can be utilized to store data over the blockchain.

In simple terms, we can say that a block is a container of information that stores the data over the blockchain. A typical block comprises transactions, a timestamp, a block identifier, a nonce value, and the hash of the previous block. Depending on the blockchain platform that is in use, a block might have additional information, such as the hash value of other blocks. The blockchain is formed by a chain of these blocks utilizing the hash values of previous blocks. Different platforms may have various data structures. For example, Hyperledger utilizes a key-value scheme for blocks [62]. The timestamp connected with the block is also important, ensuring that the blockchain is always under control according to the time. In Bitcoin, for example, a block is generated every 10 minutes [1]. Within 10 minutes, at least one block can be mined and added to the chain. Miners attempt to guess the nonce value (which is not the same as the transaction nonce) that will be appended to block data to create a specified hash result. In the case of Bitcoin, for example, this nonce number should ensure that the hash of the mined block has some leading zeros, with the number of zeros indicating the difficulty of current hash puzzle. When the miner is able to guess the nonce value, then the block

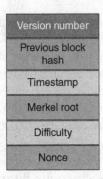

Figure 3.4 Contents of block header.

is mined and added to the chain. This process is also known as mining, and the miner receives a reward for winning the hash puzzle [1]. How can the system guarantee the block generation time is 10 minutes? The answer is by adjusting the difficulty of hash puzzle. If there is miner winning the puzzle in less than 10 minutes, then the system will increase the difficulty. Similarly, if no one can work out the solution in less than 10 minutes, then the system will lower the difficulty accordingly. The detailed information of a block generally includes block header, block identifiers, and Merkle trees. A block header contains details about a block such as a timestamp, protocol information, nonce, difficulty, and the preceding block hash needed to create the chain. Every block has a hash value linked with it, which also serves as a block identifier. If the block data changes, the hash value will change as well. Finally, a Merkle tree is included in a block. Merkle trees are hash binary trees that are used to store and verify transactions in a block.

The first field, as can be seen, is the magic number. In the Bitcoin network, for example, the magic number always has the value displayed on the screen. The block size specifies the amount of bytes in a block. The block header is the third entry, and it contains six different things, including the preceding block hash and nonce value, as shown in Fig. 3.4. The transaction counter number, which is a positive integer that specifies how many transactions are included within a block, is then followed by a list of transactions with the same counts as the transaction counter.

Merkle roots, as previously stated, work in such a way that even if one of the transactions changes, the tree's root will alter (see Fig. 2.3). Users may therefore validate transactions simply by glancing at the Merkle root. If a single piece of information within a transaction for a block changes, the Merkle root for that block changes as well. In a Merkle tree, transactions are hashed together in groups of two. Miners can earn transaction fees on transactions in their mined block, as previously mentioned. However, transaction fees alone are insufficient to cover the cost of miners.

Bitcoin mining is the process of generating new Bitcoins and confirming new transactions, which is critical to ensuring the correctness and security of the ledger. Mining requires miners to solve a hash-based math problem that is highly complicated. The block reward refers to a certain quantity of Bitcoins released by the blockchain network and is only awarded to the hash problem solver since the mining is quite costly. Block

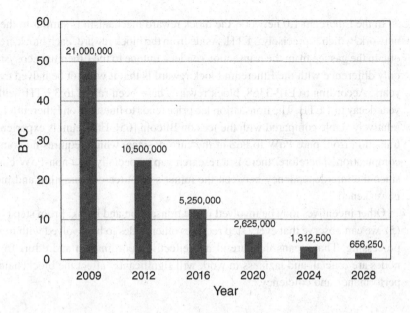

Figure 3.5 Block reward halves every four years [63].

reward is the compensation for the miner's CPU (central processing unit) time and energy consumption, and the key to ensure that a rational miner would work properly.

In addition to compensating the miners and supporting the Bitcoin network, mining is also responsible for "minting." As of April 4, 2022, the number of Bitcoins in circulation was about 19 million [64]. At the beginning of a Bitcoin project release, the number of minted coins for each block (i.e., block reward) was 50 (i.e., 50 BTC). However, the block reward is not always 50 BTC, but is halved every 210,000 blocks. The halving generally occurs every four years since the block generation takes about 10 minutes. Figure 3.5 shows that the Bitcoin reward halves every four years. As of the year of 2022, the block creator could be rewarded only 6.25 BTC. Around the year 2140, the reward is expected to be 0 BTC. The miners have to collect more transaction fees to compensate their work. The principle of the halving works like this: halved reward ⇒ half the inflation ⇒ lower supply ⇒ higher demand ⇒ higher price ⇒ miners' incentive is guaranteed. As a result, even though the reward is decreasing, miners do not lose too much as the value of Bitcoin has been increased in the market.

From the perspective of the system, block reward and miner are interdependent. The reward can attract numerous rational miners to exert their efforts on maintaining the whole network. If there is no reward, then no miner would join the network since the permissionless blockchain network cannot enforce any entry. In some other similar permissionless blockchain networks, it is possible that the sum of block reward and transaction fees is not able to compensate for a miner's computation resources. Thus, the system can assign a certain voting weight to the miners, which allows the miners to have more weight on decision-making. The miners would benefit more from this privilege.

In the Ethereum 1.0 network, the block reward mechanism is similar to the Bitcoin network, which is precisely 3 ETH. Aside from the block reward, each block creator can obtain the gas fee from the transaction senders, unique to the Ethereum ecosystem. The only difference with the Ethereum block reward is that it will not be halved every four years. According to EIP-3368, block rewards have been raised to 3 ETH, with a two-year decay to 1 ETH. The transaction fee price tends to fluctuate on Ethereum 1.0, but is relatively stable compared with the fees on Bitcoin [65]. Ethereum is experiencing the transition from pure PoW to PoS at the current stage, which requires no complicated computation. Therefore, there is a research gap, especially in a non-PoW consensus, since the interdependency between the miner's resource consumption and incentives is weakened.

Other incentives may be involved in the transaction and block: From step (2) to step (5), we can observe that every step requires other nodes to be involved with transaction processing. That means the careful and effective coordination and effort from other nodes are crucial, and laziness in work will significantly affect the blockchain system performance and efficiency.

3.2   How Economic Incentive Boosts Security

As a distributed and decentralized system, blockchain technology is considered to be a promising alternative to the traditional centralized systems which can secure the network by incentivizing the good behaviors and discouraging the bad behaviors. Here are the questions: (1) What is a good or bad behavior? (2) How do the economic incentives encourage or discourage good or bad behavior? (3) What is the relation between the users' behaviors and the system security? Below are the answers to, and thoughts on, these questions.

Firstly, good or bad behavior is always determined from the system's perspective. Behavior that is in the interest of the system is considered good. Otherwise, it is regarded as bad behavior. This book mainly focuses on the public or permissionless blockchain since only the other types of blockchain are not fully distributed and decentralized systems. The major problem of such systems is that it is impossible to enforce or monitor all the participants' behaviors since the system control is decentralized. Users may behave in many ways. Take the miners on the Bitcoin network [1] as an example. In a mining process, a hash puzzle winner creating a new block and packing the legal transactions as required are good behaviors. And the other nonwinners validating the transactions and blocks are also good behaviors, because the unmistakable transactions and blocks are the most central parts of any blockchain network. Likewise, miners tampering with the blocks or concealing validation results are bad behaviors, because these behaviors have prejudiced the system interests.

Secondly, for good behaviors, the system will issue rewards to the actors (e.g., block rewards and transaction fees). For the bad behaviors, the system will charge a penalty (e.g., a security deposit) to the actors. Such a mechanism of reward and punishment is in the interest of rational users. That is also the primary reason why the number of rational participants in a fully distributed and decentralized system must exceed a certain threshold, otherwise the system is not secure and reliable. As for the nonrational actors, if they want to initiate the double-spending attack, they have to create a new fork of blockchain that is longer than the other chains. According to the longest-chain rule, other nodes will add the new blocks to their local ledgers. However, creating new forks means that the nonrational actors have consecutively won the hash puzzles, where the cost is very high and the winning probability is extremely low. From the rationality perspective, we may explain why an attacker is unlikely to modify all the blocks or generate a longer chain than the other collaboratively generated chain, as follows.

1. **Limited budget:** Hash puzzle is a costly mining process that significantly increases the cost of creating a new block. The whole network controls the hash difficulty, and no one can change it artificially. As the core of winning a hash puzzle, the difficulty ensures a low winning rate for every participant. Therefore, with an extremely low winning rate and a relatively high mining cost, the attacker can hardly afford the total expenditure.

2. **Lack of incentives:** Suppose an attacker has created a collection of blocks at a huge cost. These blocks can hardly be finalized to the global ledger. After the block creation, the other participants must validate and confirm the blocks before finalizing them into the blockchain, where the validation and confirmation consume the computation resources. As the Schelling Coin [28] indicates, telling the truth is always the best strategy for the rational participants to get rewards.

3. **Potential punishments:** In other blockchain projects represented by Ethereum, participants are required to stake cryptocurrencies before joining the network. Even if someone wants to collude with the attacker, he risks being exposed by other honest users and thus faces a hefty fine.

Lastly, as we know, cryptography can be used to achieve system security and preserve users' privacy. Why is it necessary to use incentives to regulate the participants' behaviors? The principles behind cryptography and incentives are distinctly different. Generally, cryptography is used to resist known security attacks. However, the development cost of cryptography is very high. It always takes a lot of time to develop the cryptographic protocols and upgrade the client application and system. Thus, it would be too late to take action if some unknown attacks suddenly occurred. In contrast, developing and deploying any incentive scheme is much cheaper and more accessible. There is no need to have everyone on the network working properly. With the rationality-majority assumption, an incentive mechanism ensuring that a majority of participants act in the interests of the blockchain network can enhance system security.

Blockchain technology employs two types of incentives to encourage the majority of rational participants on the networks: block rewards and transaction fees. Briefly, every recognized consensus protocol has exploited the scarcity of something. In PoW, computational power is the scarce resource. The mining rigs, such as graphics processing units (GPU) are pretty expensive. Suppose an attacker wants to take over the blockchain network; he or she must purchase more computation power. Consequently, compromising the blockchain is financially infeasible for the attackers. The same happens within the other consensus protocols. In PoS, the scarce resource is the staked cryptocurrencies. In PoA, the scarce resource is the reputation of authorities.

Incentives doubtlessly play a significant role in the blockchain. They are crucial for security and operations. The permissionless blockchain should be built upon solid foundations of incentives. There are many areas left in the incentive mechanism to improve, ranging from the very basics of block rewards and how they interact with the consensus mechanism, through the dynamics of transaction fees, and all the other stages of the life cycle of the transactions.

3.3   Summary

This chapter provides a comprehensive survey of the incentive issues in blockchain networks. We have outlined a typical life cycle of transactions and then emphasized two essential incentives within this cycle. Furthermore, this chapter introduces the transaction fee and block reward in terms of concepts, calculation functions, and impacts. We also highlight why incentives are feasible to secure a distributed system. Based on the survey of incentives in cryptoeconomics, this chapter is trying to offer an overview of the mainstream incentives, explaining what makes the incentives possible to achieve security in a distributed system. This survey is expected to serve as an efficient guideline for further understanding incentive mechanisms and exploring potential research directions that may lead to exciting outcomes in cryptoeconomics.

Part II

Consensus Protocol Design in Blockchain Networks

4 Consensus Mechanism Basics

The consensus problem is the key issue in a multi-agent system. All agents must agree on a majority value to achieve a certain goal. The majority in this case necessitates at least one more than half of the available votes. However, one or more flawed methods may influence the eventual results, resulting in a lack of, or inaccurate, agreement.

It is quite easy to achieve consensus in a centralized system, since the central party can censor and monitor the scattered nodes. The consensus process generally occurs in a distributed or decentralized system, requiring all agents to cooperate in the presence of various faults. The practical applications of consensus include deciding the system state and transaction order. The most common scenario that requires consensus is the blockchain network. This chapter first introduces the basic network model, including centralized, decentralized, and distributed networks, in order to make it easier to understand the consensus problem.

4.1 Network Model Basics

The dispute over centralized, decentralized, and distributed systems affects both individuals and companies. It impacts nearly everyone who uses the Internet. It is crucial to the growth and expansion of networks, financial systems, businesses, applications, and web services, among other things.

While all of these systems are capable of performing their functions, some are more reliable and secure by design than others. Systems can be quite tiny, with only a few devices and a few people interconnected. They can also be massive, spanning countries and continents. We present the details of three types of network model and show the comparison of advantages and disadvantages.

4.1.1 Three types of Network: Centralized, Decentralized, and Distributed

Before introducing the networks of blockchain systems, this chapter first discusses the common types of networks, which are shown in Fig. 4.1.

As seen in the diagram, there are three different types of networks: centralized, distributed, and decentralized networks. A centralized network is controlled by a central party, which is able to determine the outcome of a whole system. Undoubtedly, consensus is simple in a centralized system. However, it would be a different case in

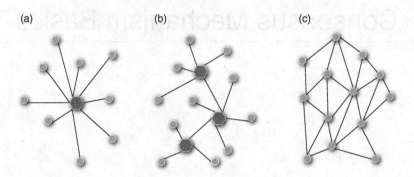

Figure 4.1 Three types of network.

a distributed or decentralized system. Since the centralized network is straightforward and easy to understand, let us start off with that one.

4.1.1.1 Centralized Network

Centralized networks are client or server architecture systems in which one or more client nodes are directly linked to a central server. The centralized networks are often used in medium and small businesses, allowing clients to make requests to a central server and get responses from it. The major components of a centralized system include: (1) clients, (2) server, and (3) communication link (cables, Wi-Fi, etc.). The key characteristics of a centralized system are listed as follows.

1. Presence of a global clock: The global clock is controlled by the central party. All the other client nodes must be in sync with the central server.
2. One single central unit: There is only one central server coordinating all the other client nodes.
3. Dependent failure of components: The security of whole system is highly associated with the central server. Once the central node is down, there is no one managing all the requests from the other client nodes.

Therefore, the client nodes in a centralized network cannot access the internal resources without the central server's permission. A typical centralized network always has a single domain controller, which is in charge of the global clock synchronization, authentication, and access control.

At the current stage, there still exist lots of common examples of the centralized network. For most of the small business companies, using a centralized network to manage the identities and access control is much easier and cheaper. For example, online social applications such as Facebook, Twitter, and Instagram are examples of centralized systems. However, they are not the same as the small business companies since they use a more complicated network architectures (maybe a hybrid model) to realize all of their network functions. Ultimately, these large companies require a central unit to manage the internal and external resources, authenticate the identities, and control the access rights.

With the growth of business, more and more firms have transformed their centralized architecture into a decentralized one because the decentralized platforms are becoming more cost effective and accessible. Thus, the advantages of a centralized network no longer seem to stand out compared with the obvious disadvantages. We conclude the disadvantages as follows.

1. **Single point failure:** A single central server presents a single point of failure on a centralized network. If the central node is down, then the entire network goes down. Consequently, any minor changes on the central part will impact the whole network performance.
2. **Security issues:** The central server is the only target for the attackers since it stores all the sensitive and valuable data and manages all the authorities. Once the central server is compromised, it will cause unexpected economic losses. Therefore, a centralized network always involves security risks and privacy risks.
3. **Scalability limitation:** It is easy and cheap to build up a small-scale centralized network. However, it is pretty challenging to scale an existing centralized network. The central server can only add more storage and processing units. Besides, a sudden increase in the requests may lead to a crash in the only central unit, causing the collapse of the whole network.

The advantages of a centralized network are listed as follows.

1. **Easy and cheap deployment:** There is only one central party processing the clients' requests. No further configuration is needed.
2. **Handy management:** The central unit is able to monitor the clients' behaviors in a more straightforward way. Once there is any malicious behavior being detected, it will be removed directly.

4.1.1.2 Decentralized Networks

Instead of a single centralized server, a decentralized network employs numerous servers to store and process the clients' requests. Relatively, the multi-server architecture can afford more traffic and workloads compared with a counter single-server architecture. A client is also able to act as a server. Thus, the major components of a decentralized network are (1) nodes and (2) communication link. A centralized network and a decentralized network are different in the control level. Compared with the centralized one, a decentralized network does not have a global clock since it has numerous servers or nodes to process requests independently, bringing some major benefits, as follows.

1. **No single point failure:** There exist numerous storage and process units holding multiple copies of the resources in the decentralized network, which solves the problem of single point of failure that always exists in a centralized network. Numerous nodes sustain the entire network. Even if any node is compromised, the whole network will be almost unaffected. The requests can also be processed more quickly since more processing units are available.

2. **High security and privacy level:** All the sensitive and confidential data is not stored in one single unit, but in multiple independent units. For any potential attacker, hacking all the storage and process units is extremely difficult and costly. Even if some of the nodes have been compromised, there are still nodes available for network operation. Therefore, a decentralized network can eliminate the cyber risk, efficiently ensuring the security and preserving the users' privacy.
3. **Scalability:** A decentralized network is easy to scale since any client node adding the storage or process units will not affect the whole network's performance.

However, the decentralized network is not always advantageous in every aspect. The disadvantages are listed as follows.

1. **Lack of regulatory oversight:** In a decentralized network, the server nodes generally act independently; it is more difficult to achieve a common goal than with a centralized network. Thus, achieving consensus is always the central issue of all decentralized network. Owing to the high availability and scalability, the decentralized network is often adopted in a large-scale system. However, this makes it harder to detect the compromised nodes.
2. **Costly deployment:** Decentralized networks are more reliable than centralized networks. Because a decentralized network relies on various nodes to support the system, it requires nodes with more storage space and more processing power.

Apparently, the decentralized network is not always suitable for all kinds of systems. Different business models may have various requirements in network deployments, so they must carefully consider the pros and cons of using a decentralized network.

According to Van Steen and Tanenbaum [67], the decentralized networks are multi-tiered client–server architectures, which have divided the applications into a user interface, processing components, and a data level. However, this does not mean that data storage and processing power have also been divided evenly across the entire network. The intensive data storage and process tasks must rely on the high-performance nodes. Different groups of nodes that are specialized to a particular set of functions refer to the vertical distribution [67]. As the network technology evolves, the other way of managing the network is referred to as horizontal distribution, in which the nodes can independently work on their own share of the complete data set for balancing the network load. The system which has realized the horizontal distribution is known as a peer-to-peer (P2P) system.

A public blockchain is built upon a decentralized network, which enables anyone to participate in the network and access to the data on the blockchain. It worth noting that a public blockchain is often depicted as a decentralized, distributed, and P2P system. This is because the underlying network architecture of the public blockchain is usually of a tremendous scale, and a hybrid construction can contribute to system robustness and functional diversity.

The InterPlanetary File System (IPFS) is a common example using a P2P storage network. It enables all data to be securely stored and exchanged throughout the whole network without the involvement of a third party.

4.1.1.3   Distributed Networks

According to the definition in [67], "A distributed system is a collection of independent computers that appears to its users as a single coherent system." A distributed system is composed of a number of computers that interact over a network and work together to accomplish a common task. The interpretation of this definition is as follows.

1. Autonomous collaboration: All the nodes must be autonomous and work on a common task like a unified system.
2. Large number of participants: A small group of computers cannot form a reliable distributed system.
3. No requirement for a single node: A distributed system can involve various heterogeneous devices. The nodes can range from high-performance machine to lightweight devices.

Distributed networks and decentralized networks share similarities in several aspects: (1) no central party; (2) suitable for a large-scale system; (3) nodes are autonomous. Decentralized networks are often recognized as the subset of distributed networks. These inherent commonalities result in them having almost the same strengths and weaknesses. Owing to the geographically dispersed structure, the distributed network has a slight advantage over the decentralized network. The advantages are listed as follows.

1. **High scalability and low latency:** Distributed networks outperform both centralized and decentralized networks in terms of scalability. There is no specific performance and location requirements for nodes in a distributed network. The data processing is dispersed evenly across multiple nodes; thus, distributed networks can present lower latency than other types of network.
2. **More security and privacy guarantee:** Data is stored and shared across the entire network; processing power is also distributed evenly. Any attacker can hardly hack all the servers. As a result, it is far more difficult to successfully censor the users and to tamper with the system.

The drawbacks of decentralized networks are similar to those of decentralized networks for example, poor regulatory oversight, but on a larger scale.

1. **Difficult to reach a consensus:** Distributed networks, compared with decentralized networks, take more resources to maintain or reconfigure the system by allowing more nodes to join the network without performance and location requirements. Since any critical update must be synchronized with all the other nodes, making timely decisions or achieving a consensus on a large-scale common project might be challenging due to the tremendous performance differences of nodes.
2. **Loosely organized:** The evenly distributed processing power allows the network to respond quickly to the other nodes' requests. However, the geographically dispersed architecture may result in unexpectable latency, which makes it even harder to locate the compromised nodes. Furthermore, designing algorithms or protocols for a distributed network can be rather troublesome.

There is no central party monitoring the activity of nodes. The distributed network must adopt some mechanism to allow the individual nodes to determine the system action, and the system state depends on the outcomes of the decisions each individual has agreed on. All the rules that nodes must be followed throughout the decision-making process will be specified in a consensus mechanism. The consensus mechanism determines the exact way through which a dispersed network makes decisions.

A large enterprise with thousands of people and systems geographically dispersed among branch offices and data centers is an example of a distributed network. Rather than placing a single server on each site, they have spread servers throughout the network, put them in various physical locations, and adopted advanced protocols and algorithms to balance the load across the entire network.

The Google search technology is based on a distributed network. Hundreds of computers work on every single request, searching the Internet and responding to the request. Google seems to be a single system to the users, but it is actually a collection of computers working together to complete a single task.

4.1.2   Two Communication Models of a Distributed System: Asynchronous and Synchronous Systems

A distributed system is an esoteric discipline, involving a great number of theories, protocols, and technologies. The aim is to use more devices and process more data, which coincides with the design of blockchain technology. That is the reason why a public blockchain uses a distributed network as its basic network layer.

Consensus is the core issue of a distributed system. Before discussing this issue, we must consider the communication model of the distributed system. The way to construct or analyze a distributed system is directly influenced by the communication modes of the distributed system, namely, synchronous or asynchronous. In a synchronous system, all information must be confirmed in a single round. As a result, no message delivered in one round can affect the actions in the same round. The second round can only be initiated after a complete information transmission and confirmation process. Modeling a synchronous system is more straightforward since everyone must wait for the final confirmation before their subsequent actions. However, the communications in real-world networks are generally asynchronous due to the unexpected failure of some nodes or channels. This discussion starts with the synchronous system.

4.1.2.1   Synchronous System

A synchronous distributed system provides strong guarantees on the system operation. It is frequently accompanied by strong assumptions and limitations when modeling and analyzing a synchronous system. It serves as an idealized model that can facilitate researchers to better understand the distributed system. The key features of the synchronous system are listed as follows [68].

1. **Upper bound on message delivery:** In a single round, every message is delivered in less than a maximum latency. Messages between any particular set of participating nodes are not anticipated to be delayed for random time periods.

2. **Ordered message delivery:** Messages are sent in a predetermined order, that is, First In First Out, which guarantees the messages can be delivered only in the order that they were originally sent. Randomly ordered messages are not acceptable.

3. **Notion of globally synchronized clocks:** Although each node has its own local clock, the clocks of all nodes are constantly in synchronization with each other. This makes it feasible to establish a global real-time ordering of events across the entire network.

4. **Lock-step-based execution:** In each single round, all processes of the whole system must be executed by all the other nodes at the same time in parallel. Suppose there is a coordinator node responsible for distributing the messages to the other nodes. It is not allowed for separate follower nodes to independently process the message and output states at different times.

Based on these features, we can have a brief understanding of the synchronous system. A message is delivered over the network in specific time duration (with a known upper bound). All the messages are sent following the same ordering rule. The follower nodes start to process the message at a predictable speed in parallel. Finally, the system can obtain a deterministic and uniform result and state. Under normal circumstances, the network has no major breakdowns, and the nodes perform well. It makes sense to use a synchronous model.

However, the problem with synchronous systems is that it is hard to calculate the upper bound, and the network connections are not always stable due to unpredictable failures. The strong assumptions and limitations that cannot be ignored make the synchronous system less practical in real-world applications. Take the public blockchain as an example. The system is not able to ask the participants to deliver messages in a fixed time duration. Large scale and open systems often have numerous unpredictable risks.

4.1.2.2 Asynchronous System

Real-world distributed systems can only be modeled as a asynchronous system since it does not have any strong assumptions regarding the delivery upper bound and event ordering. Consequently, the system behaves asynchronously, meaning that the nodes will send and process the messages independently at different times instead of taking actions at the same time in parallel. The key features of the asynchronous system are listed as follows [68].

1. **Clock may not be accurate or be out of synchronization:** Every node processes the messages and requests independently without waiting for others' confirmations. Thus, the local clock of each node is not always in synchronization with all the others.

2. **Messages can be delayed for arbitrary period of times:** Since some of nodes may go offline and the communication link is not always stable, the upper-bound latency of message transmission is difficult to calculate. There are also no constraints on the event ordering.

Compared with the synchronous systems, there are more uncertainties involved in the asynchronous systems. The most challenging aspect of designing a distributed system is how the system can tolerate various potential failures. That is the reason why the protocols and algorithms for an asynchronous model tend to be more difficult and complicated than those of a synchronous one.

To solve synchronization issues, the asynchronous paradigm requires protocol designers to make no assumptions about network latency. Here are two assumptions that can be acceptable for asynchronous system design [69]: (1) there are infinitely many computation steps for each process, and (2) every message is eventually delivered. (These are fairness conditions.)

Next, we focus on the core concept of a distributed system, consensus, presenting the critical definitions and necessary problem formulation. By introducing various consensus protocols, we discuss the requirements and limitations on designing the consensus in a synchronous or asynchronous distributed system.

4.2   Consensus in Distributed Systems

The consensus refers to a number of nodes reaching an agreement on a single value or state. It does not mean that every one in this system must agree on this value or state; opinions can be divided over the result. But the number of nodes which have a common opinion must reach a certain threshold, otherwise, the final agreed result is not reliable and trustless. Therefore, a consensus protocol must be fault tolerant. Fault tolerance is the ability of a system to continue working normally in the face of a number of failures. If its operational quality deteriorates, the deterioration is proportionate to the degree of the failure [70].

The consensus problem is a core issue in distributed systems. To reach consensus on some issues, one feasible way is to set an agreement threshold [71]. Take the blockchain as an example. For some proposed value, the amount of votes must achieve a certain threshold; then the voted result can be considered as valid. A consensus protocol tolerating faults must satisfy the following properties [71].

1. **Termination:** Nonfaulty processes can determine some values.
2. **Integrity:** If all nonfaulty processes have proposed the same value, then any nonfaulty process must decide the value.
3. **Agreement:** Every nonfaulty process must agree on the same value.

These three characteristics are known as termination, agreement, and validity. Any algorithm that possesses these three characteristics is considered to solve the consensus issue.

Time complexity and message complexity are two important aspects when evaluating the performance of consensus [72]. The number of rounds of message exchange is referred to as time complexity. The quantity of message traffic created by the protocol is referred to as message complexity. Other considerations may include the implementations of failure detectors, network latency, and the throughput.

Therefore, is there a deterministic consensus algorithm in an asynchronous distributed system that can satisfy agreement, integrity, and termination? The answer is "impossible." In the remainder of this chapter, we will introduce two theorems of great importance, Fischer, Lynch, and Patterson (FLP) and consistency, availability and partition (CAP), to present the basic design principles in distributed systems.

4.2.1   Fischer, Lynch, and Patterson (FLP) Impossibility Theorem

The FLP theorem, one of the most fundamental research on distributed system, was proposed in 1985 [73], and named after its authors Fischer, Lynch, and Paterson. It has answered the question "In an asynchronous distributed system, is there a deterministic consensus algorithm that can satisfy agreement, validity, termination, and fault tolerance?" As the title implies, it is impossible to design any consensus algorithms that tolerate even a single node fault in an asynchronous distributed system. That is "No completely asynchronous consensus protocol can tolerate even a single unannounced process death." This means that in asynchronous distributed systems, there does not exist an algorithm that can enable all nodes to achieve consensus. The above conclusion is known as the FLP impossibility. This theorem is considered one of the most important theorems in distributed systems.

The problem of consensus can be solved in a synchronous distributed system. This is because all the actions are taken at the same time in parallel. If parts of the whole system are compromised, the remaining parts will stop working when they wait for timeout. As we know, the message propagation latency from one node to another in an asynchronous paradigm is unbounded. This implies that if a node does not receive messages, it cannot tell if the sender node has crashed or if the message has simply been delayed.

The FLP theorem asserts that fault tolerant consensus cannot simultaneously satisfy agreement and termination properties under the asynchronous network paradigm. Thus, the distributed systems cannot achieve fault tolerance and correctness simultaneously. Under the asynchronous network paradigm, we cannot have all three attributes (fault tolerance, agreement, and termination) at the same time. However, under the synchronous network model (where message delays are bounded), an algorithm exists that satisfies all three required properties.

In a fully asynchronous distributed system, at least one node going down or offline is modeled as a crash failure, and at least one node telling lies is modeled as a Byzantine failure. It has been proven that a Byzantine failure is much more difficult than a crash failure [74]. The FLP theorem has two important assumptions: (1) message channels do not discard messages, and (2) non-Byzantine failures.

It worth noting that the FLP theorem does not mean that designing a deterministic consensus for a distributed system is impossible. This impossibility result derives from worst-case scheduling scenarios, which are unlikely to occur in practice. We can realize two of the three properties under the asynchronous network model. Under the synchronous network model with the bounded message delays, there exist algorithms that satisfy all three desired properties. Nonetheless, scientists have always been persisting in finding ways to deal with the impossibility of FLP. The two methods for overcoming the FLP impossibility are as follows: (1) the partially synchronous assumption and (2) the nondeterministic model [75].

4.2.2   Consistency, Availability, and Partition (CAP) Tolerance Theorem

The CAP theorem is also called Brewer's theorem, and is named after Eric Brewer, the computer scientist who proposed the concept during his talk in 2000. The concept was elaborated in his book [76] in 2012. The CAP theorem applies a similar logic to that of the FLP theorem, that is, a distributed system has difficulty processing all three properties when experiencing failures: consistency, availability, and partition tolerance, as shown in Fig. 4.2. The details of the three properties are listed as follows.

1. **Consistency:** This implies that all clients, regardless of which node they connect to, view the same data at the same time. If data is being written to one node, it must be promptly forwarded or duplicated to all other nodes in the system.
2. **Availability:** This means that every node can receive requests or get services even if one or more nodes are offline. All nonfaulty nodes can deliver a valid response to any request.
3. **Partition tolerance:** This means the network must be tolerant to partitions. Even if there exist a number of communication breakdowns between nodes or groups, the remaining parts must be able to operate normally.

Normally, the system performs all three functions. However, according to the CAP theorem, a distributed system can guarantee only two of the them when it has a network failure. More specifically, the system can provide only either consistency or availability since partition tolerance is necessary in any case. Consequently, when a system is experiencing the failures, only two options are available: (1) high consistency but low availability, and (2) high availability but low consistency.

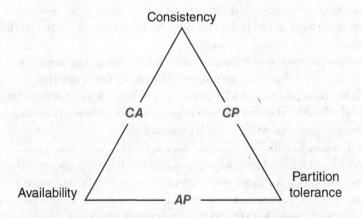

Figure 4.2 The CAP triangle [77].

4.2.3   Fault Tolerance

Fault tolerance refers to the ability of a system to continue operating despite failures [70]. Fault tolerance can be implemented into a distributed system to eliminate the impacts of node failure, ensuring the high availability of the system.

Faults (such as lying node or network interruptions) are a common cause of network unavailability. Designing a system to work normally even if parts of network are defective is known as fault tolerance. High-performance devices can improve system stability to some degree, but cannot eliminate node or line failures caused by the unexpectable attacks. The primary benefit of fault tolerance is that it can reduce the possibility of systems being unavailable due to some component failures. In the following we introduce two common fault tolerance protocols which deal with the crash failure and Byzantine failure, respectively.

4.2.3.1   Crash Fault Tolerance

Crash fault tolerance (CFT) is one level of resilience, where the system will correctly reach consensus if there exist compromised nodes and network interruption. It focuses only on the crash failure, and cannot deal with malicious nodes or behaviors. The Paxos family of protocols was proposed to solve the crash failures [78]. One of family members is named Raft [79].

Raft reaches consensus via an elected and trusted leader. A server in a Raft cluster can be either a leader or a follower; the leader is in charge of replicating logs to the followers. It sends a heartbeat message to its followers on a regular basis to notify them of its presence. Each follower has a maximum latency during which it waits for the leader's heartbeat. When the heartbeat is received, the timer is reset. If no pulse is received, the follower's status is changed to candidate, and a leader election is initiated.

The Raft protocol can guarantee the security and reach consensus through the following properties [80].

1. **Unique leader:** There is at most one leader each round.
2. **Log consistency:** The logs with the same index must have the same content.
3. **Leader completeness:** The log entries made in a particular term will always show in the logs of the leaders who follow that term.
4. **State machine safety:** Once a server has applied a certain log entry to its state machine, no other server in the server cluster can use a different command for the same log.
5. **Node crash:** When a follower node goes down, all requests submitted to that node are ignored. After the node resumes, it synchronizes its log with that of the leader node.

Raft has a strict single-leader policy, requiring all follower nodes to trust the leader. Sometime there will be network congestion issues. Furthermore, it cannot tackle the dishonest nodes and malicious behaviors.

When blockchain is utilized by businesses, however, various firms, departments, or teams may manage distinct components of the system. These many firms, departments,

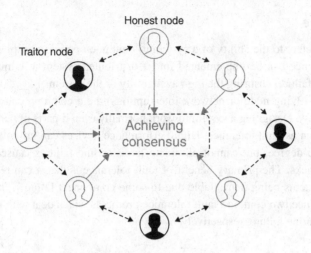

Figure 4.3 Byzantine General Problem [66].

or teams may have disparate goals, leaving the system open to malicious behavior. If any entity behaves maliciously, CFT finds it impossible to form a consensus.

4.2.3.2 Byzantine Fault Tolerance

Byzantine fault is a term for the distributed system, and it is derived from an allegory called the "Byzantine General Problem." In a basic version of the Byzantine General Problem, a group of generals surrounding an enemy must decide whether to attack or retreat (see Fig. 4.3). These generals in various locations may have different decisions. Some want to launch an attack, while others prefer to retreat. In this case, the crucial issue is that all generals must agree on a unique decision. Only if all the generals agree to launch the attack can they win a victory. Some generals may be telling lies, namely, the dishonest generals vote for the "attack" option, but they act as traitors, eventually leading to a defeat. Coordinated attack and retreat do not impact the system performance and benefit.

For example, suppose there are $(2N + 1)$ generals attacking the enemy. The best case is that all of them agree on a common decision, attack or retreat. However, in the real world, the most common case may be that $n(n < N)$ generals vote for one option, and $m(m <= N)$ generals vote for the other option, while the remaining generals $(2N + 1 - n - m)$ have no response. Consequently, the Byzantine General Problem is always the core issue that needs to be addressed in a large-scale distributed system. Furthermore, the difficulty in solving this problem will be exacerbated by the fact that generals are physically scattered, and unexpected errors may occur during transmission.

Back to the computer science area, each node in a distributed system could be considered a general. The Byzantine fault of a distributed system is defined as the unpredictable behaviors and arbitrary data that are presented and generated even by honest participants. Another similar concept in a distributed system is known as Byzantine failure. The definitions of Byzantine fault and Byzantine failure are given as [81]

(1) Byzantine fault: a fault presenting different symptoms to different observers; and (2) Byzantine failure: the loss of a system service due to a Byzantine fault. It is worth noting that if a system has exhibited Byzantine failures, then it necessarily comes with the Byzantine faults. A Byzantine fault will not always result in a Byzantine failure if there is no consensus requirement of the system.

However, a distributed system without consensus can not be considered a reliable system. And it is almost impossible to get rid of the Byzantine faults within the distributed system. A feasible solution to the Byzantine General Problem is Byzantine fault tolerance. As a result, to achieve Byzantine fault tolerance is the primary consideration for the distributed systems. Byzantine fault tolerance refers to whether the distributed system can continue functioning smoothly when some nodes go offline or act as liars. According to [82], the Byzantine fault tolerance mechanisms must be able to ensure the following conditions: (1) all loyal generals agree on the same plan of action, and (2) the presence of a small number of traitors does not cause loyal users to choose bad plans.

Byzantine failures are regarded as the most widespread and complicated class of failures, which can confuse the failure detection systems and eventually make Byzantine fault tolerance difficult. In the case of the blockchain network, the Byzantine General Problem is the core issue, and Byzantine fault tolerance is also of great concern. That is the reason why almost all blockchain systems have consensus mechanisms, which describe the rules for a blockchain to achieve Byzantine fault tolerance. The common types of consensus algorithms in blockchain networks will be discussed in Chapter 5.

4.3 Summary

In this chapter, we have introduced and compared the three types of the network model in terms of creation, maintenance, fault tolerance, and scalability. For most companies, the debate over centralized versus distributed network administration is meaningless since centralized architectures are too limited for today's service demands. However, some instances, such as data center, may benefit a lot from centralized network management. In contrast, the decentralized network is a good choice for expanding companies that need secure, flexible, and reliable access to resources. Informally, decentralized networks can be viewed as a subset of distributed networks. Cryptocurrencies, for example, use decentralized networks to make it difficult for a hacker to access the whole digital ledgers and accounts. As a truly reliable system, the distributed network must have the following characteristics [83].

1. Fault tolerant: It can recover from component failures without performing incorrect actions.
2. Highly available: It can restore operations even when some components have failed.
3. Recoverable: Failed components can restart themselves after the cause of failure has been repaired.

4. Consistent: The system can coordinate actions by multiple components often in the presence of concurrency and failure.
5. Scalable: The system can operate correctly even as it is scaled to a larger size.
6. Predictable performance: The ability to provide desired responsiveness in a timely manner.
7. Secure: The system can preserve the security of data and users' information.

Which one is the best for blockchain? When evaluating the relative benefits of various network configurations, keep in mind that no one is superior to another in all scenarios. The current Internet was built mainly on the foundation of centralized networks, and most of the earlier system features are centralized configurations. As the network technology evolves, organizations will increasingly be able to select the network architecture that best satisfies their individual requirements. If any single network architecture can not meet the needs of every aspect, a hybrid network that involves various technical components might be a better solution. Therefore, we can discover that there exist three types of blockchain networks: public blockchain, consortium blockchain, and private blockchain. This book considers only public blockchain since it has more research significance than the others.

5   Incentivized Consensus Mechanism

The core task of a blockchain network is to ensure that the trustless nodes in the network reach the agreement upon a single tamper-proof record of transactions. The network is expected to tolerate a portion of the nodes deviating from this canonical record with their local views of data. These significant functions can be achieved only through the consensus mechanisms. The focus of this chapter is revealing the consensus mechanisms underlying the popular blockchain projects from theoretic and quantitative perspectives. Moreover, bearing in mind the aforementioned design principles for consensus formation and incentive mechanism, we will provide mathematical insight into the incentive compatibility of blockchain consensus protocols in different protocol layers.

5.1   Consensus Mechanism of Blockchain

From the perspective of system design, a blockchain leverages the power of a P2P network to support the decentralized ledger of transactions. As the subset of a distributed network, a P2P network enables all necessary blockchain protocols and mechanisms to operate on top of it. Given reliable data synchronization over P2P connections, the consensus layers provide the core functionality to maintain the originality, consistency, and order of the blockchain data across the network. More specifically, the consensus protocols provide Byzantine fault tolerance [84] in blockchain networks.

Since the Byzantine Generals' objective is for all (nontraitorous) generals to agree on the same result, this indicates that, in a blockchain network, every nonmalicious entity has the same blockchain state. An agreement (i.e., consensus) on the unique common state or view of the blockchain is expected to be achieved by the consensus nodes in the condition of Byzantine or arbitrary failures. In blockchain networks, Byzantine failures refer to the arbitrary behaviors caused by faulty nodes, including malicious attacks or collusions (e.g., Sybil attacks [85] and double-spending attacks [86]), node mistakes (e.g., unexpected blockchain fork due to software inconsistency [87]), and connection errors. To be specific, in an open-access (i.e., public or permissionless) blockchain network, a node is allowed to freely join or leave the network and activate or deactivate any available system functionalities including issuing new transactions (e.g., as a client), disseminating the received transactions (e.g., as a relay), and validating/finalizing the order and content of transactions (i.e., as a consensus participant).

With the chain-of-block-based data structure and its data order being the consensus target, we can roughly consider that a sequence of transactions in the form of blocks (i.e., transaction batch) represents the state of a ledger, and the confirmation of a block's content and its order in the blockchain incurs a ledger state transition. Then, we can reinterpret the four general requirements for Byzantine fault tolerant (BFT) consensus in the blockchain-based scenarios [14, 88].

1. **Validity (correctness):** If every honest node activated on a common ledger state proposes to expand the blockchain by the same valid block, any honest node transiting to a new local replica state adopts the blockchain headed by that block. Namely, the new block is accepted into the blokchain.
2. **Agreement (consistency):** If an honest node accepts or discards a new block as the header of its local blockchain replica, then any honest node that updates its local blockchain view will update with the same decision.
3. **Liveness (Termination):** All valid transactions that originated from the honest nodes will eventually be confirmed into the canonical blockchain.
4. **Event ordering:** The order and content of the blocks accepted by every honest node will be consistent with each other, as long as the blocks are confirmed in the local blockchain views of each honest node.

The design of consensus protocols may vary with different setups or Quality-of-Service (QoS) requirements of the specific permissionless blockchain systems under consideration. Since the permissioned blockchain networks admit tighter control on the synchronization, they usually adopt the well-studied BFT consensus protocols such as Practical BFT (PBFT) [89] for reaching the consensus among a small group of authenticated nodes (e.g., HyperLedger Fabric v0.5 [90]).

As pointed out in [91], permissioned consensus protocols rely on a semicentralized consensus framework and a higher messaging overhead to provide immediate consensus finality and thus high transaction processing throughput. A typical implementation of such protocols can be found in the Ripple network [92], where a group of synchronized Ripple servers performs blockchain expansion through a voting mechanism. Further, if an external oracle is introduced to designate the primary node for block generation (e.g., with HyperLedger Fabric v0.5 [90]), PBFT [89] can be adopted to implement a three-phase commit scheme for blockchain expansion. In a network of N consensus nodes, the BFT-based protocols are able to conditionally tolerate $\lfloor \frac{N-1}{5} \rfloor$ (e.g., [92]) to $\lfloor \frac{N-1}{2} \rfloor$ faulty nodes.

On the other hand, permissionless blockchain networks admit no identity authentication or explicit synchronization schemes, which require cryptographic techniques (e.g., cryptographic puzzle systems [93], [94]) and incentive mechanisms to achieve Byzantine fault tolerance. This is because, for permissionless blockchains, the jobs of transaction proposal, data propagation, and transaction or block validation or finalization are typically performed over a free-access virtual point-to-point network. The virtual network overlays an existing network infrastructure (e.g., the Internet) and is composed of homogeneous nodes with different functionalities activated. When reliable data transmission between nodes is guaranteed by the adopted network protocols in a blockchain system, our focus will be placed on the layers of data organization and consensus management, such that the nodes of different roles (e.g., relays or consensus participants) are ensured to act on behalf of the other nodes (e.g., blockchain clients) in a trustless point-to-point environment. In the condition of bounded delay and honest majority, permissionless consensus protocols provide significantly better support for network scalability at the cost of lower processing efficiency. Owing to the lack of identity authentication, the direct voting-based BFT protocols do not fit in permissionless blockchain networks. Instead, the incentive-based consensus schemes such as the Nakamoto consensus protocol [1] are widely adopted. This chapter focuses only on the consensus protocols for the permissionless blockchain network.

5.2   Nakamoto Consensus Protocol

To jointly address the problems of pseudonymity, scalability, and poor synchronization, Nakamoto proposed in [1] a permissionless consensus protocol based on a framework of cryptographic block-discovery racing game. This is also known as the Proof of Work (PoW) scheme [95, 96]. From a single node's perspective, the Nakamoto consensus protocol defines three major procedures, namely, the procedure of chain validation, the procedure of chain comparison and extension, and the procedure of PoW solution searching [97]. The chain-validation predicate provides a Boolean judgment on whether a given chain of blocks has valid structural properties. It checks if each block in the chain provides a valid PoW solution with no conflict between transactions as well as the historical records exists. The function of chain comparison and extension compares the length of a set of chains, which may be either received from peer nodes or locally proposed. It guarantees that an honest node only adopts the longest proposal among the candidate views of the blockchain. In this way, PoW solution searching is the main "workhorse" of the protocol and defines a cryptographic puzzle-solving procedure in a computation-intensive manner.

In brief, the PoW solution requires exhaustively querying a cryptographic hash function for a partial preimage generated from a candidate block. The hashcode of that block is expected to satisfy a predefined condition. For simplicity of exposition, let $\mathcal{H}(\cdot)$ denote the hash function and let x denote the binary string assembled based on the candidate block data including the set of transactions (e.g., Merkle root), the reference hash pointers. Then, we can formally define the PoW puzzle and solution as follows.

Definition 1   Given an adjustable hardness condition parameter h, the process of PoW puzzle solution aims to search for a solution string, nonce, such that for a given string x assembled based on the candidate block data, the hashcode (i.e., the target block header bh) of the concatenation of x and nonce is smaller than a target value $D(h)$:

$$bh = \mathcal{H}(x||nonce) \leq D(h), \tag{5.1}$$

where, for some fixed length of bits L, $D(h) = 2^{L-h}$.

The Nakamoto protocol is computation-intensive since to win the puzzle-solving race, a node needs to achieve a hash querying rate as high as possible. This property financially prevents the Sybil attacks of malicious nodes by merely creating multiple pseudoidentities. On the other hand, the economic cost (mainly electricity consumption) also renders it impractical for any node to voluntarily participate in the consensus process at a consistent economic loss. To ensure proper functioning of a permissionless blockchain network, the Nakamoto protocol introduces incentives to probabilistically award the consensus participants based on an embedded mechanism of token supply and transaction tipping [1]. From a game-theoretic point of view, an implicit assumption adopted by the Nakamoto consensus protocol is that all the participant nodes are individually rational [98]. In return, the consensus mechanism is expected to be incentive compatible. In other words, the consensus protocol should ensure that any consensus node will suffer from finical loss whenever it deviates from truthfully following the protocol.

However, the incentive compatibility of the Nakamoto protocol has been openly questioned [99, 100]. Since the Nakamoto protocol allows nodes to propose arbitrary blocks from their local pending transaction set, it is inevitable for the network to experience a blockchain expansion race with a (temporary) split, namely, a fork, in the local views of the blockchain state [86, 96] (see Fig. 5.1). To guarantee the consensus properties and thus convergence to one canonical blockchain state, the Nakamoto protocol relies on the assumption that the majority of the consensus nodes follow the longest-chain rule and are altruistic in information forwarding. It has been found [101, 102]

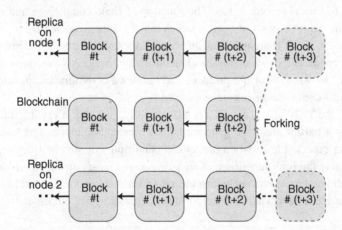

Figure 5.1 A (temporary) fork occurs at nodes 1 and 2 when their local PoW processes lead to different proposals of the new blockchain header, that is, (t+3) and (t+3)′, at the same time. Both (t+3) and (t+3)′ satisfy equation (5.1). Reprinted with permission from the paper "A survey on consensus mechanisms and mining strategy management in blockchain networks" published in *IEEE Access*.

that rational consensus nodes may not have an incentive for transaction or block propagation. As a result, the problem of blockchain forking may not be easily resolved in the current framework of the Nakamoto protocol. Special measures should be further taken in the protocol design, and a set of folklore principles has been suggested to gear the consensus mechanism towards a protocol for secure and sustainable blockchain networks [102, 103]:

1. For self-interested nodes in a permissionless blockchain network, helping to relay the information (e.g., new transactions) for other nodes and accepting the view of the longest chain of blocks may not necessarily be their monotonic strategies [104]. Therefore, an efficient consensus protocol is expected to ensure that all the substages concerning the behaviors of individual nodes during consensus formation should be incentive-compatible with the rules set by the protocol, especially in an open environment with Byzantine and unfaithful faults.
2. The interests of individual consensus participants may not align with the design goal of permissionless blockchains in terms of the principles of decentralization and fairness. Then, even when the consensus about following the rules is achieved among the nodes, an efficient incentive mechanism is necessary to address the potential issues of coalition such as botnets and mining pools [97] carefully.
3. For permissionless blockchains, the goals of security, processing throughput, and network scalability are usually contradictory at the design stage of a consensus protocol [105]. Therefore, a proper balance is expected at the stage of introducing incentive mechanisms to guarantee the financial or application value that the blockchain carries.

5.2.1 Proof-of-Work Basics

The PoW process abstracted by Definition 1 is essentially a verifiable process of weighted random coin-tossing, where the probability of winning is no longer uniformly associated with the nodes' identities but in proportion to the resources, for example, the hashrate cast by the nodes. We can consider that each new block is generated by a time-independent "lottery," where the probability of being elected as the leader for block proposal depends on the ratio between the cast resource of a node (or a node coalition) and the total resources presented in the entire network. Let w_i denote the resource held by node i in a network of node set N. Then, the probability of its winning the leader election in a PoW-like process should follow:

$$\Pr_i^{win} = \frac{w_i}{\sum_{j \in \mathcal{N}} w_j}, \tag{5.2}$$

where w_i generalizes the share of any verifiable resource such as computational power [1], memory [106], and storage [107]. In contrast to the BFT protocols, the peer nodes accept the received block proposal following the longest-chain rule after they verify the validity of the block and the transactions therein. Since no all-to-all messaging phase is needed, the Nakamoto protocol may have a much smaller message complexity (n) when the majority of the peers are honest [108].

As we have discussed previously, the primitive PoW scheme proposed in [1] works to financially disincentivize the Sybil attacks on block proposal and maintains a biased random leader-election process in proportion to the hashrate cast by each node. Recall that the input string x to the PoW puzzle is a concatenation of the previous block's hash pointer and the payload data of the proposed block. For the puzzle design of PoW, the reason for choosing the hash function $\mathcal{H}(\cdot)$ in equation (5.1), for example, SHA-256, in practice lies in the fact that a hash function is computationally indistinguishable from a pseudorandom function, if it preserves the properties of collision resistance[1] and preimage resistance [109]. Since the random output of $\mathcal{H}(\cdot)$ is time-independent and is determined only by the input string, it plays the role of an uncompromisable random oracle and outputs a unique, unpredictable result every time it is queried with a different x [110]. This means that a node in the blockchain network is able to construct a fresh random challenge solely based on its block proposal without referring to any designated verifier or third-party initializer. Meanwhile, it is well-known that, with a proper cryptographic hash function, the search for a preimage $(x, nonce)$ satisfying the condition $\mathcal{H}(x \| nonce) \leq 2^{L-h}$ in equation (5.1) cannot be more efficient than exhaustively querying the random oracle for all $nonce \in [0, 2^L]$. This leads to a puzzle time complexity of $\mathcal{O}(2^h)$ [111]. On the other hand, verifying the puzzle requires only a single hash query. Therefore, the properties of noninvertibility, completeness, soundness, and freshness are all satisfied by the PoW puzzle given by Definition 1.

For a given difficulty level $D(h)$ in equation (5.1), each single query to $\mathcal{H}(\cdot)$ is an independent and identically distributed (i.i.d.) Bernoulli trial with a success probability

$$\Pr(y: \mathcal{H}(x \| y) \leq D(h)) = 2^{-h}. \tag{5.3}$$

We adopt the typical assumption of loose network synchronization for analyzing PoW-based blockchains [97, 110]. Namely, all messages are delivered with bounded delay in one round. Then, equation (5.3) indicates that the frequency for a node to obtain the puzzle solutions during a certain number of loosely synchronized rounds is a Bernoulli process. Since the probability given in equation (5.3) is negligible for a sufficiently large h with cryptographic hash functions $\mathcal{H}(\cdot)$, the Bernoulli process of node i converges to a Poisson process as the time interval between queries or trails shrinks [108].

To analyze the PoW scheme, let w_i refer to the number of queries that node i can make to $\mathcal{H}(\cdot)$ in a single round. Then, we can approximate the rate of the Poisson process for node i's puzzle solution by $\lambda_i = w_i/2^h$ [112]. Note that every node in the network is running an independent puzzle-solving process. Since a combination of N independent Poisson processes is still a Poisson process, the collective PoW process of a network with N nodes has a rate

---

[1] The collision probability of $\mathcal{H}(\cdot)$ is $e^{-\Omega(L)}$ and thus negligible [97].

$$\lambda = \sum_{i=1}^{N} \lambda_i = \frac{\sum_{i=1}^{N} w_i}{2^h}. \tag{5.4}$$

The property of the combined Poisson processes in equation (5.4) leads to the probability distribution for leader election. From a single node's perspective, the repeated PoW puzzle-solving processes take the form of a block-proposal competition across the network. From the perspective of the network, for a given difficulty level $D(h)$, this puzzle-solving race simulates a verifiable random function for leader election. Most importantly, this randomness simulation process cannot be biased by any fraction of the Byzantine nodes in the network.

Nevertheless, PoW by itself does not guarantee any principle properties of Byzantine consensus. On top of the designed PoW puzzle and the P2P information diffusion functionality, three external functions are abstracted in [97] to describe the Nakamoto consensus protocol from a single node's perspective. These functions are

1. the *chain reading function* that receives as input a blockchain and outputs an interpretation for later use;
2. the *content validation function* that validates a blockchain replica and checks the data consistency with the applications (e.g., Bitcoin) atop the blockchain;
3. the *input contribution function* that compares the local and the received views of the blockchain and adopts the "best" one following the rule of longest chain.

From the independent Poisson processes in the block-proposal competition, more than one node may simultaneously propose to extend the blockchain using different blocks with corresponding valid PoW solutions. As a result, the nodes may read from the network multiple valid views of the blockchain and choose different forks as their "best" local views (see also Fig. 5.1). Theoretically, it has been shown [113] that deterministic consensus in permissionless blockchain networks cannot be guaranteed unless all nonfaulty nodes are reachable from one to another and the number of consensus nodes is known. For this reason, Garay et al. [97, 110, 114] propose to capture the properties of validity, agreement, and liveness of the Nakamoto protocol by the three chain-based properties in Table 5.1. Then, the PoW-based Nakamoto protocol can be modeled as a probabilistic Byzantine Agreement protocol.

In order to quantify the Byzantine Agreement properties for blockchains, three conditions, namely, the upper-bounded information diffusion delay, a "flat network" with equal and limited hashrates and the upper-bounded number of Byzantine nodes are assumed [97, 110, 114]. It is shown in [97] that the three properties in Table 5.1 are quantified by three parameters, namely, the collective hashrates of the honest nodes, the hashrate controlled by the adversaries, and the expected block arrival rate of the network-level Poisson process given in equation (5.4). It has been further proved [97] that under the condition of honest majority, the basic properties of validity and agreement are satisfied by the Nakamoto protocol with overwhelming probability. Furthermore, the common-prefix property and the chain-growth property formalize the presumption [1] that a transaction is secured when a sufficient length of subsequent blocks is appended to the chain. In other words, when a block is a certain number of blocks

Table 5.1 Three properties of Nakamoto protocols for blockchains.

Nakamoto protocol-specified properties	Corresponding properties of Byzantine Agreement	Explanation in detail
Common-prefix property	Agreement (and permanent order)	In the condition of multiple local blockchain views due to forking, the *common-prefix property* indicates that after cutting off (pruning) a certain number of blocks from the end (header) of the local chain, an honest node will always obtain a subchain that is a prefix of another honest node's local view of the blockchain.
Chain-quality property	Validity	Among a given length of consequent blocks in the local blockchain view of an honest node, the number of blocks that is proposed by Byzantine nodes (adversaries) is upper-bounded.
Chain-growth property	Liveness	For any given rounds of block proposals, the number of blocks appended to the local view of any honest node is lower-bounded.

Reprinted with permission from the paper "A survey on consensus mechanisms and mining strategy management in blockchain networks" published in *IEEE Access*.

deep from the end of the chain, or equivalently, the repeated block-proposal competition has passed sufficiently many rounds, the transaction data in that block is non-reversible or persistent and thus guaranteed to be double-spending proof. It is worth noting that the studies in [97, 115] provide a generalizable approach for evaluating the security and the efficiency of the PoX-based Nakamoto protocols in permissionless blockchains. Based on the quantitative analysis of the properties in Table 5.1, the same framework of security evaluation has been adopted by the studies in consensus protocols using other types of puzzle design such as PoS [115, 116].

Owing to the open-access nature of permissionless blockchains, the hashrate presented in a practical blockchain network is generally unstable. As indicated by Fig. 5.2, since the introduction of the Application Specific Integrated Circuit (ASIC) for hash acceleration in 2013, the practical PoW-based blockchain networks, for example, Bitcoin, have experienced an explosive increase of the total hashrate with huge fluctuations [117]. Practically, blockchain networks adopt a heuristic, periodic difficulty-adjustment policy to maintain a roughly fixed time interval, namely, λ^{-1} in equation (5.4), between two neighboring blocks. However, the expected value of λ^{-1} is usually chosen in an arbitrary manner and is frequently reduced in favor of a higher transaction throughput (see ZCash [106], for example). Following the assumption of partial synchronization [97], the roughly fixed time interval indeed implies an upper bound for the information dissemination latency in the P2P network [118].

With such a consideration in mind, a theoretical study is provided in [119] between the upper bound of the information latency and the persistence of the block data in

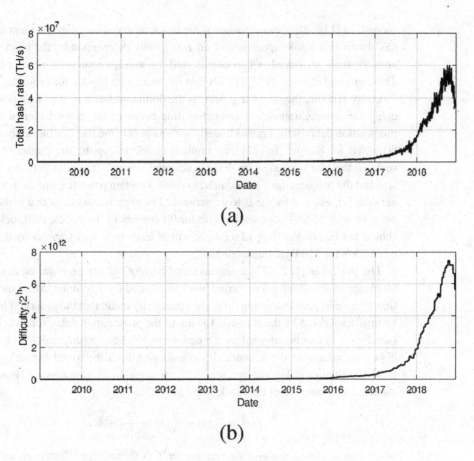

Figure 5.2 Evolution of (a) the total hashrate and (b) the PoW puzzle difficulty in the Bitcoin network over time. Data source: www.blockchain.com. Reprinted with permission from the paper "A survey on consensus mechanisms and mining strategy management in blockchain networks" published in *IEEE Access*.

a node's local view of the blockchain. Consider a flat network of N nodes with a maximum block propagation delay of T. It is found in [119] that for a given fraction of adversary node ρ ($0 \leq \rho < 0.5$), the block generation probability for each node should satisfy the following condition in order to ensure the property of data persistence (Theorem 1.1 in [119]):

$$\Pr_i^g \leq \frac{1}{T\rho \sum_{i=1}^{N} w_i}, \tag{5.5}$$

where $\Pr_i^g$ can be calculated based on equation (5.4) and a given hashrate.

Furthermore, the block interval rules the trade-off between security and efficiency. The former refers to the degree of fulfillment (i.e., the probabilistic consistency) of the Byzantine Agreement properties, whereas the latter refers to the transaction throughput, which can be measured in the number of confirmed transactions per second. In [118, 119], examination of the block propagation delay T in equation (5.5) has shown that a safe upper bound on T is jointly determined by the block size, the network scale measured in hop counts, and the average round-trip time of the links. The empirical study in [120] reveals that for small-size blocks, for example, less than 20 kB for Bitcoin, the round-trip delay is the dominant factor of the block propagation delay. Otherwise, transaction validation time becomes the major factor of the block propagation delay, which grows linearly with respect to the size of a block, for example, 80 ms/kB for Bitcoin. In [121], an implicit metric to capture the impact of network scale on the block propagation delay is adopted. Therein, the ratio between the block size and the propagation time required to reach a certain percentage of the nodes in the network is measured for the Bitcoin network. The experiments show that in the Bitcoin network with 55 kb/s propagation rate for 90 percent of the nodes, the block interval should not be smaller than 12 seconds, which leads to a peak transaction throughput of 26 TX/s for 250 Byte transactions.

The studies in [122, 123] also consider the impact of the propagation delay on the incidence of abandoning a proposed block with valid PoW solution. More specifically, finding a valid puzzle solution does not necessarily mean that the proposed block will be finally accepted by the network. Owing to the propagation delay, a blockchain fork (see Fig. 5.1) can be adopted as the canonical blockchain state only when it is first disseminated across the network. By considering both the round-trip delay and the block verification delay, the average block propagation delay across a P2P network is modeled as a function of the block size s in [122]:

$$T(s) = T_p(s) + T_v(s) = \frac{s}{aC} + bs, \qquad (5.6)$$

where a is a network scale-related parameter, C is the average effective channel capacity of each link [123], and b is a coefficient determined by both the network scale and the average verification speed of each node (cf. [120]). The probability for the network to abandon or orphan a valid block proposal of size s due to the delay of block diffusion is modeled as follows [122, 124]:

$$\mathrm{Pr}^{\mathrm{Orphan}}(s) = 1 - e^{-\lambda T(s)}, \qquad (5.7)$$

where λ is the expected block arrival rate.

From a user's perspective, it is insufficient to know only the network-level probability of block orphaning due to the latency. Alternatively, it is of more interest to determine the safe time interval between locally observing on the chain a transaction and confirming it. With this in mind, the study in [119] considers a scenario where the adversary gets additional computation time by delaying the block propagation with a certain number of rounds Δ. Based on the analysis of the common-prefix property [97], a new metric, namely, K-consistency, is proposed in [119] to examine whether any two honest nodes are able to agree on the blockchain state that is at least K blocks deep from the end of the chain. Let α and β denote the probabilities that an honest node and the attackers can propose a valid block within a round, respectively. The analytical study in [119] (cf. [118, Lemma 8]) shows that the required waiting time T is jointly determined by α, β, Δ, and the parameter determining the searching space of the hash function, that is, L in Definition 1. More specifically, as long as the following condition is satisfied with an arbitrarily small constant $\delta > 0$ (see [119, Theorem 1.2])

$$\alpha(1 - (2\Delta + 2)\alpha) \geq (1 + \delta)\beta, \tag{5.8}$$

and $K > K_0(L) = c \log(L)$ for some constant c, the Nakamoto protocol satisfies the property of K-consistency (except with negligible probability in K). However, the closed-form threshold $K_0(L)$ for K-consistency is not provided in [119].

5.2.2 Incentive Compatibility in Proof of Work

For Nakamoto protocols, monetary incentive plays the key role to ensure that most of the consensus nodes or miners follow the rules of blockchain state transition during the puzzle-solution competition. In permissionless blockchain networks, the incentive mechanism is built upon the embedded digital token issuing and transferring schemes. In a typical PoW-based blockchain network, the leader or winner in the block proposal competition not only collects transaction fees from the approved transactions in the new block, but also gets token-issuing reward, for example, the "coinbase reward" in Bitcoin, for expanding the blockchain with the new block. For this reason, the puzzle competition process is compared with the process of "gold mining," since by casting resources into the competition, the nodes expect to receive monetary rewards carried by the tokens. As a result, the consensus participant nodes are better known as block "miners" to the public.

In [103] the consensus in blockchain networks is divided into three areas, namely, the consensus about the rules, for example, about transaction dissemination and validation, the universality of the blockchain state, and the financial value that the digital token carries. Then, the studies on the Nakamoto protocol's incentive compatibility can also be categorized according to these three aspects. Since the introduction of ASIC devices and pool mining for PoW-based blockchain networks, concerns have been raised about the nodes' incentive to fully abide by the protocol [100, 103, 125, 126]. Because of the explosion of network-level hashrates (see Fig. 5.2), most of the practical blockchain networks, namely, cryptocurrency networks, are nowadays dominated by the proxies of mining pools [127]. An individual node in a mining pool is known as a mining worker, since it no longer performs the tasks of transaction validation or propagation and does not even keep any blockchain data. On the other hand, only the proxy of the pool, that is, the pool server or task operator, maintains the replica of the blockchain. The pool server divides the exhaustive preimage search for a PoW solution into a number of subtasks and outsources them to the mining workers. In this sense, only the pool server can be considered as a node in the blockchain network. Studies have shown that joining a mining pool has become the more plausible strategy than working as an individual consensus node. Such a strategy reduces the income variance and secures stable profits of the mining workers [100, 128]. However, this leads to the formation of a mining-pool Cartel [100] and is against the design goal of Nakamoto consensus in [1], that "the network is robust in its unstructured simplicity."

A further study in [99] reveals that under the current framework of Nakamoto proto-cols, no incentive is provided for nodes to propagate the transactions that they are aware of. The study considers the situation when transaction fees dominate the block rewards [129]. The analysis in [99] models the paths of transaction dissemination as a forest of d-ary directed trees, where each transaction issuer considers its peer nodes as the tree roots and the nodes on the far end of the network as the leaves. During transaction dissemination, a consensus node can add any number of pseudoidentities (that is, fake identities) before selectively relaying the transaction to any of its neighbors. It is shown that a consensus node tends not to broadcast any transaction that offers a fee. By doing so, it reduces the number of nodes that are aware of the transaction and hence the competition of mining that transaction. An improved protocol is proposed in [99] by introducing a broadcasting incentive mechanism. More specifically, the proposed mechanism requires that each relaying node in the path of transaction propagation shares a uniform portion of reward with the root (i.e., mining) node, when the height of the relaying node is smaller than a predetermined threshold in the directed tree. The analysis of the new protocol is based on the formulation of a normal form game [130], and thus the equilibrium strategy of each node can be obtained through itera-tive removal of dominated strategies. The designed incentive mechanism is shown to guarantee that only the non-Sybil and information propagating strategies survive in the iterated removal of weakly dominated strategies, as long as the miners are connected to a sufficient number of peers.

Similar studies to enforce honest block or transaction propagation can also be found [102, 131]. The study in [132] casts the problem of incentivizing block propagation into the framework of routing in k-connected networks, where each rational node can freely choose between relaying and mining (or both). A protocol of transaction fee-sharing is designed therein to guarantee that the rational strategy of honest nodes in the network is to propagate the received transactions. It is required that a mining node shares the reward of a new transaction with the relaying nodes in one path between itself and the client which issues that transaction. According to [99], creating pseu-doidentities does not increase the connectivity of a node. From such an observation, it is proved in [132] that assigning the propagation reward of each relaying node as a decreasing function of the hop count guarantees transaction propagation, as long as the computing power (or other resources for mining) controlled by each node does not dominate the network. Comparatively, the study in [133] ensures that the pay-ment made to the transaction-relaying nodes cannot be denied by the miners of the new blocks. With the proposed propagation protocol in [133], each intermediate hop adds its own signature to the transaction before sending it to the next hop. While working on their own PoW-puzzle solution, the relaying nodes freely charge their descendants at least a minimum fee for propagation. The miner whose block finally gets confirmed by the blockchain will pay for the propagation fees to one selected path of nodes. As in [99] the process of transaction propagation and relaying price competition is modeled as a noncooperative game in [133]. It is proved that with the proposed propagation protocol based on the chain of signatures, a rational miner's equilibrium strategy is always to choose the shortest path, and a rational relaying node's equilibrium strategy is always to charge its descendants the minimum fees for relaying transactions.

When block creation reward dominates the mining reward, incentive incompatibility may appear in different forms. Intuitively, it is plausible for a rational miner to pack up a proper number of transactions with decent fees in the new block for profit maximization. However, empty blocks with only coinbase transaction or blocks with a tiny number of transactions can be frequently observed in the practical blockchain networks. An informal game-theoretic analysis in [131] indicates that the consensus nodes tend to ignore the received blocks of large size in a fiat network and relay the smaller competing blocks instead. The reason is that large blocks incur longer delay due to transaction validation, hence increasing the probability of orphaning any blocks that are mined based on them. Although mining empty blocks does not violate the Nakamoto protocol, it results in the same situation as a Distributed Denial of Service (DDoS) attack [134] by blocking the confirmation of normal transactions. Furthermore, the statistical studies in [135] and [136] have shown that the consensus nodes behave rationally and are prone to prioritizing the transactions with higher transaction fees during block packing. However, when the coinbase reward dominates the block mining reward, the miners are not yet incentivized to enforce strictly positive fees [135]. In the case study of the Bitcoin network, extra delays for the small-value transactions are identified ranging from 20 minutes [135] to as long as 30 days [137]. Also, it is observed in [135] that most of the lightweight nodes still set an arbitrary transaction fee in the real-world scenarios. It is unclear whether the miners or the transaction issuers adopt best-response strategies systematically. The study in [136] simplifies the consensus process as a supply game subject to the trade of a specific type of physical goods. In the considered scenario, the miners essentially become the follower players in a two-level hierarchical or Stackelberg game led by the blockchain network, which is assumed to be able to set the transaction prices. Then, they are expected to have an incentive for including all transactions if no block size limit exists. On the other hand, it is pointed out in [123] that, since the block orphaning probability exponentially grows with the block size, a healthy transaction-fee market does not exist for unlimited block size due to the physical constraint of link capacity in the network. Finally, it is worth noting that most of the existing studies are based on the presumption that the tokens carried by a blockchain have monetary value and their exchange-rate volatility is small. An optimistic prediction is provided in [101] based on an assumption excluding any state variables on the user sider except the belief in "proper functioning of a cryptocurrency." In the absence of investors and when the blockchain is used only for the purpose of remittance, it is shown in [101] that the tokens of a blockchain network admit a unique equilibrium exchange rate in each period of the belief evolution. Conditioned on the survival of a cryptocurrency, the equilibrium state depends on the excess in users' valuation of the blockchain over the other payment options as well as the supply of the tokens in the market. Together with the Stackelberg game-based interpretation in [136], it is reasonable to consider that the equilibrium price of a blockchain token is determined by the demand–supply relation in the market. It is worth noting that the data security is only guaranteed by sufficient

PoW computation power in the blockchain network. Currently, except for a few studies such as [138], it is generally unclear how the impact of security issues is reflected in the users' valuation of the blockchain. As a result, whether the security requirement of the Nakamoto protocol is compatible with the market clearing price remains an open question.

5.2.3   Upgraded Proof of Work

Under the framework of Nakamoto protocol, a number of alternative PoW-like schemes have been proposed to replace the original PoW scheme in permissionless blockchain networks. Generally, these PoX schemes aim at two major designing goals, that is, to incentivize useful resource provision, for example, [107, 139–142], and to improve the performance, for example, in terms of security, fairness and eco-friendliness [143–145] of the blockchain networks. Starting from this subsection, we will focus on the principles of puzzle design and provide a close examination on different PoX schemes in the literature. With the purpose of useful resource provision, the idea of "Proof of Useful Resources" (PoUS) has been proposed to tackle the resource wasting problem of PoW. Instead of enforcing the consumption of computational cycles for merely hash queries, a number of studies are devoted to the design of puzzles that are attached to useful work. An early attempt, namely, Primecoin [146], proposed to replace the PoW puzzle in equation (5.1) by the puzzle of searching three types of prime number chains, that is, the Cunningham chain of the first or second kind or the bi-twin chain [147]. However, the verification stage of Primecoin puzzle is based on classical Fermat test of base two (pseudoprime) [146], and hence violates the principle of soundness in noninteractive zero-knowledge proof. Meanwhile, since the induced solution arrival does not follow the i.i.d. Bernoulli model in equation (5.3), the Primecoin puzzle does not simulate the random distribution for leader selection as required by equation (5.2).

A similar scheme, namely, the proof of exercise, is proposed to replace the preimage searching problem in PoW with the useful "exercise" of matrix product problems [148]. The scheme uses a pool of task proposals to replace the PoW-based puzzle-solving processes by the computation tasks offered by nonauthenticated clients. Each consensus node needs to bid for a specific task to determine its puzzle. For this reason, the puzzle solution-generating scheme behaves more like a Computation as a Service (CaaS) platform. Since the matrix problems in the task pool may present different complexity levels, the puzzle competition does not fully simulate on the network level the random distribution in equation (5.2). Also, the solution verification can only be done probabilistically due to the lack of $\Leftarrow n$) verification schemes. Therefore, the proposed scheme in [148] suffers from the same problems as in the Primecoin [146].

In [140], a new puzzle framework, namely, useful Proof of Work (uPoW), is designed to replace the primitive PoW puzzle in equation (5.1) with a specific set of problems satisfying not only the properties of completeness, soundness, and noninvertibility (hardness), but also the additional requirement of usefulness. Here, the usefulness is implied in the execution stage of the puzzle (cf. Table 5.1). Formally, by assuming completeness and soundness, the properties of usefulness can be defined as follows (cf. [140] and Definition 1).

Definition 2 Suppose that a challenge c_x and an accompanying puzzle solution (proof) s are generated from an input string x. If there exists an algorithm Recon(c_x, s) such that for a target function $F(\cdot)$ its output satisfies Recon$(c_x, s) = F(x)$, the challenge is known to be useful for delegating the computation of $F(x)$.

The study in [140] proposes to replace the preimage searching in equation (5.1) with a family of one-way functions satisfying the property of fine-grained hardness [149] for uPoW puzzle design. Namely, the PoW puzzle is proposed to be replaced by the problem of known worst-case-to-average-case complexity reduction. A special case of uPoW puzzles based on the problem of k-orthogonal vectors (k-OV) is discussed. In brief, the solution to k-OV performs an exhaustive search over k sets of identical-dimension vectors and determines whether for each set there exists a vector such that these k vectors are k-orthogonal. In order to construct noninteractive proofs, uPoW in [140] employs the hash function $H(\cdot)$ as a random oracle. Simply put, given the number of vectors in each set, noninteractive uPoW treats the elements of each vector as the random coefficients of polynomials with the identical order. Thus, uPoW initializes the first element of each vector, that is, the lowest-order coefficient, with a publicly known input string x and then uses it as the input to $H(\cdot)$ for generating the next-order coefficient. The output of $H(\cdot)$ will then be iteratively used as the input for generating the next-order coefficient. This can be considered as a typical example of applying the Fiat–Shamir scheme to construct non-interactive PoW out of interactive zero-knowledge proof schemes. With such an approach, uPoW does not need to explicitly define the vector sets. It also guarantees that the solutions of k-OV found by each prover follow a Bernoulli distribution. Therefore, the uPoW scheme fits well in the existing Nakamoto protocols by simulating a provable random function. As stated in [140], besides k-OV, uPoW is compatible with computation delegation for other problems such as 3SUM [149], all-pairs shortest path [149], and any problem that reduces to them.

Schemes that are similar to uPoW can also be found [142]; here, the problem of untrusted computational work assignment is addressed in a Trusted Execution Environment (TEE). The TEE can be constructed using Intel Software Guard Extensions (SGX), which is a set of new instructions available on certain Intel CPUs to protect user-level codes from attacks by hardware and other processes on the same host machine. In the permissionless network, the clients supply their workloads in the form of tasks that can be run in an SGX-protected enclave (i.e., protected address space). The study in [142] exploits the truthfulness-guaranteeing feature of the Intel attestation service [150] in the SGX-protected platform to verify and measure the software running in an enclave. With the designed puzzle, the work of each consensus node is metered on a per-instruction basis. The SGX enclave randomly determines whether the work leads to a valid block proof by treating each instruction as a Bernoulli trial. Based on the TEE, each executed useful-work instruction is analogous to one hash query in the primitive PoW, and the enclave module works as a trusted random oracle. Apart from delegation of useful computation, PoX can also be designed to incentivize distributed storage provision. For example, Permacoin [151] proposes a scheme of Proof of Retrievability (PoR) in order to distributively store an extremely large size of data provided by an authoritative file dealer. The file dealer divides the data into a number of sequential segments and publishes the corresponding Merkle root using the segments as the leaves. A consensus node uses its public key and the hash function to select a random group of segment indices for local storage. For each locally stored segment, the node also stores the corresponding Merkle proof derived from querying the Merkle tree. The challenge–proof pair is generated based on a subset of the locally stored segments and the corresponding Merkle proof. To ensure the non-interactiveness and freshness of the puzzle (e.g., interactive PoR in [152]), the node needs a publicly known and nonprecomputable puzzle ID to seed the process of segment selection called "scratch-off." To help the readers understand the puzzle generation process, we present a simplified execution stage of PoR as follows: Suppose a node is given the key pair (sk, pk), the puzzle ID ID_{puz}, the vector of locally stored segment indices $\mathbf{v}$, the required number of Merkle proofs k, the vectors of all the file segments $\mathbf{U}$, and the corresponding Merkle proof vector π. The random IDs of the local segments for challenge generation can be determined by

$$\forall 1 \leq j \leq k : r_j = \mathbf{v}(\mathcal{H}(id_{puz}\|pk\|j\|nonce) \bmod |\mathbf{v}|), \qquad (5.9)$$

where *nonce* is a random value chosen by the node. For each segment $\mathbf{U}(\mathbf{v}(r_j))$ in the challenge, the proof is in the form of $(pk_i, nonce, \mathbf{U}(\mathbf{v}(r_j)), \pi(\mathbf{v}(\mathbf{r_j})))$.

The execution stage of PoR in [151] is composed of a fixed number of queries to the random oracle $\Leftarrow H$). Thereby, although PoR satisfies the principle properties of a noninteractive zero-knowledge proof, it does not simulate the random leader-election process. In this sense, the proposed PoR scheme may not be able to achieve the claimed goal of "repurposing PoW" in [151]. Instead, it is more similar to the existing systems such as Storj [153], Sia [154], and TorCoin [141], where PoX is only used to audit the execution of the smart contracts or script-based transactions instead of facilitating the consensus mechanism.

Further improvement to PoR can be found in the proposals of KopperCoin [107] and Filecoin [139]. In [107], KopperCoin adopts the same framework of distributed storage for a single file as in Permacoin [151]. Compared with Permacoin, the main improvement of the puzzle design in KopperCoin is to simulate the random leader-election process for block proposal. KopperCoin introduces a bitwise XOR-based distance metric between the index of a locally stored data segment and a random, publicly known challenge c. A node needs to provide the valid Merkle proof (PoR) of a segment, of which the index (denoted by j) should satisfy the following condition:

$$\mathcal{H}(x) \cdot 2^{|j \oplus c|} \leq D(h), \qquad (5.10)$$

where the block payload x and the difficulty threshold $D(h)$ are defined in the same way as in Definition 1. Compared with equation (5.1), the solution searching for equation (5.10) is now performed within the range of the locally stored segment indices. The more segments a node offers to store, the better chance the node has to find a solution to equation (5.10). Again, the generation of the public unpredictable random challenge

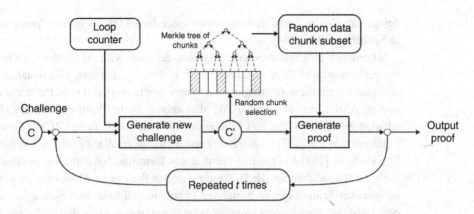

Figure 5.3 Illustration of the PoST scheme based on iterative PoR over time. Reprinted with permission from the paper "A survey on consensus mechanisms and mining strategy management in blockchain networks" published in *IEEE Access*.

c can be derived based on hashing the header of the most recent block. This approach presents another example of applying the Fiat–Shamir transformation to realize non-interactiveness [155]. In the Filecoin network [139], the concept of "spacetime" is introduced to allow metering the data stored in the network with an expiry time. Filecoin aims to provide the functionality of recycling and reallocating the storage on the provider (miner) side as well as easing the file retrieval process on the client side. As in the proof-of-exercise scheme, Filecoin designs the market for storage and retrieval of multiple files based on smart contracts. A new puzzle, namely, Proof of SpaceTime (PoST) [143], is adopted based on the intuition of generating a PoR sequence during a certain period to prove the holding time of useful storage. As illustrated by Fig. 5.3, the major difference of PoST from PoR lies in the repeated execution phases for challenge updating without rerunning the initialization stage. Namely, a consensus node is required by the Filecoin network to submit PoR (e.g., in a similar way to Permacoin [151]) every time when the blockchain is extended by a certain number of blocks. Instead of simulating random leader election based on adjustable difficulty [107], the Filecoin network uses the following mechanism to determine whether a node i is elected for block proposal:

$$\frac{1}{2^L}\mathcal{H}(t|rand(t)) \leq \frac{w_i}{\sum_{j\in\mathcal{N}}w_j}, \tag{5.11}$$

where t is the index of consensus round (i.e., block index), L is the output string length of the hash function (see equation (5.1)), $rand(\cdot)$ is an assumed random oracle, and w_i represents the storage power of node i (see also equation (5.2)). It is worth noting that the evaluation of w_i in equation (5.11) can only be done through PoST. Thus, the Filecoin network admits a double-challenge scheme, where the leader election is performed based on a second challenge, namely, equation (5.11). The nodes with the better quality of PoST proofs (storage power) are more likely to win the second challenge. Under the framework of double challenges, a similar approach of puzzle design can also be found in the proof of space-based cryptocurrency proposal known as SpaceMint [143, 144].

Alternative PoX schemes have also been designed with the emphasis on improving the performance of PoW in aspects such as security, fairness, and sustainability. To alleviate the problem of computation power centralization due to the massive adoption of ASICs, memory-hard PoW, also known as the Proof of Memory (PoM), is adopted by ZCash [106] and Ethereum [156] networks. In the ZCash network, the Equihash scheme [157] is adopted based on the generalized birthday problem [158]. The study in [157] has pointed out that any identified NP-complete problem can be the natural candidate for the PoX puzzle due to their proved hardness, as long as the solution verification can be completed in polynomial time. However, a puzzle design only satisfying the hardness requirement may not be able to combat the botnet or ASIC-based manipulation of hashrate. Thus, a suitable PoX is expected to be "optimization-free" and "parallelism-constraint." Namely, the solution-searching process cannot be speeded up by using alternative algorithms or through parallelization.

An ideal approach of imposing a parallelism constraint is to ensure that the PoW scheme is inherently sequential. However, an inherently sequential nondeterministic polynomial time (NP) problem that is known to be verified in short time is yet to be found [157]. Therefore, the study in [157] adopts an alternative approach by imposing enormous memory bandwidth to the parallel solution of the puzzle. According to [158], the generalized k-dimensional birthday problem is to find k strings of n bits from k sets of strings, such that their XOR operation leads to zero. Equihash employs the hash function $\mathcal{H}(\cdot)$ to randomly generate the k strings using the block payload data x and a *nonce* (as in equation (5.9)), such that both the XOR-based birthday problem solution and a PoW preimage of a given difficulty are found. It is shown in [158] that the best solution algorithm to this problem presents $\mathcal{O}(2^{n/k})$ complexity in both time and space and thus is memory-intensive. More importantly, for a k-dimensional problem, a discounting factor $1/q$ in memory usage leads to $\mathcal{O}(q^{k/2})$ times more queries to the hash function. Because of the physical memory bandwidth limit, the computation advantage of parallelization is limited. These properties guarantee the ASIC-resistance of Equihash. With the same purpose of preventing the "super-linear" profit through hashrate accumulation, Ethereum currently adopts a different puzzle design known as Ethash for ASIC resistance [159]. Ethash requires the consensus nodes to search for the PoW puzzle solution based on a big pseudorandom dataset, which increases linearly over time. The dataset is organized as the adjacency matrix of a directed acyclic graph (DAG), where each vertex represents a randomly generated data field of 128 bits. In the execution stage of Ethash, the node starts a onetime search of the solution with a hash query, and uses the concatenation of the block payload and a nonce to seed the hash function for locating a random vertex in the DAG. Then, the search is completed in a fixed-iteration loop of queries to the hash function, for which the output of the last iteration, that is, the data field of the last vertex in the path, is used as the input to determine the position of the next vertex in the DAG. The final output of the loop is used to check against the preimage condition as in equation (5.1). As illustrated in Fig. 5.4, the designed puzzle of Ethash makes the searching algorithm inherently

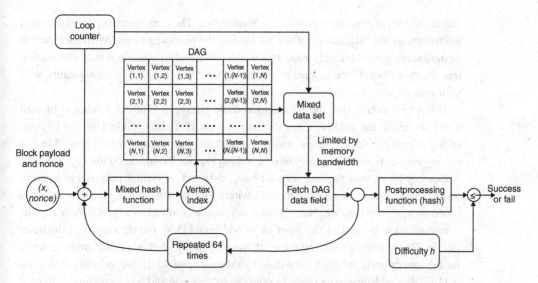

Figure 5.4 One query to the random oracle in Ethash for a given nonce based on the iterative mixed hash operation for vertex searching. Reprinted with permission from the paper "A survey on consensus mechanisms and mining strategy management in blockchain networks" published in *IEEE Access*.

sequential. With Ethash, the rate of data field fetching from the DAG is limited by the memory bandwidth. Then, paralleling the hash queries with ASICs cannot lead to much performance improvement in a single search of the puzzle solution.

Ethash [159] only makes the puzzle solution partially sequential within a single attempt of preimage search. Therefore, Ethash still faces the problem of PoW outsourcing since a consensus node can divide the puzzle-solution search into multiple subproblems and outsource them to different "mining workers" (i.e., puzzle solvers). Such a problem is also known as the formation of mining coalition (pool) [100] and may result in a serious problem of consensus manipulation by a handful of full nodes [128]. In [160], a nonoutsourceable "scratch-off puzzle" is proposed to disincentivize the tendency of mining task outsourcing. Intuitively, when a node effectively outsources its puzzle-solving work to some mining machines, we call the puzzle nonoutsourceable if these miners can steal the block proposal reward of that node without producing any evidence to implicate themselves. The study in [160] employs Merkle proofs for puzzle design, which can be considered as a generalization of the PoR [151]. In [160], a Merkle tree is created based on a number of random strings. To generate a fresh puzzle, a node queries the hash function for the first time with a random nonce and the constructed Merkle root. The output of this query is used to select a random subset of distinct leaves on the Merkle tree. Then, the concatenation of the Merkle proofs for each leaf in the subset and the same nonce is used as the input to the second query of the hash function. The output is used to compare with the preimage condition as given in equation (5.1). If a solution (nonce) is found, the payload of the proposed block is used as the input of the third query to the hash function, and the output is used to select another subset of random leaves on the Merkle tree. The corresponding Merkle proofs are treated as the "signature" of the payload of the proposed block. With such puzzle design, mining workers only need to know a sufficiently large fraction of the Merkle tree leaves to "steal" the reward by replacing the Merkle proof-based signature with their own proofs.

It is worth noting that the nonoutsourceable puzzle in [160] is generated in such a way to make the preimage search for equation (5.1) independent of the payload of the proposed block, that is, using the randomly generated Merkle tree. Then, a mining worker is able to replace the original payload including the public keys from the outsourcer by its own payload without being detected. A similar proposal of nonoutsourceable puzzle can be found in [161], where a nonoutsourceable puzzle is designed based on a two-fold puzzle. Namely, an inner puzzle is solved as a typical PoW puzzle, whose solution is used as the input of an additional PoW puzzle known as the outer puzzle. To prevent outsourcing the work load, a mining worker's signature is required for the inner puzzle solution to be used by the outer puzzle. However, it is pointed out in [161] that such design can only be considered heuristic and is not guaranteed to have the formal properties of "weak outsourceability" [160]. Apart from the manipulation-resistant puzzles, other puzzles are proposed in [145] and [146] with the emphasis on eco-friendliness. Therein, the major goal is to reduce or remove the repeated hash queries to curb energy consumption due to hash queries. In [144], the SpaceMint network is proposed based on Proof of SPace (PoSP) [162]. Similar to PoR [151], PoSP requires the consensus nodes to provide noninteractive proofs of storage dedication during puzzle solution searching. The major difference from PoR lies in the fact that PoSP does not need the prover to store useful data (from the verifiers), and the proof is based on a large volume of random data stored on the prover's hard drive. As in Ethash [159], the committed space is also organized as a DAG, where the value of each vertex is determined based on the hash of its parent vertices (see Fig. 5.5). A consensus node is required to use the hash of an earlier block as the seed to sample a random set of vertex values. The set of the vertex values forms the challenge of the node's local PoSP puzzle. If the node is able to provide the Merkle proofs for all the vertices in the challenge set, namely, the sibling vertices that lie on the path between each challenge vertex and the end vertex in the DAG with no outgoing edge, the proposed block is considered a valid block candidate. SpaceMint also proposes to measure the quality of a set of Merkle proofs based on the hash value of the concatenated vertex in a Merkle tree. Then, the blockchain network is able to select the block with the best quality of proof from the candidate blocks when a fork occurs. The study in [145] proposes to introduce a human-in-the-loop puzzle, namely, the Proof of Human-work (PoH), into the Nakamoto protocol. The design goal of PoH is to guarantee the properties of eco-friendliness, usefulness, and centralization resistance at the same time. It is proposed in [145] that PoH should be able to provide noninteractive, computer-generated puzzles which are moderately hard for a human but hard for a computer to solve, even for the computer that generates the puzzles. Note that PoH is inspired by the widely–adopted systems of Completely Automated Public Turing-Test to tell Computers and Humans Apart (CAPTCHA) [163]. Traditional CAPTCHA systems

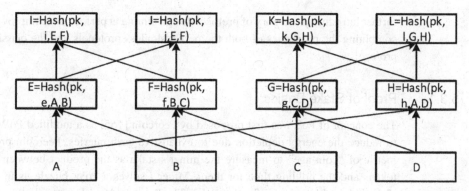

pk: public key
A, B, C...: vertex values
a, b, c...: vertex indices

Figure 5.5 An example of DAG formation based on the hash of the parent vertices: for miner i adopting a public key pk_i, the value v_j of j's vertex in its DAG with m parent vertices $p_1, \ldots, p_m$ is obtained as $v_j = H(pk_i, j, v_{p1}, \ldots, v_{pm})$. Reprinted with permission from the paper "A survey on consensus mechanisms and mining strategy management in blockchain networks" published in *IEEE Access*.

usually take human-efficient input (e.g., images) with a known solution and generate the puzzle based on distortion as the solution. For PoH, a universal sampler [164] is assumed to be available to generate a random CAPTCHA instance for the consensus node such that the puzzle-generating machine is not able to directly obtain the puzzle solution. Then, the node (i.e., miner) needs human work to obtain the corresponding solution of the CAPTCHA puzzle. A two-challenge puzzle design is adopted and the solution of the CAPTCHA puzzle is used as the input of a small PoW puzzle as defined in equation (5.1). A complete PoH solution includes a CAPTCHA solution and a nonce such that they together satisfy the preimage condition in equation (5.1). So PoH implicitly assumes that some Artificial Intelligence (AI) problems (e.g., recognition of distorted audios or images) are human-efficient but difficult for machines. Then, by selecting a proper underlying CAPTCHA scheme, it is possible to extend the PoH with a variety of meaningful human activities ranging from educational purposes to a number of socially beneficial programs [164].

5.3   Other Consensus Protocols in Blockchain

In Section 5.2, we reviewed the consensus protocols in the Nakamoto framework and the related issues of mining strategy management. Now, a natural question arises: Is it possible to simulate the random leader-election process among permissionless nodes in an approach other than the Nakamoto-like protocols? To answer this question, in this section we focus on the design methodology of the virtual-mining protocols. Then, we further introduce a category of protocol design aiming at performance improvement by combining the properties of both the permissionless protocols and the classical BFT protocols.

5.3.1   Proof of Stake Basics

The concept of PoS was first proposed by Peercoin [165] as a modified PoW scheme to reduce the energy depletion due to exhaustive hash queries. Peercoin proposes a metric of "coin age" to measure the miner's stake as the product between the held tokens and the holding time for them. Miner i solves a PoW puzzle as in equation (5.1) with an individual difficulty $D(h_i)$. The Peercoin kernel protocol allows a miner to consume its "coin ages" to reduce the difficulty, namely, h_i, for puzzle solution. The public verification of the "coin ages" is done through empirically estimating the holding time of the miner's Unspent Transaction Output (UTXO) based on the latest block on the public chain.

By completely removing the structure of PoW-based leader election, the protocols of pure PoS are proposed in [139, 143, 166, 167]. To simulate a verifiable random function following the stake distribution (see also equation (5.2)), an algorithm, follow-the-coin (also known as, follow-the-satoshi), has been proposed by [168] and widely adopted by these works. Here, the terms "coin" or "satoshi" are used to indicate the minimum unit of the digital tokens carried by the blockchain. Briefly, all the tokens in circulation are indexed, for example, between 0 and the total number of available coins in the blockchain network. A simplified PoS protocol can use the header of block $t - 1$ to seed the follow-the-coin algorithm and determine the random mining leader for block t. Specifically, the hash function $\mathcal{H}(\cdot)$ is queried with the header of block $t - 1$, and the output is used as the random token index to initialize the searching algorithm. The algorithm traces back to the minting block (i.e., the first coinbase transaction [169]) for that token or the UTXO account that currently stores it [168]. Then, the creator or the holder of the token is designated as the leader for generating block t. To enable public verification of the block, the valid leader is required to insert in the new block its signature, which replaces the data field "nonce" for PoW-based blockchains.

It is worth emphasizing that the pure PoS protocols do not rely on a Poisson process-based puzzle-solution competition to simulate the random generator of the block leader. Therefore, the zero-knowledge puzzle-solving process can be simply replaced by the process of asymmetric key-based signing and verification, and the proof of resource dedication is no longer needed. For this reason, PoS is also known as a process of "virtual mining" [128] since the block miners do not consume any resources. In the literature, a number of protocol proposals are also claimed to be able to (partially) achieve the same purpose. However, these protocols either need special hardware support, for example, Intel SGX-enabled TEEs for proof of luck or elapsed-time or ownership [166, 167], or are still under the framework of PoW, for example, Proof of Burn (PoB) [165], Proof of Stake-Velocity (PoSV) [170] and "PoS" using coin age [165]. Strictly speaking, they cannot be considered as the real virtual mining schemes in permissionless blockchains.

Compared with the PoX-based protocols, PoS keeps the longest-chain rule but adopts an alternative approach for simulating the verifiable random function of block-leader generation. For this reason, the same framework for analyzing the properties of Byzantine Agreements in PoW-based blockchain networks [97] can be readily used for the quantitative analysis of PoS protocols. For example, the investigations in [139] and [171] mathematically evaluate the properties of common prefix, chain quality and chain growth.

Kiayias and coworkers [139] propose the "Ouroboros" protocol, and consider that the stakes are distributed at the genesis block by an ideal distribution functionality. By assuming an uncorrupted ideal sampling functionality, Ouroboros guarantees that a unique leader is elected in each block-generation round following the stake distribution among the stakeholders (see also equation (5.2)). With Ouroboros, forking no longer occurs when all the nodes are honest. However, when adversary exists, forking may be caused by the adversarial leader through broadcasting multiple blocks in a single round. The study in [116] shows that the probability for honest nodes to fork the blockchain with a divergence of k blocks in m rounds is no more than $\exp\{-\Omega(k) + \ln(m)\}$ under the condition of honest majority. It is further shown that the properties of chain growth and chain quality are also guaranteed with negligible probability of being violated. The studies in [166] and [171] introduce the mechanism of epoch-based committee selection, which dynamically selects a committee of consensus nodes for block generation/validation during an epoch (i.e., a number of rounds). Compared with the single-leader PoS protocol, namely, Ouroboros [116], and its asynchronous variation [171], the committee-based PoS gears the protocol design toward the leader-verifier framework of traditional BFT protocols (see also Fig. 5.6). In [168], the scheme of Proof of Activity (PoA) is proposed with the emphasis that only the active stake-holding nodes get rewarded. The PoA is featured by the design that the leader is still elected

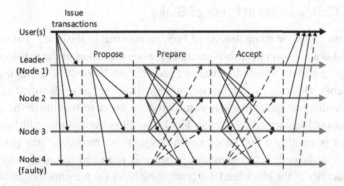

Figure 5.6 The BFT-based message pattern of a three-way handshake in permissioned blockchains. The message is formed based on the granularity level of blocks, namely, a batch of transactions. Reprinted with permission from the paper "A survey on consensus mechanisms and mining strategy management in blockchain networks" published in *IEEE Access*.

through a standard PoW-based puzzle competition, and is only responsible for publishing an empty block. Using the header of this block to seed the follow-the-coin algorithm, a committee of N ordered stakeholders is elected and guaranteed to be publicly verifiable. The first $N - 1$ stakeholders work as the endorsers of the new empty block by signing it with their private keys. The Nth stakeholder is responsible for including the transactions into that block. The transaction fees are shared among the committee members and the block miner. In this sense, PoA can be categorized as a hybrid protocol that integrates both PoW and PoS schemes.

Bentov et al. [171] propose a protocol called "Snow White," which uses a similar scheme to select a committee of nodes as in [168]. However, only the selected committee members are eligible for running for the election of the block generation leader. Under the Snow White protocol, the leader of an epoch is elected through a competition based on repeated preimage search with the hash function. At this stage, the difference of Snow White from the standard PoW puzzle in equation (5.1) is that the hash function is seeded with the time stamp instead of an arbitrary nonce. Like PoA, Snow White also pertains to the characteristics of a hybrid protocol. The analysis in [172] shows that the proposed protocol supports frequent committee reconfigurations and is able to tolerate nodes that are corrupted or offline in the committee.

The recent proposal by Ethereum, Casper [18], provides an alternative design of PoS that is more similar to traditional BFT protocols. The current proposal of Casper does not aim to be an independent blockchain consensus protocol, since it provides no approach of leader election for block proposal. Instead, the stakeholders join the set of validators and work as the peer nodes in a BFT protocol. The validators can broadcast a vote message specifying which block in the blockchain is to be finalized. The validator's vote is not associated with its identity, but with the stake that it holds. According to [18], Casper provides plausible liveness (instead of probabilistic liveness with PoW) and accountable safety, which tolerates up to one third of the overall voting power (weighted by stake) that is controlled by the Byzantine nodes.

5.3.2   Incentive Compatibility in Proof of Stake

Regarding the incentive compatibility of PoS, an informal analysis in [116] shows that being honest is a $\sigma-$Nash equilibrium strategy when the stakes of the malicious nodes are less than a certain threshold and the endorsers are insensitive to the transaction validation cost. However, a number of vulnerabilities are also identified in PoS. In [173], the nothing-at-stake attack is considered. In order to maximize the profits, a block leader could generate conflicting blocks on all possible forks with "nothing at stake," since generating a PoS block consumes no more resources than generating a signature. A dedicated digital signature scheme is proposed to enable any node to reveal the identity of the block leader if conflicting blocks at the same height are found. Alternatively, a rule of "three strikes" is proposed in [169] to blacklist the stakeholder who is eligible for block creation but fails to do so properly for three consecutive times. In addition, an elected mining leader is also required to sign an auxiliary output to prove that it provides some extra amount tokens as the "deposit." In case this node is malicious and broadcasts more than one block, any miner among the consecutive block-creation leaders can include this output as an evidence in their block to confiscate the attacker's deposit. Such a scheme is specifically designed to disincentivize block forking by the round leader.

Grinding attack is another type of attack targeting PoS [116]. With PoS, the committee or the leader is usually determined before a round of mining starts. Then, the attacker has an incentive to influence the leader or committee election process in an epoch to improve its chances of being selected in the future. When the verifiable random generator takes as input the header of the most recent block for leader or committee election, the attacker may test several possible block headers with different content to improve the chance of being selected in the future (e.g., [116, 168]). It is expected to use an unbiased, unpredictable random generator to neutralize such a risk [116]. In practice, the protocol usually selects an existing block that is a certain number of blocks deep to seed the random function instead of using the current one [168, 172].

With all the aforementioned studies, a significant limit of the existing analyses about PoS-based protocols lies in the simplified assumption that ignores the stake trade outside the blockchain network (e.g., at an exchange market) [174]. A study in [175] provides a counterexample for the persistence of PoS in such a situation. The study in [175] assumes no liquidity constraint in a blockchain network, where nodes own the same stake at the beginning stage. Houy [175] considers a situation where a determined, powerful attacker attempts to destroy the value of the blockchain by repeatedly buying the stake from each of the other nodes at a fixed price. After taking into account the belief of the nodes that the attacker will buy more tokens, the interaction between the attackers and the stakeholders is modeled as a Bayesian repeated game. The study concludes that the success of the attack depends on two factors, namely, the attacker's valuation of the event "destroying the blockchain" and the profit (e.g., monetary interest) that the nodes can obtain from holding the stake. When the former factor is large and the latter is small, the nodes in the network will end up in a competition to sell their stakes to the attackers. As a result, the blockchain can be destroyed at no cost.

5.3.3 Hybrid Consensus Protocols

Despite the unique characteristics of permissionless consensus protocols, public blockchain networks are known to be limited in performance (e.g., transaction throughput) due to the scalability-performance trade-off [91]. To boost permissionless consensus without undermining the inherent features such as scalability, a plausible approach is to combine a permissionless consensus mechanism (e.g., Nakamoto protocol) with a fast permissioned consensus protocol (e.g., BFT). Following our previous discussion (cf. PoA [168] and Casper [18]), we study in this subsection how a standard permissionless consensus protocol can be improved by incorporating (part of) another consensus protocol in the blockchain networks.

In [176], the protocol "Bitcoin-NG" (where "NG" means "next generation") is proposed to extend the PoW-based Nakamoto protocols. The prominent feature of Bitcoin-NG is to decouple the consensus process in a blockchain network (e.g., Bitcoin network) into two planes: leader election and transaction serialization. To bootstrap the transaction throughput, the protocol introduces two types of blocks, namely, the key blocks that require a PoW puzzle solution for leader election and the microblocks that require no puzzle solution and are used for transaction serialization. The time interval between two key blocks is known as an epoch. In an epoch, the same leader is allowed to publish microblocks with the limited rate and block size. Although operation decoupling in Bitcoin-NG does not ensure strong consistency, it paves the way for incorporating additional mechanisms on the basis of standard Nakamoto protocols. Following the methodology of [176], hybrid consensus mechanisms atop Nakamoto protocols are proposed in [177] and [178] with the goal of providing strong consistency and immediate finality. In [179], the "PeerCensus" protocol is proposed by decoupling block creation and transaction committing or confirmation. PeerCensus consists of two core components, namely, a PoW scheme named BlockChain (BC) and a BFT-based scheme named Chain Agreement (CA). With the proposed BC protocol, nodes acquire the voting right of the CA protocol when they propose new blocks through PoW and are approved by the committee of CA. The CA protocol is adapted from BFT protocols such as PBFT [89] and the Secure Group Membership Protocol (SGMP) [178]. Through the four stages of propose, preprepare, prepare, and commit of BFT protocols (cf. Fig. 5.6), CA designates the miner of the newest block in the chain as the leader for the next block proposal. The leader proposes one from the multiple candidate blocks obtained in BC. The peer nodes in the committee extend the preprepare stage with an operation of block validation. The design of PeerCensus ensures that committing transactions (i.e., CA) is independent of block generation (i.e., BC). Therefore, no forking occurs in the condition of honest majority and strong consistency is guaranteed.

In [177], a hybrid consensus protocol is proposed by combining the data framework of two-type blocks in Bitcoin-NG and the hybrid PoW-BFT design in PeerCensus. As in PeerCensus, the Nakamoto protocol is used to construct a "snailchain," which is allowed to commit transactions from a specific mempool of outstanding transactions known as the "snailpool." Following the quantitative analysis of the common prefix blocks in a chain in [97], only a fixed number of miners whose recently minted blocks are a certain number of blocks deep in the chain can be used to form the committee for the BFT protocol. In contrast to PeerCensus, the BFT committee of miners in the proposed protocol has no influence on how the next block on the snailchain is determined. Instead, it is responsible for committing transactions from an independent mempool known as the "txpool." For this reason, the transactions approved by the BFT protocol are committed off the snailchain without relying on any mining mechanism. In this sense, these transactions can be considered similar to those in the microblocks of Bitcoin-NG. The hybrid consensus protocol in [177] explicitly addresses the problem of BFT-committee scalability in PeerCensus and provides a secured (with theoretical proof) consensus property of immediate finality. Namely, the

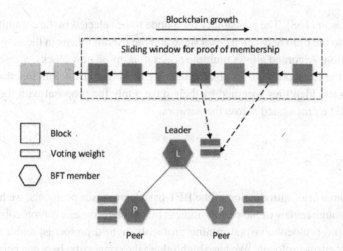

Figure 5.7 Illustration of BFT-committee formation with weighted voting power. Valid weights are credited only to the miners of the blocks in the sliding window. Reprinted with permission from the paper "A survey on consensus mechanisms and mining strategy management in blockchain networks" published in *IEEE Access*.

transaction confirmation time from the txpool depends only on the network's actual propagation delay. The method of using Nakamoto protocols to select nodes into a BFT committee is also known as the consensus mechanism with the proof of membership [180]. A sliding-window mechanism is proposed in [180] to generalize the mechanisms of dynamic BFT-committee selection in [177] and [178]. As illustrated in Fig. 5.7, the BFT committee is maintained by a fixed-size sliding window over the PoW-based blockchain. The sliding window moves forward along the blockchain as new blocks are appended or confirmed. Consensus nodes minting multiple blocks in the window are allowed to create the same number of pseudoidentities in the BFT consensus process to gain the proportional voting power for approving new blocks. For hybrid consensus using BFT protocols to guarantee strong consistency, a natural thinking is to replace the Nakamoto protocols with virtual mining (e.g., PoS) for selecting the leader or committee in BFT-consensus processes. A typical example for such an approach can be found in the "Tendermint" protocol [181], where a node joins the BFT committee of block validators by posting a bond-deposit transaction. The validator no longer needs to prove its membership by competing for the PoW-puzzle solution. Alternatively, its voting power is equal to the amount of stake measured in bonded tokens. Meanwhile, instead of randomly electing the leader of block proposal in the committee (cf. [176]), Tendermint adopts a round-robin scheme to designate the leader in the committee.

A similar design can be found in a number of recent proposals such as Proof of Authority (PoAu) [182] and Delegated Proof of Stake (DPoS) [183]. To generalize the mechanisms of BFT-committee selection based on virtual mining, Gilad et al. [184] further propose a consensus protocol called "Algorand." Like the other hybrid protocols, Algorand relies on BFT algorithms for committing transactions. It assumes a verifiable random function to generate a publicly verifiable BFT committee of random nodes, just as in [168]. The probability for a node to be selected in the committee is in proportion to the ratio between its own stake and the overall tokens in the network. For leader election, Algorand allows multiple nodes to propose new blocks. Subsequently, an order of the block proposals is obtained through hashing the random function output with the nodes' identities specified by their stake. Only the proposal with the highest priority will be propagated across the network.

5.4   Summary

Starting from a brief introduction of the BFT-based consensus protocols, we have provided a thorough review of the permissionless blockchain consensus protocols, including Nakamoto protocols, virtual mining protocols, hybrid protocols, and a series of parallel consensus protocols. We have highlighted the connection between permissionless consensus protocols and the traditional Byzantine Agreement protocols, as well as their distinctive characteristics. We have also highlighted the analysis of incentive compatibility in the permissionless protocol design. From a game-theoretic perspective, we have also investigated their influence on the strategy adoption of the consensus participants in the blockchain networks.

Based on our comprehensive survey of the consensus protocol design and its consequent influence on the blockchain networks, we have provided an outlook on the emerging applications of blockchain networks in different areas. This chapter is expected to serve as an efficient guideline for further understanding of blockchain consensus mechanisms and exploring potential research directions that may lead to exciting outcomes in related areas.

Part III

Mechanism Design in Blockchain Networks and Beyond

6   Mechanism Design Basics

A game designer attempts to analyze all alternative games and select the one that has the most effect on the strategies of other players. Mechanism design is a branch of game theory that studies solutions for solving a specific type of private information game. The following are the distinguishing characteristics of these games. To begin, a game "designer" chooses the game structure rather than inheriting one. As a result, the mechanism design is commonly referred to as "reverse game theory." Second, the game's outcome is important to the creator. A "game of mechanism design" is such a game and is generally solved by incentivizing players to provide individual information. Leonid Hurwicz, Eric Maskin, and Roger Myerson were awarded the Nobel Memorial Prize in Economic Sciences in 2007 for "for having laid the foundations of mechanism design theory." Mechanism design is used to set game rules in order to accomplish the desired game result. This differs from game analysis, in which the game rules are predefined and the game outcome is examined. Furthermore, the game creator must address the possibility that the players will lie. Fortunately, the reveal principle requires simply that games in which players truly divulge their private information be considered. In this chapter, we go through mechanism design in depth.

6.1   Definitions

First, we have the basic definitions for the following mechanisms.

- Outcome set: Ω.
- Players $i \in \mathcal{I}$, where $\mathcal{I}$ is the set of the players of size $|\mathcal{I}| = N$, with preference types $\theta_i \in \Theta_i$.
- Utility $u_i(o, \theta_i)$, over outcome $o \in \Omega$.
- Mechanism $M = (S, g)$ defines:
  - a strategy space $S^N = S_1 \times \cdots \times S_N$, s.t. player i chooses a strategy $s_i(\theta_i) \in S_i$ with $s_i \colon \Theta_i \to S_i$;
  - an outcome function $g \colon S^N \to \Omega$, s.t. outcome $g(s_i(\theta_1), \ldots, s_N(\theta_N))$ is implemented given strategy profile $s = (s_1(\cdot), \ldots, s_N(\cdot))$.
- Game: The utility to player i from strategy profile s, is $u_i(g(s(\theta)), \theta_i)$, which is denoted as $u_i(s, \theta_i)$.

The objective of a mechanism $M = (S, g)$ is to achieve the desired game outcome

$f(\theta)$ such that

$$g(s_1^*(\theta_1), \ldots, s_N^*(\theta_N)) = f(\theta), \ \forall \theta \in \Theta^N \tag{6.1}$$

for an equilibrium strategy $(s_1^*, \ldots, s_N^*)$. The desired properties of a mechanism can be listed as follows.

- Efficiency: Select the outcome that maximizes total utility.
- Fairness: Select the outcome that achieves a certain fairness criterion in utility.
- Revenue maximization: Select the outcome that maximizes revenue to a seller (or more generally, utility to one of the players).
- Budget-balanced: Implement outcomes that have balanced transfers across players.
- Pareto optimality: Only implement outcomes o^*, for which for all $o' \neq o^*$, either $u_i(o'; \theta_i) = u_i(o^*; \theta_i)$ for all i, or $\exists i \in \mathcal{I}$ with $u_i(o', \theta_i) < u_i(o^*, \theta_i)$.

In the next section, we will first explore different design possibilities, then describe the revelation principle, and then explain the impossibility and possibility. As an example, the Groves mechanism is investigated.

6.1.1   Equilibrium Concepts

We define three equilibrium concepts: Nash implementation, Bayes–Nash implementation, and dominant implementation, with increasing difficulty.

Definition 3   Nash implementation: Mechanism $M = (S, g)$ implements $f(\theta)$ in Nash equilibrium if, for all $\theta \in \Theta$, $g(s^*(\theta)) = f(\theta)$, where $s^*(\theta)$ is a Nash equilibrium, that is,

$$u_i(s_i^*(\theta_i), s_{-i}^*(\theta_{-i}), \theta_i) \geq u_i(s_i'(\theta_i), s_{-i}'(\theta_{-i}), \theta_i), \ \forall i, \forall \theta_i, \forall s_i' \neq s_i^*. \tag{6.2}$$

Definition 4   Bayes–Nash implementation: With common prior $F(\theta)$, mechanism $M = (S, g)$ implements $f(\theta)$ in Bayes–Nash equilibrium if, for all $\theta \in \Theta$, $g(s^*(\theta)) = f(\theta)$, where $s^*(\theta)$ is a Bayes–Nash equilibrium; that is,

$$E_{\theta_{-i}}[u_i(s_i^*(\theta_i), s_{-i}^*(\theta_{-i}), \theta_i)] \geq E_{\theta_{-i}}[u_i(s_i'(\theta_i), s_{-i}'(\theta_{-i}), \theta_i)], \ \forall i, \forall \theta_i, \forall s_i' \neq s_i^*. \tag{6.3}$$

Definition 5   Dominant implementation: Mechanism $M = (S, g)$ implements $f(\theta)$ in a dominant strategy equilibrium if, for all $\theta \in \Theta$, $g(s^*(\theta)) = f(\theta)$, where $s^*(\theta)$ is a dominant strategy equilibrium; that is,

$$u_i(s_i^*(\theta_i), s_{-i}^*(\hat{\theta}_{-i}), \theta_i) \geq u_i(s_i'(\theta_i), s_{-i}'(\hat{\theta}_{-i}), \theta_i), \ \forall i, \forall \theta_i, \forall \hat{\theta}_{-i}, \forall s_i' \neq s_i^*. \tag{6.4}$$

Then, with increasing complexity, we identify three rationality concepts: ex-ante individual rationality, intermediate individual rationality, and ex-post individual rationality.

Let $\bar{u}_i(\theta_i)$ denote the (expected) utility to player i with type θ_i as its outside option, and recall that $u_i(f(\theta); \theta_i)$ is the equilibrium utility of player i from the mechanism. We have the following three definitions of rationality.

- Ex-ante individual rationality. Players choose to participate before they know their own types:

$$E_{\theta \in \Theta}[u_i(f(\theta); \theta_i)] \geq E_{\theta_i \in \Theta_i}[\bar{u}_i(\theta_i)]. \tag{6.5}$$

- Interim individual rationality. Players can withdraw once they know their own type:

$$E_{\theta_{-i} \in \Theta_{-i}}[u_i(f(\theta, \theta_{-i}); \theta_i)] \geq \bar{u}_i(\theta_i). \tag{6.6}$$

- Ex-post individual rationality. Players can withdraw from the mechanism at the end:

$$u_i(f(\theta); \theta_i) \geq \bar{u}_i(\theta_i). \tag{6.7}$$

A special kind of mechanisms is called the direct-revelation mechanism (DRM), which has a strategy space $S = \Theta$ and which has a player who simply reports a type to the mechanism with outcome rule $g: \Theta \rightarrow \Omega$. For DRM, we have the following definitions for incentive compatible and strategy proof.

Definition 6 Incentive compatible: A DRM is (Bayes–)Nash incentive compatible if truth revelation is a (Bayes–)Nash equilibrium; that is, $s_i^*(\theta_i) = \theta_i$, for all $\theta \in \Theta$.

Definition 7 Strategy proof: A DRM is strategy proof if truth revelation is a dominant strategy equilibrium, for all $\theta \in \Theta$.

6.1.2 Revelation Principle

The revelation principle states that for any Bayesian Nash equilibrium there corresponds a Bayesian game with the same equilibrium outcome but in which players truthfully report type. The principle allows one to solve for a Bayesian equilibrium by assuming all players truthfully report type (subject to an incentive-compatibility constraint), which eliminates the need to consider either strategic behavior or lying. So, no matter what the mechanism, a designer can confine attention to equilibria in which players truthfully report type.

Theorem 1 *For any mechanism, M, there is a direct, incentive-compatible mechanism with the same outcome.*

Proof Consider mechanism $M = (S, g)$, that implements $f(\theta)$, in a dominant strategy equilibrium. In other words, $g(s^*(\theta)) = f(\theta)$, for all $\theta \in \Theta$, where s^* is a dominant strategy equilibrium. We construct the direct mechanism $M = (S, g)$. By contradiction, we suppose

$$\exists \theta_i' \neq \theta_i, \text{ s.t. } u_i(f(\theta_i', \theta_{-i}), \theta_i) > u_i(f(\theta_i, \theta_{-i}), \theta_i) \tag{6.8}$$

for some $\theta_i' \neq \theta_i$. But because $f(\theta) = g(s^*(\theta))$, this implies that

$$u_i(g(s_i^*(\theta_i'), s_{-i}^*(\theta_{-i})), \theta_i) > u_i(g(s_i^*(\theta_i), s_{-i}^*(\theta_{-i})), \theta_i), \tag{6.9}$$

which contradicts the strategy proof-ness of s^* in mechanism M. □

The practical implications are obvious for the above theorem. First, incentive-compatibility is free, that is, any outcome implemented by mechanism, M, can be implemented by an incentive-compatible mechanism, M'. Second, fancy mechanisms are unnecessary, namely, any outcome implemented by a mechanism with complex strategy space, S, can be implemented by a DRM.

6.1.3   Budget Balance and Efficiency

Before we define the budget balance, we first introduce transfers or side payments. Define the outcome space $\mathcal{O} = \mathcal{K} \times \mathbb{R}^N$, such that an outcome rule, $o = (k, t_1, \ldots, t_N)$, defines a choice, $k(s) \in \mathcal{K}$, and a transfer, $t_i(s) \in \mathbb{R}$ from player i to the mechanism, given strategy profile $s \in S$. For example, the utility can be written as

$$u_i(o, \theta_i) = v_i(k, \theta_i) - t_i, \tag{6.10}$$

where $v_i(k, \theta_i)$ is the value of player i and t_i is the payment (transfer) to the auctioneer.

Definition 8   Budget balance introduces constraints over the total transfers made from the players to the mechanism. Let $s^*(\theta)$ denote the equilibrium strategy of a mechanism. We have the following.

1. Weak budget balance
   (a) ex-post: $\sum_t t_i(s^*(\theta)) \geq 0, \forall \theta$;
   (b) ex-ante: $E_{\theta \in \Theta}[\Sigma_t t_i(s^*(\theta))] \geq 0$.
2. Strong budget balance
   (a) ex-post: $\sum_t t_i(s^*(\theta)) = 0, \forall \theta$;
   (b) ex-ante: $E_{\theta \in \Theta}[\Sigma_t t_i(s^*(\theta))] = 0$.

Obviously, strong budget balance is harder than weak budget balance, and ex-post is harder than ex-ante.

Next, we define the efficiency and discuss the trade-off between efficiency and budget balance.

Definition 9   A choice rule, $k^*: \Theta \to \mathcal{K}$, is (ex-post) efficient if for all $\theta \in \Theta$, $k^*(\theta)$ maximizes the sum of individual value functions $\sum_{k \in \mathcal{K}} v_i(k, \theta_i)$.

Unfortunately, according to the Green–Laffont impossibility theorem [185], if Θ allows all valuation functions from $\mathcal{K}$ to $\mathbb{R}$, then no mechanism can implement an efficient and ex-post budget-balanced in dominant strategy. So we can either (1) restrict space of preferences, (2) drop budget balance, (3) drop efficiency, or (4) drop dominant strategy.

6.1.4   Groves Mechanisms

Now, we discuss a special mechanism, the Groves mechanisms, as an example.

Definition 10   A Groves mechanism, $M = (\Theta, k, t_1, \ldots, t_N)$, is defined with choice rule,

$$k^*(\hat{\theta}) = \arg\max_{k \in \mathcal{K}} \sum_i v_i(k, \hat{\theta}_i), \tag{6.11}$$

and transfer rules

$$t_i(\hat{\theta}) = h_i(\hat{\theta}_{-i}) - \sum_{j \neq i} v_j(k^*(\hat{\theta}), \hat{\theta}_j), \tag{6.12}$$

where $h_i(\cdot)$ is an (arbitrary) function that does not depend on the reported type, $\hat{\theta}_i$, of player i.

It has been proved that Groves mechanisms are strategy proof and efficient [186]. Groves mechanisms are unique, in the sense that any mechanism that implements efficient choice, $k^*(\theta)$, in truthful dominant strategy must implement Groves transfers.

6.1.5   Impossibility and Possibility

For the different desired properties discussed so far, some combinations are possible, while others are impossible. We list some well-known results for impossibility and possibility as the following theorems:

Theorem 2   Gibbard–Satterthwaite Impossibility Theorem [187, 188] *If agents have general preferences, there are at least two agents, and at least three different optimal outcomes over the set of all agent preferences; then a social-choice function is dominant-strategy implementable if and only if it is dictatorial (i.e., one (or more) agents always receive one of its most preferred alternatives).*

Theorem 3   Hurwicz Impossibility Theorem [189] *It is impossible to implement an efficient, budget-balanced, and strategy-proof mechanism in a simple exchange economy[1] with quasilinear preferences.*

Theorem 4   Myerson–Satterthwaite Theorem [190] *It is impossible to achieve allocative efficiency, budget balance, and (interim) individual rationality in a Bayesian–Nash incentive-compatible mechanism, even with quasilinear utility functions.*

An interesting extension of the Groves mechanism, the dAGVA (or "expected Groves" [191, 192]) mechanism, demonstrates that it is possible to achieve efficiency and budget balance in a Bayesian–Nash equilibrium, even though this is impossible in dominant-strategy equilibrium (Hurwicz impossibility theorem). However, the dAGVA mechanism is not individual rational, which we should expect by the Myerson–Satterthwaite impossibility theorem.

6.2   Incentivizing Blockchain Consensus: A Game-Theoretic Perspective

Public blockchain networks using Proof of Work (PoW)-based consensus protocols are considered a promising platform for decentralized resource management with

---

[1] A simple exchange environment is one in which there are buyers and sellers, selling single units of the same good.

financial incentive mechanisms. In order to maintain a secured, universal state of the blockchain, PoW-based consensus protocols financially incentivize the nodes in the network to compete for the privilege of block generation through cryptographic puzzle solving. For rational consensus nodes, namely, miners with limited local computational resources, offloading the computation load for PoW to the cloud–fog providers (CFPs) becomes a viable option. In this chapter, we study the interaction between the CFPs and the miners in a PoW-based blockchain network using a game-theoretic approach. In particular, we propose a lightweight infrastructure of the PoW-based blockchains, where the computation-intensive part of the consensus process is offloaded to the cloud–fog. We formulate the computation resource management in the blockchain consensus process as a two-stage Stackelberg game, where the profit of the CFP and the utilities of the individual miners are jointly optimized. In the first stage of the game, the CFP sets the price of the offered computing resource. In the second stage, the miners decide on the amount of service to purchase accordingly. We apply backward induction to analyze the subgame perfect equilibria in each stage for both uniform and discriminatory pricing schemes. For uniform pricing where the same price applies to all miners, the uniqueness of the Stackelberg equilibrium is validated by identifying the best response strategies of the miners. For discriminatory pricing where the different prices are applied, the uniqueness of the Stackelberg equilibrium is proved by capitalizing on the variational inequality theory. Further, real experimental results are employed to justify our proposed model.

6.2.1   Introduction and Contribution

Blockchain networks were first designed to be the backbone of a distributed, permissionless or public database for recording the transactional data of cryptocurrencies in a tamper-proof and totally ordered manner [1, 193]. The blockchain network is essentially organized as a virtual overlay P2P network, where the database state is maintained in a purely decentralized manner and any node in the network is allowed to join the state maintenance process without the need of identity authentication. As indicated by the name "blockchain," the records of transactions between nodes in the network are organized in a data structure known as the "block." A series of blocks are arranged in a strictly increasing-time order by a linked-list-like data structure known as the chain of blocks (i.e., "blockchain"). The blockchain is maintained as the appending-only local replicas by the nodes participating in the replicated consensus process. Unlike the traditional distributed ledger systems using the PBFT [194] or Paxos [195] protocols, a permissionless blockchain network no longer needs any centralized authorities (e.g., authenticating or authorizing servers) and is able to accommodate a much larger number of consensus nodes in the network [196]. Such an objective is achieved by blockchain networks with the Nakamoto consensus protocol [1] (or protocols alike). Per the Nakamoto protocol, financial incentive is introduced into the consensus process to ensure that the best strategies of the pseudonymous consensus nodes is to follow the given rules of blockchain maintenance or extension. Otherwise they will suffer from monetary loss.

The core component of the Nakamoto consensus protocol is a computation-intensive process known as Proof of Work (PoW). For the consensus nodes that propose their local blockchain view to be the new state of the blockchain database, PoW requires them to solve a cryptographic puzzle, that is, to find a partial preimage satisfying certain conditions of a hash mapping based on the proposed blockchain state. According to [97], a typical PoW process is executed in the following steps. First, with an input contribution function, a consensus node validates and bundles a subset of unconfirmed transactions into a new block. Then, the consensus node computes the PoW solution to the cryptographic puzzle, which is formed based on the value of the new block. Immediately after the puzzle solution is obtained, the consensus node broadcasts the new block to the entire network as its own proposal of the new blockchain head. On the other hand, the rest of nodes in the network run a chain validation-comparison function to determine whether to accept such a proposal or not. In the blockchain network, an honest consensus node follows "the-longest-chain" rule and adopts the longest one among the received blockchain proposals to update its local view of the blockchain state. In such a process, the nodes that devote their computational resources to the generation of new blocks (i.e., PoW solutions) are also known as the block "miners." This is mainly because, according to the Nakamoto protocol, a certain amount of blockchain tokens will be awarded to the node that has its proposed blockchain state accepted by the majority of the network. The theoretic proof and analysis for secure and private communication with the Nakamoto protocol can be found in [97].

With the blossoming of various cryptocurrencies, permissionless blockchains are considered to be especially appropriate for constructing the decentralized autonomous resource management framework in (wireless) communication networks. Specifically, when the resource management relies on the design of incentive mechanisms (e.g., resource access control [197] and proactive edge caching [198]), permissionless blockchains are able to provide fast implementation of the self-organized trading platform with small investment in the operational infrastructure. Furthermore, with the PoW-based Nakamoto consensus protocol, the users of a Decentralized Application (DApp) are incentivized to turn themselves from the free riders of the blockchain network into consensus nodes (i.e., block miners) for more profit. However, owing to the required computation contribution by the PoW, the computationally lightweight nodes such as the Internet of Things (IoT) devices may be prevented from directly participating in the consensus process. To alleviate such limitation, "cloud mining" becomes a viable option where the mobile devices offload their storage load and/or computation tasks in PoW to the CFPs or even other edge devices [199, 200]. In the case of computation offloading, the lightweight devices may employ the existing cloud-mining protocols such as Stratum [201] without causing any significant transmission overhead. From the perspective of the blockchain-based DApp's designer, the benefit of encouraging cloud-based mining is multi-fold. First, by incorporating more consensus nodes, the robustness of the blockchain network is naturally improved [97]. Second, the user devices may improve their valuation of the DApps, thanks to the additional reward obtained in the consensus process. Also, the high level of user activities may attract more users and in return further improve the robustness of the underlying blockchain network. In this chapter, we study the interaction between the computationally lightweight devices and a CFP, where the lightweight devices (i.e., block miners) purchase the computing power from the CFP to participate in the consensus process of a PoW-based blockchain for block-mining revenues. Game theory can be leveraged as a promising mathematical tool to analyze the interactions among the CFP and block miners. For example, in [202], the authors formulated a Stackelberg game to solve the resource management in fog computing networks, where the game-theoretic study of the market and pricing strategies are presented. In [203], the authors studied the spectrum resource allocation in order to mitigate the interference management among multiple cellular operators in the unlicensed system. A multi-leader multi-follower Stackelberg game is proposed to model the interactions among the operators and users in unlicensed spectrum. Similarly, we also model the resource offloading market as a two-stage Stackelberg game. In the first stage, the CFP sets the unit price for computation offloading. In the second stage, the miners decide on the amount of services to purchase from the CFP. In particular, we analyze two pricing schemes [204], namely, uniform pricing where a uniform unit price is applied to all the miners and discriminatory pricing where different unit prices are assigned to different miners. The uniform pricing leads to a straightforward implementation as the CFP does not need to keep track of information of every miner, and charging the same prices is fair to all miners. However, from the perspective of the CFP, discriminatory pricing yields a higher profit by allowing price adjustment for different miners [205]. The main contributions of this chapter are summarized as follows.

1. We explore the possibility of implementing a permissionless, PoW-based blockchain in a network of computationally lightweight devices. By allowing computation offloading to the cloud–fog, we model the interactions between the rational blockchain miners and the CFP as a two-stage Stackelberg game.
2. We study both the uniform pricing scheme and the discriminatory pricing scheme for the CFP. Through backward induction, we provide a series of analytically results with respect to the properties of the Stackelberg equilibrium in different situations.
3. In particular, the existence and uniqueness of Stackelberg equilibrium are validated by identifying the best response strategies of the miners under the uniform pricing scheme. Likewise, the Stackelberg equilibrium is proved to exist and be unique by capitalizing on the Variational Inequalities (VI) theory under discriminatory pricing scheme.
4. We conduct extensive numerical simulations to evaluate the performance of the proposed price-based resource management in blockchain networks. The results show that the discriminatory pricing helps the CFP to encourage more service demand from the miners and achieve greater profit. Moreover, under uniform pricing, the CFP has an incentive to set the maximum price for the profit maximization.

The rest of the chapter is organized as follows. Section 6.2.2 presents a brief review of the related work. We describe the model of the consensus formation in a permissionless PoW-based blockchain network and formulate the two-stage Stackelberg game between the lightweight nodes and the CFP in Section 6.2.3. In Section 6.2.4, we analyze the optimal service demand of block miners as well as the profit maximization of the CFP using backward induction for both uniform and discriminatory pricing schemes. We present the performance evaluations in Section 6.2.5. Section 6.3 concludes the work with a summary and future directions.

6.2.2 Related Work and Motivation

6.2.2.1 Public Blockchains, DApps, and Incentive Mechanism

For blockchain networks, the core technological "building blocks" have been recognized as the distributed database (i.e., ledger), the consensus protocol, and the executable scripts (i.e., smart contract) based on network consensus [95]. From a data processing point of view, a DApp is essentially a collection of smart contracts and transactional data residing on the blockchain. The realization of a DApp relies on the distributed ledger to identify the state or ownership changes of the tokenized assets. The smart contracts are implemented as transaction (data)-driven procedures to autonomously determine the state transition regarding the asset redistribution among the DApp users [95]. With public blockchains, the implementation of a DApp does not require a centralized infrastructure, namely, dedicated storage and computation provision for the ledger and smart contracts. Instead, the DApp users are allowed to freely enable their functionalities among transaction issuing or validation, information propagation or storage, and consensus participation [95, 96]. More specifically, the token-based incentive mechanisms in public blockchains offload the tasks of resource provision and system maintenance from the DApp providers to the DApp users. Thereby, public blockhain networks are considered to be a suitable platform for implementing the incentive-driven Distributed Autonomous Organization (DAO) systems.

In recent years, a line of work has been dedicated to the study in DAO for wireless networking applications based on public blockchains. In [206], a trading platform for Device-to-Device (D2D) computation offloading is proposed using a dedicated cryptocurrency network. Therein, resource offloading is executed between neighbor D2D nodes through smart contract-based auctions, and the block mining tasks are offloaded to the cloudlets. In [207], a PoW-based public blockchain is adopted as the backbone of a P2P file storage market, where the privacy of different parties in a transaction is enhanced by techniques such as ring signatures and one-time payment addresses. When identity verification is required for market access granting, for example, in the senarios of autonomous network slice brokering [208] and P2P electricity trading [209], the public blockchains can be adapted into consortium blockchains by introducing membership-authorizing servers with little modification to the consensus protocols and smart contract design.

Our work also relates to the classical literature on incentive mechanisms in crowdsensing [210–212]. In crowdsensing, the crowdsensing platform as the service provider offers a reward as the incentive to attract more crowdsensing user participation. In the pioneering work [210], the authors considered two system models: the platform-centric model where the provider offers a certain amount of reward that will be shared by the participating users, and the user-centric model where the users have their reserve prices for the participation. In [211], the authors designed the incentive mechanisms for crowdsensing with multiple crowdsourcers, that is, service providers. The interactions among the service providers are modeled as the noncooperative game. Therein, the authors proposed a discrete time dynamic algorithm utilizing the best response dynamics to compute the Nash equilibrium of the modeled game. The authors in [212] presented the incentive mechanism in a sealed market where the users have incomplete information on other users' behavior. The convergence to the Nash equilibrium in such a market is then analyzed using the well-known best-response dynamics.

6.2.2.2 Consensus and Game-Theoretic Mining Models in PoW-based Blockchains

By the Nakamoto protocol, from a single miner's point of view, the process of solving a PoW puzzle involves an exhaustive query to a collision-resistant hash function (e.g., SHA-256), which aims to find a fixed-length hashcode output with no less than a given number of prefix zeros [1, 97]. For each individual miner, such a process simulates a Poisson process when the required number of prefix zeros is sufficiently large. For a group of miners independently running their own PoW processes at the same time, the first miner to obtain the PoW puzzle solution will have a high probability of getting its block head proposal acknowledged by the entire network. Therefore, block mining under the Nakamoto protocol can also be viewed as a hashing competition, where the probability of a miner winning the competition is roughly proportional to the ratio between its devoted hash power[2] and the total hash power in the network.

According to the theoretical analysis in [97], when the PoW-based blockchain network satisfies the condition of honest majority in terms of computing power, the probability for the blockchain state machine to be compromised is negligible. Therefore, the mainstream research on the PoW-based consensus protocols focuses on the protocol's incentive compatibility and thus the search of miners' rational strategy to optimize the reward obtained in the mining process. A plethora of recent studies [213–215] model the mining process in PoW-based blockchain networks as a noncooperative game, where rational miners may withhold their newly found blocks with valid PoW solutions to internationally cause the fork of the blockchain. In certain conditions of hash power distribution, it is proved in [213–215] that by postponing the newly mined blocks, rational miners may obtain a higher expected payoff than fully abiding by the Nakamoto protocol.

In the literature, the most relevant works to this chapter are about the pool-based mining mechanisms. In public blockchains based on outsourceable PoW schemes, a mining pool is essentially a proxy node in the network that only enables its local functionalities of transaction issuing or validation and information propagation or storage. The proxy node offloads the queries to the hash function to the mining workers that subscribe to the pool for mining payment [95, 96]. It is worth noting that most of the existing studies consider the pool-based mining from the perspective of mining workers (i.e., cloud-side resource providers) [216–219]. In [216], the process of mining pool

---

[2] We use the hash power and computing power interchangeably throughout the book.

formation is modeled as a coalitional game among the mining workers, which is found to have an empty core under the proportional payment scheme. In contrast, the social welfare of miners is considered in [217] and a geometric-payment pooling strategy is found to be able to achieve the optimal steady-state utility for the miners. In [218], the group bargaining solution is adopted by considering the P2P relationship of the miners. In [219], instead of limiting the miner subscription to a single mining pool, a computing power-splitting game is proposed. With the proposed scheme, the miners play a puzzle-solution game by distributing their computing power into different pools in order to maximize the mining reward.

6.2.3 System Model and Game Formulation

In this section, we first propose the system model of blockchain under our consideration [220]. Then, we present the Stackelberg game formulation for the price-based computing resource management in blockchain networks assisted by cloud–fog computing.

6.2.3.1 Chain Mining Assisted by Cloud/Fog Computing

We consider a public blockchain network using the PoW-based consensus protocol [221–223]. The blockchain network dedicatedly works as the backbone of a specific DApp, where most of the nodes are limited in their local computing power (e.g., the IoT devices and smart phones in a typical crowdsensing market). We assume that the adopted PoW protocol is ASIC-resistant [96], for example, using the Ethash-based PoW scheme [159] or the schemes alike. Then, to participate in the consensus process, a node only has to solve the PoW puzzle with general-purpose computing devices. In the blockchain network, a set of N nodes, denoted as $\mathcal{N} = \{1, \ldots, N\}$, are interested in participating in the consensus process and make extra profit through block mining. In order to achieve this, these block miners purchase the necessary hash power from a public CFP (e.g., Amazon EC2) without hassle of managing the infrastructure such as seeking extra electricity sources [224]. In addition, we consider that the CFP is able to provide the near-to-end computing units such as fog nodes or even edge devices which are closer to the miners [225].[3] As such, the aforementioned PoW puzzle can be offloaded to the remote cloud or the nearby fog computing unit. The computing resources offered to the miners is priced by the CFP.[4] Figure 6.1 shows the system model of the blockchain network under our consideration. Note that we assume the link between the miners and cloud–fog computing units is sufficiently reliable and

---

[3] Note that this fog unit deployment is also more appropriate in hostile environment where the communications with remote cloud are limited and for the access from personal devices which keep moving, for example, mobile devices.

[4] Note that the resource may also include a communication resource. Specifically, we can consider that the communication cost is part of the price charged by the CFP. In other words, the CFP offers the service as a bundle which is composed of computing and wireless or wired communication resources. The energy consumption for the computing and communication is naturally accounted in the bundle.

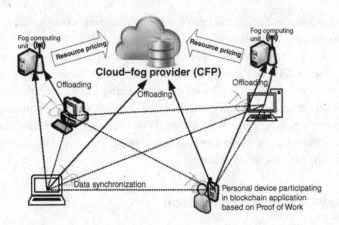

Figure 6.1 System model of public blockchain application involving PoW. Reprinted with permission from the paper "Cloud/fog computing resource management and pricing for blockchain networks" published in *IEEE Internet of Things Journal*.

secured, and is guaranteed by certain ready-to-use communication protocols (e.g., Stratum [201]).

The CFP, that is, the seller, sells the computing services, and the miners, that is, the buyers, access and consume this service from the remote cloud or the nearby fog computing unit. Each miner $i \in \mathcal{N}$ determines their individual service demand, denoted by x_i. Additionally, we consider $x_i \in [\underline{x}, \overline{x}]$, in which $\underline{x}$ is the minimum service demand, for example, for blockchain data synchronization, and $\overline{x}$ is the maximum service demand governed by the CFP. Note that each miner has no incentive to unboundedly increase its service demand due to its financial burden. Then, let $\mathbf{x} \triangleq (x_1, \dots, x_N)$ and $\mathbf{x}_{-i}$ represent the service demand profile of all the miners and all other miners except miner i, respectively. As such, the miner $i \in \mathcal{N}$ with the service demand x_i has a relative computing power (hash power) α_i with respect to the total hash power of the network, which is defined as follows:

$$\alpha_i(x_i, \mathbf{x}_{-i}) = \frac{x_i}{\sum_{j \in \mathcal{N}} x_j}, \quad \alpha_i > 0, \tag{6.13}$$

such that $\sum_{j \in \mathcal{N}} \alpha_j = 1$.

In the blockchain network, miners compete against each other in order to be the first one to solve the PoW puzzle and receive the reward from the speed game accordingly. The occurrence of solving the puzzle can be modeled as a random variable following a Poisson process with mean $\lambda = \frac{1}{600\,s}$ [213]. Note that our model is general and can be applied with other values of λ easily. The set of transactions to be included in a block chosen by miner i is denoted as t_i. Once the miner successfully solves the puzzle, the miner needs to propagate its solution to the whole blockchain network and its solution needs to reach consensus. Because there is no centralized authority to verify or validate a newly mined block, a mechanism for reaching network consensus must be employed. In this mechanism, the verification needs to be processed by other miners before the new mined block is appended to the current blockchain.

The first miner to successfully mine a block that reaches consensus earns the reward. The reward consists of a fixed reward denoted by R, and a variable reward which is defined as rt_i, where r denotes a given variable reward factor and t_i denotes the number of transactions included in the block mined by miner i [213]. Additionally, the process of solving the puzzle incurs an associated cost, that is, the payment from miner i to the CFP, p_i. The objective of the miners is to maximize their individual expected utility, and for miner i, it is defined as follows:

$$u_i = (R + rt_i)P_i\left(\alpha_i(x_i, \mathbf{x}_{-i}), t_i\right) - p_i x_i, \tag{6.14}$$

where $P\left(\alpha_i(x_i, \mathbf{x}_{-i}), t_i\right)$ is the probability that miner i successfully mines the block and its solutions reach consensus, that is, miner i wins the mining reward.

The process of successfully mining a block consists of two steps, that is, the mining step and the propagation step. In the mining step, the probability that miner i mines the block is directly proportional to its relative computing power α_i. Furthermore, there are diminishing chances of winning if one miner chooses to propagate a block that propagates slowly to other miners in the propagation step. In other words, even though one miner may find the first valid block, if its mined block is large, then this block will be likely to be discarded because of long latency, which is called orphaning [213]. Considering this fact, the probability of successful mining by miner i is discounted by the chances that the block is orphaned, $\mathbb{P}_{\text{orphan}}(t_i)$, which is expressed by

$$P_i(\alpha_i(x_i, \mathbf{x}_{-i}), t_i) = \alpha_i(1 - \mathbb{P}_{\text{orphan}}(t_i)). \tag{6.15}$$

Using the fact that block mining times follow the Poisson distribution aforementioned, the orphaning probability is approximated as [226]:

$$\mathbb{P}_{\text{orphan}}(t_i) = 1 - e^{-\lambda \tau(t_i)}, \tag{6.16}$$

where $\tau(t_i)$ is the block propagation time, which is a function of the block size. In other words, the propagation time needed for a block to reach consensus is dependent on its size t_i, that is, the number of transactions in it [213, 227]. Thus, the bigger the block is, the more time needed to propagate the block to the whole blockchain network [120]. As in [213], we assume this time function is linear, that is, $\tau(t_i) = z \times t_i$ with $z > 0$ represents a given delay factor. Note that this linear approximation is acceptable according to the numerical results from [213]. Additionally, it would be more appropriate to add a constant term in this function [120], but apparently this constant term has no effect on our subsequent analytical results. Thus, the probability that the miner i successfully mines a block and its solution reaches consensus is expressed as follows:

$$P_i(\alpha_i(x_i, \mathbf{x}_{-i}), t_i) = \alpha_i e^{-\lambda z t_i}, \tag{6.17}$$

where $\alpha_i(x_i, \mathbf{x}_{-i})$ is given in equation (6.13).

6.2.3.2   Two-Stage Stackelberg Game Formulation

The interaction between the CFP and miners can be modeled as a two-stage Stackelberg game, as illustrated in Fig. 6.2. The CFP, that is, the leader, sets the price in the upper Stage I. The miners, that is, the followers, decide on their optimal computing service

Upper Stage I
(leader)

Stackelberg game

Lower Stage II
(followers)

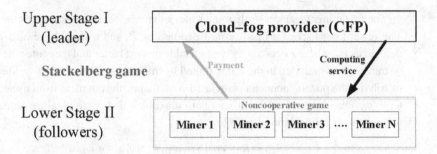

Figure 6.2 Two-stage Stackelberg game model of the interactions among the CFP and miners in the blockchain network. Reprinted with permission from the paper "Cloud/fog computing resource management and pricing for blockchain networks" published in *IEEE Internet of Things Journal*.

demand for offloading in the lower Stage II, being aware of the price set by the CFP. By using backward induction, we formulate the optimization problems for the leader and followers as follows.

Miners' mining strategies in Stage II

Given the pricing of the CFP and other miners' strategies, the miner i determines its computing service demand for its hash power maximizing the expected utility which is given as:

$$u_i(x_i, \mathbf{x}_{-i}, p_i) = (R + rt_i)\frac{x_i}{\sum_{j \in \mathcal{N}} x_j} e^{-\lambda z t_i} - p_i x_i, \qquad (6.18)$$

where p_i is the price per unit for service demand of miner i. The miner subgame problem can be written as follows:

Problem 1 (Miner i subgame)

$$\underset{x_i}{\text{maximize}} \quad u_i(x_i, \mathbf{x}_{-i}, p_i)$$
$$\text{subject to} \quad x_i \in [\underline{x}, \overline{x}]. \qquad (6.19)$$

CFP's pricing strategies in Stage I

The profit of the CFP is the revenue obtained from charging the miners for computing service minus the service cost. The service cost is directly related to the time that the miner takes to mine a block, the cost of electricity, c, and the other cost that is a function of the service demand x_i. Therefore, the CFP decides the pricing within the strategy space $\{\mathbf{p} = [p_i]_{i \in \mathcal{N}} : 0 \leq p_i \leq \overline{p}\}$ to maximize its profit which is represented as:

$$\Pi(\mathbf{p}, \mathbf{x}) = \sum_{i \in \mathcal{N}} p_i x_i - \sum_{i \in \mathcal{N}} cT x_i. \qquad (6.20)$$

Note that practically the price is bounded by maximum price constraint that is denoted by $\overline{p}$. Then, the profit maximization problem of the CFP is formulated as follows.

Problem 2 (CFP subgame)

$$\text{maximize} \quad \Pi(\mathbf{p}, \mathbf{x})$$
$$\text{subject to} \quad 0 \le p_i \le \bar{p}. \tag{6.21}$$

Problem 1 and Problem 2 together form the Stackelberg game, and the objective of this game is to find the Stackelberg equilibrium. The Stackelberg equilibrium ensures that the profit of the CFP is maximized given that the miners generate their demands following the best responses, namely, the Nash equilibrium. This means that the demands from the miners maximize the utility. In our problem, the Stackelberg equilibrium can be written as follows.

Definition 11   Let $\mathbf{x}^*$ and $\mathbf{p}^*$ denote the optimal service demand vector of all the miners and optimal unit price vector of computing service, respectively. Then, the point $(\mathbf{x}^*, \mathbf{p}^*)$ is the Stackelberg equilibrium if the following conditions,

$$\Pi(\mathbf{p}^*, \mathbf{x}^*) \ge \Pi(\mathbf{p}, \mathbf{x}^*) \tag{6.22}$$

and

$$u_i(x_i^*, \mathbf{x}_{-i}^*, \mathbf{p}^*) \ge u_i(x_i, \mathbf{x}_{-i}^*, \mathbf{p}^*), \quad \forall x_i \ge 0, \forall i \tag{6.23}$$

are satisfied, where $\mathbf{x}_{-i}^*$ is the best response service demand vector for all the miners except miner i.

Note that the same or different prices can be applied to the miners, and we refer to them as the uniform and discriminatory pricing schemes, respectively. In the following, we investigate these two pricing schemes for resource management in blockchain networks. The Stackelberg equilibrium ensures that the profit of the CFP is maximized given that the miners generate their demands following the best responses, namely, the Nash equilibrium. This means that the demands from the miners maximize the utility. The Stackelberg equilibrium under the uniform pricing scheme contains only one single price that the CFP imposes on the miners identically. On the other hand, the equilibrium under the discriminatory pricing scheme contains different prices, each of which the CFP imposes to each miner separately.

The significance of each pricing scheme is as follows. Under the uniform pricing scheme, the equilibrium ensures a fair price applied to all miners. The miners are indifferent to choosing the services. However, the CFP has limited degrees of freedom to maximize its profit. By contrast, under the discriminatory pricing scheme, the CFP can customize the price for each miner, matching with the miner's demand and preference. As such, the profit obtained under the discriminatory pricing scheme is expected to be superior to that of the uniform pricing scheme in terms of the higher profit for the CFP.

6.2.4   Equilibrium Analysis for Cloud–Fog Computing Resource Management

In this section, we propose the uniform pricing and discriminatory pricing schemes for resource management in blockchain application involving PoW assisted by the CFP.

We then analyze the optimal service demand of miners as well as the profit maximization of the CFP under both pricing schemes.

6.2.4.1 Uniform Pricing Scheme

We first consider the uniform pricing scheme, in which the CFP charges all the miners the same unit price for their computing service demand, that is, $p_i = p, \forall i$. Given the payoff functions defined in Section 6.2.3, we use backward induction to analyze the Stackelberg game.

Stage II: Miners' Demand Game

Given the price p decided by the CFP, in Stage II, the miners compete with each other to maximize their own utility by choosing their individual service demand, which forms the noncooperative Miners' Demand Game (MDG) $\mathcal{G}^u = \{\mathcal{N}, \{x_i\}_{i \in \mathcal{N}}, \{u_i\}_{i \in \mathcal{N}}\}$, where $\mathcal{N}$ is the set of miners, $\{x_i\}_{i \in \mathcal{N}}$ is the strategy set, and u_i is the utility, that is, payoff, function of miner i. Specifically, each miner $i \in \mathcal{N}$ selects its strategy to maximize its utility function $u_i(x_i, \mathbf{x}_{-i}, p)$. We next analyze the existence and uniqueness of the Nash equilibrium in the MDG.

Definition 12 A demand vector $\mathbf{x}^* = (x_1^*, \ldots, x_N^*)$ is the Nash equilibrium of the MDG $\mathcal{G}^u = \{\mathcal{N}, \{x_i\}_{i \in \mathcal{N}}, \{u_i\}_{i \in \mathcal{N}}\}$, if, for every miner $i \in \mathcal{N}$, $u_i(x_i^*, \mathbf{x}_{-i}^*, p) \geq u_i(x_i', \mathbf{x}_{-i}^*, p)$ for all $x_i' \in [\underline{x}, \overline{x}]$, where $u_i(x_i, \mathbf{x}_{-i})$ is the resulting utility of the miner i, given the other miners' demand $\mathbf{x}_{-i}$:

$$
x_i^* = \mathscr{F}_i(\mathbf{x}) = \begin{cases} \underline{x}, & \sqrt{\frac{(R+rt_i)\sum_{i \neq j} x_j}{pe^{\lambda z t_i}}} - \sum_{i \neq j} x_j < \underline{x} \\[2ex] \sqrt{\frac{(R+rt_i)\sum_{i \neq j} x_j}{pe^{\lambda z t_i}}} - \sum_{i \neq j} x_j, & \underline{x} \leq \sqrt{\frac{(R+rt_i)\sum_{i \neq j} x_j}{pe^{\lambda z t_i}}} - \sum_{i \neq j} x_j \leq \overline{x} \\[2ex] \overline{x}, & \sqrt{\frac{(R+rt_i)\sum_{i \neq j} x_j}{pe^{\lambda z t_i}}} - \sum_{i \neq j} x_j > \overline{x} \end{cases}. \quad (6.24)
$$

Theorem 5 *A Nash equilibrium exists in MDG $\mathcal{G}^u = \{\mathcal{N}, \{x_i\}_{i \in \mathcal{N}}, \{u_i\}_{i \in \mathcal{N}}\}$.*

Proof Firstly, the strategy space for each miner is defined to be $[\underline{x}, \overline{x}]$, which is a nonempty, convex, compact subset of the Euclidean space. From equation (6.18), u_i is apparently continuous in $[\underline{x}, \overline{x}]$. Then, we take the first-order and second-order derivatives of equation (6.18) with respect to x_i to prove its concavity, which can be written as follows:

$$
\frac{\partial u_i}{\partial x_i} = (R + rt_i)e^{-\lambda z t_i}\frac{\partial \alpha_i}{\partial x_i} - p, \quad (6.25)
$$

$$
\frac{\partial^2 u_i}{\partial x_i^2} = (R + rt_i)e^{-\lambda z t_i}\frac{\partial^2 \alpha_i}{\partial x_i^2} < 0, \quad (6.26)
$$

where $\frac{\partial \alpha_i}{\partial x_i} = \frac{\sum_{i \neq j} x_j}{\left(\sum_{i \in \mathcal{N}} x_j\right)^2} > 0$, and $\frac{\partial^2 \alpha_i}{\partial x_i^2} = -2\frac{\sum_{i \neq j} x_j}{\left(\sum_{i \in \mathcal{N}} x_j\right)^3} < 0$.

Therefore, we have proved that u_i is strictly concave with respect to x_i. Accordingly, the Nash equilibrium exists in this noncooperative MDG $\mathcal{G}^u$ [228]. The proof is now completed. $\qquad\square$

Further, based on the first-order derivative condition, we have

$$\frac{\partial u_i}{\partial x_i} = (R + rt_i)e^{-\lambda z t_i}\frac{\partial \alpha_i}{\partial x_i} - p = 0, \qquad (6.27)$$

and we obtain the best-response function of miner i by solving equation (6.27), as shown in equation (6.24).

Theorem 6 *The uniqueness of the Nash equilibrium in the noncooperative MDG is guaranteed given the following condition*

$$\frac{2(N-1)e^{\lambda z t_i}}{R + rt_i} < \sum_{j\in\mathcal{N}}\frac{e^{\lambda z t_j}}{R + rt_j} \qquad (6.28)$$

is satisfied.

Proof Let $\mathbf{x}^*$ denote the Nash equilibrium of the MDG. By definition, the Nash equilibrium needs to satisfy $\mathbf{x} = \mathcal{F}(\mathbf{x})$, in which $\mathcal{F}(\mathbf{x}) = (\mathcal{F}_1(\mathbf{x}), \mathcal{F}_2(\mathbf{x}), \ldots, \mathcal{F}_N(\mathbf{x}))$. In particular, $\mathcal{F}_i(\mathbf{x})$ is the best response function of miner i, given the demand strategies of other miners. The uniqueness of the Nash equilibrium can be proved by showing that the best-response function of miner i, that is, as given in equation (6.24), is the standard function [228].

Definition 13 A function $\mathcal{F}(\mathbf{x})$ is a standard function when the following properties are guaranteed [228].

(1) Positivity: $\mathcal{F}(\mathbf{x}) > \mathbf{0}$.
(2) Monotonicity: If $\mathbf{x} \leq \mathbf{x}'$, then $\mathcal{F}(\mathbf{x}) \leq \mathcal{F}(\mathbf{x}')$.
(3) Scalability: For all $\phi > 1$, $\phi\mathcal{F}(\mathbf{x}) > \mathcal{F}(\phi\mathbf{x})$.

Firstly, for the positivity, under the condition in equation (6.28), we have (from Lemma 1)

$$\sum_{i\neq j} x_j < \frac{R + rt_i}{4pe^{\lambda z t_i}} < \frac{R + rt_i}{pe^{\lambda z t_i}}, \qquad (6.29)$$

then we can conclude that

$$\sum_{i\neq j} x_j < \sqrt{\frac{(R + rt_i)\sum_{i\neq j} x_j}{pe^{\lambda z t_i}}}. \qquad (6.30)$$

Thus, we can prove that

$$\mathcal{F}_i(\mathbf{x}) = \sqrt{\frac{(R + rt_i)\sum_{i\neq j} x_j}{pe^{\lambda z t_i}}} - \sum_{i\neq j} x_j > 0, \qquad (6.31)$$

which is the positivity condition. Secondly, we prove the monotonicity of equation (6.24). Let $\mathbf{x}' > \mathbf{x}$, we can further simplify the expression of $\mathcal{F}_i(\mathbf{x}') - \mathcal{F}_i(\mathbf{x})$, which is shown in equation (6.32).

$$
\begin{aligned}
\mathcal{F}_i(\mathbf{x}') - \mathcal{F}_i(\mathbf{x}) &= \sqrt{\frac{(R + rt_i)\sum_{i \neq j} x_j'}{pe^{\lambda z t_i}}} - \sum_{i \neq j} x_j' - \sqrt{\frac{(R + rt_i)\sum_{i \neq j} x_j}{pe^{\lambda z t_i}}} - \sum_{i \neq j} x_j \\
&= \left(\sqrt{\frac{(R + rt_i)}{pe^{\lambda z t_i}}} - \sqrt{\sum_{i \neq j} x_j'} - \sqrt{\sum_{i \neq j} x_j} \right) \left(\sqrt{\sum_{i \neq j} x_j'} - \sqrt{\sum_{i \neq j} x_j} \right).
\end{aligned}
$$

(6.32)

$$
\begin{aligned}
\phi \mathcal{F}_i(\mathbf{x}) - \mathcal{F}_i(\phi \mathbf{x}) &= \phi \sqrt{\frac{(R + rt_i)\sum_{i \neq j} x_j}{pe^{\lambda z t_i}}} - \phi \sum_{i \neq j} x_j - \sqrt{\frac{(R + rt_i)\sum_{i \neq j} \phi x_j}{pe^{\lambda z t_i}}} - \sum_{i \neq j} \phi x_j \\
&= \left(\phi - \sqrt{\phi} \right) \sqrt{\frac{(R + rt_i)\sum_{i \neq j} x_j}{pe^{\lambda z t_i}}} > 0, \quad \forall \phi > 1.
\end{aligned}
$$

(6.33)

In particular, we have $\sqrt{\sum_{i \neq j} x_j'} - \sqrt{\sum_{i \neq j} x_j} > 0$, and we can easily verify that

$$
\sqrt{\frac{R + rt_i}{pe^{\lambda z t_i}}} - \sqrt{\sum_{i \neq j} x_j'} - \sqrt{\sum_{i \neq j} x_j} \in
$$

$$
\left(\sqrt{\frac{R + rt_i}{pe^{\lambda z t_i}}} - 2\sqrt{\sum_{i \neq j} x_j'}, \sqrt{\frac{R + rt_i}{pe^{\lambda z t_i}}} - 2\sqrt{\sum_{i \neq j} x_j} \right).
$$

(6.34)

Under the condition we will see in equation (6.42), we can prove that

$$
\sqrt{\frac{R + rt_i}{pe^{\lambda z t_i}}} - 2\sqrt{\sum_{i \neq j} x_j} > 0, \quad \forall x_j.
$$

(6.35)

Thus, the best-response function of miner i in equation (6.24) is always positive.

At last, as for scalability, we need to prove that $\phi \mathcal{F}(x) > \mathcal{F}(\phi x)$, for $\lambda > 1$. The steps of proving the positivity of $\phi \mathcal{F}(x) - \mathcal{F}(\phi x)$ are shown in equation (6.33). Therefore, $\phi \mathcal{F}(x) > \mathcal{F}(\phi x)$ is always satisfied for $\phi > 1$. Until now, we have proved that the best-response function in equation (6.24) satisfies three properties described in Definition 2. Therefore, the Nash equilibrium of MDG $\mathcal{G}^u = \{\mathcal{N}, \{x_i\}_{i \in \mathcal{N}}, \{u_i\}_{i \in \mathcal{N}}\}$ is unique. The proof is now completed. $\qquad\square$

Theorem 7 *The unique Nash equilibrium for miner i in the MDG is given by*

$$x_i^* = \frac{N-1}{\sum_{j \in \mathcal{N}} \frac{pe^{\lambda z t_j}}{R+rt_j}} - \left(\frac{N-1}{\sum_{j \in \mathcal{N}} \frac{pe^{\lambda z t_j}}{R+rt_j}} \right)^2 \frac{pe^{\lambda z t_i}}{R+rt_i}, \quad \forall i, \tag{6.36}$$

provided that the condition in equation (6.28) holds.

Proof According to equation (6.25), for each miner i, we have the mathematical expression

$$\frac{\sum_{i \neq j} x_j}{\left(\sum_{j \in \mathcal{N}} x_j \right)^2} = \frac{pe^{\lambda z t_i}}{R+rt_i}. \tag{6.37}$$

Then, we calculate the summation of this expression for all the miners as follows:

$$\frac{(N-1) \sum_{j \in \mathcal{N}} x_j}{\left(\sum_{j \in \mathcal{N}} x_j \right)^2} = \sum_{i \in \mathcal{N}} \frac{pe^{\lambda z t_i}}{R+rt_i}, \tag{6.38}$$

which means $\frac{(N-1)}{\sum_{j \in \mathcal{N}} x_j} = \sum_{i \in \mathcal{N}} \frac{pe^{\lambda z t_i}}{R+rt_i}$. Thus, we have

$$\sum_{j \in \mathcal{N}} x_j = \frac{N-1}{\sum_{i \in \mathcal{N}} \frac{pe^{\lambda z t_i}}{R+rt_i}}. \tag{6.39}$$

Recall from equation (6.24), according to the first-order derivative condition, we have

$$\sum_{j \in \mathcal{N}} x_j = \sqrt{\frac{(R+rt_i) \sum_{i \neq j} x_j}{pe^{\lambda z t_i}}}. \tag{6.40}$$

By substituting equation (6.40) into equation (6.39), we have

$$\frac{N-1}{\sum_{i \in \mathcal{N}} \frac{pe^{\lambda z t_i}}{R+rt_i}} = \sqrt{\frac{R+rt_i}{pe^{\lambda z t_i}} \left(\frac{N-1}{\sum_{i \in \mathcal{N}} \frac{pe^{\lambda z t_i}}{R+rt_i}} - x_i \right)}. \tag{6.41}$$

After squaring both sides, we have $\left(\frac{N-1}{\sum_{i \in \mathcal{N}} \frac{pe^{\lambda z t_i}}{R+rt_i}} \right)^2 = \frac{R+rt_i}{pe^{\lambda z t_i}} \left(\frac{N-1}{\sum_{i \in \mathcal{N}} \frac{pe^{\lambda z t_i}}{R+rt_i}} - x_i \right)$. With simple transformations, we obtain the Nash equilibrium for miner i as shown in equation (6.36). $\qquad \square$

Lemma 1 *Given*

$$\frac{2(N-1)e^{\lambda z t_i}}{R+r t_i} < \sum_{i \in \mathcal{N}} \frac{e^{\lambda z t_i}}{R+r t_i}, \tag{6.42}$$

the following condition

$$\sum_{i \neq j} x_j < \frac{R+r t_i}{4p e^{\lambda z t_i}} \tag{6.43}$$

is satisfied.

Proof   According to equations (6.36) and (6.39), we can obtain

$$\sum_{j \neq i} x_j = \left(\frac{N-1}{\sum_{j \in \mathcal{N}} \frac{p e^{\lambda z t_j}}{R+r t_j}} \right)^2 \frac{p e^{\lambda z t_i}}{R+r t_i}. \tag{6.44}$$

After substituting equation (6.43) into equation (6.44), we have

$$\frac{2(N-1)p e^{\lambda z t_i}}{R+r t_i} < \sum_{i \in \mathcal{N}} \frac{p e^{\lambda z t_i}}{R+r t_i}, \tag{6.45}$$

which means that the condition in equation (6.42) needs to be ensured. On the contrary, if the condition in equation (6.42) holds, then, the condition in equation (6.45) is satisfied. The proof is now completed. □

Generally, we can use the best-response dynamics for obtaining the Nash equilibrium of the N-player noncooperative game in Stage II [228]. In the following, we analyze the profit maximization of the CFP in Stage I under uniform pricing.

Stage I: CFP's Profit Maximization

Based on the Nash equilibrium of the computing service demand in the MDG $\mathcal{G}^u = \{\mathcal{N}, \{x_i\}_{i \in \mathcal{N}}, \{u_i\}_{i \in \mathcal{N}}\}$ in Stage II, the leader of the Stackelberg game, namely, the CFP, can optimize its pricing strategy in Stage I to maximize its profit defined in equation (6.20). Thus, the optimal pricing can be formulated as an optimization problem. By substituting equation (6.36) into equation (6.20), the profit maximization of the CFP is simplified as follows:

$$\underset{p>0}{\text{maximize}} \quad \Pi(p) = (p - cT) \frac{N-1}{\sum_{j \in \mathcal{N}} \frac{p e^{\lambda z t_j}}{R+r t_j}} \tag{6.46}$$

$$\text{subject to} \quad 0 \leq p \leq \bar{p}.$$

Theorem 8 *Under uniform pricing, the CFP achieves the globally optimal profit, that is, profit maximization, under the unique optimal price.*

Proof From equation (6.46), we have

$$\Pi(p) = \frac{p - cT}{p} \frac{N - 1}{\sum_{j \in \mathcal{N}} \frac{e^{\lambda z t_j}}{R + r t_j}}. \tag{6.47}$$

The first and second derivatives of profit $\Pi(p)$ with respect to price p are given as follows:

$$\frac{d\Pi(p)}{dp} = \frac{cT}{p^2} \frac{N - 1}{\sum_{j \in \mathcal{N}} \frac{e^{\lambda z t_j}}{R + r t_j}} \tag{6.48}$$

and

$$\frac{d^2\Pi(p)}{dp^2} = -\frac{2cT}{p^2} \frac{N - 1}{\sum_{j \in \mathcal{N}} \frac{e^{\lambda z t_j}}{R + r t_j}} < 0. \tag{6.49}$$

Because of the negativity of equation (6.49), the strict concavity of the objective function is ensured. Thus, the CFP is able to achieve the maximum profit with the unique optimal price. The proof is now completed. □

Note that the profit maximization defined in equation (6.46) is a convex optimization problem, and thus it can be solved by standard convex optimization algorithms, for example, gradient-assisted binary search. Under uniform pricing, we have proved that the Nash equilibrium in Stage II is unique and the optimal price in Stage I is also unique. Thus, we can conclude that the Stackelberg equilibrium is unique and accordingly the best-response dynamics algorithm can achieve this unique Stackelberg equilibrium [228].

6.2.4.2 Discriminatory Pricing Scheme

Now we consider the discriminatory pricing scheme, in which the CFP is able to set different unit prices of service demand for different miners. Again, we use backward induction to analyze the optimal service demand of miners and the profit maximization of the CFP.

Stage II: Miners' Demand Game

Under a discriminatory pricing scheme, the strategy space of the CFP becomes $\{\mathbf{p} = [p_i]_{i \in \mathcal{N}}: 0 \leq p_i \leq \bar{p}\}$. Recall that we can prove the existence and uniqueness of MDG $\mathcal{G}^u = \{\mathcal{N}, \{x_i\}_{i \in \mathcal{N}}, \{u_i\}_{i \in \mathcal{N}}\}$, given the fixed price from the CFP. Thus, under discriminatory pricing, the existence and uniqueness of the MDG can be still guaranteed. With a minor change from Theorem 3, we have the following theorem immediately.

Theorem 9 *Under uniform pricing, the unique Nash equilibrium demand of miner i can be obtained as follows:*

$$x_i^* = \frac{N-1}{\sum_{j\in\mathcal{N}}\frac{p_j e^{\lambda z t_j}}{R+r t_j}} - \left(\frac{N-1}{\sum_{j\in\mathcal{N}}\frac{p_j e^{\lambda z t_j}}{R+r t_j}}\right)^2 \frac{p_i e^{\lambda z t_i}}{R+r t_i}, \quad \forall i, \tag{6.50}$$

if the following condition

$$\frac{2(N-1)p_i e^{\lambda z t_i}}{R+r t_i} < \sum_{j\in\mathcal{N}}\frac{p_j e^{\lambda z t_j}}{R+r t_j} \tag{6.51}$$

holds.

Proof   The steps of proof are similar to those in the case of uniform pricing as shown previously in Section 6.2.4.1, and thus we omit them for brevity.   □

We next analyze the profit maximization of the CFP in Stage I under discriminatory pricing to further investigate the Stackelberg equilibrium.

Stage I: CFP's Profit Maximization

As in Section 6.2.4.1, we analyze the profit maximization with the analytical result from Theorem 5, that is, the Nash equilibrium of the computing service demand in Stage II. After substituting equation (6.50) into equation (6.20), we have the following optimization,

$$\underset{\mathbf{p}>0}{\text{maximize}} \quad \Pi(\mathbf{p}) = \sum_{i\in\mathcal{N}}\left(p_i - cT\frac{N-1}{\sum_{j\in\mathcal{N}}\frac{p_j e^{\lambda z t_j}}{R+r t_j}}\right) \tag{6.52}$$

$$\text{subject to} \quad 0 \le p_i \le \bar{p}, \forall i.$$

Theorem 10 $\Pi(\mathbf{p})$ *is concave on each* p_i, *when* $\sum_{i\ne j}(a_i+a_j)\left(1-\frac{N\frac{p_j}{a_j}}{\sum_{j\in\mathcal{N}}\frac{p_j}{a_j}}\right) \le 0$,

and decreasing on each p_i *when* $\sum_{i\ne j}(a_i+a_j)\left(1-\frac{N\frac{p_j}{a_j}}{\sum_{j\in\mathcal{N}}\frac{p_j}{a_j}}\right) > 0$, *provided that the*

following condition

$$\frac{p_i}{a_i} \ge \frac{\sum_{j\in\mathcal{N}}\frac{p_j}{a_j}}{(N-1)^2} \tag{6.53}$$

is satisfied, where $a_i = (R+r t_i)e^{-\lambda z t_i}$.

$$g(\mathbf{p}) = \sum_{j\ne h}\left(a_h\left(1-\frac{p_h}{a_h}\frac{N-1}{\sum_{h\in\mathcal{N}}\frac{p_h}{a_h}}\right)\left(1-\frac{p_j}{a_j}\frac{N-1}{\sum_{h\in\mathcal{N}}\frac{p_h}{a_h}}\right)\right). \tag{6.54}$$

$$\frac{\partial g(\mathbf{p})}{\partial p_i} = \sum_{j \neq i} \left((a_i + a_j) \left(\frac{-\frac{N-1}{a_i} \sum_{h \neq i} \frac{p_h}{a_h}}{\left(\sum_{h \in \mathcal{N}} \frac{p_h}{a_h} \right)^2} \left(1 - \frac{N-1}{\sum_{h \in \mathcal{N}} \frac{p_h}{a_h}} \frac{p_j}{a_j} \right) + \frac{\frac{N-1}{a_i} \frac{p_j}{a_j}}{\left(\sum_{h \in \mathcal{N}} \frac{p_h}{a_h} \right)^2} \left(1 - \frac{N-1}{\sum_{h \in \mathcal{N}} \frac{p_h}{a_h}} \frac{p_i}{a_i} \right) \right) \right).$$

(6.55)

$$\sum_{i \neq j} \left((a_i + a_j) \left(\sum_{h \in \mathcal{N}} \frac{\lambda p_h' + (1-\lambda) p_h''}{a_h} - N \frac{\lambda p_j' + (1-\lambda) p_j''}{a_j} \right) \right)$$

$$= \sum_{i \neq j} \left((a_i + a_j) \left(\lambda \sum_{h \in \mathcal{N}} \frac{p_h'}{a_h} - (1-\lambda) \sum_{h \in \mathcal{N}} \frac{p_h''}{a_h} - \lambda N \frac{p_j'}{a_j} - (1-\lambda) N \frac{p_j''}{a_j} \right) \right)$$

$$= \lambda \sum_{i \neq j} \left((a_i + a_j) \left(\sum_{h \in \mathcal{N}} \frac{p_h'}{a_h} - N \frac{p_j''}{a_j} \right) \right) + (1-\lambda) \sum_{i \neq j} \left((a_i + a_j) \left((1-\lambda) \sum_{h \in \mathcal{N}} \frac{p_h'}{a_h} - N \frac{p_j''}{a_j} \right) \right) \leq 0.$$

(6.56)

$$\frac{\partial \Pi(\mathbf{p})}{\partial p_i} = \sum_{j \neq i} \left((a_i + a_j) \left(\frac{\frac{N-1}{a_i} \sum_{h \neq i} \frac{p_h}{a_h}}{\left(\sum_{h \in \mathcal{N}} \frac{p_h}{a_h} \right)^2} \left(1 - \frac{N-1}{\sum_{h \in \mathcal{N}} \frac{p_h}{a_h}} \frac{p_j}{a_j} \right) + \frac{\frac{N-1}{a_i a_j} p_j}{\left(\sum_{h \in \mathcal{N}} \frac{p_h}{a_h} \right)^2} \left(1 - \frac{N-1}{\sum_{h \in \mathcal{N}} \frac{p_h}{a_h}} \frac{p_i}{a_i} \right) \right) \right) + \frac{\frac{N-1}{a_i} cT}{\left(\sum_{h \in \mathcal{N}} \frac{p_h}{a_h} \right)^2}$$

$$\leq \frac{\frac{N-1}{a_i}}{\left(\sum_{h \in \mathcal{N}} \frac{p_h}{a_h} \right)^2} \left(\sum_{j \neq i} \left((a_i + a_j) \left(-\sum_{h \in \mathcal{N}} \frac{p_h}{a_h} \left(1 - \frac{N-1}{\sum_{h \in \mathcal{N}} \frac{p_h}{a_h}} \frac{p_j}{a_j} \right) + \frac{p_j}{a_j} \left(1 - \frac{N-1}{\sum_{h \in \mathcal{N}} \frac{p_h}{a_h}} \frac{p_i}{a_i} \right) \right) \right) + cT \right)$$

$$= -\frac{\frac{N-1}{a_i}}{\left(\sum_{h \in \mathcal{N}} \frac{p_h}{a_h} \right)^2} \underbrace{\sum_{j \neq i} \left((a_i + a_j) \left(\sum_{h \in \mathcal{N}} \frac{p_h}{a_h} \left(1 - \frac{N}{\sum_{h \in \mathcal{N}} \frac{p_h}{a_h}} \frac{p_j}{a_j} \right) \right) \right)}_{<0} + \frac{\frac{N-1}{a_i}}{\left(\sum_{h \in \mathcal{N}} \frac{p_h}{a_h} \right)^2} \left(cT - \sum_{j \neq i} \left((a_i + a_j) \frac{N-1}{\sum_{h \in \mathcal{N}} \frac{p_h}{a_h}} \frac{p_i}{a_i} \frac{p_j}{a_j} \right) \right)$$

$$= -\frac{\frac{N-1}{a_i}}{\left(\sum_{h \in \mathcal{N}} \frac{p_h}{a_h} \right)^2} \sum_{j \neq i} \left((a_i + a_j) \left(-\sum_{h \in \mathcal{N}} \frac{p_h}{a_h} \left(1 - \frac{N}{\sum_{h \in \mathcal{N}} \frac{p_h}{a_h}} \frac{p_j}{a_j} \right) \right) \right) + \frac{\frac{N-1}{a_i}}{\left(\sum_{h \in \mathcal{N}} \frac{p_h}{a_h} \right)^2} \left(cT - \sum_{j \neq i} \underbrace{\frac{a_i + a_j}{a_j}}_{<1} \frac{N-1}{\sum_{h \in \mathcal{N}} \frac{p_h}{a_h}} \frac{p_i p_j}{a_i} \right)$$

$$\leq -\frac{\frac{N-1}{a_i}}{\left(\sum_{h \in \mathcal{N}} \frac{p_h}{a_h} \right)^2} \sum_{j \neq i} \left((a_i + a_j) \left(-\sum_{h \in \mathcal{N}} \frac{p_h}{a_h} \left(1 - \frac{N}{\sum_{h \in \mathcal{N}} \frac{p_h}{a_h}} \frac{p_j}{a_j} \right) \right) \right) + \frac{\frac{N-1}{a_i}}{\left(\sum_{h \in \mathcal{N}} \frac{p_h}{a_h} \right)^2} \left(cT - p_{\min} \frac{N-1}{\sum_{h \in \mathcal{N}} \frac{p_h}{a_h}} \frac{N-1}{a_i} \frac{p_i}{a_i} \right)$$

$$= \underbrace{-\frac{\frac{N-1}{a_i}}{\left(\sum_{h \in \mathcal{N}} \frac{p_h}{a_h} \right)^2} \sum_{j \neq i} \left((a_i + a_j) \left(-\sum_{h \in \mathcal{N}} \frac{p_h}{a_h} \left(1 - \frac{N}{\sum_{h \in \mathcal{N}} \frac{p_h}{a_h}} \frac{p_j}{a_j} \right) \right) \right)}_{<0} + \underbrace{\frac{\frac{N-1}{a_i}}{\left(\sum_{h \in \mathcal{N}} \frac{p_h}{a_h} \right)^2} \left(cT - p_{\min} \frac{(N-1)^2}{\sum_{h \in \mathcal{N}} \frac{p_h}{a_h}} \frac{p_i}{a_i} \right)}_{<0} < 0.$$

(6.57)

Proof We firstly decompose the objective function in equation (6.52) into two parts, namely, $\sum_i cT x_i^*$ and $\sum_i p_i x_i^*$. Then, we analyze the properties of each part. We define

$$f(\mathbf{p}) = -cT x_i^* = -cT \frac{N-1}{\sum_{j \in \mathcal{N}} \frac{p_j e^{\lambda z t_j}}{R + r t_j}}.$$

(6.58)

Let $a_j = (R + r t_j) e^{-\lambda z t_j}$, and we have $f(\mathbf{p}) = \frac{-cT(N-1)}{\sum_{j \in \mathcal{N}} \frac{p_j}{a_j}}$. Then, we obtain the first and the second partial derivatives of equation (6.58) with respect to p_i as follows:

$$\frac{\partial f(\mathbf{p})}{\partial p_i} = \frac{(N-1)cT}{a_i \left(\sum_{j \in \mathcal{N}} \frac{p_j}{a_j} \right)^2},$$

(6.59)

$$\frac{\partial^2 f(\mathbf{p})}{\partial p_i{}^2} = \frac{-2(N-1)cT}{a_i{}^2 \left(\sum_{j \in \mathcal{N}} \frac{p_j}{a_j}\right)^3}. \tag{6.60}$$

Further, we have

$$\frac{\partial f(\mathbf{p})}{\partial p_i p_j} = \frac{-2(N-1)cT}{a_i a_j \left(\sum_{j \in \mathcal{N}} \frac{p_j}{a_j}\right)^3}. \tag{6.61}$$

Thus, we can obtain the Hessian matrix of $f(\mathbf{p})$, which is expressed as:

$$\nabla^2 f(\mathbf{p}) = \frac{-2(N-1)cT}{\left(\sum_{j \in \mathcal{N}} \frac{p_j}{a_j}\right)^3} \begin{bmatrix} \frac{1}{a_1{}^2} & \frac{1}{a_1 a_2} & \cdots & \frac{1}{a_1 a_N} \\ \frac{1}{a_2 a_1} & \frac{1}{a_2{}^2} & \cdots & \frac{1}{a_2 a_N} \\ \vdots & \vdots & \ddots & \vdots \\ \frac{1}{a_N a_1} & \frac{1}{a_N a_2} & \cdots & \frac{1}{a_N{}^2} \end{bmatrix}. \tag{6.62}$$

For each $i \in \mathcal{N}$, we have $\frac{1}{a_i{}^2} > 0$. Thus, the diagonal elements of the Hessian matrix are all larger than zero, and the principle minors are equal to zero. Therefore, the Hessian matrix of $f(\mathbf{p})$ is seminegative definite.

Then, we analyze the properties of $\sum_i p_i x_i^*$. We first define

$$g(\mathbf{p}) = \sum_{i \in \mathcal{N}} p_i x_i^* = \frac{\sum_{j \neq i} a_i x_i x_j}{\left(\sum_{j \neq i} x_j\right)^2}. \tag{6.63}$$

By substituting equation (6.50) into equation (6.63), we can obtain the final expression for $g(\mathbf{p})$, which can be rewritten as in equation (6.54). Then, we derive the first-order and the second-order partial derivatives of equation (6.54) with respect to p_i as shown in equations (6.55) and (6.64). Since we have $x_i = \frac{N-1}{\sum_{h \in \mathcal{N}} \frac{p_h}{a_h}} - \frac{p_i}{a_i} \left(\frac{N-1}{\sum_{h \in \mathcal{N}} \frac{p_h}{a_h}}\right)^2 = \frac{N-1}{\sum_{h \in \mathcal{N}} \frac{p_h}{a_h}} \left(1 - \frac{N-1}{\sum_{h \in \mathcal{N}} \frac{p_h}{a_h}} \frac{p_i}{a_i}\right) > 0$, $1 - \frac{N-1}{\sum_{h \in \mathcal{N}} \frac{p_h}{a_h}} \frac{p_i}{a_i} > 0$. When $\sum_{i \neq j} (a_i + a_j) \left(1 - \frac{N\frac{p_j}{a_j}}{\sum_{j \in \mathcal{N}} \frac{p_j}{a_j}}\right) \leq 0$, it is observed that $\frac{\partial^2 g(\mathbf{p})}{\partial p_i{}^2} < 0$, that is, $g(\mathbf{p})$ is concave on each p_i. Now we prove that $\Pi(\mathbf{p})$ is a monotonically decreasing function with respect to p_i, when $\sum_{i \neq j} (a_i + a_j) \left(1 - \frac{N\frac{p_j}{a_j}}{\sum_{j \in \mathcal{N}} \frac{p_j}{a_j}}\right) > 0$. The steps are shown in equation (6.57), where $p_{\min} = \min\{p_1, p_2, \ldots, p_N\}$. Practically, $p_{\min} > cT$. Thus, with some manipulations, we can prove $\frac{\partial \Pi}{\partial p_i} < 0$ when $\sum_{i \neq j} (a_i + a_j) \left(1 - \frac{N\frac{p_j}{a_j}}{\sum_{j \in \mathcal{N}} \frac{p_j}{a_j}}\right) > 0$, if the condition in equation (6.53) holds. The proof is now completed. $\qquad \square$

Theorem 11 *Under discriminatory pricing, the CFP achieves the profit maximization by finding the unique optimal pricing vector.*

Proof From Theorem 6, we know that $\Pi(\mathbf{p})$ is concave on each p_i, when $\sum_{i \neq j} (a_i + a_j)$ $\left(1 - \dfrac{N \frac{p_j}{a_j}}{\sum_{j \in \mathcal{N}} \frac{p_j}{a_j}} \right) \leq 0$, and decreasing on each p_i when $\sum_{i \neq j} (a_i + a_j) \left(1 - \dfrac{N \frac{p_j}{a_j}}{\sum_{j \in \mathcal{N}} \frac{p_j}{a_j}} \right) >$ 0. In other words, when $\Pi(\mathbf{p})$ is concave on p_i, p_i needs to be smaller than a certain threshold, and $\Pi(\mathbf{p})$ is decreasing on p_i when p_i is larger than this threshold.

$$\frac{\partial^2 g(\mathbf{p})}{\partial p_i^2} = \sum_{j \neq i} \left((a_i + a_j) \left(\frac{2 \frac{N-1}{a_i^2} \sum_{h \neq i} \frac{p_h}{a_h}}{\left(\sum_{h \in \mathcal{N}} \frac{p_h}{a_h} \right)^3} \left(1 - 2 \frac{N-1}{\sum_{h \in \mathcal{N}} \frac{p_h}{a_h}} \frac{p_j}{a_j} \right) - \frac{2 \frac{N-1}{a_i^2} \frac{p_j}{a_j}}{\left(\sum_{h \in \mathcal{N}} \frac{p_h}{a_h} \right)^3} \left(1 - \frac{N-1}{\sum_{h \in \mathcal{N}} \frac{p_h}{a_h}} \frac{p_i}{a_i} \right) \right) \right).$$

$$(6.64)$$

$$\frac{\partial^2 g(\mathbf{p})}{\partial p_i^2} = \frac{2 \frac{N-1}{a_i^2} \sum_{h \neq i} \frac{p_h}{a_h}}{\left(\sum_{h \in \mathcal{N}} \frac{p_h}{a_h} \right)^3} \sum_{j \neq i} \left((a_i + a_j) \left(1 - 2 \frac{N-1}{\sum_{h \in \mathcal{N}} \frac{p_h}{a_h}} \frac{p_j}{a_j} \right) \right) - \frac{2 \frac{N-1}{a_i^2}}{\left(\sum_{h \in \mathcal{N}} \frac{p_h}{a_h} \right)^3} \sum_{j \neq i} \left((a_i + a_j) \frac{p_j}{a_j} \left(1 - \frac{N-1}{\sum_{h \in \mathcal{N}} \frac{p_h}{a_h}} \frac{p_i}{a_i} \right) \right)$$

$$\leq \frac{2 \frac{N-1}{a_i^2} \sum_{h \neq i} \frac{p_h}{a_h}}{\left(\sum_{h \in \mathcal{N}} \frac{p_h}{a_h} \right)^3} \underbrace{\sum_{j \neq i} \left((a_i + a_j) \left(1 - \frac{N}{\sum_{h \in \mathcal{N}} \frac{p_h}{a_h}} \frac{p_j}{a_j} \right) \right)}_{\leq 0} - \frac{2 \frac{N-1}{a_i^2}}{\left(\sum_{h \in \mathcal{N}} \frac{p_h}{a_h} \right)^3} \sum_{j \neq i} \left((a_i + a_j) \frac{p_j}{a_j} \underbrace{\left(1 - \frac{N-1}{\sum_{h \in \mathcal{N}} \frac{p_h}{a_h}} \frac{p_i}{a_i} \right)}_{\geq 0} \right).$$

$$(6.65)$$

Then, it can be concluded that if the price is higher than the threshold, the miner is not willing to purchase the computing service from the CFP. Therefore, we know that the optimal value of profit of the CFP, that is, $\Pi^*(\mathbf{p})$ is achieved in the concave parts when $\sum_{i \neq j} (a_i + a_j) \left(1 - \dfrac{N \frac{p_j}{a_j}}{\sum_{j \in \mathcal{N}} \frac{p_j}{a_j}} \right) \leq 0$. Clearly, the maximization of profit $\Pi(\mathbf{p})$ is achieved either in the boundary of the domain area or in the local maximization point. We know that the optimal value of profit, that is, $\Pi^*(\mathbf{p})$, is achieved in the interior area, and thus $\mathbf{p}^*$ exists. In the following, we prove that there exists at most one optimal solution by using Variational Inequality theory [229], from which the uniqueness of the optimal solution, namely, the Stackelberg equilibrium, follows. Let the set $\mathcal{K} = \left\{ \mathbf{p} = [p_1, \ldots, p_N]^\top \middle| \sum_{i \neq j} (a_i + a_j) \left(1 - \dfrac{N \frac{p_j}{a_j}}{\sum_{j \in \mathcal{N}} \frac{p_j}{a_j}} \right) \leq 0, \forall i \in \mathcal{N} \right\}$. The constraint can be rewritten as follows:

$$\sum_{i \neq j} \left((a_i + a_j) \left(\sum_{h \in \mathcal{N}} \frac{p_h}{a_h} - N \frac{p_j}{a_j} \right) \right) \leq 0. \qquad (6.66)$$

Thus, we redefine the set $\mathcal{K}$ as

$$\left\{ \mathbf{p} = [p_1, \ldots, p_N]^\top \, \bigg| \, \sum_{i \neq j} \left((a_i + a_j) \left(\sum_{h \in \mathcal{N}} \frac{p_h}{a_h} - N \frac{p_j}{a_j} \right) \right) \leq 0, \forall i \in \mathcal{N} \right\}.$$

Then, we formulate an equivalent problem to equation (6.52) as follows:

$$\begin{aligned} \underset{\mathbf{p} > 0}{\text{minimize}} \quad & -\Pi(\mathbf{p}) \\ \text{subject to} \quad & \mathbf{p} \in \mathcal{K}. \end{aligned} \tag{6.67}$$

Let $F(\mathbf{p}) = \nabla(-\Pi(\mathbf{p})) = -[\nabla_{p_i} \Pi]_{i \in \mathcal{N}}^\top$. Accordingly, the optimization problem in equation (6.67) is equivalent to find a point set $\mathbf{p}^* \in \mathcal{K}$, such that $(\mathbf{p} - \mathbf{p}^*) F(\mathbf{p}^*) \geq 0, \forall \mathbf{p} \in \mathcal{K}$, which is the Variational Inequality (VI) problem: $\text{VI}(\mathcal{K}, F)$.

Definition 14   If F is strictly monotone on $\mathcal{K}$, then $\text{VI}(\mathcal{K}, F)$ has at most one solution, where $\mathcal{K} \in \mathbb{R}^N$ is a convex closed set, and the mapping $F \colon \mathcal{K} \mapsto \mathbb{R}^N$ is continuous [229].

Let $\lambda \in (0, 1)$, $\mathbf{p}', \mathbf{p}'' \in \mathcal{K}$; it can be concluded that $\lambda \mathbf{p}' + (1 - \lambda) \mathbf{p}' \in \mathcal{K}$, which is shown in equation (6.56). Accordingly, $\mathcal{K}$ is a convex and closed set. To prove that the mapping $F \colon \mathcal{K} \mapsto \mathbb{R}^N$ is strictly monotone on $\mathcal{K}$, we check the positivity of $(\mathbf{p}' - \mathbf{p}'')^\top (F(\mathbf{p}') - F(\mathbf{p}'')), \forall \mathbf{p}', \mathbf{p}'' \in \mathcal{K}$ and $\mathbf{p}' \neq \mathbf{p}''$. We know

$$\begin{aligned} & (\mathbf{p}' - \mathbf{p}'')^\top (F(\mathbf{p}') - F(\mathbf{p}'')) \\ &= \sum_{i \in \mathcal{N}} \left((p_i' - p_i'') \left(-\nabla_{p_i} \Pi \big|_{p_i = p_i'} + \nabla_{p_i} \Pi \big|_{p_i = p_i''} \right) \right), \end{aligned} \tag{6.68}$$

and from Theorem 6, we have

$$\frac{\partial^2 \Pi(\mathbf{p})}{\partial p_i^2} = \frac{\partial^2 (f(\mathbf{p}) + g(\mathbf{p}))}{\partial p_i^2} < 0. \tag{6.69}$$

Thus, $\nabla_{p_i} \Pi$ is decreasing on each p_i, and $-\nabla_{p_i} \Pi$ is increasing on each p_i. It can be concluded that

$$-\nabla_{p_i} \Pi \big|_{p_i = p_i'} + \nabla_{p_i} \Pi \big|_{p_i = p_i''} = \begin{cases} \geq 0, p_i' \geq p_i'' \\ < 0, p_i' < p_i''. \end{cases} \tag{6.70}$$

Then, we have

$$\left((p_i' - p_i'') \left(-\nabla_{p_i} \Pi \big|_{p_i = p_i'} + \nabla_{p_i} \Pi \big|_{p_i = p_i''} \right) \right) \geq 0, \quad \forall i \in \mathcal{N}, \tag{6.71}$$

and we know $\mathbf{p}' \neq \mathbf{p}''$, and accordingly there exists at least one $j \in \mathcal{N}$ which satisfies the constraint in equation (6.71). Therefore, we have proved that F is strictly monotone on $\mathcal{K}$ and continuous. Until now, we have proved that $\text{VI}(\mathcal{K}, F)$ has at most one solution according to Definition 4 in [229]. Thus, the equivalent problem admits at most one optimal solution. Since we know the existence of a single optimal solution, thus the uniqueness of the optimal solution is validated. The proof is now completed.   □

As in Section 6.2.4.1, we can apply the low-complexity gradient-based searching algorithm to achieve the maximized profit $\Pi(\mathbf{p})$ of the CFP. In particular, we adopt Algorithm 1 to obtain the unique Stackelberg equilibrium, under which the CFP achieves the profit maximization according to Theorem 7. The basic description is explained as follows: For the given prices imposed by the CFP, the followers' subgame is solved first. After substituting the best responses of the followers' subgame into the leader subgame, the optimal prices can be obtained by a gradient-based algorithm. The similar algorithm can be used for uniform pricing as well.

Algorithm 1 Gradient iterative algorithm to find Stackelberg equilibrium under discriminatory pricing.

1: **Initialization:**
   Select initial input $\mathbf{p} = [p_i]_{i \in \mathcal{N}}$ where $p_i \in [0, \overline{p}]$, $k \leftarrow 1$, precision threshold ε;
2: **repeat**
3:     Each miner i decides its computing service demand $x_i^{[k]}$ based on (6.24);
4:     CFP updates the prices using a gradient assisted searching algorithm, that is,

$$\mathbf{p}(t+1) = \mathbf{p}(t) + \mu \nabla \Pi(\mathbf{p}(t)), \qquad (6.72)$$

   where μ is the step size of the price update and $\mu \nabla \Pi(\mathbf{p}(t))$ is the gradient with $\frac{\partial \Pi(\mathbf{p}(t))}{\partial \mathbf{p}(t)}$. The price information is sent to all miners;
5:     $k \leftarrow k + 1$;
6: **until** $\frac{\|\mathbf{p}^{[k]} - \mathbf{p}^{[k-1]}\|_1}{\|\mathbf{p}^{[k-1]}\|_1} < \varepsilon$
7: **Output:** optimal demand $\mathbf{x}^{*[k]}$ and optimal price $\mathbf{p}^{*[k]}$.

6.2.5 Performance Evaluation

In this section, we first perform a real experiment on the PoW-based blockchain mining to validate the proposed utility function of the miner. Then, we conduct extensive numerical simulations to evaluate the performance of our proposed price-based computing resource management to support blockchain application involving PoW; see Figs. 6.3 and 6.4.

6.2.5.1 Environmental Setup

We first set up a real blockchain mining experiment based on Ethereum, and consider smart phones as limited devices, as illustrated in Fig. 6.4. The experiment is performed on a workstation with Intel Xeon CPU E5-1630, and Android devices (smart phones) installing a mobile blockchain client application. The mobile blockchain client application is implemented by the Android Studio and Software Development Kits

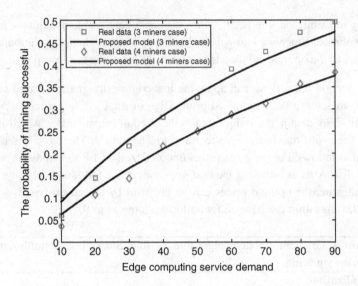

Figure 6.3 The comparison of real experiment results with our proposed model. Reprinted with permission from the paper "Cloud/fog computing resource management and pricing for blockchain networks" published in *IEEE Internet of Things Journal*.

(SDK) tools. All transactions are created by the mobile blockchain client application.[5] Each miner's working environment has one CPU core as its processor. The miner's processor and its CPU utilization rate are generated and managed by the Docker platform [231]. The mobile device of each miner has installed Ubuntu 16.04 LTS (Xenial Xerus) and Go-Ethereum [232] as the operation system and the blockchain framework, respectively.

In Fig. 6.4, from Box 1 and 2, the screen of computer terminal shows that the Ethereum is running on the host, namely, edge device (Box 5). The mobile devices in Box 4 are connected to the edge computing node through the network hub (Box 3) using a mobile blockchain client application. The basic steps can be implemented as follows. The mobile users, namely, miners, use the Android device to connect to the edge computing node through network hub, that is, access point. Then, the miners can request the service from edge node, and mine the block with the assistance of the Ethereum service provided accordingly.

We create 1000 blocks employing Node.js and use the mobile device to mine these blocks in the experiment. We consider two cases with three miners and four miners. In the three-miner case, we first fix the other two miners' service demand

---

[5] In our experiment, each mobile device sends transactions to the server, and the size of each transaction is around 1 kilobyte [230]. Then, the server will collect and pack all the transactions into a block and proceed to solve the PoW puzzle, where each block consists of block information and hash numbers. As mentioned in [230], the number of transactions in each mined block is 10, and thus the size of the data from mobile device sent to the server is approximately 10 kilobytes in total. Likewise, the size of a block including 10 hash numbers that is sent from the server to the mobile device is around 1.5 kilobytes. A detailed description can be found in our previous work [230].

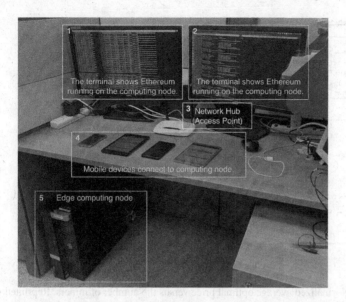

Figure 6.4 Real mobile blockchain mining experimental setup with Ethereum that is a popular open ledger. Reprinted with permission from the paper "Cloud/fog computing resource management and pricing for blockchain networks" published in *IEEE Internet of Things Journal*.

(CPU utilization) at 40 and 60, and then vary one miner's service demand. In the four-miner case, we first fix the other three miners' service demand as 40, 50, and 60, and then vary one miner's service demand. For our experiment, the number of transactions in each mined block is 10, that is, the size of block is the same. The comparison of the real experimental results and our proposed analytical model is shown in Fig. 6.3. As expected, there is not much difference between the real results and our analytical model. This is because the probability that the miner successfully mines the block is directly proportional to its relative computing power when the block sizes are identical. Note that the delay effects are negligible. In the sequel, we present the numerical results to evaluate the performance of the proposed price-based computing resource management for supporting blockchain application involving PoW.

6.2.5.2   Numerical Results

To illustrate the impacts of different parameters from the proposed model on the performance, we consider a group of N miners, for example, mobile users in the blockchain application involving PoW assisted by the CFP. We assume the size of a block mined by miner i follows the normal distribution $\mathcal{N}(\mu_t, \sigma^2)$. The default parameter values are set as follows: $\underline{x} = 10^{-2}$, $\bar{x} = 100$, $\bar{p} = 100$, $\mu_t = 200$, $\sigma^2 = 5$, $R = 10^4$, $r = 20$, $z = 5 \times 10^{-3}$, $c = 10^{-3}$, and $N = 100$. Further, we employ the "fix" function in MATLAB to round each t_i to the nearest integer toward zero. Note that some of these parameters are varied according to the evaluation scenarios. We evaluate the performance of uniform pricing and discriminatory pricing in the following.

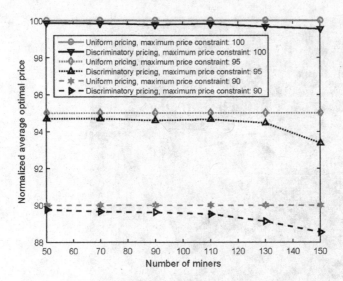

Figure 6.5 Normalized average optimal price versus the number of miners. Reprinted with permission from the paper "Cloud/fog computing resource management and pricing for blockchain networks" published in *IEEE Internet of Things Journal*.

Investigation on Total Service Demand of Miners and the Profit of the CFP

(1) The Comparison of Uniform Pricing and Discriminatory Pricing We first address the comparison of uniform pricing and discriminatory pricing schemes. Figure 6.5 demonstrates the comparison of the normalized average optimal price under two proposed pricing schemes. It is worth noting that the optimal price under uniform pricing is the same as the maximum price, which can be explained by equation (6.48). Specifically, the expression in equation (6.48) is always positive, and thus the profit of the CFP increases with the increase of price. This means that the maximum price is the optimal value for profit maximization of the CFP under uniform pricing. Thus, we have the following conclusion: The CFP intends to set the maximum possible value as the optimal price under uniform pricing. This conclusion is still useful even when the CFP does not have complete information about the miners.

Further, we find that the average optimal price of discriminatory pricing is slightly lower than that of uniform pricing. The intuition is that, under discriminatory pricing, the CFP can set different unit prices of service demand for different miners. For the details of operation of discriminatory pricing, we will conduct the case study in the next subsection. In this case, the CFP can significantly encourage the higher total service demand from miners and achieve greater profit gain under discriminatory pricing, which is also consistent with the following results. As shown in Figs. 6.6–6.8, in all cases, the total service demand from miners and the profit of the CFP under the uniform pricing scheme is slightly smaller than that under the discriminatory pricing scheme.

From Fig. 6.6, we find that when σ^2 decreases, the results under uniform pricing scheme is close to that under discriminatory pricing. This is because the heterogeneity of miners in blockchain is reduced as σ^2 decreases. We may consider one symmetric

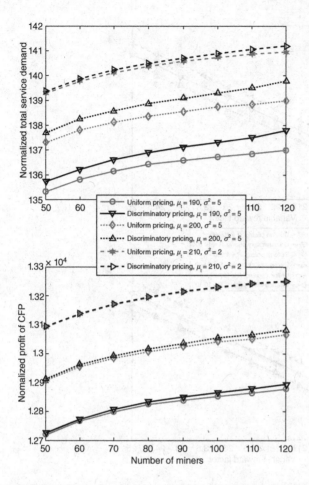

Figure 6.6 Normalized total service demand of miners and the profit of the CFP versus the number of miners. Reprinted with permission from the paper "Cloud/fog computing resource management and pricing for blockchain networks" published in *IEEE Internet of Things Journal*.

case, where the miners are homogeneous with the same size of blocks to mine, that is, $\sigma^2 = 0$. In this case, the discriminatory pricing scheme yields the same results as those of the uniform pricing scheme.

(2) The Impacts of the Number of Miners We next evaluate the impacts brought by the number of miners, and the results are shown in Fig. 6.6. From Fig. 6.6, we find that the total service demand of miners and the profit of the CFP increase with the increase of the number of miners in the blockchain. This is because having more miners will intensify the competition among the miners, which potentially motivates them to have a higher service demand. Further, the coming miners have their service demand, and thus the total service demand from miners is increased. In turn, the CFP extracts more surplus from miners and thereby has greater profit gain. Additionally, it is observed

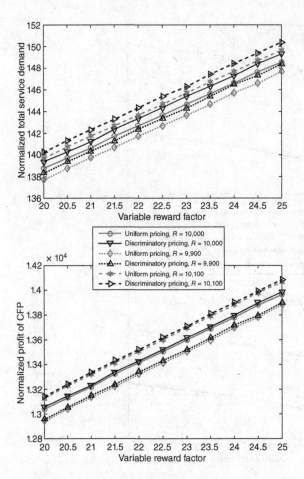

Figure 6.7 Normalized total service demand of miners and the profit of the CFP versus the variable reward factor. Reprinted with permission from the paper "Cloud/fog computing resource management and pricing for blockchain networks" published in *IEEE Internet of Things Journal*.

that the rate of service demand increment decreases as the number of miners increases. This comes from the fact that the incentive of miners to increase their service demand is weakened because the probability of their successful mining is reduced when the number of miners is increasing. Comparing different results, it is also observed that the total service demand of miners and the profit of the CFP increase as μ_t increases. This is because when μ_t increases, that is, the average size of one block becomes larger, the variable reward for each miner also increases. The potential incentive of miners to increase their service demand is improved, and accordingly the total service demand of miners increases. Consequently, the CFP achieves greater profit gain.

(3) The Impacts of Reward for Successful Mining Then, we investigate the impacts of variable reward and fixed reward on miners and the CFP, which are shown in Fig. 6.7.

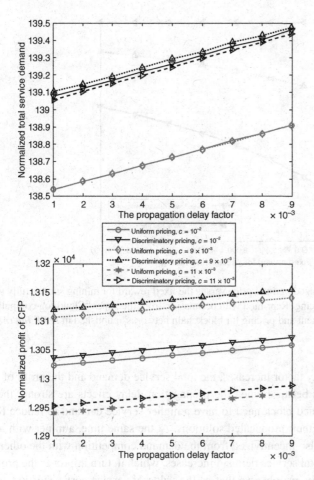

Figure 6.8 Normalized total service demand of miners and the profit of the CFP versus the propagation delay factor. Reprinted with permission from the paper "Cloud/fog computing resource management and pricing for blockchain networks" published in *IEEE Internet of Things Journal*.

It is observed that with the increase of variable reward factor, both the total service demand of miners and the profit of the CFP increase. This is because the increased variable reward enhances the motivation of miners for a higher service demand, and the total service demand is enhanced accordingly. As a result, the CFP achieves greater profit gain. Further, by comparing curves with different values of fixed reward, we find that as the fixed reward increases, the total service demand of miners and the profit of the CFP also increase. Similarly, this is because the increased fixed reward induces greater incentive for miners, which in turn improves the total service demand of miners and the profit of the CFP.

(4) The Impacts of Propagation Delay At last, we examine the impact of propagation delay on miners and the CFP, as illustrated in Fig. 6.8. It is observed that as the

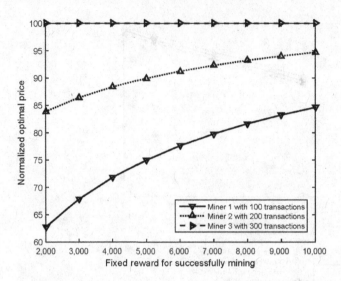

Figure 6.9 Normalized optimal price versus the fixed reward for mining successfully under discriminatory pricing. Reprinted with permission from the paper "Cloud/fog computing resource management and pricing for blockchain networks" published in *IEEE Internet of Things Journal.*

propagation delay factor increases, the total service demand and the profit of the CFP increase. This is because when the propagation delay effects are strong, the miners with a larger mined block need to have a higher service demand to reduce the propagation delay of their propagated solutions. At the same time, a miner with a smaller mined block is also incentivized from the demand competition with the other miners. Therefore, the total service demand increases, which in turn improves the profit of the CFP. Additionally, we observe that as the value of service cost factor increases, the total service demand decreases under discriminatory pricing and remains unchanged under uniform pricing. However, the profit of the CFP increases in both schemes. Recall from Fig. 6.5, the reason is that the optimal price under uniform pricing remains unchanged from varying the value of service cost factor, and thus the service demand remains unchanged under uniform pricing. Correspondingly, the CFP achieves greater profit gain from the lower cost under uniform pricing. However, under discriminatory pricing, when the service cost decreases, the CFP has an incentive to set a lower price for some miners to encourage higher total service demand. On the contrary, when the value of service cost factor increases, the CFP has no incentive to set a lower price for these miners, since the higher total service demand results in higher cost for the CFP. Therefore, as the value of service cost factor decreases, the total service demand and the profit of CFP increase.

Investigation on Optimal Price under Uniform and Discriminatory Pricing Schemes

Now, to explore the impacts of discriminatory pricing on each specific miner, we investigate the optimal price and resulting individual computing service demand from miners. We conduct a case study for three-miner mining with the following parameters:

$t_1 = 100$, $t_2 = 200$, $t_3 = 300$, $\underline{x} = 10^{-2}$, $\bar{x} = 100$, $\bar{p} = 100$, $R = 10^4$, $r = 20$, $z = 5 \times 10^{-3}$, and $c = 10^{-3}$.

As expected, we observe from Figs. 6.9 and 6.10 that the optimal price charging to the miners with the smaller blocks is lower, for example, miners 1 and 2. This is

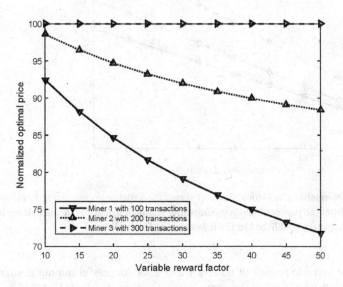

Figure 6.10 Normalized optimal price versus the variable reward factor under discriminatory pricing. Reprinted with permission from the paper "Cloud/fog computing resource management and pricing for blockchain networks" published in *IEEE Internet of Things Journal*.

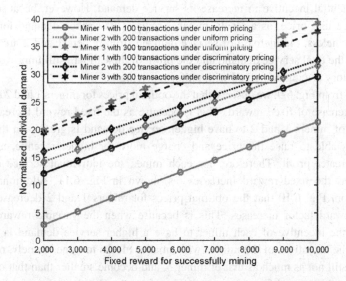

Figure 6.11 Normalized individual demand versus the fixed reward for mining successful. Reprinted with permission from the paper "Cloud/fog computing resource management and pricing for blockchain networks" published in *IEEE Internet of Things Journal*.

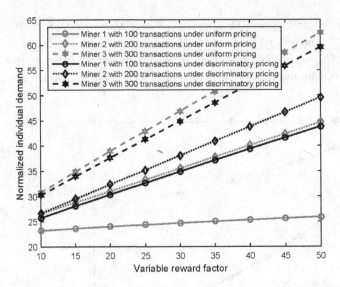

Figure 6.12 Normalized individual demand versus the variable reward factor. Reprinted with permission from the paper "Cloud/fog computing resource management and pricing for blockchain networks" published in *IEEE Internet of Things Journal*.

because the variable reward of miners 1 and 2 for successful mining is smaller than that of miner 3. Thus, miners 1 and 2 have no incentive to pay as high a price for their service demand as miner 3. In this case, the CFP can greatly improve the individual service demand of miners 1 and 2 by setting lower prices to attract them, as illustrated in Figs. 6.11 and 6.12. Owing to the competition from other two miners, miner 3 also has the potential incentive to increase its service demand. However, because of the high service unit price, as a result, miner 3 reduces its service demand for saving cost. Nevertheless, the increase of service demand from miners 1 and 2 are greater. Therefore, the total service demand and the profit of the CFP are still improved under discriminatory pricing compared with uniform pricing.

Further, from Fig. 6.9, we observe that the optimal prices for miners 1 and 2 increase with the increase of fixed reward. This is because as the fixed reward increases, the incentives of miners 1 and 2 to have higher service demand is greater. In this case, the CFP is able to raise the price and charge more for higher revenue, and thus achieves greater profit. Therefore, for each miner, the individual service demand increases as the fixed reward increases, as shown in Fig. 6.11. Additionally, we observe from Fig. 6.10 that the optimal prices for miners 1 and 2 decrease as the variable reward factor increases. This is because when the variable reward factor increases, the incentive of each miner to have a higher service demand is greater. However, the incentives of the miners with smaller blocks to mine, namely, miners 1 and 2, are still not as much as that of miner 3, and become smaller than that of miner 3 as the variable reward factor increases. Therefore, the CFP intends to set the lower price for miners 1 and 2 which may induce more individual service demand, as shown in Fig. 6.12.

Note that the Stackelberg game of the edge–fog computing service for blockchain aims at maximizing the profit of the CFP. Alternatively, social welfare, that is, utility of miners, is also important and should be maximized. As such, auction [233] is a suitable tool to achieve this objective, and some preliminary modeling and results are presented in [223].

6.3   Conclusion

In this chapter, we first outlined the basics of mechanism design, including the equilibrium concepts, revelation principle, and some necessary theorems. To better illustrate the application of the mechanism in cryptoeconomics, we investigated the price-based computing resource management for supporting offloading mining tasks to CFPs in PoW-based public blockchain networks. In particular, we have adopted the two-stage Stackelberg game model to jointly study the profit maximization of CFPs and the utility maximization of miners. Through backward induction, we have derived the unique Nash equilibrium point of the game among the miners. The optimal resource management schemes have been presented and examined, including the uniform and discriminatory pricing for the CFP. Further, the existence and uniqueness of the Stackelberg equilibrium have been proved analytically for both pricing schemes. We have performed multiple experiments to validate the proposed analytical model. Additionally, we have conducted numerical simulations to evaluate the network performance, which helps the CFP to achieve optimal resource management and gain the highest profit. For future work, we will study the oligopoly market with multiple CFPs, where providers compete with each other to sell computing services to miners. Another direction is to explore the optimal strategies of the provider and miners considering cyber-attacks, such as [138].

7 Auction Theory

Auction theory is an applied area of game theory that studies the game-theoretic features of auction markets and deals with how individuals behave in auction markets. There are several different auction designs (or sets of rules), and common concerns explored by auction theorists include the efficiency of a particular auction design, optimum and equilibrium bidding methods, and revenue comparison. Auction theory is also used to guide the design of real-world auctions, most notably auctions for the privatization of public-sector businesses or the sale of electromagnetic spectrum licenses. In this chapter, we first define the concepts and definitions of auctions. Then, we provide the mathematical problem formulation of the auction model. Some basic properties are also discussed.

7.1   Auction Basics

Auctions can take numerous forms, but they must always meet two criteria. They are universal for two reasons: First, they may be used to sell any object, and second, the outcome of the auction is not dependent on the identity of the bidders, that is, auctions are anonymous. Most auctions allow participants to enter bids, or the sums of money they are ready to spend. The definition of an auction is as follows.

Definition 15   A market mechanism in which an object, service, or set of objects, is exchanged on the basis of bids submitted by participants. An *auction* provides a specific set of rules that will govern the sale or purchase (procurement auction) of an object to the submitter of the most favorable bid. The specific mechanisms of the auction include first-price, second-price, English, and Dutch auctions.

A game-theoretic auction model is a mathematical game that consists of a set of players, a set of actions (strategies) accessible to each player, and a reward vector for each combination of strategies. In most cases, the players are the buyer(s) and the seller(s). Each player's action set consists of a collection of bid functions or reservation prices. Each bid function converts the value (in the case of a buyer) or cost (in the case of a seller) of the player to a bid price. The expected utility (or expected profit) of each player under a combination of tactics is the payout of that player under that combination of strategies.

Auction and strategic bidding game-theoretic models often fall into one of two groups. Each participant (bidder) in a private-values model assumes that each competing bidder derives a random private value from a probability distribution. In a common-values model, each bidder thinks that any other bidder will get a random signal from a probability distribution shared by all bidders. A private-values model typically, but not always, implies that the values are independent among bidders, whereas a common-values model typically assumes that the values are independent up to the common parameters of the probability distribution.

When specific assumptions about bidders' value distributions are required, most published research assumes symmetric bidders. This indicates that the probability distribution from which bidders get their values (or signals) is the same for all bidders. Symmetry means that the bidders' values are independently and identically distributed in a private-values model that presupposes independence (i.i.d.).

7.1.1 Types of Auctions

There are a variety of properties for auction. To begin, allocative efficiency implies that the highest bidder always wins in all of these auctions (i.e., there are no reserve prices). Second, a computationally efficient auction is preferable. Finally, we have the following theorem to examine the income (anticipated selling price) of several auctions.

Theorem 12 *Revenue Equivalence Theorem: Any two auctions such that:*

- *the bidder with the highest value wins,*
- *the bidder with the lowest value expects zero profit,*
- *bidders are risk-neutral,*[1]
- *value distributions are strictly increasing and atomless,*

have the same revenue and also the same expected profit for each bidder. The theorem can help find some equilibrium strategy.

The winner's curse phenomena, which may arise in common-value situations where the real values to the individual bidders are unknown but associated, and the bidders make bidding decisions based on estimated values, is worth addressing. In such circumstances, the winner is usually the bidder with the highest estimate, and that winner has typically bid too high for the auctioned item.

There are several methods to classify various sorts of auctions. Standard auctions, for example, require the winner to be the person with the highest bid. This is not required in a nonstandard auction (e.g., a lottery). There are four types of auctions that are usually used for the allocation of a single item, and these are as follows.

Definition 16 **First-price auction:** An auction in which the bidder who placed the highest offer receives the object being auctioned and pays the bid. In a procurement auction, the bidder who submits the lowest bid wins and gets paid the amount of his or her bid. In reality, first-price auctions are either sealed-bid (bidders make bids at the same time) or Dutch. Bidders in first-price auctions shade their bids below their true value.

---

[1] In economics, risk-neutral behavior is in between risk aversion and risk seeking. If offered either $50 or a 50 percent chance of $100, a risk-averse person will take the $50, a risk-seeking person will take the 50 percent chance of $100, and a risk-neutral person will have no preference between the two options.

Definition 17   **Second-price auction:** An auction in which the bidder who submitted the highest bid is awarded the object being sold and pays a price equal to the second-highest amount bid. Alternately, in a procurement auction, the winner is the bidder who submits the lowest bid, and is paid an amount equal to the next-lowest submitted bid. In practice, second-price auctions are either sealed-bid, in which bidders submit bids simultaneously, or English auctions, in which bidders continue to raise each other's bids until only one bidder remains. The theoretical nicety of second-price auctions, first pointed out by William Vickrey, is that bidding one's true value is a dominant strategy. Alternately, first-price auctions also award the object to the highest bidder, but the payment is equal to the amount bid.

Definition 18   **English auction (open ascending-bid auctions):** A type of sequential second-price auction in which an auctioneer directs participants to beat the current standing bid. New bids must increase the current bid by a predefined increment. The auction ends when no participant is willing to outbid the current standing bid. Then, the participant who placed the current bid is the winner and pays the amount bid. An English auction, in which the highest bidder pays the amount bid, is termed a second-price auction since the winning bidder need only outbid the next-highest bidder by the minimum increment. Thus, the winner effectively pays an amount equal to (slightly higher than) the second-highest bid.

Definition 19   **Dutch auction (open descending-bid auctions):** A type of first-price auction in which a "clock" initially indicates a price for the object for sale substantially higher than any bidder is likely to pay. Then, the clock gradually decreases the price until a bidder "buzzes in" or indicates his or her willingness to pay. The auction is then concluded, and the winning bidder pays the amount reflected on the clock at the time he or she stopped the process by buzzing in. These auctions are named after a common market mechanism for selling flowers in Holland, but they also reflect stores successively reducing prices on sale items.

The "standard" auction types listed above are the focus of most auction theory. Other auction types, such as the following, have also been studied academically.

Definition 20   **Japanese auction:** A type of sequential second-price auction, similar to an English auction, in which an auctioneer regularly raises the current price. Participants must signal at every price level their willingness to stay in the auction and pay the current price. Thus, unlike an English auction, each participant must bid at each level to stay in the auction. The auction concludes when only one bidder indicates his willingness to stay in. This auction format is also known as the button auction.

Definition 21   **All-pay auctions:** Bidders place their bids in sealed envelopes and present them to the auctioneer at the same time. The envelopes are opened, and the person with the highest bet wins, paying the exact amount that he or she bid. In an all-pay auction, all losing bidders must also pay the auctioneer an amount equal to their own bid. This auction format is not standardized, but it may be used to better comprehend topics like political campaigns (where bids can be read as campaign money) or waiting for a limited product (in which your bid is the amount of time that you are prepared to remain in the queue).

A Tullock auction, sometimes known as a Tullock lottery, is the most basic type of all-pay auction in which everyone places a bid but both losers and winners pay their bids. This is useful for describing some concepts in public choice economics. Only the two highest bidders pay their bids in the dollar auction, which is a two-player Tullock auction or multi-player game.

There are other types of all-pay auctions, such as the war of attrition, in which the highest bidder wins but all (or both, as is more common) bidders pay just the reduced bid. Biologists utilize the war of attrition to mimic traditional contests or agonistic interactions that are settled without the use of physical force.

Definition 22 **Unique bid auction:** A strategy game similar to traditional auctions in which the winner is normally the one with the lowest unique bid, while the auction rules may state that the individual with the highest unique bid is the winner in some cases. Auctions with unique bids are frequently utilized as a type of competition or lottery.

Definition 23 **Generalized second-price auction (GSP):** A nontruthful auction mechanism for multiple items. Initially conceived as a logical extension of the Vickrey auction, it really does not preserve some of the Vickrey auction's beneficial properties. It is most commonly used in the context of keyword auctions, in which sponsored search spaces are offered at auction.

The next section describes various unique forms of auctions and their attributes, as well as an example of how to use auction theory to resource allocation on a blockchain system.

7.1.1.1 VCG Auction

A Vickrey auction [234] is a type of sealed-bid auction, in which bidders (players) submit written bids without knowing the bid of the other people in the auction. Although the highest bidder wins, the winning price is the second-highest bid. William Vickrey designed the auction. This sort of auction is comparable to an English auction in terms of strategy, and it encourages bidders to bid their true value.

The phrases Vickrey auction and second-price sealed-bid auction are interchangeable when only a single, indivisible good is being sold. When several identical units (or a divisible good) are sold in a single auction, the most obvious generalization is that all winning bidders must pay the same price as the highest nonwinning bidder. A uniform-price auction is what this is called. Unless each bidder has desire for only one item, the uniform-price auction does not result in buyers bidding their real valuations as they do in a second-price auction.

The Vickrey–Clarke–Groves (VCG) mechanism is a generalization of the Vickrey auction that preserves the incentive to bid honestly [234]. The principle behind VCG is that each player pays the opportunity cost that their presence brings to the other players. The VCG auction is then formally defined and some of its attributes are explained.

Definition 24   The VCG mechanism implements efficient outcome, $k^* = \max_k \sum_j v_j(k, \hat{\theta}_j)$, and computes transfers

$$t_i(\hat{\theta}) = \sum_{j \neq i} v_j(k^{-i}, \hat{\theta}_j) - \sum_{j \neq i} v_j(k^*, \hat{\theta}_j), \qquad (7.1)$$

where $k^{-i} = \max_k \sum_{j \neq i} v_j(k, \hat{\theta}_j)$.

In other words, the payment equals the performance loss of all other users because of including user i.

Assume two apples are being auctioned off among three bidders. Bidder A just wants one apple and offers \$5 for it. Bidder B is looking for one apple and is ready to pay \$2 for it. Bidder C wants two apples and is ready to pay \$6 for each, but is not interested in purchasing one without the other. To begin, the auction outcome is chosen by maximizing bids: The apples are awarded to bidders A and B. The opportunity cost imposed by each bidder on the other bidders is then examined in order to determine compensation. B's utility is now \$2. If bidder A had not been there, C would have won with a utility of \$6, hence A must pay \$6 – \$2 = \$4. For bidder B's payment, presently A has a utility of \$5 and C has a value of 0. If bidder B had not been there, C would have won and would have had a utility of \$6, hence B pays \$6 – \$5 = \$1. Because the outcome is the same whether or not bidder C participates, C is not required to pay anything.

Each bidder optimizes his or her expected utility by bidding (revealing) his or her real valuation in a Vickrey auction with independent private values (IPV). Under the most general conditions, a Vickrey auction is ex-post efficient (the winner is the bidder with the highest value); it thus serves as a baseline model against which the efficiency attributes of other types of auctions may be evaluated. The auction is likewise immune to strategy. VCG auctions are commonly employed in wireless networking because of the advantages listed above, particularly in cases where it is critical to prevent participants from lying.

Despite the Vickrey auction's strengths, it has shortcomings.

- It does not allow for price discovery – that is, discovery of the market price if the buyers are unsure of their own valuations – without sequential auctions.
- Sellers may use shill bids to increase profit.
- In iterated Vickrey auctions, the strategy of revealing true valuations is no longer dominant.

The VCG mechanism has the additional shortcomings.

- It is vulnerable to collusion by losing bidders.
- It is vulnerable to shill bidding with respect to the buyers.
- It does not necessarily maximize seller revenues; seller revenues may even be zero in VCG auctions. If the purpose of holding the auction is to maximize profit for the seller rather than just allocate resources among buyers, then VCG may be a poor choice.
- The seller's revenues are nonmonotonic with regard to the sets of bidders and offers.

7.1.1.2   Share Auction

A share auction [235–237] is concerned with distributing a perfect divisible good among a group of bidders. The financial market (such as the auction of treasury notes) is the most widely cited example in the literature [238–240]. Other instances are pollution permit allocation [241] and power selling [242]. A share auction has two fundamental price systems. In a uniform-price auction, each winner (usually more than one) receives some of the product and pays the same unit price. Winning bids are filled at the bid price in a discriminatory pricing auction (also known as a pay-you-bid auction [236]). The works mentioned above largely focus on examining how different pricing and information structures affect the auction results, such as the final price, the seller's revenue, and the allocations of the divisible good.

In contrast to the well-studied single-unit good auction, in which buyers normally submit one-dimensional offers, certain share auctions enable bidders to submit various price and quantity combinations as bids (e.g., [238, 239, 241]). Because bidders have wide strategy areas, this considerably complicates auction design. Researchers generally use basic one-dimensional bidding rules when utilizing a share auction to allocate resources such as bandwidth in communication networks, as in [243–248]. The allocation is based on the bids. Some scholars have focused on finding efficiency loss constraints in such basic bidding games: According to Johari and Tsitsiklis [243], using a uniform-pricing method, the NE of a share auction achieves at least three-quarters of the total utility at a socially optimal solution. According to Sanghavi and Hajek [245], if discriminating pricing (pay-you-bid) is employed, the efficiency loss can be minimized to about one-eighth. Yang and Hajek [244] and Maheswaran and Basar [246] extend the results by demonstrating that more sophisticated pricing functions can decrease the efficiency loss to zero, given specific constraints on the bidders' utility functions. Maheswaran and Basar have considered several network resource allocation games using share auctions, with focus on studying the effects of coalition [247] or designing decentralized negotiation methods [248].

Users make one-dimensional bids b_i expressing their willingness to pay in a share auction, and the management simply assigns the available resource P in proportion to the bids. Users are then charged a fee according to their performance gain γ_i. The management makes a nonnegative reserve bid of β public. In contrast to the case when the management makes a reserve bid in order to extract more income from the other bidders [249], the major goal of the reserve bid in this case is to ensure a unique desired outcome of the auction. The following is an example of a share auction mechanism.

Share Auction Mechanism

1. The manager announces a reserve bid $\beta \geq 0$, and a price $\pi > 0$.
2. After observing β, π, user i submits a bid $b_i \geq 0$.
3. The resources are allocated to each user i, and its share p_i is proportional to its bid, that is,

$$p_i = \frac{\beta}{\sum_i b_i + \beta} P. \tag{7.2}$$

The resulting performance of user i is γ_i.

For example, if P is the overall transmitted power, for the interference case, we can have the resulting signal to interference and noise ratio (SINR) for user i as

$$\gamma_i(\boldsymbol{p}) = \frac{p_i h_{ii}}{n_0 + \sum_{j \neq i} p_j h_{ji}}, \tag{7.3}$$

where h_{ij} is the channel gain for user i to receiver j and n_0 is the noise level.

4. In a share auction, user i pays $C_i = \pi \gamma_i$.

A *bidding profile* is the vector containing the users' bids $\boldsymbol{b} = (b_1, ..., b_N)$. The *bidding profile of user i's opponents* is defined as $b_{-i} = (b_1, ..., b_{i-1}, b_{i+1}, ..., b_N)$, so that $\boldsymbol{b} = (b_i; b_{-i})$. Typically, each user i submits a bid b_i to maximize its *surplus function*

$$S_i (b_i; b_{-i}) = U_i \left(\gamma_i (b_i; b_{-i}) \right) - C_i.$$

We ignore the dependence on β and p_i in this case. An auction's NE is a fixed point of all users' best answers. These auction mechanisms vary from previously suggested auction-based network resource allocation techniques (e.g., [243, 246]) in that the bids and payouts are not the same. Instead, bids are indications of willingness to pay. The management may thus affect the NE by selecting β and p_i. This reduces the NE's normal inefficiency and, in some situations, permits us to obtain socially optimum solutions. The share auction can accomplish fair (efficient, respectively) allocation under correctly determined price. Users gain performance in a fair allocation by meeting certain established fairness criteria. The entire utility of the network is maximized in an efficient allocation.

7.1.1.3   Double Auction

There are I buyers and N sellers in a double auction [250]. Each buyer i wishes to buy x_i products, whereas each seller n wishes to sell y_n items. The data for x_i and y_n are publicly available. A buyer i reports price $p(b)_i$ (i.e., bidding price) in a double auction, whereas a seller n reports price $p(s)_n$ (i.e., asking price). These are the pricing per item. Without sacrificing generality, we may assume $p_1^{(b)} \geq p_2^{(b)} \geq \cdots \geq p_I^{(b)}$ and $p_1^{(s)} \leq p_2^{(s)} \leq \cdots \leq p_N^{(s)}$. It is worth noting that if two prices are equivalent, their indices are interchangeable. Furthermore, if the seller and buyer sell and buy each item independently, each seller or buyer can establish various pricing for different goods.

To calculate the trading price in a double auction, the demand quantity from all purchasers is organized in ascending price order. Similarly, the supply amounts from all sellers are placed in ascending price order. At the trading point T^*, aggregate demand and supply cross, and so K sellers will sell T^* things to L buyers. There are two scenarios for determining the trading price and trading quantity.

- *Case 1* The bidding and asking prices satisfy the condition $p_{i'}^{(b)} \geq p_{n'}^{(s)} \geq p_{i'+1}^{(b)}$ and aggregate demand and supply satisfy $\sum_{n=1}^{n'-1} y_n \leq \sum_{i=1}^{i'} x_i \leq \sum_{n=1}^{n'} y_n$. In this case, the sellers $n = \{1, \ldots, n'\}$ sell all their items y_n at price $p_{n'}^{(s)}$, and the buyers

$i = \{1, \ldots, i'\}$ buy at price $p_{i'}^{(b)}$. Each buyer buys with quantity $\left\lfloor x_i - \frac{\sum_{j=1}^{i'-1} x_j - \sum_{j=1}^{n'-1} y_j}{i'-1} \right\rfloor$ where $\lfloor x \rfloor$ denotes the floor function.

- *Case 2* The bidding and asking prices satisfy the condition $p_{n'+1}^{(s)} \geq p_{i'}^{(b)} \geq p_{i'}^{(s)}$ and aggregate demand and supply satisfy $\sum_{i=1}^{i'-1} x_i \leq \sum_{n=1}^{n'} y_n \leq \sum_{i=1}^{i'} x_i$. In this case, the buyers $i = \{1, \ldots, i'\}$ buy at price $p_{i'}^{(b)}$, and the sellers $n = \{1, \ldots, n'\}$ sell at price $p_{n'}^{(s)}$. Each seller sells with quantity $\left\lfloor y_n - \frac{\sum_{j=1}^{n'-1} y_j - \sum_{j=1}^{i'-1} x_j}{n'-1} \right\rfloor$.

When a central controller is accessible in this double auction, however, an optimization problem may be developed to determine the number of goods to be exchanged. Let the reserved price of each buyer and seller be fixed and denoted by $\hat{p}_i^{(b)}$ and $\hat{p}_n^{(s)}$. Let $\hat{x}_{i,n}$ and $\hat{p}_{i,n}$ be the solutions in terms of the quantity of buyer i to buy from seller n and the trading price, respectively. The utility of buyer i from a double auction can be defined as follows:

$$U_i^{(b)} = \sum_{n=1}^{\hat{n}} \left(p_i^{(b)} - \hat{p}_{i,n} \right) \hat{x}_{i,n}, \tag{7.4}$$

and that of seller n is defined as follows:

$$U_n^{(s)} = \sum_{i=1}^{\hat{i}} \left(\hat{p}_{i,n} - p_n^{(s)} \right) \hat{x}_{i,n}. \tag{7.5}$$

To maximize the utility of both seller and buyer, an optimization can be formulated as a linear programming problem as follows:

$$\max \sum_{i=1}^{\hat{i}} \sum_{n=1}^{\hat{n}} \hat{x}_{i,n} \left(p_i^{(b)} - p_n^{(s)} \right), \tag{7.6}$$

$$\text{s.t.} \sum_{i=1}^{\hat{i}} \hat{x}_{i,n} \leq y_n, \forall n, \quad \sum_{n=1}^{\hat{n}} \hat{x}_{i,n} \leq x_i, \forall i, \hat{x}_{i,n} \geq 0, \forall i, n. \tag{7.7}$$

The constraints limit the quantity of the item to be traded less than the supply and demand quantity for the seller and buyer, respectively.

7.1.2 Problem Formulation of Auction

We now investigate a basic first-price auction model with two buyers bidding for an object. Because F is symmetric between the two purchasers, this is an auction model with symmetric bidders. We suppose that (1) the seller's value of the object is 0 and (2) the seller's reservation price is also 0. Each buyer's expected utility U can be written as

$$U(p) = (v - p)\text{Pr}[p > B(v_o)], \tag{7.8}$$

where p is the bid price, $(v - p)$ is the consumer surplus that the buyer will receive conditional up on winning, and $\text{Pr}[p > B(v_o)]$ is the likelihood that he or she is going to be the buyer with the highest bid price. That likelihood is given by the probability that this buyer's bid price p exceeds the other buyer's bid price B (expressed as a function of the other buyer's value v_o).

Assume that each buyer's equilibrium bid price increases monotonically over time; this implies that the bid function B has an inverse function. Let Y be the inverse of B: $Y = B^{-1}$. Then $U(p) = (v - p)\Pr[Y(p) > v_o]$. Since v_o is distributed $F(v_o)$, we have

$$\Pr[Y(p) > v_o] = F(Y(p)) = Y(p), \tag{7.9}$$

which implies $U(p) = (v - p)Y(p)$. A bid price p maximizes U if $U'(p) = 0$. Differentiating U with respect to p and setting to zero, we have

$$U'(p) = -Y(p) + (v - p)Y'(p) = 0. \tag{7.10}$$

Since the buyers are symmetric, in equilibrium it must be the case that $p = B(v)$ or (equivalently) $Y(p) = v$. Therefore, we have

$$-Y(p) + (Y(p) - p)Y'(p) = 0. \tag{7.11}$$

A solution $\hat{Y}$ of this differential equation is an inverse Nash equilibrium strategy of this game.

At this point, we may conjecture that the (unique) solution is the linear function $\hat{Y}(p) = \alpha p$ and $\hat{Y}'(p) = \alpha$ for some real number α. Substituting into $U'(p) = 0$, we have

$$-\alpha p + (\alpha p - p)\alpha = 0. \tag{7.12}$$

When we solve for α, then get $\hat{\alpha} = 2$. As a result, $\hat{Y}(p) = 2p$ satisfies $U'(p) = 0$. The expression $\hat{Y}(p) = \hat{\alpha}p$ implies $\hat{Y}(p)/\hat{\alpha} = p$, or $v/\hat{\alpha} = \hat{B}(v)$. Thus, inside the set of invertible bidding functions, the (unique) Nash equilibrium strategy bidding function of this game is determined as $\hat{B}(v) = v/2$.

7.2   Example: Auctions for Resource Allocation in Public Blockchain Networks

As an emerging decentralized secure data-management platform, blockchain has gained much popularity recently. To maintain a canonical state of blockchain data record, PoW-based consensus protocols provide the nodes, referred to as miners, in the network with incentives for confirming a new block of transactions through a process of "block mining" by solving a cryptographic puzzle. Under the circumstance of limited local computing resources, for example, mobile devices, it is natural for rational miners, that is, consensus nodes, to offload computational tasks for PoW to the cloud–fog computing servers. Therefore, we focus on the trading between the cloud–fog computing service provider and miners, and propose an auction-based market model for efficient computing resource allocation. In particular, we consider a PoW-based blockchain network, which is constrained by the computing resource and deployed as an infrastructure for decentralized data-management applications. Owing to the competition among miners in the blockchain network, the allocative externalities are particularly taken into account when designing the auction mechanisms. Specifically, we consider two bidding schemes: the constant-demand scheme where each miner bids for a fixed quantity of resources, and the multi-demand scheme where the miners can submit their preferable demands and bids. For the constant-demand bidding scheme, we propose an auction mechanism that achieves optimal social welfare. In the multi-demand bidding scheme, the social welfare maximization problem is NP-hard. Therefore, we design an approximate algorithm which guarantees the truthfulness, individual rationality, and computational efficiency. Through extensive simulations, we show that our proposed auction mechanisms with the two bidding schemes can efficiently maximize the social welfare of the blockchain network and provide effective strategies for the cloud–fog computing service provider.

7.2.1   Introduction and Contribution

In contrast to traditional currencies, cryptocurrencies are traded among participants over a P2P network without relying on third parties such as banks or financial regulatory authorities [1]. As the backbone technology of decentralized cryptocurrencies, blockchain has also heralded many applications in various fields, such as finance [251], IoT [252] and resource offloading [253]. According to the market research firm Tractica's report, it is estimated that the annual revenue for enterprise applications of blockchain will increase to $19.9 billion by 2025 [254]. Essentially, blockchain is a tamper-proof, distributed database that records transactional data in a P2P network. The database state is decentrally maintained, and any member node in the overlay blockchain network is permitted to participate in the state maintenance without identity authentication. The transactions among member nodes are recorded in cryptographic hash-linked data structures known as *blocks*. A series of confirmed blocks are arranged in chronological order to form a sequential chain, hence the name *blockchain*. All member nodes in the network are required to follow the Nakamoto consensus protocol [1] (or other protocols alike), to agree on the transactional data, cryptographic hashes, and digital signatures stored in the block to guarantee the integrity of the blockchain.

The Nakamoto consensus protocol integrates a critical computing-intensive process, called *Proof of Work (PoW)*. In order to have their local views of the blockchain accepted by the network as the canonical state of the blockchain, consensus nodes (i.e., block miners) have to solve a cryptographic puzzle, that is, find a nonce to be contained in the block such that the hash value of the entire block is smaller than a preset target. This computational process is called *mining*, where the consensus nodes which contribute their computing power to mining are known as *miners*. Typically, the mining task for PoW can be regarded as a tournament [97]. First, each miner collects and verifies a certain number of unconfirmed transaction records which are aggregated into a new block. Next, all miners chase each other to be the first one to obtain the desired nonce value as the PoW solutions for the new block which combines the collected transactional data[2] and block metadata. Once the PoW puzzle is solved, this new block

---

[2] We refer to all transaction records stored in the block simply as transactional data in the rest of the book.

will be immediately broadcasted to the entire blockchain network. Meanwhile, the other miners receive this message and perform a chain validation-comparison process to decide whether to approve and add newly generated block to the blockchain. The miner which successfully has its proposed block linked to the blockchain will be given a certain amount of reward, including a fixed bonus and a variable transaction fee, as an incentive of mining.

Since no prior authorization is required, the permissionless blockchain is especially suitable for serving as a platform for decentralized autonomous data management in many applications. Some representative examples can be found in data sharing [255], electricity trading in smart grids [256], and personal data access control [257]. Apart from the feature of public access, permissionless blockchains have the advantage in quickly establishing a self-organized data-management platform to support various decentralized applications (DApps). This is a breakthrough in production relations in that people can independently design smart contracts and freely build decentralized applications themselves without the support or permission from trusted intermediaries. By the PoW-based Nakamoto consensus protocol, people are encouraged to become consensus nodes, that is, miners, with the mining reward. Unfortunately, solving the PoW puzzle needs continuous, high computing power which mobile devices and IoT devices cannot afford. As the number of mobile phone users is forecast to reach nearly 5 billion in 2019,[3] it is expected that DApps would usher in explosive growth if mobile devices can join in the mining and consensus process and self-organize a blockchain network to support DApps [258]. To alleviate the computational bottleneck, the consensus nodes can access the cloud–fog computing service to offload their mining tasks, thus enabling blockchain-based DApps. As the cloud–fog computing service can breed more consensus nodes to be able to execute the mining task, it would significantly improve the robustness of the blockchain network and then raise the valuation of DApps, which further attracts more DApp users to join, forming a virtuous circle.

In this book, we mainly investigate the trading between the cloud–fog computing service provider (CFP) and the computationally lightweight devices, namely, *miners*. From the system perspective, we aim to maximize the *social welfare* which is the total utility of the CFP and all miners in the blockchain network. The social welfare can be interpreted as the system efficiency [259]. For an efficient and sustainable business ecosystem, there are some critical issues about cloud–fog resources allocation and pricing for the service provider. First, which miner can be offered the computing resources? Too many miners will cause service congestion and incur high operation cost to the service provider. By contrast, a very small group of miners may erode the integrity of the blockchain network. Second, how to set a reasonable service price for miners such that they can be incentivized to undertake the mining tasks? The efficient method is to set up an auction where the miners can actively submit their bids to the CFP for decision making. We should also consider how to make miners truthfully expose their private valuation. A miner's valuation on the computing service is directly related to its privately collected transactional data which determines its expected reward from

---

[3] Source: www.statista.com/statistics/274774/forecast-of-mobile-phone-users-worldwide.

the blockchain. To address the above questions, we propose an auction-based cloud–fog computing resource market model for blockchain networks. Moreover, we design truthful auction mechanisms for two different bidding schemes. One is the *constant-demand scheme* where the CFP imposes the restriction that each miner can bid only for the same quantity of computing resources. The other one is the *multi-demand scheme* where miners can request their demands and express the corresponding bids more freely. The major contributions of this work can be summarized as follows.

- In the auction-based cloud–fog computing resources market, we take the competition among miners [260] and the network effects of blockchain by nature [261] into consideration. We study the auction mechanism with allocative externalities to maximize the social welfare.[4]
- From the perspective of the CFP, we formulate social welfare maximization problems for two bidding schemes: the constant-demand scheme and the multi-demand scheme. For the constant-demand bidding scheme, we develop an optimal algorithm that achieves optimal social welfare. For the multi-demand bidding scheme, we prove that the formulated problem is NP-hard and equivalent to the problem of nonmonotone submodular maximization with knapsack constraints. Therefore, we introduce an approximate algorithm that generates suboptimal social welfare. Both algorithms are designed to be truthful, individually rational, and computationally efficient.
- Based on the real-world mobile blockchain experiment, we define and verify two characteristic functions for system model formulation. One is the hash power function that describes the relationship between the probability of successfully mining a block and the corresponding miner's computing power. The other one is the network effects function that characterizes the relationship between security of the blockchain network and total computing resources invested into the network.
- Our simulation results show that the proposed auction mechanisms not only help the CFP make practical and efficient computing resource trading strategies, but also offer insightful guidance to the blockchain developer in designing the blockchain protocol.

To the best of our knowledge, this is the first work that investigates resource management and pricing for blockchain networks in the auction-based market. This chapter is an extended version of our conference work [262], in which we considered only the miners with constant demand and did not perform the real-world experiment to verify the network effects function.

The rest of this chapter is organized as follows. Section 7.2.2 reviews related work. The system model of cloud–fog computing resource market for blockchain networks is introduced in Section 7.2.3. Section 7.2.4 discusses the constant-demand bidding scheme and the optimal algorithm for social welfare maximization. In Section 7.2.5, the approximate algorithm for multi-demand bidding scheme is presented in detail.

---

[4] The allocative externalities occur when the allocation result of the auction affects the valuation of the miners.

Table 7.1 Frequently used notations.

Notation	Description
$\mathcal{N}, N$	Set of miners and the total number of miners
$\mathcal{M}$	Set of winners, i.e., the selected miners by the auction
$\mathbf{d}, d_i$	Miners' service demand profile and miner i's demand for cloud–fog computing resource
$\mathbf{b}, b_i$	Miners' bid profile and miner i's bid for its demand d_i
$\mathbf{x}, x_i$	Resource allocation profile and allocation result for miner i
$\mathbf{p}, p_i$	Price profile and cloud–fog computing service price for miner i
γ_i	Miner i's hash power
T, r	Fixed bonus from mining a new block and the transaction fee rate
s_i	Miner i's block size
λ	Average block time
D	Total supply of computing resources from CFP
w	Network effects function
q	Quantity of computing resource required by constant-demand miner
β	Demand constraint ratio for multi-demand miner

Reprinted with permission from the paper "Auction mechanisms in cloud/fog computing resource allocation for public blockchain networks" published in *IEEE Transactions on Parallel and Distributed Systems*.

Experimental results of mobile blockchain and the performance analysis of the proposed auction mechanisms are presented in Section 7.2.6. Finally, Section 7.3 concludes the chapter. Table 7.1 lists notations frequently used herein.

7.2.2   Related Work and Motivation

As the core part of the blockchain network, creating blocks integrates the distributed database (i.e., ledger), the consensus protocol and the executable scripts (i.e., smart contract) [95]. From the perspective of data processing, a DApp is essentially developed on the basis of smart contracts and transactional data stored in the blockchain. DApps usually use the distributed ledger to monitor the state or ownership changes of the tokenized assets. The implementation of smart contracts is driven by the transaction or data change to autonomously determine the blockchain state transition, for example, the asset redistribution among the DApp users [95, 252]. With the public blockchain, DApps do not have to rely on a centralized infrastructure and intermediary that supports ledger maintenance and smart contracts execution with dedicated storage and computing resources. Instead, DApp providers adopt the token-based reward mechanisms which incentivize people to undertake the tasks of resource provision and system maintenance. In this way, the functionalities of DApps can be freely activated and realized among transaction issuing or validation, information propagation or storage and consensus participation [95, 96]. Therefore, the public blockchain network is a suitable platform for incentive-driven Distributed Autonomous Organization (DAO) systems. To date, a line of literature study the DAO in wireless networking based on the public blockchain. The authors in [253] established a trading platform for D2D computation offloading based on a dedicated cryptocurrency network. They introduced smart contract-based auctions between neighboring D2D nodes to execute resource offloading and offload the block mining tasks to the cloudlets. The authors in [263] adopted a PoW-based public blockchain as the backbone of a P2P file storage market, where the privacy of different parties in a transaction is enhanced by the techniques such as ring signatures and one-time payment addresses. When identity verification is required for market access granting, for example, in the scenarios of autonomous network slice brokering [264] and P2P electricity trading [256], the public blockchain can be adapted into a consortium blockchain by introducing membership-authorizing servers with little modification to the consensus protocols and the smart contract design.

Recently, there have already been some studies on the blockchain network from the point of game theory. The author in [213] proposed a game-theoretic model where the occurrence of working out the PoW puzzle was modeled as a Poisson process. Since a miner's expected reward largely depends on the block size, each miner's response is to choose a reasonable block size before mining for its optimal expected reward. An analytical Nash equilibrium in a two-player case was discussed. In [265], the authors presented a cooperative game model to investigate the mining pool. In the pool, miners form a coalition to accumulate their computing power for steady rewards. Nevertheless, these works mainly focused on the block mining strategies and paid little attention to the deployment of the blockchain network for developing DApps and corresponding resource allocation problems. As a branch of game theory, the auction mechanism has been widely used to deal with resource allocation issues in various areas, such as mobile crowdsensing [266–268], cloud–edge computing [269, 270], and spectrum trading [271]. In [268], the authors proposed incentive mechanisms for efficient mobile task crowdsourcing based on reverse combinatorial auctions. They considered data quality constraints in a linear social welfare maximization problem. The authors in [269] designed optimal and approximate strategy-proof mechanisms to solve the problem of physical machine resource management in clouds. They formulated the problem as a linear integer program. In [270], the authors proposed an auction-based profit maximization model for hierarchical mobile edge computing. Unfortunately, it did not take any economic properties, for example, incentive compatibility, into account. While guaranteeing the strategyproofness, the authors in [271] investigated the problem of redistributing wireless channels and focused on the social welfare maximization. They not only considered strategyproofness, but also took the channel spatial reusability, channel heterogeneity, and bid diversity into account. However, in their combinatorial auction setting, the bidder's requested spectrum bundle is assumed to be always truthful. In fact, none of these works can be directly applied to allocating computing resources for the blockchain mainly due to its unique architecture. In the blockchain network, the allocative externalities [272, 273] should be particularly taken into consideration. For example, besides its own received computing resources, each miner also cares much about the other miners' computing power.

In our work, the social welfare optimization in the multi-demand bidding scheme is proved to be a problem of nonmonotone submodular maximization with knapsack constraints, which has not been well studied in auction mechanism design to date. The most closely related papers are [267] and [274] in mobile crowdsourcing. In [267], the authors presented a representative truthful auction mechanism for crowdsourcing tasks. They studied a nonmonotone submodular maximization problem without constraints. In [274], the authors formulated a monotone submodular function maximization problem when designing a truthful auction mechanism. The total payment to the mobile users is constrained by a fixed budget. Technically, the algorithms in the aforementioned works cannot be applied in our models. In addition, the authors in [275] used deep learning to recover the classical optimal auction for revenue maximization and applied it in the edge computing resources allocation in mobile blockchain. However, it considers only one unit of resource in the auction.

7.2.3   System Model: Blockchain Mining and Auction Based Market Model

7.2.3.1   Cloud–Fog Computing Resource Trading

Our system model is built under the assumptions that (1) the public blockchain network adopts the classical PoW consensus protocol [1], and (2) miners do not use their own devices, for example, computationally lightweight or mobile devices, to execute the mining tasks. We consider a scenario where there is one CFP and a community of miners $\mathcal{N} \Im \{1, \ldots, N\}$. Each miner runs a blockchain-based DApp to record and verify the transactional data sent to the blockchain network. Owing to insufficient energy and computing capacity of their devices, the miners offload the task of solving PoW to a nearby cloud–fog computing service which is deployed and maintained by the CFP. To perform the trading, the CFP launches an auction. The CFP first announces auction rules and the available service to miners. Then, the miners submit their resource demand profile $\mathbf{d} = (d_1, \ldots, d_N)$ and corresponding bid profile $\mathbf{b} = (b_1, \ldots, b_N)$ which represents the valuations of their requested resources. After having received miners' demands and bids, the CFP selects the winning miners and notifies all miners the allocation $\mathbf{x} = (x_1, \ldots, x_N)$ and the service price $\mathbf{p} = (p_1, \ldots, p_N)$, that is, the payment for each miner.[5] We assume that miners are single minded [276], that is, each miner only accepts its requested quantity of resources or none. The setting $x_i = 1$ means that miner i is within the winner list and allocated resources for which it submits the bid, while $x_i = 0$ means no resource allocated. The payment for a miner which fails the auction is set to be zero, that is, $p_i = 0$ if $x_i = 0$. At the end of the auction, the selected miners or winners make the payment according to the price assigned by the CFP and access the cloud–fog computing service.

7.2.3.2   Blockchain Mining with Cloud–Fog Computing Service

With the allocation x_i and demand d_i, miner i's hash power γ_i can be calculated from

$$\gamma_i(\mathbf{d}, \mathbf{x}) = \frac{d_i x_i}{d_\mathcal{N}}, \tag{7.13}$$

---

[5] Throughout this chapter, the terms price and payment are used interchangeably.

which is a linear fractional function. The function depends on other miners' allocated computing resources and satisfies $\sum_{i \in \mathcal{N}} \gamma_i = 1$. Here, $d_{\mathcal{N}} = \sum_{i \in \mathcal{N}} d_i x_i$ is the total quantity of allocated resources. The hash power function $\gamma_i(\mathbf{d}, \mathbf{x})$ is verified by a real-world experiment as presented later in Section 7.2.6.

Before executing the miner selection by the auction, each miner has collected unconfirmed transactional data into its own block. We denote each miner's *block size*, that is, the total size of transactional data and metadata, by $\mathbf{s} = (s_1, \ldots, s_N)$. In the mining tournament, the generation of new blocks follows a Poisson process with a constant mean rate $\frac{1}{\lambda}$ throughout the whole blockchain network [112]; λ is also known as the *average block time*. If the miner i finds a new block, the time for propagation and verification of transactions in the block is dominantly affected by s_i. The first miner which successfully has its block reach consensus can receive a *token reward R*. The token reward is composed of a *fixed bonus* $T \geq 0$ for mining a new block and a variable transaction fee $t_i = rs_i$ determined by miner i's block size s_i and a predefined *transaction fee rate* r [213]. Thus, miner i's token reward R_i can be expressed as follows:

$$R_i = (T + rs_i)\mathbb{P}_i(\gamma_i(\mathbf{d}, \mathbf{x}), s_i), \qquad (7.14)$$

where $\mathbb{P}_i(\gamma_i(\mathbf{d}, \mathbf{x}), s_i)$ is the probability that miner i receives the reward for contributing a block to the blockchain.

We note that obtaining the reward rests with successful mining and instant propagation. Miner i's probability of discovering the nonce value P_i^m is equal to its hash power γ_i, i.e., $P_i^m = \gamma_i$. However, a lucky miner may even lose the tournament if its broadcast block is not accepted by other miners at once, that is, failing to reach consensus. The newly mined block that cannot be added onto the blockchain is called an *orphan block* [213]. A larger block needs more propagation and verification time, thus resulting in larger delay in reaching consensus. As such, a larger block size means a higher chance that the block suffers orphaned. According to the statistics displayed in [277], miner i's block propagation time τ_i is linear to the block size, that is, $\tau_i = \xi s_i$, where ξ is a constant that reflects the impact of s_i on τ_i. Since the arrival rate of new blocks follows the Poisson distribution, miner i's orphaning probability is

$$P_i^o = 1 - e^{-\frac{1}{\lambda}\tau_i}. \qquad (7.15)$$

Substituting τ_i, we can express $\mathbb{P}_i$ as follows:

$$\mathbb{P}_i(\gamma_i(\mathbf{d}, \mathbf{x}), s_i) = P_i^m(1 - P_i^o) = \gamma_i e^{-\frac{1}{\lambda}\xi s_i}. \qquad (7.16)$$

7.2.3.3 Business Ecosystem for Blockchain-Based DApps

Here, we describe the business ecosystem for blockchain-based DApps in Fig. 7.1. In developing blockchain-based DApps, there exists a blockchain developer which is responsible for designing or adopting the blockchain operation protocol. The developer specifies the fixed bonus T, the transaction fee rate r, and so on. Through adjusting the difficulty of finding the new nonce, the blockchain developer keeps the average block time λ at a reasonable constant value. To support the DApps, in the deployed

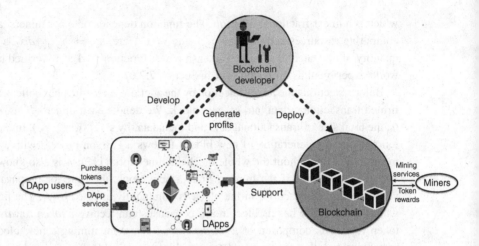

Figure 7.1 Business ecosystem for blockchain-based DApps. Reprinted with permission from the paper "Auction mechanisms in cloud/fog computing resource allocation for public blockchain networks" published in *IEEE Transactions on Parallel and Distributed Systems*.

blockchain network, miners perform mining and token reward, namely, R, is used to incentivize them. The reward may come from the token that DApps users pay to the blockchain network.

When bidding for computing resources, miners always evaluate the value of the tokens. In fact, the intrinsic value of tokens depends on the trustworthiness and robustness, that is, the value of the blockchain network itself. From the perspective of trustworthiness, the PoW-based blockchain is only as secure as the amount of computing power dedicated to mining tasks [261]. This results in positive network effects [261] in that as more miners participate and more computing resources are invested, the security of the blockchain network is improved, and hence the value of a reward given to miners increases. A straightforward example is that if the robustness of the blockchain network is very low, that is, vulnerable to manipulation (51% attack, double-spending attack, etc.), that means this blockchain is insecure and cannot support any decentralized application effectively. Naturally, this blockchain network losses its value and its distributed tokens (including the rewards to miners) would be worthless. On the other hand, if there are many miners and computing resources invested, the blockchain would be more reliable and secure [278]. Thus, users would trust it more and like to use its supported decentralized applications through purchasing the tokens and then miners would also gain more valuation on their received tokens (reward). To confirm this fact, we conduct a real-world experiment (see Section 7.2.6.1) to evaluate the value of the tokens and the reward by examining the impact of the total computing power on preventing double-spending attacks. By curve fitting of the experimental data, we define the network effects by a nonnegative utility function as follows:

$$w(\pi) = a_1 \pi - a_2 \pi e^{a_3 \pi}, \tag{7.17}$$

where $\pi = \frac{d_{\mathcal{N}}}{D} \in [0,1]$ is the normalized total computing power of the blockchain network, $d_{\mathcal{N}} = \sum_{i \in \mathcal{N}} d_i x_i$ is the total quantity of allocated computing resources, and D

is the maximum quantity that CFP can supply. Note that $a_1, a_2, a_3 > 0$ are curve fitting parameters, and this network effect function in the feasible domain is monotonically increasing with a diminishing return.

7.2.3.4 Miner's Valuation on Cloud–Fog Computing Resources

In the auction, a miner's bid represents the valuation of computing resources for which it demands. Since miner i cannot know the number of winning miners and the total quantity of allocated resources until the end of auction, we assume that miner i can only give the bid b_i according to its expected reward R_i and demand d_i without considering network effects and other miners' demands, that is, setting $w(d_\mathcal{N}) = 1$ and $\sum_{j \in \mathcal{N} \setminus \{i\}} d_j x_j = 0$. In other words, miner i has an ex-ante valuation v'_i which can be written as ($P_i^m = \gamma_i = 1$):

$$v'_i = R_i d_i = (T + rs_i)\, e^{-\frac{1}{\lambda}\xi s_i} d_i. \tag{7.18}$$

Here, we assume that R_i represents miner i's valuation for one unit of computing resource and d_i is decided according to miner i's own available budget. Since our proposed auction mechanisms are truthful (to be proved later), b_i is equal to the true ex-ante valuation v'_i, that is, $b_i = v'_i$.

After the auction is completed, miners receive the allocation result, that is, $\mathbf{x}$, and are able to evaluate the network effects. Hereby, miner i has an ex-post valuation v''_i as follows:

$$
\begin{aligned}
v''_i &= v'_i w(\pi) \gamma_i(\mathbf{d}, \mathbf{x}) \\
&= \frac{d_i^2 x_i}{d_\mathcal{N}} \left(a_1 \pi - a_2 \pi e^{a_3 \pi} \right) (T + rs_i)\, e^{-\frac{1}{\lambda}\xi s_i} \\
&= \frac{d_i^2 x_i}{D} \left(a_1 - a_2 e^{a_3 \frac{d_\mathcal{N}}{D}} \right) (T + rs_i)\, e^{-\frac{1}{\lambda}\xi s_i}.
\end{aligned}
\tag{7.19}
$$

7.2.3.5 Social Welfare Maximization

The CFP selects winning miners, that is, winners, and determines corresponding prices in order to maximize the social welfare. Let c denote the unit cost of running the cloud–fog computing service, so the total cost to the CFP can be expressed by $C(d_\mathcal{N}) = cd_\mathcal{N} = \sum_{i \in \mathcal{N}} cd_i x_i$. Thus, we define the social welfare of the blockchain network S as the difference between the sum of all miners' ex-post valuations and the CFP's total cost, namely,

$$
\begin{aligned}
S(\mathbf{x}) &= \sum_{i \in \mathcal{N}} v''_i - C(d_\mathcal{N}) \\
&= \sum_{i \in \mathcal{N}} \frac{d_i^2 x_i}{D} \left(a_1 - a_2 e^{a_3 \frac{d_\mathcal{N}}{D}} \right) (T + rs_i)\, e^{-\frac{1}{\lambda}\xi s_i} \\
&\quad - cd_\mathcal{N}.
\end{aligned}
\tag{7.20}
$$

Therefore, the primary objective of designing the auction mechanism is to solve the following integer programming:

$$\max_{\mathbf{x}} \quad S(\mathbf{x}) = \sum_{i \in \mathcal{N}} \left(\frac{d_i^2 x_i}{D} \left(a_1 - a_2 \mathrm{e}^{\frac{a_3}{D} \sum_{i \in \mathcal{N}} d_i x_i} \right) \right.$$

$$\left. (T + rs_i) \, \mathrm{e}^{-\frac{1}{\lambda} \xi s_i} \right) - \sum_{i \in \mathcal{N}} c d_i x_i, \tag{7.21}$$

$$\text{s.t.} \quad \sum_{i \in \mathcal{N}} d_i x_i \le D, \tag{7.22}$$

$$x_i \in \{0, 1\}, \forall i \in \mathcal{N}, \tag{7.23}$$

where (7.22) is the constraint on the quantity of computing resources that CFP can offer. In the next two sections, we consider two types of bidding scheme in the auction design: the constant-demand bidding scheme and the multi-demand bidding scheme. Accordingly, there are two types of miners: constant-demand miners and multi-demand miners. We aim to maximize the social welfare, while guaranteeing the truthfulness, individual rationality, and computational efficiency.

7.2.3.6   Example Application: Mobile Data Crowdsourcing

As shown in Fig. 7.2, we take an example of mobile data crowdsourcing to illustrate the use of our model and and to demonstrate an effectiveness of the related concepts. Initially, there is a group of mobile users. Each of the mobile users can be either a

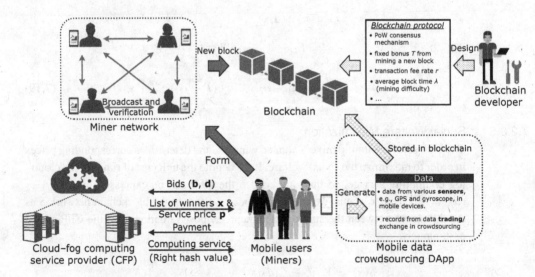

Figure 7.2 An example mobile data crowdsourcing application illustrating the system model and the cloud–fog computing resource market for blockchain networks. Reprinted with permission from the paper "Auction mechanisms in cloud/fog computing resource allocation for public blockchain networks" published in *IEEE Transactions on Parallel and Distributed Systems*.

worker that collects data from the sensors in its mobile device or a requester that wants to buy the sensing data from other users (workers). However, there is often no trusted or authorized crowdsourcing platform to process the data trading and record the transactions. Moreover, no mobile user has enough trust, right, or capability to establish and operate such a centralized platform. In this case, a viable solution is to design and deploy a blockchain-based crowdsourcing DApp by a blockchain developer. Based on the designed protocol, the mobile users can utilize the available cloud–fog computing resources to self-organize a reliable blockchain network. Thus, their data trading activities can be facilitated by the established decentralized crowdsourcing platform with smart contracts.

The blockchain developer adopts the PoW protocol and sets the parameters, such as the fixed reward T, the transaction fee rate r and the average block time λ. Because of limited energy and computational capability, mobile users (miners) need to buy computing resources from the CFP through an auction process and then join the miner network. Before the auction begins, miner i may possess a certain amount of data to be stored in the blockchain and knows its block size s_i. According to equation (7.18), miner i will evaluate its expected reward and the ex-ante value v_i' of the computing resources based on the protocol parameters, its block size, and demand. Next, miner i submits the bid b_i and the demand d_i to the CFP. Using our proposed auction algorithm, the CFP can select the winning miners, that is, the allocation x_i, and determine the price p_i to maximize the social welfare. Meanwhile, it can guarantee the miner's truthfulness and nonnegative utility, which is the difference between the ex-post valuation v_i'' and its payment p_i. Once the auction ends, the winning miners which are allocated the computing resources form a miner network. With the CFP service in solving the PoW puzzle and calculating the hash values, the winning miners can start the mining and consensus process to verify and contribute new blocks containing the crowdsourced data and corresponding transaction records to the blockchain. For more details about the blockchain-based crowdsourcing, please refer to [279].

7.2.4   Auction-Based Mechanism for Constant-Demand Miners

In this section, we first consider a simple case where all miners submit bids for the same quantity of computing resources. Here, each miner's demand is q units, that is, $d_i = q \in (0, D), \forall i \in \mathcal{N}$. Thus, the optimization problem for the CFP can be expressed as follows:

$$\max_{\mathbf{x}} \ S(\mathbf{x}) = \sum_{i \in \mathcal{N}} \left(\frac{q^2 x_i}{D} \left(a_1 - a_2 e^{\frac{a_3}{D} \sum_{i \in \mathcal{N}} q x_i} \right) \right.$$

$$\left. (T + r s_i) e^{-\frac{1}{\lambda} \xi s_i} \right) - \sum_{i \in \mathcal{N}} c q x_i, \tag{7.24}$$

$$\text{s.t.} \ \sum_{i \in \mathcal{N}} q x_i \leq D, \tag{7.25}$$

$$x_i \in \{0, 1\}, \forall i \in \mathcal{N}. \tag{7.26}$$

Algorithm 2 CDB auction.

Require: Miners' bid profile **b** and demand profile **d**.
Ensure: Resource allocation **x** and service price **p**.

1: **for** $i \in \mathcal{N}$ **do**
2:   $x_i \leftarrow 0, p_i \leftarrow 0$;
3: **end for**
4: Sort bids **b** in descending order.;
5: $j \leftarrow \arg\max_{j \in \mathcal{N}} b_j$;
6: $\mathcal{M} \leftarrow \{j\}, S \leftarrow \frac{q}{D} \left(a_1 - a_2 e^{\frac{a_3 q}{D}} \right) b_j - cq$;
7: **while** $\mathcal{M} \neq \mathcal{N}$ **and** $|\mathcal{M}| \leq D$ **do**
8:   $j \leftarrow \arg\max_{j \in \mathcal{N} \setminus \mathcal{M}} b_j$;
9:   $\mathcal{M}_t \leftarrow \mathcal{M} \cup \{j\}$;
10:   $S_t \leftarrow \sum_{i \in \mathcal{M}_t} \frac{q}{D} \left(a_1 - a_2 e^{a_3 q |\mathcal{M}_t|} \right) b_i - cq |\mathcal{M}_t|$;
11:   **if** $S_t < S$ **or** $S_t < 0$ **then**
12:     **break**;
13:   **end if**
14:   $\mathcal{M} \leftarrow \mathcal{M} \cup \{j\}$;
15: **end while**
16: **for** $i \in \mathcal{M}$ **do**
17:   $x_i \leftarrow 1, \mathcal{N}_{-i} \leftarrow \mathcal{N} \setminus \{i\}, \mathcal{M}_{-i} \leftarrow \mathcal{M} \setminus \{i\}$;
18:   $j \leftarrow \arg\max_{j \in \mathcal{N}_{-i}} b_j$;
19:   $\mathcal{M}' \leftarrow \{j\}, S' \leftarrow \frac{q}{D} \left(a_1 - a_2 e^{\frac{a_3 q |\mathcal{M}'|}{D}} \right) b_j - cq$;
20:   **while** $\mathcal{M}' \neq \mathcal{N}$ **and** $|\mathcal{M}'| \leq D$ **do**
21:     $j \leftarrow \arg\max_{i \in \mathcal{N}_{-i} \setminus \mathcal{M}'} b_j$;
22:     $\mathcal{M}'_t \leftarrow \mathcal{M}' \cup \{j\}$;
23:     $S'_t \leftarrow \sum_{i \in \mathcal{M}'_t} \frac{q}{D} \left(a_1 - a_2 e^{\frac{a_3 q |\mathcal{M}'_t|}{D}} \right) b_i - cq |\mathcal{M}'_t|$;
24:     **if** $S'_t < S'$ **or** $S'_t < 0$ **then**
25:       **break**;
26:     **end if**
27:     $\mathcal{M}' \leftarrow \mathcal{M}'_t, S' \leftarrow S'_t$
28:   **end while**
29:   $p_i = S' - \sum_{i \in \mathcal{M}_{-i}} \frac{q}{D} \left(a_1 - a_2 e^{\frac{a_3 q |\mathcal{M}_{-i}|}{D}} \right) b_i - cq |\mathcal{M}_{-i}|$;
30: **end for**

The first proposed truthful auction for Constant-Demand miners in Blockchain networks (CDB auction), as presented in Algorithm 2, is an optimal one and its rationale is based on the well-known Myerson's characterization [280] provided in Theorem 13.

Theorem 13 ([276, Theorem 13.6]) *An auction mechanism is truthful if and only if it satisfies the following two properties.*

1. *Monotonicity: If miner i wins the auction with bid b_i, then it will also win with any higher bid $b_i' > b_i$.*
2. *Critical payment: The payment by a winner is the smallest value needed in order to win the auction.*

As illustrated in Algorithm 2, the CDB auction consists of two consecutive processes: winner selection (lines 5–16) and service price calculation (lines 17–31). The winner selection process is implemented with a greedy method. For the convenience of later discussion, we define a set of winners as $\mathcal{M}$. Adding a miner i in $\mathcal{M}$ means setting $x_i = 1$. Thus, we transform the original problem in equations (7.24)–(7.26) to an equivalent set function form as follows:

$$\max_{\mathcal{M} \subseteq \mathcal{N}} S(\mathcal{M}) = \sum_{i \in \mathcal{M}} \left(a_1 - a_2 e^{\frac{a_3 q |\mathcal{M}|}{D}} \right) \frac{q b_i}{D} - cq |\mathcal{M}|, \quad (7.27)$$

$$\text{s.t. } q|\mathcal{M}| \leq D, \quad (7.28)$$

where $|\mathcal{M}|$ represents the cardinality of set $\mathcal{M}$ which is the number of winners in $\mathcal{M}$ and $b_i = v_i' = (T + rs_i) e^{-\frac{1}{\lambda} \xi s_i} q$. In the winner selection process (lines 5–11), miners are first sorted in descending order according to their bids. Then, they are sequentially added to the set of winners $\mathcal{M}$ until the social welfare $S(\mathcal{M})$ begins to decrease. Finally, the set of winners $\mathcal{M}$ and the allocation $\mathbf{x}$ are output by the algorithm.

Proposition 1 *The resource allocation $\mathbf{x}$ output by Algorithm 2 is globally optimal to the social welfare maximization problem given in equations (7.24)–(7.26).*

Proof With the proof by contradiction, this result is found from the following Claim. □

Claim Let $\mathcal{M}_A$ be the solution output by Algorithm 2 on input $\mathbf{b}$, and let $\mathcal{M}_O$ be the optimal solution. If $\mathcal{M}_A \neq \mathcal{M}_O$, then we can construct another solution $\mathcal{M}_O^*$ whose social welfare $S(\mathcal{M}_O^*)$ is even larger than the optimal social welfare $S(\mathcal{M}_O)$.

Proof We assume $b_1 \geq \cdots \geq b_N$ and $\mathcal{M}_A \neq \mathcal{M}_O$. Next, we consider two cases.

(1) Case 1: $\mathcal{M}_O \subset \mathcal{M}_A$. According to Algorithm 2, it is obvious that we can construct a solution $\mathcal{M}_O^*$ with higher social welfare by adding a member from $\mathcal{M}_A$ to $\mathcal{M}_O$.

(2) Case 2: $\mathcal{M}_O \not\subset \mathcal{M}_A$. Let m be the first element (while-loop lines 7–14) that $m \notin \mathcal{M}_O$. Since m is maximal (b_m is minimal by assumption), we have $1, \ldots, m - 1 \in \mathcal{M}_O$ and the corresponding set of winning bids $\mathbf{b}_{\mathcal{M}_O} = \{b_1, \ldots, b_{m-1}, b_m', b_{m+1}', \ldots, b_{|\mathcal{M}_O|}'\}$, where the bids $\{b_1, \ldots, b_{|\mathcal{M}_O|}'\}$ are listed in the descending order. Meanwhile, Algorithm 2 chooses

$$\mathbf{b}_{\mathcal{W}_A} = \{b_1, \ldots, b_{m-1}, b_m, b_{m+1}, \ldots, b_{|\mathcal{M}_A|}\},$$

and there must be $b_m > b_j'$ for all $j \geq m$. In particular, we have $b_m > b_m'$. Hence, we define $\mathbf{b}_{\mathcal{M}_O^*} = \mathbf{b}_{\mathcal{M}_O} \cup \{b_m\} \setminus \{b_m'\}$, that is, we obtain $\mathbf{b}_{\mathcal{M}_O^*}$ by removing b_m' and adding b_m to $\mathbf{b}_{\mathcal{M}_O}$. Thus, the social welfare of $\mathbf{b}_{\mathcal{W}_O^*}$ is calculated as follows:

$$S(\mathcal{M}_O^*) = S(\mathcal{M}_O) + \frac{q}{D} \left(a_1 - a_2 e^{\frac{a_3 q |\mathcal{M}|}{D}} \right) (b_m - b_m').$$

As $b_m - b'_m > 0$, $(a_1 - a_2 e^{\frac{a_3 q |\mathcal{M}|}{D}})\frac{q}{D} > 0$, and $|\mathcal{M}_O^*| = |\mathcal{M}_O|$, $S(\mathcal{M}_O^*)$ is strictly larger than $S(\mathcal{M}_O)$. This is in contradiction to that $\mathcal{M}_O$ is the optimal solution and thus proves the claim. $\qquad\square$

We apply the VCG mechanism [234] in the service price calculation. In lines 16–30, for each iteration, we exclude one selected miner from the set of winners and reexecute the winner selection process to calculate the social cost of the miner as its payment. The VCG-based payment function is defined as follows:

$$p_i = S(\mathcal{M}_{\mathcal{N}\setminus\{i\}}) - S(\mathcal{M}_\mathcal{N} \setminus \{i\}), \qquad (7.29)$$

where $S(\mathcal{M}_{\mathcal{N}\setminus\{i\}})$ is the optimal social welfare obtained when the selected miner i is excluded from the miner set $\mathcal{N}$, and $S(\mathcal{M}_\mathcal{N} \setminus \{i\})$ is the social welfare of the set of winners which is obtained by removing miner i from the optimal winner set selected from $\mathcal{N}$.

Proposition 2 *The CDB auction (Algorithm 2) is truthful.*

Proof Since the payment calculation in the algorithm relies on the VCG mechanism, it directly satisfies the second condition in Theorem 13 [276]. For the first condition about monotonicity in Theorem 13, we need to show that if a winning miner i raises its bid from b_i to b_i^+, where $b_i^+ > b_i$, it still stays in the winner set. We denote the original winner set by $\mathcal{M}$ and the new winner set by $\mathcal{M}_+$ after miner i changes its bid to b_i^+. The original set of bids is $\mathbf{b} = \{b_1, \ldots, b_i, \ldots, b_N\}$ ($i \leq |\mathcal{M}|$) sorted in descending order. In addition, we define $S(\mathbf{b}_\mathcal{K}) = S(\mathcal{K}), \forall \mathcal{K} \subseteq \mathcal{N}$, which means the social welfare of a set of bids is equal to that of the set of corresponding miners. We discuss the monotonicity in two cases.

(1) Case 1: $b_{i-1} \geq b_i^+ \geq b_i \geq b_{i+1}$. The new set of ordered bids is $\mathbf{b}^+ = \{b_1, \ldots, b_{i-1}, b_i^+, b_{i+1}, \ldots, b_N\}$. We have

$$S(\{b_1, \ldots, b_i^+\}) = \frac{q}{D}\left(a_1 - a_2 e^{\frac{a_3 q i}{D}}\right)\left(\sum_{j=1}^{i-1} b_j + b_i^+\right) - cqi$$

$$> S(\{b_1, \ldots, b_i\}) = \frac{q}{D}\left(a_1 - a_2 e^{\frac{a_3 q i}{D}}\right)\sum_{j=1}^{i} b_j - cqi. \qquad (7.30)$$

The social welfare of the new set of bids $\{b_1, \ldots, b_i^+\}$ is larger than that of the original set of bids $\{b_1, \ldots, b_i\}$, which guarantees b_i^+ being in the set of winning bids.

(2) Case 2: $b_{k-1} \geq b_i^+ \geq b_k \geq \cdots \geq b_i$, $1 < k < i$. The new set of ordered bids is $\mathbf{b}^+ = \{b_1, \ldots, b_{k-1}, b_i^+, b_k, \ldots, b_{i+1}, \ldots, b_N\}$. We have

$$S(\{b_1, \ldots, b_{k-1}, b_i^+\}) = \frac{q}{D}\left(a_1 - a_2 e^{\frac{a_3 q k}{D}}\right)\left(\sum_{j=1}^{k-1} b_j + b_i^+\right) - cqk, \qquad (7.31)$$

$$S(\{b_1, \ldots, b_{k-1}, b_k\}) = \frac{q}{D}\left(a_1 - a_2 e^{\frac{a_3 q k}{D}}\right)\sum_{j=1}^{k} b_j - cqk, \qquad (7.32)$$

$$S(\{b_1,\ldots,b_{k-1}\}) = \frac{q}{D}\left(a_1 - a_2 e^{\frac{a_3 q(k-1)}{D}}\right)\sum_{j=1}^{k-1} b_j - cq(k-1). \tag{7.33}$$

As the coefficient $\frac{q}{D}\left(a_1 - a_2 e^{\frac{a_3 q|\mathcal{M}|}{D}}\right)$ in $S(\mathcal{M})$ is a monotonically decreasing function of $\mathcal{M}$, increasing b_i may change the set of winners $\mathcal{M}$ and reduce the number of winning miners. However, the first i bids $\{b_1,\ldots,b_{k-1},b_k,\ldots,b_i\}$ in the original set of bids **b** have already won the auction, so we have $S(\{b_1,\ldots,b_{k-1},b_k\}) > S(\{b_1,\ldots,b_{k-1}\})$. From the following equation (7.34),

$$S(\{b_1,\ldots,b_{k-1},b_k\}) = \frac{q}{D}\left(a_1 - a_2 e^{\frac{a_3 qk}{D}}\right)\left(\sum_{j=1}^{k-1} b_j + b_k\right)$$

$$< \frac{q}{D}\left(a_1 - a_2 e^{\frac{a_3 qk}{D}}\right)\left(\sum_{j=1}^{k-1} b_j + b_i^+\right) = S\left(\{b_1,\ldots,b_{k-1},b_i^+\}\right) \tag{7.34}$$

the proof can be finally concluded by

$$S(\{b_1,\ldots,b_{k-1},b_i^+\}) > S(\{b_1,\ldots,b_{k-1}\}), \tag{7.35}$$

which implies that b_i^+ still remains the bid of a winner in the auction. □

Proposition 3 *The CDB auction (Algorithm 2) is computationally efficient and individually rational.*

Proof Sorting the bids has the complexity of $O(N \log N)$. Since the number of winners is at most $\min(\frac{D}{q}, N)$, the time complexity of the winner selection process (while-loop, lines 7–15) is $O(\min^2(\frac{D}{q}, N))$. In each iteration of the payment calculation process (lines 16–30), a similar winner selection process is executed. Therefore, the whole auction process can be performed in polynomial time with the time complexity of $O(\min^3(\frac{D}{q}, N) + N \log N)$.

According to Proposition 1 and the properties of the VCG mechanism [234], the payment scheme in Algorithm 2 guarantees the individual rationality. □

7.2.5 Auction-Based Mechanisms for Multi-demand Miners

In this section, we investigate a more general scenario where miners request multiple demands of cloud–fog computing resources.

7.2.5.1 Social Welfare Maximization for the Blockchain Network

We first investigate the winner selection problem defined in equations (7.21)–(7.23) from the perspective of an optimization problem. Evidently, it is a nonlinear integer programming problem with linear constraints, which is NP-hard to obtain the optimal solution. Naturally, we can find an approximate method with a lower bound guarantee. Similar to Section 7.2.4, the original problem is rewritten as a subset function form:

$$\max_{\mathcal{M} \subseteq \mathcal{N}} S(\mathcal{M}) = \sum_{i \in \mathcal{M}} \frac{d_i}{D} \left(a_1 - a_2 e^{\frac{a_3 \sum_{i \in \mathcal{M}} d_i}{D}} \right) b_i$$

$$-c \sum_{i \in \mathcal{M}} d_i, \tag{7.36}$$

$$\text{s.t.} \sum_{i \in \mathcal{M}} d_i \leq D, \tag{7.37}$$

where $S(\mathcal{M})$ is the social welfare function of the selected set of winners $\mathcal{M}$ and $b_i = v_i' = (T + rs_i) e^{-\frac{1}{\lambda} \xi s_i} d_i$. This form means that we can view it as a subset sum problem [281]. We assume that there is at least one miner i such that $S(\{i\}) > 0$. Additionally, although the miners can submit demands that they want instead of the same constant quantity of computing resources, it is reasonable to assume that the CFP puts a restriction on the purchase quantity, namely, $\beta_1 D < d_i \leq \beta_2 D$, where $\beta_1 D, \beta_2 D$ are respectively the lower and upper limit on each miner's demand, and $0 < \beta_1 < \beta_2 < 1$ are predetermined demand constraint ratios. Clearly, $S(\emptyset) = 0$.

Definition 25 (Submodular Function [282]) Let $\mathcal{X}$ be a finite set. A function $f : 2^{\mathcal{X}} \to \mathbb{R}$ is submodular if

$$f(\mathcal{A} \cup \{x\}) - f(\mathcal{A}) \geq f(\mathcal{B} \cup \{x\}) - f(\mathcal{B}), \tag{7.38}$$

for any $\mathcal{A} \subseteq \mathcal{B} \subseteq \mathcal{X}$ and $x \in \mathcal{X} \setminus \mathcal{B}$, where $\mathbb{R}$ is the set of reals. A useful equivalent definition is that f is submodular if and only if the derived set-function

$$f_x(\mathcal{A}) = f(\mathcal{A} \cup \{x\}) - f(\mathcal{A}) \qquad (\mathcal{A} \subseteq \mathcal{X} \setminus \{x\}) \tag{7.39}$$

is monotonically decreasing for all $x \in \mathcal{X}$.

Proposition 4 *The social welfare function $S(\mathcal{M})$ in equation (7.36) is submodular.*

Proof By Definition 25, we need to show that $S_u(\mathcal{M})$ in equation (7.43) is monotonically decreasing, for every $\mathcal{M} \subseteq \mathcal{N}$ and $u \in \mathcal{N} \setminus \mathcal{M}$. Let $g(z) = a_1 - a_2 e^{\frac{a_3}{D} z}$, where $z \in \mathbb{R}^+$.

$$S_u(\mathcal{M}) = S(\mathcal{M} \cup \{u\}) - S(\mathcal{M}) \tag{7.40}$$

$$= \sum_{i \in \mathcal{M} \cup \{u\}} \frac{d_i}{D} \left(a_1 - a_2 e^{\frac{a_3 \sum_{i \in \mathcal{M} \cup \{u\}} d_i}{D}} \right) b_i$$

$$- \sum_{i \in \mathcal{M}} \frac{d_i}{D} \left(a_1 - a_2 e^{\frac{a_3 \sum_{i \in \mathcal{M}} d_i}{D}} \right) b_i - c d_u \tag{7.41}$$

$$= \underbrace{\left(\left(a_1 - a_2 e^{\frac{a_3 \sum_{i \in \mathcal{M} \cup \{u\}} d_i}{D}} \right) - \left(a_1 - a_2 e^{\frac{a_3 \sum_{i \in \mathcal{M}} d_i}{D}} \right) \right) \sum_{i \in \mathcal{M}} \frac{d_i b_i}{D}}_{①} \tag{7.42}$$

$$+ \underbrace{\left(a_1 - a_2 e^{\frac{a_3 \sum_{i \in \mathcal{M} \cup \{u\}} d_i}{D}} \right) \frac{d_u b_u}{D} - c d_u}_{②}. \tag{7.43}$$

Then, the first derivative and second derivative of $g(z)$ are expressed respectively as follows:

$$\frac{dg(z)}{dz} = -\frac{a_2 a_3}{D} e^{\frac{a_3}{D} z}, \quad \frac{d^2 g(z)}{dz^2} = -\frac{a_2 a_3^2}{D^2} e^{\frac{a_3}{D} z}. \tag{7.44}$$

Because $a_2, a_3, D > 0$, we have $-\frac{a_2 a_3}{D} e^{\frac{a_3}{D} z} < 0$ and $-\frac{a_2 a_3^2}{D^2} e^{\frac{a_3}{D} z} < 0$, which indicates that $g(z)$ is monotonically decreasing and concave.

Next, we discuss the monotonicity of $S_u(\mathcal{M})$ in equation (7.43). Note that expanding $\mathcal{M}$ means increasing the total quantity of allocated resources $d_{\mathcal{M}} = \sum_{i \in \mathcal{M}} d_i$. Substituting $z = d_{\mathcal{M}}$ and $z = d_{\mathcal{M} \cup \{u\}}$ into $g(z)$, we observe that

$$g(d_{\mathcal{M} \cup \{u\}}) - g(d_{\mathcal{M}}) = \left(a_1 - a_2 e^{\frac{a_3}{D} \sum_{i \in \mathcal{M} \cup \{u\}} d_i} \right) - \left(a_1 - a_2 e^{\frac{a_3}{D} \sum_{i \in \mathcal{M}} d_i} \right) < 0$$

is decreasing and negative due to $d_{\mathcal{M}} < d_{\mathcal{M} \cup \{u\}}$ and the monotonicity and concavity of $g(z)$. Additionally, it is clear that when $\mathcal{M}$ expands, $\sum_{i \in \mathcal{M}} d_i b_i > 0$ is positive and increasing. Therefore, ① in equation (7.42) is proved to be monotonically decreasing. Because $g(z)$ is monotonically decreasing, it is straightforward to see that ② in equation (7.43) is also monotonically decreasing with the expansion of $\mathcal{M}$. Finally, we can conclude that $S_u(\mathcal{M})$ is monotonically decreasing, thus proving the submodularity of $S(\mathcal{M})$. □

It is worth noting that there is a constraint in equation (7.22), also called a knapsack constraint. This constraint not only affects the resulting social welfare and the number of the selected miners in the auction, but also needs a careful auction mechanism design to guarantee the truthfulness. Essentially, the optimization problem appears to be a *nonmonotone submodular maximization with knapsack constraints*. It is known that there is a $(0.2 - \eta)$-approximate algorithm which applies the fractional relaxation and local search (FRLS) method [283, Figure 5]. Note that $\eta > 0$ is a preset constant parameter that specifies the approximation ratio $(0.2 - \eta)$. For the ease of expression, we name this approximate algorithm the FRLS algorithm. In general, the FRLS algorithm first solves a linear relaxation of the original integer problem using local search, and then it rounds the obtained fractional solution to an integer value. However, the algorithm requires the objective function to be nonnegative. To address this issue, let $H(\mathcal{M}) = S(\mathcal{M}) + c \sum_{i \in \mathcal{N}} d_i$. Clearly, $H(\mathcal{M}) \geq 0$ for any $\mathcal{M} \subseteq \mathcal{N}$ and it remains submodular since $c \sum_{i \in \mathcal{N}} d_i$ is a constant. Additionally, maximizing $S(\mathcal{M})$ is equivalent to maximizing $H(\mathcal{M})$. Hence, we attempt to design the FRLS auction which selects the winner based on the FRLS algorithm and let the service price $p_i = b_i$. As to the specific input to the FRLS algorithm, it takes 1 as the number of knapsack constraints, the normalized demand profile $\frac{d}{D}$ as its knapsack weights parameter, η as the approximate degree, and $H(\mathcal{M})$ as the value oracle which allows querying for function values of any given set. The FRLS auction is computationally efficient, as the running time of the FRLS algorithm is polynomial [283]. Furthermore, miners just need to pay their submitted bids to the CFP and cannot suffer deficit, so the FRLS auction also satisfies the individual rationality requirement. However, we find that an FRLS auction cannot guarantee truthfulness. The corresponding proof is omitted due to space constraints.

7.2.5.2   Multi-demand Miners in Blockchain Networks (MDB) Auction

Although the FRLS auction is capable of solving the social welfare maximization problem approximately, it is not realistic to be directly applied in a real market since it cannot prevent the manipulation of bids by bidders, namely, lacking of truthfulness. As mentioned before, we aim to design an auction mechanism that not only achieves a good social welfare, but also possesses the desired properties, including computational efficiency, individual rationality and truthfulness. Therefore, we present a novel auction mechanism for Multi-Demand miners in Blockchain networks (MDB auction). In this auction, the bidders are limited to be single-minded in the combinatorial auctions. That is, we can assume safely that the mechanism always allocates to the winner i exactly the d_i items that it requested and never allocates anything to a losing bidder. The design rationale of the MDB auction relies on Theorem 14.

Theorem 14   ([284]) *In the multi-unit and single minded setting, an auction mechanism is truthful if it satisfies the following two properties.*

1. *Monotonicity: If a bidder i wins with bid (d_i, b_i), then it will also win with any bid which offers at least as much price for at most as many items. That is, bidder i will still win if the other bidders do not change their bids and bidder i changes its bid to some (d'_i, b'_i) with $d'_i \leq d_i$ and $b'_i \geq b_i$.*
2. *Critical payment: The payment of a winning bid (d_i, b_i) by bidder i is the smallest value needed in order to win d_i items, that is, the infimum of b'_i such that (d_i, b'_i) is still a winning bid, when the other bidders do not change their bids.*

Auction Design

Before presenting the MDB auction, we first introduce the *marginal social welfare density*. It is the density of miner i's marginal social welfare contribution to the existing set of winners $\mathcal{M}$, which is defined as follows:

$$S'_i(\mathcal{M}) = \frac{S_i(\mathcal{M})}{d_i} = \frac{S(\mathcal{M} \cup \{i\}) - S(\mathcal{M})}{d_i}$$

$$= \underbrace{\frac{\left(a_2 e^{\frac{a_3 \sum_{j \in \mathcal{M}} d_j}{D}} - a_2 e^{\frac{a_3 \sum_{j \in \mathcal{M} \cup \{i\}} d_j}{D}} \right) \sum_{j \in \mathcal{M}} d_j b_j}{D d_i}}_{\textcircled{1}}$$

$$+ \underbrace{\left(a_1 - a_2 e^{\frac{a_3 \sum_{j \in \mathcal{M} \cup \{i\}} d_j}{D}} \right) \frac{b_i}{D}}_{\textcircled{2}} - c. \tag{7.45}$$

For the sake of brevity, we simply call it *density*.

As illustrated in Algorithm 3, the MDB auction allocates computing resources to miners in a greedy way. According to the density, all miners are sorted in a nonincreasing order:

$$S'_1(\mathcal{M}_0) \geq S'_2(\mathcal{M}_1) \geq \cdots \geq S'_i(\mathcal{M}_{i-1}) \geq \cdots \geq S'_N(\mathcal{M}_{N-1}). \qquad (7.46)$$

The ith miner has the maximum density $S'_i(\mathcal{M}_{i-1})$ over $\mathcal{N} \setminus \mathcal{M}_{i-1}$, where $\mathcal{M}_{i-1} = \{1, 2, \ldots, i-1\}$ and $\mathcal{M}_0 = \emptyset$. From the sorting, the MDB auction finds the set of winners $\mathcal{M}_{L_m}$ containing L_m winners, such that $d_{\mathcal{M}_{L_m}} \leq D$, $S'_{L_m}(\mathcal{M}_{L_m-1}) \geq 0$ and $S'_{L_m+1}(\mathcal{M}_{L_m}) < 0$ (lines 6–13).

To determine the service price for each winner $i \in \mathcal{M}_{L_m}$ (lines 14–36), the MDB auction reexecutes the winner selection process and similarly sorts other winners in $\mathcal{N}_{-i} = \mathcal{N} \setminus \{i\}$ as follows:

$$S'_{i_1}(\mathcal{T}_0) \geq S'_{i_2}(\mathcal{T}_1) \geq \cdots \geq S'_{i_k}(\mathcal{T}_{k-1}) \geq \cdots \geq S'_{i_{N-1}}(\mathcal{T}_{N-2}), \qquad (7.47)$$

where $\mathcal{T}_{k-1}$ denotes the first $k-1$ winners in the sorting and $\mathcal{T}_0 = \emptyset$. From the sorting, we select the first L_p winners where the L_pth winner is the last one that satisfies $S'_{i_{L_p}}(\mathcal{T}_{L_p-1}) \geq 0$ and $d_{\mathcal{T}_{L_p-1}} \leq D - d_i$. Let $\tilde{S}$ denote the $(L_p + 1)$th winner's virtual density. If the $(L_p + 1)$th winner has a negative density on $\mathcal{T}_{L_p}$, that is, $S'_{i_{L_p+1}}(\mathcal{T}_{L_p}) < 0$, or its demand is larger than that of winner i, namely, $d_{L_p+1} > d_i$, we set $\tilde{S} = 0$. Otherwise, $\tilde{S} = S'_{i_{L_p+1}}(\mathcal{T}_{L_p})$. Meanwhile, Algorithm 3 forms a price list $\mathbf{L} = \{S'_{i_1}(\mathcal{T}_0), \ldots, S'_{i_{L_p}}(\mathcal{T}_{L_p-1}), \tilde{S}\}$ containing $(L_p + 1)$ density values. According to the list, we find the winner i's minimum bid b'_i such that $S'_i(\mathcal{T}_{k-1}) \geq S'_{i_k}(\mathcal{T}_{k-1}), \exists k \in \{0, 1, \ldots, L_p\}$ or $S'_i(\mathcal{T}_{L_p}) \geq \tilde{S}$. Here, b'_i is called miner i's ex-ante price, which is the payment without considering the allocative externalities. Then, we set $p_i = \left(a_1 - a_2 e^{\frac{a_3 \sum_{j \in \mathcal{M}_{L_m}} d_j}{D}} \right) \frac{b'_i}{D}$ as the winner i's final payment.

Properties of MDB Auction

We show the computational efficiency (Proposition 5), the individual rationality (Proposition 6), and the truthfulness (Proposition 7) of the MDB auction in the following.

Proposition 5 *MDB auction is computationally efficient.*

Proof In Algorithm 3, finding the winner with the maximum density has the time complexity of $O(N)$ (line 7). Since the number of winners is at most N, the winner selection process (the while-loop lines 6–13) has the time complexity of $O(N^2)$. In the service price determination process (lines 14–36), each for-loop executes similar steps as the while-loop in lines 6–13. Hence, lines 14–36 have the time complexity of $O(N^3)$ in general. Hence, the running time of Algorithm 3 is dominated by the for-loop, which is bounded by polynomial time $O(N^3)$. $\qquad \square$

Proposition 6 *MDB auction is individually rational.*

Proof Let i_i be the miner i's replacement which appears in the ith place in the sorting (7.47) over $\mathcal{N}_{-i}$. Since miner i_i would not be in the ith place if winner i is considered, we have $S'_{i_i}(\mathcal{T}_{i-1}) \leq S'_i(\mathcal{T}_{i-1})$. Note that Algorithm 3 chooses the minimum bid b'_i for miner i, which means that given the bid b'_i, miner i's new density $S''_i(\mathcal{T}_{i-1})$

Algorithm 3 MDB auction.

Require: Miners' demand profile $\mathbf{d}$ and bid profile $\mathbf{b}$;
Ensure: Resource allocation $\mathbf{x}$ and service price profile $\mathbf{p}$;
1: **for** $i \in \mathcal{N}$ **do**
2:     $x_i \leftarrow 0, p_i \leftarrow 0$;
3: **end for**
4: $\mathcal{M} \leftarrow \varnothing, d \leftarrow 0$;
5: **while** $\mathcal{M} \neq \mathcal{N}$ **do**
6:     $j \leftarrow \arg\max_{i \in \mathcal{N} \setminus \mathcal{M}} S_i'(\mathcal{M})$;
7:     **if** $d + d_j > D$ **or** $S_j'(\mathcal{M}) < 0$ **then**
8:         **break**;
9:     **end if**
10:     $\mathcal{M} \leftarrow \mathcal{M} \cup \{j\}$;
11:     $d \leftarrow d + d_j$;
12: **end while**
13: **for** $i \in \mathcal{M}$ **do**
14:     $x_i \leftarrow 1, \mathcal{N}_{-i} \leftarrow \mathcal{N} \setminus \{i\}$;
15:     $\mathcal{T}_0 \leftarrow \varnothing, d' \leftarrow 0, k \leftarrow 0, L_p \leftarrow 0$;
16:     **while** $\mathcal{T}_k \neq \mathcal{N}_{-i}$ **do**
17:         $i_{k+1} \leftarrow \arg\max_{l \in \mathcal{N}_{-i} \setminus \mathcal{T}_k} S_l'(\mathcal{T}_k)$;
18:         $b_{i_{k+1}}' \leftarrow \arg_{b_i \in \mathbb{R}^+} S_i'(\mathcal{T}_k) = S_{i_{k+1}}'(\mathcal{T}_k)$;
19:         **if** $d' + d_{i_{k+1}} > D$ **or** $S_{i_{k+1}}'(\mathcal{T}_k) < 0$ **then**
20:             **break**;
21:         **else if** $d' + d_{i_{k+1}} \leq D - d_i$ **then**
22:             $L_p \leftarrow L_p + 1$;
23:         **end if**
24:         $\mathcal{T}_{k+1} \leftarrow \mathcal{T}_k \cup \{i_{k+1}\}, d' \leftarrow d' + d_{i_{k+1}}$;
25:         $k \leftarrow k + 1$;
26:     **end while**
27:     **if** $S_{i_{L_p+1}}'(\mathcal{T}_{L_p}) < 0$ **or** $d_{i_{L_p+1}} > d_i$ **then**
28:         $\widetilde{S} \leftarrow 0$;
29:     **else**
30:         $\widetilde{S} \leftarrow S_{i_{L_p+1}}'(\mathcal{T}_{L_p})$;
31:     **end if**
32:     $b_{i_{L_p+1}}' \leftarrow \arg_{b_i \in \mathbb{R}^+} S_i'(\mathcal{T}_{L_p}) = \widetilde{S}$;
33:     $b_i' \leftarrow \min_{k \in \{0, 1, ..., L_p+1\}} b_{i_k}'$;
34:     $p_i \leftarrow (a_1 - a_2 e^{\frac{a_3 \sum_{j \in \mathcal{M}} d_j}{D}}) \frac{b_i'}{D}$;
35: **end for**

---

at least satisfies $S_i''(\mathcal{T}_{i-1}) \leq S_{i_i}'(\mathcal{T}_{i-1}) \leq S_i'(\mathcal{T}_{i-1})$. According to the definition of the density in equation (7.45), $S_i'(\mathcal{T}_{i-1})$ is a monotonically increasing function of b_i. Hence, we have $b_i - b_i' \geq 0$ as $S_i'(\mathcal{T}_{i-1}) \geq S_i''(\mathcal{T}_{i-1})$. Therefore, the final payment for miner

i is not more than its ex-post valuation, that is, $p_i = \left(a_1 - a_2 e^{\frac{a_3 \sum_{j \in \mathcal{M}_{Lm}} d_j}{D}}\right) \frac{b_i'}{D} \le$

$v_i'' = \left(a_1 - a_2 e^{\frac{a_3 \sum_{j \in \mathcal{M}_{Lm}} d_j}{D}}\right) \frac{b_i'}{D}$. Thus, the individual rationality of MDB auction is ensured. □

Proposition 7 *MDB auction is truthful.*

Proof Based on Theorem 14, it suffices to prove that the selection rule of the MDB auction is monotone, and the ex-ante payment b_i' is the critical value for winner i to win the auction.

We first discuss the monotonicity of the MDB auction in terms of winner i's bid and subsequent demand. Recalling the density $S_i'(\mathcal{M})$ in equation (7.45), it is clear that $S_i'(\mathcal{M})$ is a monotonically increasing function of miner i's bid b_i. As miner i takes the ith place in the sorting (7.46), when winner i raises its bid from b_i to b_i^+, it at least has a new larger density $S_{i+}'(\mathcal{T}_{i-1}) > S_i'(\mathcal{T}_{i-1}) \ge 0$. Because of the submodularity of $S(\mathcal{M})$, miner i can only have a larger density when it is ranked higher in the sorting, that is, $S_{i+}'(\mathcal{M}_{i-k}) > S_{i+}'(\mathcal{M}_{i-1}) \ge 0, \forall k \in \{2, 3, \ldots, i\}$. Therefore, miner i with a higher bid can always win the auction. Similarly, when it comes to miner i's demand d_i, we only need to show that $S_i'(\mathcal{M})$ is a monotonically decreasing function of d_i. Let

$$h(z) = \frac{a_4 \left(1 - e^{\frac{a_3}{D} z}\right)}{z}, \tag{7.48}$$

where $z \in \mathbb{R}^+$ and all parameters are positive. The first derivative of $h(z)$ is

$$\frac{dh(z)}{dz} = -\frac{a_4 (\frac{a_3}{D} e^{\frac{a_3}{D} z} z + 1 - e^{\frac{a_3}{D} z})}{z^2}. \tag{7.49}$$

Since the first derivative of $(\frac{a_3}{D} e^{\frac{a_3}{D} z} z + 1 - e^{\frac{a_3}{D} z})$ is $\frac{a_3^2}{D^2} e^{\frac{a_3}{D} z} z > 0$, we can have $\frac{dh(z)}{dz} < 0$ with $a_3, a_4, D, z > 0$. Thus, $h(z)$ is monotonically decreasing with z. By substituting $z = d_i$, we can easily observe that ① in equation (7.45) is a monotonically decreasing function with respect to d_i. Finally, $S_i'(\mathcal{M})$ is proved to be monotonically decreasing with d_i since ② in equation (7.45) is clearly a monotonically decreasing function of d_i as well.

Next, we prove that b_i' is the critical ex-ante payment. This means that bidding lower $b_i^- < b_i'$ can lead to miner i's failure in the auction. Given that d_i is fixed, we note that b_i' is the minimum bid such that miner i's new density $S_i''(\mathcal{T}_k)$ is no more than any value in the kth place in the sorting (7.47), where $k \in \{0, 1, \ldots, L_p - 1\}$. If miner i submits a lower bid b_i^-, it must be ranked after the L_pth winner in (7.47) due to submodularity of $S(\mathcal{M})$. Then, its density has to be compared with $\tilde{S}$. Considering the $(L_p + 1)$th winner in the sorting (7.47), if its density $S_{i_{L_p+1}}'(\mathcal{T}_{L_p}) \ge 0$ and $d_{i_{L_p+1}} \le d_i$, $\tilde{S}$ is set to be $S_{i_{L_p+1}}'(\mathcal{T}_{L_p})$. In this case, miner i with bid b_i^- cannot take the $(L_p + 1)$th place as its new density is $S_i''(\mathcal{T}_{L_p}) < S_i'(\mathcal{T}_{L_p}) \le \tilde{S} = S_{i_{L_p+1}}'(\mathcal{T}_{L_p})$. Also, it can no longer win the auction by taking the place after the $(L_p + 1)$th because the remaining supply $D - d_{\mathcal{T}_{L_p+1}}$ cannot meet its demand d_i, that is, $D - d_{\mathcal{T}_{L_p+1}} < d_i$. If $S'_{i_{L_p+1}}(\mathcal{T}_{L_p}) < 0$ or $d_{i_{L_p+1}} > d_i$, $\tilde{S}$ is just set to be 0. Apparently, b_i^- is not a winning bid as $S''_i(\mathcal{T}_{L_p}) < b_i' = \tilde{S} = 0$.   □

7.2.6   Experimental Results and Performance Evaluation

In this section, we first perform experiments to verify the proposed hash power function and network effects function. Then, from simulation results, we examine the performance of the proposed auction mechanisms in social welfare maximization and provide useful decision-making strategies for the CFP and the blockchain developer.

7.2.6.1   Verification for Hash Power Function and Network Effects Function

Similar to the experiments on mobile blockchain mining in [258, 285], we design a mobile blockchain client application in the Android platform and implement it on each of three mobile devices (miners). The client application can not only record the data generated by internal sensors or the transactions of the mobile P2P data trading, but also allows each mobile device to be connected to a computing server through a network hub. The miners request the computing service from the server. Then, the server allocates the computing resources and starts mining the block for the miners. At the server side, each miner's CPU utilization rate is managed and measured by the Docker platform.[6] In our experiment, all mining tasks (solving the PoW puzzle) are under the Go-Ethereum[7] blockchain framework.

To verify the hash power function in equation (7.13), we vary the service demand of one miner i in terms of CPU utilization, namely, d_i, while fixing the other two miners' service demand at 40 and 60. Here, the total amount of computing resources is $d_{\mathcal{N}} = d_i + 40 + 60$. Besides, we initially broadcast 10 of the same transaction records to the miners in the network so that all mined blocks have the same size. Figure 7.3a shows the change of the hash power, that is, the probability of successfully mining a block with different amount of computing resources. We note that the hash power function defined in equation (7.13) can fit the real experimental results well.

To verify the network effects function in equation (7.17), we investigate the capability of the blockchain to prevent double-spending attacks. We add a malicious miner with fixed computing powers, that is, an attacker performing double-spending attacks, to the blockchain network. Then, we conduct several tests by varying the CPU resources of the other miners, that is, the sum of existing honest miners' computing resources $d_{\mathcal{N}}$, to measure the probability of the successful attacks. Specifically we count the number of fake blocks which successfully join the chain every 10,000 blocks generated in each test. Based on the above results, we finally calculate the proportion of the genuine blocks every 10,000 blocks (that is, each data point in Fig. 7.3b) as the security measure or the network effects of the blockchain network. As illustrated in Fig. 7.3b, it is evident that the network effects function in equation (7.17) also well fits the real experiment

---

[6] www.docker.com/community-edition.
[7] https://ethereum.github.io/go-ethereum.

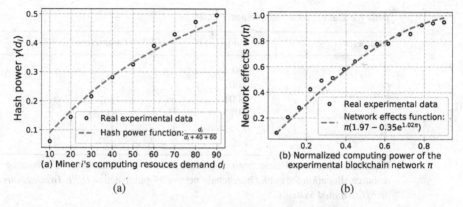

(a)   (b)

Figure 7.3 Estimation of (a) the hash power function $\gamma(d_i)$ in equation (7.13) and (b) the network effects function $w(\pi)$ in equation (7.17). Reprinted with permission from the paper "Auction mechanisms in cloud/fog computing resource allocation for public blockchain networks" published in *IEEE Transactions on Parallel and Distributed Systems*.

results. Based on the experiments, we set $a_1 = 1.97, a_2 = 0.35, a_3 = 1.02$ in the following simulations.

7.2.6.2   Numerical Results

To demonstrate the performance of the proposed auction mechanisms and the impacts of various parameters on the social welfare of the blockchain network, we consider a set of N miners, for example, mobile users in a PoW-based blockchain application supported by the CFP. Each miner's block size is uniformly distributed over $(0, 1024]$. Instead of being restricted to submit a constant demand as in the CDB auction, each miner in the MDB auction and FRLS auction can choose its desired demand which follows the uniform distribution over $[\beta_1 D, \beta_2 D]$. Each measurement is averaged over 600 instances and the associated 95 percent confidence interval is given. We can find that the confidence intervals are very narrowly centered around the mean. The default parameter values are presented in Table 7.2. Note that setting $q = 10, \beta_1 = 0$, and $\beta_2 = 0.02$ means the expected demand of miners in the MDB auction is equal to the constant demand of miners in the CDB auction. Hence, we can compare the performance of both proposed auction mechanisms.

7.2.6.3   Evaluation of MDB Auction versus FRLS Auction in Terms of Social Welfare Maximization

We evaluate the performance of the MDB auction in maximizing the social welfare by comparing it with the FRLS auction. Table 7.3 shows the social welfare obtained by the MDB auction and the FRLS auction. The social welfare generated from the MDB auction is lower than that from the FRLS auction when dealing with a small number of miners. As the group of interested miners grows, the MDB auction can achieve slightly larger social welfare although it has to preserve necessary economic properties, including individual rationality and truthfulness. The main reason is that the

Table 7.2 Default parameter values.

Parameters	Values	Parameters	Values
N	300	T	12.5
r	0.007	λ	15
c	0.001	q	10
a_1	1.97	β_1, β_2	0, 0.02
a_2	0.35	ξ	0.001
a_3	1.02	D	1000

Reprinted with permission from the paper "Auction mechanisms in cloud/fog computing resource allocation for public blockchain networks" published in *IEEE Transactions on Parallel and Distributed Systems*.

Table 7.3 MDB auction versus FRLS auction in social welfare maximization.

Number of miners	10	15	20	25
MDB auction	33.954	50.368	65.421	80.135
FRLS auction	34.656	49.935	65.060	79.853

Reprinted with permission from the paper "Auction mechanisms in cloud/fog computing resource allocation for public blockchain networks" published in *IEEE Transactions on Parallel and Distributed Systems*.

FRLS auction is an algorithm which provides a theoretical lower bound guarantee only in the worst case for approximately maximizing the social welfare, and may have more severe performance deterioration when the number of interested miners increases.

Impact of the Number of Miners N

Besides the social welfare, we introduce the satisfaction rate, that is, the percentage of winners selected from all interested miners, as another metric. Here, we compare the social welfare as well as the satisfaction rate of the CDB auction and the MDB auction with various number of miners, as shown in Fig. 7.4. From Fig. 7.4, we observe that the social welfare S in both auction mechanisms increases as the base of interested miners becomes larger. We observe that the satisfaction rate decreases and the rise of the social welfare also slows down with the increase of N. The main reason is that the competition among miners becomes more obvious when more miners take part in the auction, and, with more winners selected by the auction, the subsequent winner's density decreases due to the network effects. When choosing between the CDB auction and the MDB auction, Fig. 7.4 clearly shows that there is a trade-off between the social welfare and the satisfaction rate. The MDB auction can help the CFP achieve more social welfare than the CDB auction because of its advantage in relaxing restrictions on miners' demand. However, the CDB is relatively more fair because the MDB auction allows miners with large demand to take up more computing resources and this leads to a lower satisfaction rate.

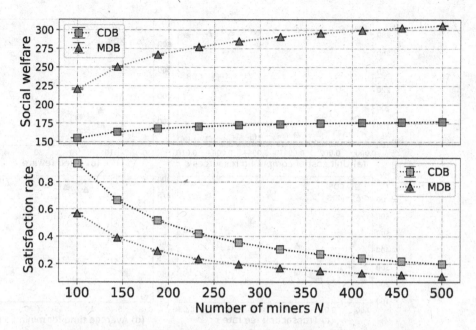

Figure 7.4 Impact of the number of miners N. Reprinted with permission from the paper "Auction mechanisms in cloud/fog computing resource allocation for public blockchain networks" published in *IEEE Transactions on Parallel and Distributed Systems*.

7.2.6.4 Impact of the Unit Cost c, the Fixed Bonus T, the Transaction Fee Rate r, and the Block Time λ

The CFP organizes the auction and cares about the unit cost of the computing resource. It is obvious from Fig. 7.5a that as the computing resources become expensive, the social welfare in each auction mechanism decreases linearly. The blockchain developer may be more interested in optimizing the blockchain protocol parameters, including the fixed reward, the transaction fee rate and the block time. In Figs. 7.5b–d, we study their impacts on the social welfare of the blockchain network. Figures 7.5b and 7.5c illustrate that if the blockchain developer raises the fixed bonus T or the transaction fee rate r, higher social welfare will be generated nearly in proportion. This is because the miner's valuation increases with higher T and r, according to the definition in equation (7.18). Moreover, by increasing T and r, we observe that the difference of the social welfare between the CDB auction and the MDB auction amplifies. The reason is that raising T and r can significantly improve the valuation of miner i which possesses large block size s_i and high demand d_i. As shown in Fig. 7.5d, when the blockchain developer raises the difficulty of mining a block, that is, extending the block time λ, the social welfare goes up. This is because a long block time λ gives the miner which has solved the PoW puzzle a higher probability to successfully propagate the new block and reach consensus. However, different from adjusting T and r, the marginal gains in social welfare gradually become smaller if the blockchain developer continues to increase the difficulty of the blockchain mining. This is mainly because the increasing

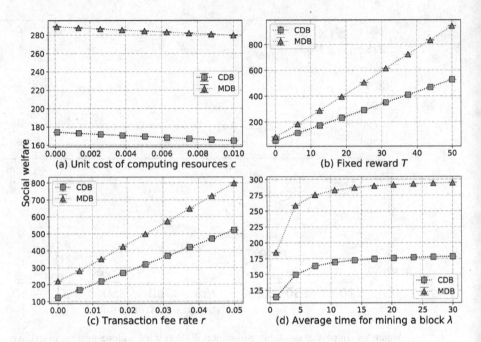

Figure 7.5 Impact of unit cost c, fixed bonus T, transaction fee rate r, and block time λ. Reprinted with permission from the paper "Auction mechanisms in cloud/fog computing resource allocation for public blockchain networks" published in *IEEE Transactions on Parallel and Distributed Systems.*

value of λ has less impact on the miner's valuation, as can be seen from the equations (7.16) and (7.18).

Miner's Utility and Individual Demand Constraints in the MDB Auction

In the MDB auction, we randomly choose a miner (ID = 120) to see its utility, which is defined by the difference between its ex-post valuation and its payment, that is, $v''_{120} - p_{120}$. The miner's block size is respectively at a low level ($s_{120} = 300$) and a high level ($s_{120} = 1000$). We investigate the impact of the miner's true demand on its utility, which also reflects the impact of its available budget. Figure 7.6a shows that when miner 120's true demand rises, its utility initially stays at 0 and then suddenly increases. This indicates that only when the miner's demand is above a threshold can it be selected as the winner by the MDB auction, that is, x_i changes immediately from 0 to 1, obtains the computing resources and finally has a positive utility. Otherwise, the miner would not be allocated the resources, namely, $x_i = 0$, and then both its ex-post valuation and payment should be 0 according to the MDB auction algorithm, which results in zero utility. Additionally, if the miner's generated block is larger, it can obtain higher utility with the same true demand. This implies that miners with large block size and high demand are easier to be selected by the MDB auction for social welfare maximization.

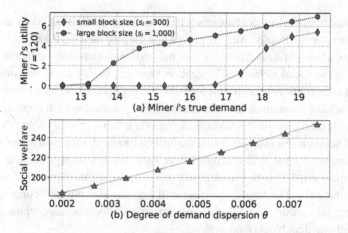

Figure 7.6 Relationship between miner i's ($i = 120$) utility and its true demand, and the impact of the degree of demand dispersion θ. Reprinted with permission from the paper "Auction mechanisms in cloud/fog computing resource allocation for public blockchain networks" published in *IEEE Transactions on Parallel and Distributed Systems*.

In Fig. 7.6b, we investigate the impact of the demand constraints on the social welfare in the MDB auction. To fix the miner's expected demand at q, we set demand constraints $\beta_1 D = q - \theta D$ and $\beta_2 D = q + \theta D$, where $\theta \in [0, \min(\frac{q}{D}, 1 - \frac{q}{D})]$ characterizes the degree of demand dispersion. It is clear that social welfare increases as the degree of demand dispersion rises and miners have more freedom to submit their desired demands.

7.3   Conclusion

To begin with, this chapter provides a detailed discussion on auction theory, including three major types of auction, namely, VCG auction, share auction, and double auction. VCG is the only type of mechanism that is allocatively efficient and strategy proof. In a share auction, the resources are allocated to users proportional to their bids. A double auction is a process of buying and selling goods when potential buyers submit their bids and potential sellers simultaneously submit their ask prices to an auctioneer, and then the auctioneer chooses some price p that clears the market: All the sellers who asked less than p sell and all buyers who bid more than p buy at this price p. Based on the auctions, we have investigated the applications of auction theory in cloud–fog computing services. To allocate computing resources efficiently, we have presented an auction-based market model to study the social welfare optimization and considered allocative externalities that particularly exist in blockchain networks, including the competition among the miners as well as the network effects of the total hash power. For miners with constant demand, we have proposed an auction mechanism (CDB auction) that achieves optimal social welfare. For miners with multiple demands, we have transformed the social welfare maximization problem to a nonmonotone submodular maximization with knapsack constraint problem. Then, we have designed two efficient mechanisms (FRLS auction and MDB auction) maximizing social welfare approximately. We have proven that the proposed CDB and MDB auction mechanisms are truthful, individually rational and computationally efficient and are able to solve the social welfare maximization problem. In this work, we consider the energy and computational constraints for PoW-based public blockchain network while assuming an ideal communication environment. For practical system implementation, the communication constraint is actually an important factor in establishing the mobile blockchain network. An example is that the limited bandwidth for each miner's mutual wireless communication will not only affect each miner's utility, but also have an adverse impact on the block broadcasting process and the throughput of the whole blockchain network. For future work, we will take the complicated communication environment into account, and design new spectrum allocation algorithms for more efficient and practical blockchain systems.

8   Contract Theory

For decades, contract theory has been a thriving and vibrant research area in economics, finance, management, and corporate law. Contract theory framework can be applied to study the information and incentives between the principals and agents. In a real market, there always exists asymmetric information. Contract theory analyzes how the principals and agents behave when the incentives vary under different conditions. Some agents may prefer not to reveal their true identities, while in some cases, the agents want to persuade the principal to trust the information that they submit. As for the principals, in some cases, they care about the agents' ex-post efforts, which are difficult to observe directly. Therefore, contract theory is used to design the incentive mechanism that motivates agents to take appropriate actions and exert sufficient efforts.

The solution to the formulated problems under the contract theory framework is a menu of contracts for the agents to maximize the principal's profit or utility. Generally, the problem is formulated to maximize an objective function that represents the principal's payoff, subject to the incentive compatibility constraint that the agent's expected payoff is maximized when signing the contract and the individual rationality constraint that the agent's payoff under the contract is greater than or equal to its reservation payoff when not participating.

8.1   Basic Concepts

Contract theory was developed to study the theory of incentives, information, and economics institutions, which provides the tools for analyzing the "ownership" and "control rights." [286]. To formulate the interactions between the principals and agents, contract theory framework provides several models to deal with the various circumstances. The most common models include adverse selection and moral hazard.

8.1.1   Classification of Contract Theory

Adverse Selection This refers to a situation where the seller does not have the preference information of buyers. In a more general case, the adverse selection problem is that the principal has no idea about the private information regarding some key traits of the agents, such as their dislike for specific duties and their level of competence or productivity. One of the most common problems in adverse selection is the screening problem, in which the contract is offered by the uninformed party, namely, the principal.

The uninformed party often responds to adverse selection through the revelation principle, which drives the informed party, namely, the contractor, to choose the contract that best reflects their real situation. Based on the revelation principle, the contract seller can offer numerous contracts (q, T) to contract buyers, where q refers to the services or products that the seller can provide, and T is the total amount paid to the seller. The buyer's utility function is given by

$$u(q, T, \theta) = \theta v(q) - T, \tag{8.1}$$

where $v(0) = 0$, $v'(q) > 0$, and $v''(q) < 0$ for all q, θ denotes the private information of buyers, and $v(\cdot)$ is the evaluation function of q. The seller can obtain the distribution of the private information only according to some prior knowledge. Equation (8.1) is the uniform utility function for the most of adverse selection models. There is no uniform utility function for the contract sellers. By using this utility function, the seller is trying to induce the buyer to select a contract that can maximize the seller's profit. In other cases, q can also indicate the work time, a needed performance, or anything else that the company desires from the contract seller, and T refers to the salary that is paid to the contract buyers.

Moral Hazard This refers to the situations where the agent's ex-post actions are hidden from the principal. Unlike the problem of adverse selection, moral hazard occurs only after the contracts between the seller and buyers have been signed. In this case, the seller has no idea about the buyers' actions and outcomes. The contract form of moral hazard is a menu of action–reward bundles (q, w), where q is the observed action or effort after accepting the contracts, w is the wage paid to contract buyers. The utility function of a contract buyer is given by

$$u(w) - \psi(a), \tag{8.2}$$

where $u(\cdot)$ is the evaluation function with $u'(\cdot) > 0$, $u''(\cdot) \leq 0$, and $\psi''(\cdot) \geq 0$. There is a simplifying assumption that $\psi(a) = a$ without loss of generality. The principle behind the solution to the problem of moral hazard is that the contract buyers' final rewards are highly associated with their outcomes. They can get a higher wage only by exerting more efforts and presenting better performance.

In a general moral hazard case, the contract buyers tend to be lazy or have unacceptable behaviors since they feel that no penalty is required in the signed contract. However, bad behaviors can increase the risk of financial loss to the contract seller. Thus, relating the reward to the buyer's outcome is the most straightforward way to prevent the problem of moral hazard.

8.1.2   Individual Rationality and Incentive Compatibility

The main goal of mechanism design is to maximize the objective function over all the mechanism participants' utility functions. Meanwhile, two important constraints must be satisfied: individual rationality (IR) and incentive compatibility (IC). Depending on the various circumstances, the objective functions can be expressed in different forms. As for the case of contract theory, the utility functions of different contract buyers generally have the similar form.

Individual Rationality (IR) Before we introduce the individual rationality, we will first explain what is a rational individual. A rational individual always make the best decision so that he or she can obtain the greatest benefit. Briefly, the rational individual makes decisions in terms of self-interest. The concepts that are associated with rationality are often used in the economics and game theory field. Individual rationality is the basis of a contract that allows the contract buyers to purchase contracts voluntarily. It refers to a situation that only when the contract provides more benefit than the case of noncontract will the rational individuals purchase the contracts. It is expressed mathematically as

$$u(q,T,\theta) = \theta v(q) - T > 0, \quad u(w) - \psi(a) > 0. \tag{8.3}$$

Incentive Compatibility (IC) This constraint ensures that all the rational contract buyers can obtain the greatest benefits by truthfully revealing their private information. As for the adverse selection model, the contract seller offers set contracts for the different types of contract buyers. Suppose there are N types of contracts in total; here are four definitions regarding the IC constraints between type-i and type-j ($i \neq j, 0 \leq i \leq N, 0 \leq j \leq N$).

(a) If $\forall j \in \{1, \ldots, i - 1\}$, the constraints are called Downward Incentive Constraints (**DICs**).
(b) If $j = i - 1$, the constraint is called the Local Downward Incentive Constraint (**LDIC**).
(c) If $\forall j \in \{i + 1, \ldots, N\}$, the constraints are called Upward Incentive Constraints (**UICs**).
(d) If $j = i + 1$, the constraint is called the Local Upward Incentive Constraint (**LUIC**).

Specifically, IC refers a validator of type-i obtaining the maximum profit only by choosing their own contract instead of all the others' contracts. The basic idea of IC constraint reduction is that if for type-i the LDIC holds, then all its the DICs hold, and the same for its LUIC and UICs.

As a result, by exploiting IR and IC restrictions, the contract seller can induce contract buyers to divulge their true information and incentivize them to exert more desired efforts, thus maximizing the seller's benefit.

8.2 Example: Contract-Theoretic Approach for Pricing Security Deposits

In this section, we introduce a flexible pricing scheme for security deposits. Considering the limited budgets of the IoT, we propose two joint models under the contract theory framework to determine the optimal price of different types of security deposits.

8.2.1   Introduction and Related Work

As a network of connected devices, the IoT is capable of collecting, sharing, and analyzing data with each other [287]. Specifically, the IoT is the collection of technologies, including identification and tracking technologies, wired and wireless sensor networks, machine-to-machine interfaces, enhanced communication protocols, and so on. Owing to the flexible and powerful data management, there are multiple industrial solutions based on the IoT, for example, IBM Industrial 4.0 [288] and Ericsson Industrial 4.0 [289]. However, the traditional IoT system has limited scalability and single point of failure issues because of its centralized architecture. With the advent of blockchain technology, the combination of the IoT and blockchain has a promising application in the future.

In the last decade, the blockchain technology has been considerably researched and developed by both academic communities and industrial circles [193]. A blockchain is a distributed ledger of transaction records, which is jointly maintained and supported by all participating parties [1]. The transactions can be initiated by any party in the system, and then verified by all of the participants after being recorded in the blocks of the public ledger. Because of the cryptographic design, the transaction records of the same block are organized in a Merkle hash tree, and all the blocks are sequentially connected before and after with each other, which makes it difficult to tamper with a single transaction record, let alone a single block. As a distributed, decentralized, and tamper-resistant public ledger, blockchain has found a wide range of applications in both the financial and nonfinancial worlds, for example, the stablecoin project called Libra that is initiated by Facebook [290] and Vehicle Passport of SHIFTMobility [291].

As the development of industry, the blockchain-based IoT platform has been a research focus. As a result of the intensive computation required by PoW, IoT nodes, as the computationally lightweight nodes, are unable to participate in mining. There are multiple related researches regarding resource management and allocation. In order to reduce the cost and increase the availability of data management, Feng et al. [292] construct a decentralized platform for data storage and trading in a wireless powered IoT crowd-sensing system. Asheralieva and Niyato [293] introduce mobile-edge computing and unmanned aerial vehicles to help relay and run the blockchain tasks that include the data collected from the IoT. Other related works are [294–296]. The other application of blockchain in the IoT is to preserve the data security and privacy. Zhao et al. [297] have designed a secure and privacy-preserving system by applying the federal learning the blockchain technology. Gai et al. [298] combine the edge computing with the blockchain-based IoT together, which is called blockchain-based Internet of Edge model and becomes a scalable, controllable privacy-preserving, and efficient system. In the industrial area, the first blockchain IoT platforms is IOTA [299]. Other blockchain-based solutions include IoT Chain [300], Atonomi [301], Chain of Things [302], and so on.

Proof of Work (PoW), known as the original consensus protocol, is applied for the Bitcoin project [1]. It requires all the participants to solve a hash puzzle based on SHA-256 by brute-force, wherein the first one that solves the problem (i.e., miner) has the right to generate a block and obtains a reward for its work. Under the similar framework of PoW, a number of alternative protocols have been proposed to improve the performance of original PoW protocols, for example, Proofs of Useful Work [140] and REM [142]. However, the competition of solving a hash puzzle incurs huge energy expenditure for all the participants. To solve this problem, a new idea of the consensus protocol called Proof of Stake (PoS) was first suggested on Bitcoin Forum [303] and improved by Peercoin [165]. PoS shares the same purpose as PoW, but unlike PoW's leader selection depending on the hash puzzle calculation, it relies on the number of coins (i.e., stake), together with the ownership duration (i.e., coin age). Bentov et al. [169] point out the rationale behind PoS is that the entities with stake are more suitable to retain the security in order to prevent losses caused by the system erodes. Based on these core ideas of PoS, numerous frameworks with different puzzle designs have been proposed in [116, 171, 172, 304].

Despite the rapid development, there is still a huge gap between the blockchain technology and real applications. Take the Bitcoin blockchain and Ethereum as examples; Bitcoin blockchain could handle 3–6 transactions per second (tps) [305], and Ethereum 1.0 can only process 7–15 transactions per second [306]. Compared with Visa [307], which is capable of handling more than 65,000 transaction messages per second, it is clear that neither of them can be considered as an alternative for daily transactions. One straightforward method to increase the throughput and reduce the latency is to partition the entities into parallel subgroups (i.e., committees), which are responsible for generating and sustaining the subblocks (i.e., sharding) synchronously. Sharding is a term derived from distributed database and can be applied to the blockchain network for realizing the scalability [121].

To further satisfy the requirements in the blockchain network with shards, protocols that support high-throughput such as those in [308] and [309] were proposed. Take the ongoing Ethereum 2.0 project as the example; it publishes two possible PoS consensus protocols, namely, Casper CBC [310] and Casper FFG [304]. Since the project is always up to date and well-maintained, we adopt the latter in this work according to the latest document of github [311], which is a security-deposit based economic consensus protocol that can be deployed atop any *proposal mechanism*. The security of PoS is deemed to derive from the size of **security deposits** rather than the number of participants, which can be set to greatly exceed the gains from the reward, and thus, proof of stake provides strictly stronger security incentives than PoW [304]. Here we clarify two novel concepts: **security incentive** and **economic incentive**. For security incentive, participants have to behave in a legitimate way in the case that their deposits are slashed due to violating the rules. In this case, the penalty is regarded as the cost to motivate the majority of participants to sustain the security of the whole system. For economic incentive, the participants are motivated to follow the rules by the rewards issued from the system.

Ethereum 2.0 adopts the combination of sharding and Casper to handle the scalability issue. It requires all participants to initiate a one-way transaction of 32 ETH to a deposit contract on Ethereum 1.0 [317]. However, 32 ETH blocks out the participant whose stake is lower than that. For the participants whose stake values are far more

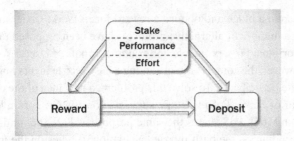

Figure 8.1 Relationship between the features (i.e., stake, performance, and effort), reward, and deposit of a participant. Reprinted with permission from the paper "Contract-theoretic pricing for security deposits in sharded blockchain with Internet of Things (IoT)" published in *IEEE Internet of Things Journal*.

than 32 ETH, the security incentive constraint is weakened. Moreover, it is not fair to issue the same reward to the participants who have different stakes, performances and efforts. As shown in Fig. 8.1, we list the relationship between the features (i.e., stake, performance, and effort), reward and deposit of a participant. Rationally speaking, the reward should be issued according to the participant's stake, performance, or effort, which leads to an effective economic incentive for the participant; the deposit that is submitted to system should be greater than the reward and less than the stake. This means that it is affordable to the participant. There are some existing research work designing the economic incentive for a blockchain network by various game models, such as Evolutionary Game [122], Stackelberg Game [138] and Contract Theory [313]. However, none of them is applicable to the scenario considered in this work. Although [313] adopted the adverse selection model of contract theory, they only have a single consideration, that is, the principal cannot determine agents' capability.

8.2.2   Motivation and Contribution

A sharded blockchain with PoS is a promising framework that allows the participants to run the transaction-related functions at a lower cost than the PoW-based blockchain. However, the steep security deposit price is an obstacle to the lower stake participants, such as the IoT device owners. The IoT refers to a wide range of kinds of stuff and techniques, that benefit not only the industrial fields but also the individual life experiences, including smart wearables, smart homes, and smart communities. In this work, any individual or institute who possesses the IoT devices can be viewed as the "validator." The diversity of heterogeneous devices owned by the validators indicates various distribution of stake and performance. According to [304] and [317], staking the deposit is only a method to prohibit illegal behaviors in the participating blockchain rather than an extra cost. Moreover, any honest participant will be rewarded accordingly for their efforts in processing the transaction-related tasks. After exiting the blockchain network, the honest participants will get the security deposit returned. Considering both the disadvantage and advantage of participating in such a blockchain network, we dedicate to studying the mathematical models of security deposit pricing for these owners with a different stake and performance.

Before designing an incentive scheme in the similar scenario (e.g., Ethereum 2.0), we analyze the problems that lead to the difficulty in designing an economic incentive mechanism, from the perspective of the intrinsic characteristics in blockchain. For a blockchain network with shards, even though there is a beacon chain in charge of the administrative transactions, the problem of *information asymmetry* still exists. Owing to the anonymity of a blockchain network and weak leadership of the beacon chain [311], the problem is mainly manifested in the following aspects. (a) The beacon chain cannot determine the exact stake value of a single participant. (b) The real performance and effort exerted by the participant are unknown to others except themselves. Note that even though the timestamps contained in the work (i.e., block proposal, transaction or block confirmation) can be used as a metric of performance, they are not accurate [318], for example, the block proposal times are accurate only to within an hour or two in general. (c) The stake, performances and efforts are not uniformly distributed among these heterogeneous nodes. The blockchain network should set the deposit to greatly exceed the reward to regulate a validator's behavior [304]. But the validators cannot afford it if the deposit exceeds the stake in their accounts. In other words, the reward for each participant is the lower bound of their deposit, while the personal stake is the upper bound. Consequently, the reward is the key to determine the deposit. One easy way is to set a uniform reward and deposit for all validators with the same weights [319]. However, designing an adaptive deposit pricing scheme is challenging in terms of asymmetric information. As the study of how incentivizing the different parties in the presence of asymmetric information [286], contract theory is advantageous in mechanism design, benefiting the designer, and accordingly offering feasible mechanisms for rational game players. However, in practice, there must be a contract designer able to obtain the prior distribution of participants and design the contract items to the potential participants, which is against the conventional blockchain network with a single chain. That is also why contract theory cannot be applied in such a decentralized and autonomous system. In contrast, a sharded blockchain network consists of one main chain, one beacon chain, and various committees. With a weak leadership due to the decentralized architecture, the beacon chain can be the contract designer and can deploy the contract items among the validators during each epoch.

In this work chapter, with the consideration of all the above aspects, we utilize the contract theory [286] to formulate the problems. In particular, contract theory can help overcome information asymmetry when designing the mechanisms. As shown in Table 8.1, contract theory has been widely applied to variety of areas, for example, Wireless Edge Caching Networks [312], Fog computing [203], Cognitive Radio Network [315] and Mobile Crowdsourcing [316]. Compared with the other research studies regarding the blockchain and our previous work [314], we consider more sophisticated cases in the blockchain network with shards. Generally, there is a positive correlation between the performance and effort of a participant, but the stake has nothing to do with the performance or effort, which can be purchased online. When taking stake and effort or both of them into consideration at the same time, we present two different cases in the

Table 8.1 Related works comparison.

Paper	Scenario	Model	Hidden information	Hidden action
[312]	Wireless communication		✓	✗
[313]	Blockchain & Internet of vehicles	AS[1]	✓	✗
[314]	Blockchain		✓	✗
[203]	Fog computing	MH[2]	✗	✓
[315]	Cognitive radio networks	JAM[3]	✓	✓
[316]	Mobile networks	TM[4]	✗	✓
Our work	Blockchain & IoT	JAM JAT[5]	✓	✓

[1] AS represents Adverse Selection.
[2] MH represents Moral Hazard.
[3] JAM represents Joint Adverse Selection and Moral Hazard.
[4] TM represents Tournament Model.
[5] JAT represents Joint Adverse Selection and Tournament Model.
Reprinted with permission from the paper "Contract-theoretic pricing for security deposits in sharded blockchain with Internet of Things (IoT)" published in *IEEE Internet of Things Journal*.

following. (a) **Stake-oriented**: There is a significant difference among the validators' stakes, but they vary slightly in performances (or efforts), or in other words, their performances are far better than the task needs. (b) **Effort-oriented**: There is a significant difference among the validators' performances (efforts), or in other words, the system values performances (efforts) more than stakes.

Here we summarize the main contributions of this work in the following.

1. We proposed two joint models based on contract theory, aiming to determine the participants' rewards according to their stakes and performances (efforts). Then the deposits can be specified based on the different rewards. That means the participants obtain the different rewards and submit the different deposits, in which the deposits exceed the rewards. Compared with the mainly emphasized security incentive in Ethereum 2.0, the two proposed schemes are able to balance the security incentive and economic incentive for the beacon chain and the participants.

2. The first joint model is the combination of *adverse selection* and *moral hazard*. The *adverse selection* is used for distinguishing participants' stake type, and the *moral hazard* is used for determining the performance (or effort) exerted by a participant of a certain stake type.

3. The second joint model is the combination of *tournament* and *adverse selection*, which is applied to the second case. We utilize *tournament*, a competition of performances (or efforts), to distinguish the participants' capability. Then in a certain performance (or effort) type, *adverse selection* can help to determine the minimum stake threshold for the participants.

4. The simulation results and the related analysis are provided for both joint models. We compare the impacts from the results of different key parameters, and present optimal rewards and security deposits to prove the feasibility and efficacy of the two models.

8.2.3 System Model

As shown in Fig. 8.2, a complete blockchain network with shards consists of a PoW-based blockchain (main chain), a PoS-based blockchain (beacon chain), a validator pool, and a number of committees. In PoS, the consensus nodes (i.e., IoT devices or nodes in this work) are known as validators. The main chain is constituted by verified blocks with all the finalized transactions, the beacon chain contains the administrative transactions that are associated with all the validators and shards. More details of the work process are included in Fig. 8.2. The major terminologies are listed in Table 8.2. Let the beacon chain with weak leadership be responsible for designing the contracts. At the beginning of each epoch, even before the first step described in Fig. 8.2, the validators will sign the contracts according to their own stake or effort. The optimal reward and deposit are determined by the contracts based on the previous statistics. The details of designing and issuing contracts are listed in Fig. 8.3. Throughout the work, we set the temporary manager of the beacon chain as the contract designer. We classify the

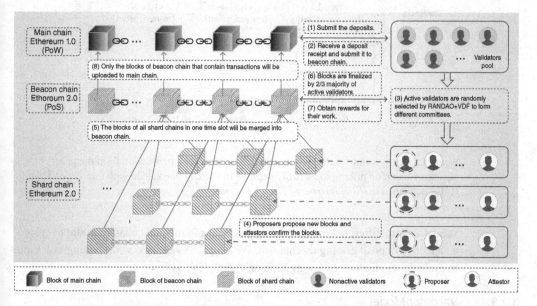

Figure 8.2 An overview of the blockchain network with shards. Reprinted with permission from the paper "Contract-theoretic pricing for security deposits in sharded blockchain with Internet of Things (IoT)" published in *IEEE Internet of Things Journal*.

Table 8.2 Terminology [311].

Term	Description
Beacon chain	The central proof-of-stake chain that is the base of the sharding system.
Shard chain	One of the chains on which user transactions take place and account data is stored.
Validator	A registered participant in the beacon chain. Anyone can become one by sending ether into Ethereum 1.0 deposit contract.
Proposer	A validator who proposes a new block.
Attestor	A validator who verifies and confirms the blocks.
Slot	A period during which one proposer creates a beacon chain block.
Epoch	An aligned span of slots during which all validators get exactly one chance to make an attestation.

Reprinted with permission from the paper "Contract-theoretic pricing for security deposits in sharded blockchain with Internet of Things (IoT)" published in *IEEE Internet of Things Journal*.

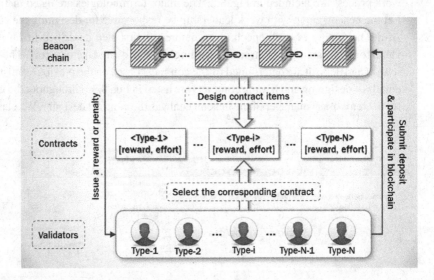

Figure 8.3 An overview of the system model. Reprinted with permission from the paper "Contract-theoretic pricing for security deposits in sharded blockchain with Internet of Things (IoT)" published in *IEEE Internet of Things Journal*.

validators into different types regarding their stake in the blockchain account to design an adaptive deposit pricing mechanism. We adopt the validator's completing task time to evaluate its effort (e.g., voting time on chain [304, 317]).

8.2.3.1   Validator Model

Definition 26   We classify the validator nodes into different types: type-1, type-2, ..., type-$\mathbb{N}$. The classification criterion is based on their stake or performance (effort). Let θ_i represent the type, and the type θ_i follows the inequation:

$$\theta_1 < \theta_2 < \cdots < \theta_{\mathbb{N}}. \tag{8.4}$$

In this work, a validator who has more stake or higher performance will be identified as a higher type, which is set to be an index in Section 8.2.4 without loss of generality. The utility function of a validator node is defined as follows:

$$U_V = \omega(\mathbb{R}) - \psi(e) - \xi(s) - \varphi(\theta, \mathbb{R}, e), \tag{8.5}$$

where $\mathbb{R}$ represents the reward that should be paid for the validator nodes, e denotes the efforts made by the validators, $\omega(\cdot)$ is the evaluation function of the reward $\mathbb{R}$, $\psi(\cdot)$ is the cost function of the effort e, and $\xi(\cdot)$ is defined to evaluate the lock-up cost. According to [304] and [317], the penalty for any violation is a validator's entire deposit, so we set $\varphi(\cdot)$ as the function of expected penalty (i.e., deposit).

8.2.3.2 Beacon Chain Model

The utility function of beacon chain is defined as follows:

$$U_{BC} = \pi(q) - \mu(\mathbb{R}), \tag{8.6}$$

where $\pi(\cdot)$ is the metric functions that evaluate the quality of effort received from a validator and increasing in the observed quality q, and $\mu(\cdot)$ is defined to evaluate the reward issued to the validator and increasing in the issued reward $\mathbb{R}$. The gap between the two terms denotes the beacon chain's utility obtained from the validator. From the beacon chain's perspective, it expects to extract the maximized utility by requiring a higher quality of validator's effort and offering a lower reward.

8.2.3.3 Definitions of Contract Theory

Definition 27 (Spence–Mirrlees Single–Crossing Property) For any contract $(\mathbb{R}_i, e_i)$ with different type θ_i, if the utility function of validators satisfies the inequation:

$$\frac{\partial}{\partial \theta}\left[-\frac{\partial U_V/\partial \mathbb{R}}{\partial U_V/\partial e}\right] > 0, \tag{8.7}$$

the number of constraints can be effectively reduced [320].

Definition 28 (Individual Rationality) IR means that only when a positive utility is assigned by the beacon chain, can the validator accept the contract, that is,

$$U_{V(i)} \geq 0, \quad \forall i \in \{1, \ldots, i, \ldots, N\}. \tag{8.8}$$

The basic idea of IR constraint reduction is that the constraints of all types will hold if the IR constraint of type-1 can be satisfied.

Definition 29 (Incentive Compatibility) Here are four definitions regarding the IC constraints between type-i and type-j.

(a) If $\forall j \in \{1, \ldots, i-1\}$, the constraints are called Downward Incentive Constraints (**DICs**).

(b) If $j = i-1$, the constraint is called Local Downward Incentive Constraint (**LDIC**).

(c) If $\forall j \in \{i+1, \ldots, N\}$, the constraints are called Upward Incentive Constraints (**UICs**).

(d) If $j = i+1$, the constraint is called Local Upward Incentive Constraint (**LUIC**).

So, IC refers to a validator of type-i obtaining the maximum profit only by choosing their own contract instead of all the others' contracts. The basic idea of IC constraint reduction is that if for type-i the LDIC holds, then all the DICs hold, and the same as its LUIC and UICs.

8.2.4   The Joint Design of Adverse Selection and Moral Hazard

In this section, we consider the scenario that there is a significant difference among the validators' stake values, but they vary relatively little in performance, or in other words, their performances are far better than that the task needs. So the stake value will be considered to be the main criterion of rewarding level. However, the stake value information of a single validator node is unknown to the beacon chain. This assumes that it can obtain only part of the information about the validator nodes, such as their stake value distribution and the possible value range.

In a PoS-based blockchain network, all the participants can lock their coins (i.e., stake) in the network and will be randomly selected as the future block manager. According to [304] and [321], any holder of ether (i.e., the cryptocurrency issued by Ethereum) in Ethereum 1.0 can participate in Eth2 by submitting the security deposit. For ease of description, we call the account saving of an ether holder in Ethereum 1.0 the "stake." The main idea of pricing the security deposit is that the price must greatly exceed the reward issued by the network [304]. Our goal is to design an affordable security deposit without impacting the security incentive. Consequently, an affordable security deposit should be greater than the validator's reward, but less than its stake. Moreover, the reward, security deposit, and the voting weight of a validator should be positively associated with its stake. Thus, we classify the validators into different types based on their stake, for example, $\theta \in \{\theta_1, ..., \theta_i, ..., \theta_N\}$. A higher-type participant needs to stake a much higher deposit to obtain more reward and more significant weight in blockchain, such as voting. Nevertheless, it will be fined much higher if any violation occurs. Opposite to a higher-type participant, the lower one needs only to stake a minor deposit in exchange for a meager income and far less weight, which hardly impacts the voting results. We list the main notations of this model in Table 8.3.

For the different type θ_i, we set the different fixed salary f_i (a reward for one's participation) and the different bonus b_i (a reward for one's effort). Intuitively, for $\forall \theta_i, i \in \{1, ..., N\}$, the salaries and bonuses satisfy the inequalities as follow:

$$f_1 < \cdots < f_i < \cdots < f_N, \quad b_1 < \cdots < b_i < \cdots < b_N. \tag{8.9}$$

Thus, the reward $\mathbb{R}$ distributed by the beacon chain now is described as a tuple (f_i, b_i).

The base salary depends on a validator's type, but the bonus varies in the validator's effort. It is difficult to measure validators' efforts directly. As we know, an extensively applied metric of the whole blockchain network performance is *throughput* (e.g., [319, 322]), which is the total number of transactions processable within a second. Thus, we consider that the completion time of a single task (i.e., transaction verification or voting) can be the metric of a validator's effort. For a specific validator belonging to

Table 8.3 Main notations (1).

Symbol	Definition
θ_i	Validators' type
f_i	Fixed salary
b_i	Bonus for the type-i validator's effort
T_i	Observed time of type-i validator completes the task
t_i	Actual completing time
ε	Network delay
e_i	The effort exerted by a validator
q_i	The observable quality of effort
$\rho(\theta_i, \mathbb{R}_i)$	The deposit submitted by type-i validators
ω_i	The evaluation function of reward
ψ	The cost function of effort
ξ	The cost function of stake
φ	The penalty function
π	The evaluation function of response' quality
μ	Total salary

Reprinted with permission from the paper "Contract-theoretic pricing for security deposits in sharded blockchain with Internet of Things (IoT)" published in *IEEE Internet of Things Journal*.

type i, the time T_i of completing the task observed by the system consists of two parts: actual completing time t_i and the network delay ε, and we have

$$T_i = \begin{cases} t_i + \varepsilon, & \varepsilon > 0, \\ t_i, & \varepsilon = 0, \end{cases} \qquad (8.10)$$

where the whole network delay is assumed to follow a normal distribution [323] with mean μ and variance σ.

A direct connection between effort and time is that making more effort in the same task will take less time. That is, the exerted effort e_i is decreasing in the actual completing time t_i and the observed quality of effort q_i is decreasing in the observed time T_i. Similar to [313], we define a time-related metric function to measure the effort of a validator and the observed quality of a response, which is expressed as follow:

$$e_i = \alpha_1(T_{max} - t_i)^{a_1}, \qquad (8.11)$$

$$q_i = \alpha_2(T_{max} - T_i)^{a_2}, \qquad (8.12)$$

where T_{max} is the maximum acceptable response time of the beacon chain, $e_{i,k} \geq q_{i,k}$, α_1, α_2, a_1, and a_2 are the predefined coefficients, and $e'(t) < 0, q'(t) < 0$. That means, by virtue of the network delay, the observed task quality is always less than or equal to the actual effort that is made by the validator node, and the effort level and the response quality decrease with the increment of time.

With the assumption of risk neutrality, we define an evaluation function $\omega_{i,k}$ regarding the base salary f_i, bonus b_i and effort e_i, which derives from the linear incentive schemes in [286, 324]. If a validator k of type i signs the corresponding contract (f_i, b_i), its evaluation function of total reward is expressed by:

$$\omega_{i,k} = \theta_i \beta_1 f_i + \theta_i \beta_2 b_i e_{i,k}. \tag{8.13}$$

According to the cost model in [324], the cost function is associated with the effort level and the observation error. In the proposed model, the total cost consists of three parts: the cost of exerting effort, the cost of staking deposit into blockchain, and the potential penalty due to the inefficient performance. For a given unit effort cost c, and the maximum acceptable response time T_{max}, we define cost functions of the effort, staking and penalty as follows:

$$\psi(e_{i,k}) = c^2(e_{i,k})^2, \tag{8.14}$$

$$\xi(\theta_i, b_i) = \theta_i^2 b_i^2 + b_i, \tag{8.15}$$

$$\varphi(\theta_i, \mathbb{R}_i, e_{i,k}) = \rho(\theta_i, \mathbb{R}_i)\gamma(1 - e_{i,k}/T_{max})^2. \tag{8.16}$$

Similar to [286] and [313], we set a quadratic cost function with respect to effort level. Equation (8.15) is not the actual lock-up cost (e.g., the lock-up cost function is generally denoted by an increasing natural exponential function), but an individual evaluation function with respect to the deposit. Considering the deposit is positively correlated with the reward, we adopt the bonus instead of the deposit to simplify the calculation. This quadratic function is convex, where $\sum(\xi(\theta_i, b_i)) \leq \xi(\theta_i, \sum b_i)$. It incurs more cost for those who intend to collude together. Consequently, the function in equation (8.15) is increasing in the validator's type and deposit, which is monotonic, just like the actual lock-up cost function. Here, $\rho(\theta_i, \mathbb{R}_i)$ denotes the evaluation function of the deposit that the validator node should submit to the beacon chain, which is related to the validator nodes' type and reward. We also use $\gamma(1 - e_{i,k}/T_{max})^2 \in (0, 1]$ to express the failure probability of inefficient performance. Obviously, if the validator exerts no effort at all (i.e., $e_{i,k} = 0$), then $U_{i,k} = -b_{i,k}\varepsilon - \gamma\rho(\theta_i, \mathbb{R}_i) < 0$.

Therefore, according to the redefined functions (8.13)–(8.16), we can rewrite the utility function (8.5) of the validator node k as follows:

$$U_{V(i,k)} = \theta_i \beta_1 f_i + \theta_i \beta_2 b_i e_{i,k} - c^2(e_{i,k})^2 - \theta_i^2 b_i^2 - b_i - \rho(\theta_i, \mathbb{R}_i)\gamma\left(1 - \frac{e_{i,k}}{T_{max}}\right)^2. \tag{8.17}$$

Owing to the features of blockchain, the beacon chain can obtain only limited information about the validators. Set λ_i as the probability of the validator node k belonging to the certain type-i, where $\sum_{i=1}^{N} \lambda_i = 1$. Assume that there are $\mathbb{K}$ validator nodes in each type, the utility function of beacon chain is rewritten as follows:

$$U_{BC} = \sum_{i=1}^{N} \lambda_i \left(\sum_{k=1}^{\mathbb{K}} \pi(q_{i,k}) - \mu(\mathbb{R}_{i,k}) \right). \tag{8.18}$$

For given fixed salary f_i and bonus b_i,

$$\mu(\mathbb{R}_{i,k}) = \mathbb{R}_{i,k} = f_i + b_i q_{i,k}, \tag{8.19}$$

where $q_{i,k}$ is the observed performance of type-i validator k, and $b_i q_{i,k}$ denotes the reward for its effort.

8.2.4.1 Problem Formulation

According to the constraint **IR**, for any rational validator node with any effort greater than zero, only when its utility given by the contract is greater than zero can it accept the contract. So we have

$$U_{V(i,k)} \geq 0. \tag{8.20}$$

The constraint **IC** can guarantee that the rational validator nodes will sign the contracts that are designed specifically for their own types, since the validator nodes can obtain the greatest utilities only from their own contracts instead of others. We set $U_{V(i,k)}(\mathbb{R}_i, e_i)$ as the type-i validator node k's utility that is obtained from its own type contract, and set $U_{V(i,k)}(\mathbb{R}_j, e_j)$ as the utility that is obtained from the type-j contract. Thus, according to the IC constraint, we have

$$U_{V(i,k)}(\mathbb{R}_i) \geq U_{V(i,k)}(\mathbb{R}_j). \tag{8.21}$$

Therefore, with the constraints (8.20) and (8.21), the optimization problem is described as follows:

$$\max_{(f_i, b_i)} \quad U_{BC} = \sum_{i=1}^{N} \lambda_i \left(\sum_{k=1}^{K} \pi(q_{i,k}) - f_i - b_i q_{i,k} \right), \tag{8.22}$$

s.t.

$$(a) \quad U_{V(i,k)}(\mathbb{R}_i) \geq 0,$$

$$(b) \quad U_{V(i,k)}(\mathbb{R}_i) \geq U_{V(i,k)}(\mathbb{R}_j).$$

However, problem (8.22) is not a convex problem, and thus cannot be directly solved by the convex optimization tools. We solve this problem by the proposed method in the following subsections.

8.2.4.2 Optimal Solution of Contract

Since the problem is formulated with the joint moral hazard and adverse selection, from the perspective of contract theory [286], its optimal solutions will vary under the different cases. However, in our scenario, the stake value of a validator node is always unknown to the system. That means the adverse selection problem always exists, and there is no probability that only the moral hazard case exists. Thus, we present the optimal solutions for the joint model (i.e., the joint model of adverse selection and moral hazard) and adverse selection model, respectively. Moreover, we explain the physical meaning behind these mathematical models.

For a certain type-i, we can easily determine that the utility of a validator is a concave function with respect to its effort. Thus, in order to obtain the optimal effort choice for validator k, we first differentiate the utility function of validators with respect to e and set it to zero:

$$\frac{\partial U_{V(i,k)}}{\partial e} = 0. \tag{8.23}$$

For ease of analysis and without loss of generality, we conduct the following steps to simplify the calculation. For the effort $e_{i,k} = \alpha_1(T_{max} - t_{i,k})^{a_1}$ and $q_{i,k} = \alpha_2(T_{max} - T_{i,k})^{a_2}$, we set $\alpha_1 = \alpha_2 = a_1 = a_2 = 1$, since the time is one of the general performance metrics, as in [323]. Given the historical performance data and $\tau(e_i) = \gamma(1 - e_{i,k}/T_{max})^2$, we can obtain that $\tau(e_i) \in (0, \tau(\underline{e})]$, where $\underline{e}$ represents the lowest level of effort accepted by system. Then we reduce $\tau(e_i)$ to a constant $\tau(\underline{e})$ without impacting the monotonicity and incentive compatibility of all types of validators. According to our previous analysis of *reward, deposit, and stake* in Fig. 8.1, deposit (also known as penalty if any illegal behavior occurs) should be greater than all the rewards issued by the system, where $\rho(\theta_i, \mathbb{R}_i) \geq \mu(\mathbb{R}_{i,k})$. Therefore, we define $\rho(\theta_i, \mathbb{R}_i) = \kappa\theta_i(f_i + b_ie_{i,k})$, where $1 \leq \kappa$. Finally, the optimal choice of effort for validator k belonging to type-i can be obtained according to the first derivative as follows:

$$e_i^* = \frac{\theta_i b_i}{2c^2}(\beta_2 - \kappa\tau). \tag{8.24}$$

Since β_2 is a predefined parameter, then if $\beta_2 = 2c + \kappa\tau$ holds, regardless of the value of right side, e_i^* can be rewritten as $e_i^* = \theta_i b_i/c$. For a certain type-i, $e_{i,k}^*$ can represent all the validator nodes' optimal choice of efforts, so we use e_i^* instead. Similarly, if the type-i validator node signs the contract that is designed for type-j, its optimal effort choice is as follows:

$$e_{i,j}^* = \frac{\theta_i b_j}{c}. \tag{8.25}$$

From equation (8.24), we can reach the conclusion that the optimal effort choice e_i^* for all types θ_i is greater than zero, and it will increase with its type θ_i and bonus b_i and decrease with the cost c. From the validator node's perspective, it will have more incentives to respond to the beacon chain to the best of its abilities, if it is identified as a higher type and rewarded with a higher bonus [286]. By substituting the effort $e_{i,k}$ with e_i^*, we first rewrite the type-i validator node's utility function (8.17) as

$$U_{V(i)}(\mathbb{R}_i) = \theta_i(\beta_1 - \kappa\tau)f_i - b_i. \tag{8.26}$$

In the pure adverse selection model, the effort e_i for its type will be a fixed value, namely, $\hat{e}_i$, which means that a type-i validator is required to exert e_j^* if he or she signs the type-j contract rather than the optimal effort $e_{i,j}^*$. From equation (8.26), we can conclude that this validator can obtain the maximum utility from the joint model, which is $\theta_i(\beta_1 - \kappa\tau)f_j - b_j$. However, the validator's maximum utility in the pure model is only $\theta_i(\beta_1 - \kappa\tau)f_j - b_j - (\theta_j - \theta_i)^2b_j^2$, which is apparently less than that of the joint model. Therefore, even if signing the wrong contract, the rational validators are more willing to maximize their utility by adjusting the efforts. Therefore, we only give the solution of joint model below. After solving the moral hazard problem and obtaining the optimal choice of efforts, we assume that the validators' performance can be obtained (the performance can be expressed as a function of f_i and b_i). However, the validator nodes' stake values are still unknown to the beacon chain. Here we set the contract as (f_i, b_i), that is, the fixed salary f_i and bonus b_i. However, from equation (8.22) we can see that there are $\mathbb{N}(\mathbb{N} - 1)$ IC constraints and $\mathbb{N}$ IR constraints in total. Consequently, it is still difficult to solve the problem. Thus, we will first reduce the constraints by utilizing the definitions that we described in Section 8.2.3.3. The monotonicity of f_i and b_i is predefined, and the monotonicity of e_i^* is explained in the previous analysis (8.24). So we omit the proof of monotonicity here.

- **Reduction of IR Constraints**

According to the IC constraints in equation (8.22), for type $\forall i \in \{1, ..., \mathbb{N}\}$, we first have

$$U_{V(i)}(f_i, b_i) \geq U_{V(i)}(f_1, b_1). \tag{8.27}$$

Then based on the monotonic condition (8.4), we have

$$U_{V(i)}(f_1, b_1) \geq U_{V(1)}(f_1, b_1). \tag{8.28}$$

Obviously, given equation (8.27) and (8.28), we can come to the conclusion that

$$U_{V(i)}(f_i, b_i) \geq U_{V(1)}(f_1, b_1). \tag{8.29}$$

- **Reduction of IC Constraints**

According to the IC constraints, for given three adjacent types, namely, type-$i - 1$, type-i and type-$i + 1$, which follow $\forall i \in \{2, \ldots, \mathbb{N} - 1\}$, we have the following two inequations:

$$U_{V(i+1)}(f_{i+1}, b_{i+1}) \geq U_{V(i+1)}(f_i, b_i), \tag{8.30}$$

$$U_{V(i)}(f_i, b_i) \geq U_{V(i)}(f_{i-1}, b_{i-1}). \tag{8.31}$$

To proceed with the reduction of IC constraints, we set two parameters l and r, where

$$l = (\theta_{i+1} - \theta_i)(\beta_1 - \kappa\tau)f_i, \tag{8.32}$$

$$r = (\theta_{i+1} - \theta_i)(\beta_1 - \kappa\tau)f_{i-1}. \tag{8.33}$$

Then based on the monotonic conditions (8.4), (8.9), and the optimal result analysis (8.24), we easily have $l \geq r$. So we add equations (8.32) and (8.33) to (8.31), and obtain a new inequation $U_{V(i)}(f_i, b_i) + l \geq U_{V(i)}(f_{i-1}, b_{i-1}) + r$, that is,

$$U_{V(i+1)}(f_i, b_i) \geq U_{V(i+1)}(f_{i-1}, b_{i-1}). \tag{8.34}$$

Based on expressions (8.30) and (8.34), we have

$$U_{V(i+1)}(f_{i+1}, b_{i+1}) \geq U_{V(i+1)}(f_{i-1}, b_{i-1}). \tag{8.35}$$

Repeat the steps (8.30), (8.31), (8.34), and (8.35), and we can obtain the following constraints:

$$
\begin{aligned}
U_{V(i+1)}(f_{i+1}, b_{i+1}) &\geq U_{V(i+1)}(f_{i-1}, b_{i-1}) \\
&\geq U_{V(i+1)}(f_{i-3}, b_{i-3}) \\
&\geq \cdots \\
&\geq U_{V(i+1)}(f_2, b_2) \\
&\geq U_{V(1)}(f_1, b_1).
\end{aligned}
\tag{8.36}
$$

Similarly, for the type θ_{i-1} and all the contracts which follow $\forall i \in \{2, \ldots, \mathbb{N}\}$, we can easily obtain the following inequations by the same steps above:

$$
\begin{aligned}
U_{V(i-1)}(f_{i-1}, b_{i-1}) &\geq U_{V(i-1)}(f_{i+1}, b_{i+1}) \\
&\geq \cdots \\
&\geq U_{V(i-1)}(f_{\mathbb{N}}, b_{\mathbb{N}}).
\end{aligned}
\tag{8.37}
$$

Therefore, the proof of expressions (8.36) indicates that if the LDICs are satisfied, all the DICs also hold, as well as the LUICs and UICs proved in (8.37).

With the reduced constraints, we set the profit metric function as $\pi(\cdot) = d\theta_i q_i^*$. If there is no network delay, then $q_i = e_i$ holds. The optimization problem can be redefined as follows:

$$
\max_{(f_i, b_i)} \quad U_{BC} = \sum_{i=1}^{\mathbb{N}} \lambda_i \left[\frac{d\theta_i^2 b_i}{c} - f_i - \frac{\theta_i b_i^2}{c} \right],
\tag{8.38}
$$

s.t.

(a) $U_{V(i)}(f_i, b_i) = U_{V(i)}(f_{i-1}, b_{i-1}), \quad \forall i \in \{1, \ldots, \mathbb{N}\},$

(b) $U_{V(1)}(f_1, b_1) = 0.$

To solve this problem, we first set

$$
\Delta_j = (\theta_{j+1} - \theta_j) f_j (\beta_1 - \kappa\tau).
\tag{8.39}
$$

Based on the $\mathbb{N}$ IR constraints of equation (8.38), we add all the equations that are numbered from 1 to i together and get

$$
U_{V(i)} = \sum_{j=1}^{i-1} \Delta_j.
\tag{8.40}
$$

According to equation (8.40), we derive an expression for f_i:

$$
f_i = \frac{b_i + \sum_{j=1}^{i-1} \Delta_j}{\theta_i(\beta_1 - \kappa\tau)}, \quad \forall i \in \{2, \ldots, \mathbb{N}\}.
\tag{8.41}
$$

Note that $f_1 = b_1/\theta_1(\beta_1 - \kappa\tau)$. After substituting equation (8.41) into (8.38), (8.38) will be converted into a new problem; we differentiate U_{BC} with respect to b_i and then get

$$
\frac{\partial U_{BC}}{\partial b_i} = \frac{d\theta_i^2}{c} - \frac{1}{\theta_i(\beta_1 - \kappa\tau)} - \frac{2\theta_i b_i}{c}.
\tag{8.42}
$$

Next, by differentiating $\frac{\partial U_{BC}}{\partial f_i}$ with respect to b_i, we have

$$\frac{\partial^2 U_{BC}}{\partial (b_i)^2} = -\frac{2\theta_i}{c} < 0. \tag{8.43}$$

Clearly, we can reach the conclusion that the problem is a convex problem with the result (8.43). Therefore, we can get the optimal solution (f_i^*, b_i^*) by setting the first derivative as zero:

$$b_i = \frac{d\theta_i}{2} - \frac{c}{2\theta_i^2(\beta_1 - \kappa\tau)}. \tag{8.44}$$

The network failure occurs mostly within the information propagation among nodes and can cause an extra time cost, which is viewed as the network delay in this book for simplicity. The network delay of the whole network is assumed to follow a normal distribution with mean μ and variance σ^2 [323]. When we take the network delay into consideration, that is, $\varepsilon > 0$, and with $q_i = e_i - \varepsilon$, we can rewrite the optimization problem as follows:

$$\max_{(f_i, b_i)} \quad U_{BC} = \sum_{i=1}^{N} \lambda_i \left[d\theta_i \int_0^{\Delta T} (e_i^* - t)\mathrm{d}F(t; \mu) - f_i - b_i \int_0^{\Delta T} (e_i^* - t)\mathrm{d}F(t; \mu) \right]. \tag{8.45}$$

where $\varepsilon \sim f(t; \mu, \sigma)$ is a normal distribution, and ΔT is the acceptable tolerant delay for blockchain network. The optimal solutions to such problem is similar as above.

We present the optimal results of e_i^*, f_i, and b_i in the following subsection.

8.2.4.3 Simulation Results and Analysis

In this subsection, we present the simulation results and give the analysis for each illustration with the parameter setting. Then we present the numerical results in the following steps.

According to the utility function earlier in Section 8.2.4, we set the different parameters β_1 and β_2 to evaluate the fixed salary f_i and bonus b_i. That means, the parameter setting will affect the fixed salary and bonus. Since $\beta_2 = 2c + \kappa\tau$, we first keep the parameters κ and τ fixed and set $d = 5.5$ and $c = 5$, and then increase β_1. With the x-axis representing the different types of validator nodes, from Fig. 8.4, we can see that β_1 significantly affects the fixed salary f_i, but has slight effect on the bonus b_i. Moreover, the monotonicity shown in Fig. 8.4 is consistent with our premise (8.9).

According to the optimal solutions f_i^*, b_i^* and the optimal effort choice e_i^*, we observe that another important parameter that may affect them is the unit cost c. We increase the cost and try to determine the different impacts on the results. So we first keep the parameters κ and τ fixed and set $d = 3.1$, $\beta_1 = 5$, and then change the value of c. Finally, from Figs. 8.5a–c we can see that the fixed salary, an optimal effort choice, and total reward decrease along with the increasing of c. We do not list the bonus b_i here, since it varies little as the the cost changes, which is similar to Fig. 8.4. In fact, even for the fixed salary, the variation is tiny as well.

As shown in Fig. 8.6, the validators of type-2, type-4, type-6, type-8, and type-10 signing the different contracts have various utilities. It shows apparently that the

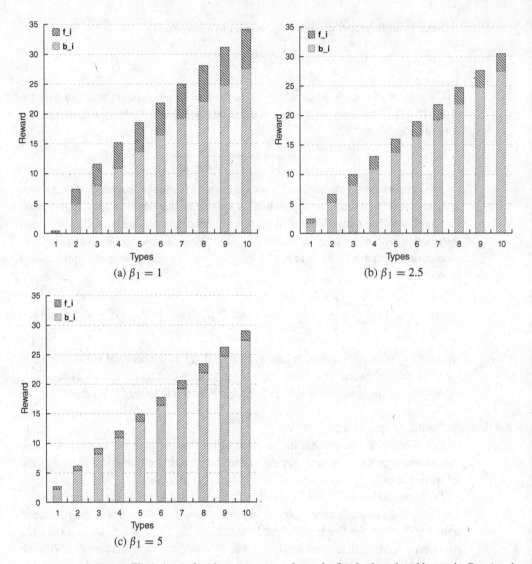

Figure 8.4 The impact of evaluate parameter β_1 on the fixed salary f_i and bonus b_i. Reprinted with permission from the paper "Contract-theoretic pricing for security deposits in sharded blockchain with Internet of Things (IoT)" published in *IEEE Internet of Things Journal.*

validators have the maximum utilities only when choosing the contract designed for their own, which proves the IC constraint. Besides, all these maximum incentives are positive, which explains the IR constraint.

Finally, Fig. 8.7 represents the comparison of the proposed scheme and the fixed-deposit scheme (e.g., Ethereum 2.0). The reward curve is the same as the one marked with "$c = 10$" of Fig. 8.5c. The stake curve is not obtained from the real data, just from a simulation in this model. However, it is easy to adapt the real data to a curve of this model by adjusting the parameters and setting an "exchange rate." In Ethereum 2.0,

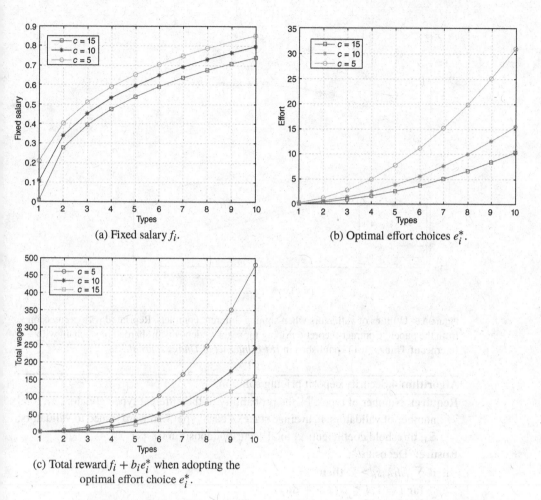

(a) Fixed salary f_i.

(b) Optimal effort choices e_i^*.

(c) Total reward $f_i + b_i e_i^*$ when adopting the optimal effort choice e_i^*.

Figure 8.5 The impact of cost c on the fixed salary f_i, optimal effort choice e_i^* and the total reward $f_i + b_i e_i^*$. Reprinted with permission from the paper "Contract-theoretic pricing for security deposits in sharded blockchain with Internet of Things (IoT)" published in *IEEE Internet of Things Journal*.

only the validators whose stakes are greater than 32 ETH can afford it and are eligible for operation and maintenance within a blockchain. We assume that these validators belong to the types that are greater than 7 in our model. Obviously, 32 ETH blocks out these validators whose types are less than 7 and leads' to their disqualification from the participation of a blockchain. Not only that, 32 ETH cannot ensure an adequate security incentive for the system against the higher-type validators. For a better comparison, take the type-10 validator as an example, let D_1 denote the difference between the stake and 32 ETH, let D_2 denote the difference between the proposed deposit and stake, and let D_3 denote the difference between the proposed deposit and 32 ETH. Thus, it is clear that owing to $D_2 < D_1$ and $D_3 > 0$, the proposed model can provide a better security incentive than that of the fixed-deposit model for the system, which motivates

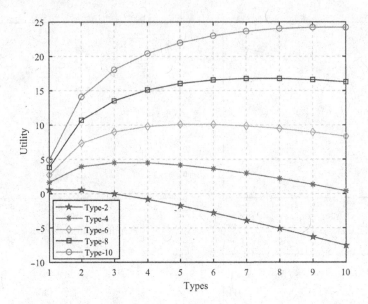

Figure 8.6 Utilities of validators when signing different contracts. Reprinted with permission from the paper "Contract-theoretic pricing for security deposits in sharded blockchain with Internet of Things (IoT)" published in *IEEE Internet of Things Journal*.

Algorithm 4 Security deposit pricing solution.

Require: Number of types: $\mathbb{N}$, the probability of the different type validator: λ_i, total number of validators: n, average stake of each type: s_i, reward issued to validators: $\mathbb{R}_i$, threshold coefficient: κ, total security deposit in Casper: $\mathbb{D}$;

Ensure: Deposit d_i^*;

1: **if** $\sum_1^N n\lambda_i s_i \geq \mathbb{D}$ **then**
2:     **for** $i = 1; i \leq \mathbb{N}; i + +$ **do**
3:         Set $\delta = \frac{\lambda_i s_i}{\sum_{j=1}^N \lambda_j s_j}$;
4:         $d_i^* = \min\left\{s_i, \max(\frac{\delta\mathbb{D}}{n\lambda_i}, \kappa \cdot \mathbb{R}_i)\right\}$;
5:     **end for**
6: **end if**

---

the validators who possess more stake to behave in a legal way. Additionally, there is no restriction for the lower-type validators. All of them are required to submit an affordable deposit, and obtain reward for their work by signing the contracts. In this model, reward, deposit and stake of all types always follow the rule that we analyzed before, namely, reward < deposit < stake. According to [304], security derives from the size of the penalty, which equals the amount of deposit submitted by validators, not the number of validators. Thus, we can easily have the relation of a deposit's amount between [304] and our work as follows: $\sum_{i=1}^{10} \lambda_i \mathbb{D}_i \geq \sum_{i=7}^{10} \lambda_i \mathbb{D}_7$, where the left-hand term denotes the total amount of deposits in our work and the right-hand term represents the size of deposits in [304] with $\mathbb{D}_i$ viewed as the required deposit. Together

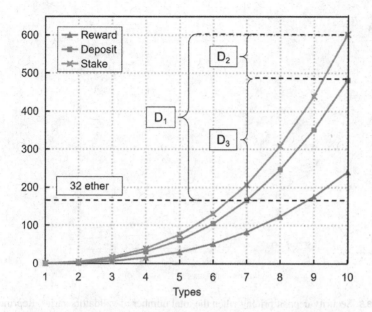

Figure 8.7 Comparison of reward, deposit, stake, and the fixed deposit (e.g., 32 ETH). Reprinted with permission from the paper "Contract-theoretic pricing for security deposits in sharded blockchain with Internet of Things (IoT)" published in *IEEE Internet of Things Journal.*

with the same distribution of validators, the deposits required in this model exceed Ethereum 2.0, which means the security is retained rather than being reduced.

An extreme case is that all the potential validators do not have as many as 32 ETH in their accounts. However, if the total number of these potential validators n is far greater than that of validators in the original committee (e.g., 128 in [325]), the following inequality may hold:

$$\sum_{i=1}^{N} n\lambda_i s_i \geq \mathbb{D}, \tag{8.46}$$

where $\mathbb{D}$ is the total amount of security deposit required by one committee. We adopt a proportional assignment to determine the security deposit d_j for each validator:

$$d_j = \frac{\lambda_j s_j}{\sum_{i=1}^{N} \lambda_i s_i} \cdot \frac{\mathbb{D}}{n\lambda_j}. \tag{8.47}$$

With the inequality (8.46), we can prove that:

$$d_i \leq s_i. \tag{8.48}$$

Obviously, any assigned deposit is less than or equal to the stake in the validator's account, which indicates such an assignment is feasible. Additionally, Algorithm 4 is proposed to obtain the optimal deposit. We assume the validators are uniformly distributed for ease of analysis, and type-7 validators have an average stake of 32

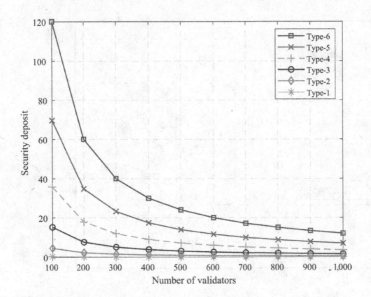

Figure 8.8 Security deposit pricing when the total number of validators varies. Reprinted with permission from the paper "Contract-theoretic pricing for security deposits in sharded blockchain with Internet of Things (IoT)" published in *IEEE Internet of Things Journal*.

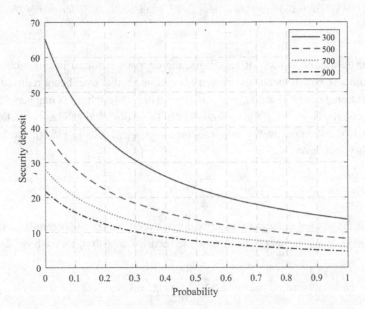

Figure 8.9 Security deposit pricing when the probability of type-6 validators varies. Reprinted with permission from the paper "Contract-theoretic pricing for security deposits in sharded blockchain with Internet of Things (IoT)" published in *IEEE Internet of Things Journal*.

ETH, so all the lower types cannot afford 32 ETH. We further investigate the security deposit pricing when the total number of validators varies in Fig. 8.8. We can see that the security deposit is decreasing in the number of validators. However, some of the

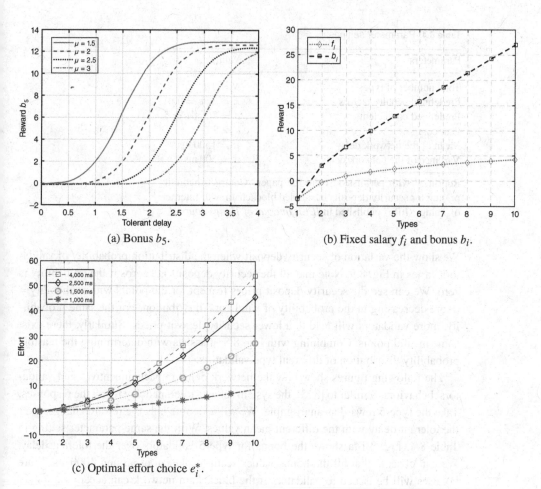

(a) Bonus b_5.

(b) Fixed salary f_i and bonus b_i.

(c) Optimal effort choice e_i^*.

Figure 8.10 The impact of network delay on validators' rewards and efforts. Reprinted with permission from the paper "Contract-theoretic pricing for security deposits in sharded blockchain with Internet of Things (IoT)" published in *IEEE Internet of Things Journal*.

deposit pricing points are not valid. Take type-6 as an example. It needs to submit up to 120 ETH security deposit if the total number is 100. With the previous assumptions, inequality (8.46) and equation (8.47), we can easily obtain the minimum number of validators: 476. Together with the total number, we also have the security deposit for each validator satisfying the equation: $d_i = s_i$. Moreover, we can also obtain the upper bound and lower bound of the penalty coefficient: $\overline{\kappa} = \frac{s_i}{\mathbb{R}_i}$ and $\underline{\kappa} = \frac{d_i}{\mathbb{R}_i}$. According to our contract design, κ is predetermined. Through the calculation of boundaries, we can conclude that $\kappa \cdot \mathbb{R}_i$ will be adopted as the security deposit if $\kappa \in [\underline{\kappa}, \overline{\kappa}]$. Consequently, the security deposits charged on the validators exceed $\mathbb{D}$: $\sum_{i=1}^{N} n\lambda_i \kappa \mathbb{R}_i > \mathbb{D}$. As mentioned in [304], security derives from the security deposit. Thus, the proposed security deposit pricing can even provide more security.

Apart from the total number of validators, another factor may affect the security deposit pricing is the probability of validators' distribution. Take type-6 as an example.

Table 8.4 Parameter settings.

Parameters	Values
Total number of types	$N = 10$
Predefined penalty factors	$\kappa = 2, \tau = 0.01$
Predefined coefficients	$d = 5.5, \beta_1 = 5$
Unit cost	$c = 5$
Mean of the network delay	$\mu = 1500 \, \text{ms}$
Variance of the network delay	$\sigma = 500 \, \text{ms}$

Reprinted with permission from the paper "Contract-theoretic pricing for security deposits in sharded blockchain with Internet of Things (IoT)" published in *IEEE Internet of Things Journal*.

We show the variation of security deposit when the distribution probability of validators varies in Fig. 8.9. Note that all the security deposits are zeros if the probability is zero. We can see the security deposit prices (except for the points with probability = 0) are decreasing in the probability of validators' distribution. For the same probability, more validators will lead to a lower security deposit prices. Similarly, there exist some invalid points. Combining with Fig. 8.8, it assists with determining the feasible probability distribution of different type validators.

The following figures show how the network delay impacts incentives and validators' behaviors. Similar to [323], the system set up a tolerant delay for all the responses. Take the type-5 reward as an example. We will examine how the reward changes over the tolerant delay with the different mean values. With the same parameter setting in Table 8.4, Fig. 8.14a shows the bonus for type-5 validators over the tolerant delay. We can observe that all the bonus values seem to plateau at around 4000 ms. More bonuses will be issued to validators if the blockchain network can accept the longer delay. Moreover, the solid curve demonstrates that a lower network delay can result in a higher bonus. However, the maximum values are still lower than that of the no-delay case in Fig. 8.4a. With $\mu = 1500 \, \text{ms}$ and $\Delta T = 3000 \, \text{ms}$, Fig. 8.14b plots the base salary and bonus over all the validator types. As the type increases, the rewards for each type of validator are gradually increasing. Similarly, all the rewards are less than that of the no-delay case in Fig. 8.4a. Note that the rewards for type-1 and type-2 are lower than zero. Thus, some lowest types of validators can be filtered out due to the network delay. Finally, Fig. 8.14c compares all the effort levels with the different tolerance delay. As is observed, the effort level increases in types and tolerance delay, which indicates that more effort is required to compensate for the loss caused by network delay. Combining with Fig. 8.14a, we can figure out that network delay can decrease the bonus, which means the network delay also acts as a disincentive to effort level.

8.2.5   The Joint Design of Adverse Selection and Tournament

To take this research one step further, we additionally consider that the network places more weight on the performance (e.g., a higher quality of task completion contributes more market value for the blockchain network) than on the stake. The performance also varies significantly throughout all the validators. In this case, we consider performance as the main criterion of classification. However, a validator node's effort is a hidden action that can be scheduled by itself and is unknown to the beacon chain. To supplement this, "stake" should be considered as a minor criterion of rewarding. We further utilize *adverse selection* to formulate the optimization problem and determine the minimum threshold of stake s required from different types of validators. We assume that the devices' ability distribution can be acquired through the prescreening in the PoW context. To reduce the monitoring cost [286] and maintain the ex-ante effort level, we develop a joint design of adverse selection and tournament to deal with this intricate problem. The beacon chain, as the contract designer, divides the time into $\mathbb{K}$ intervals, and each interval Δt is represented by a type $\theta \in \{\theta_1, ..., \theta_i, ..., \theta_{\mathbb{K}}\}$. Note that the first interval Δt_1 belongs to the $\mathbb{K}$th type $\theta_{\mathbb{K}}$, and the last interval $\Delta_{\mathbb{K}}$ belongs to the first type θ_1. Assume that time t is a random variable whose distribution depends on the reciprocal of effort, namely, e^{-1}. We can intuitively determine that the more effort results in the shorter time. That is, for different effort levels i and j, if $e_i > e_j$ and $e_i^{-1} < e_j^{-1}$, then there is a high probability that $t_i < t_j$.

For better understanding, we clarify the monotonicity and mapping relation of *type*, *effort*, *reciprocal of effort*, and *performance* as shown in Table 8.5.

From Table 8.5, we can conclude that a validator node wins the jth place if and only if its effort is the jth order and it belongs to type-j of all the orders $\{1, ... j, ..., \mathbb{K}\}$. An important point is that the first place of type order denotes the lowest performance level and the $\mathbb{K}$th place denotes the highest one. Take θ_j as an example; the validator's effort level is e_j and the corresponding time interval is $\Delta t_{(\mathbb{K}+1-j)}$ rather than Δt_j. We list the main notations of this model in Table 8.6.

Given the analysis regarding the performance, effort, stake and reward, it is clear that the joint model given earlier in Section 8.2.4 does not apply to the scenario that we consider in this section. The basic rationale of tournament is first to check the performance rank order, and then to reward the validator according to the orders. Through prescreening [326], the beacon chain obtains an ex-ante task completion time distribution. Assume that the computation power distribution is relatively constant during a certain period, and the winning probability of a validator is positively associated with its optimal effort on computing. In other words, a validator can achieve its

Table 8.5 Monotonicity and mapping relation.

Term	Parameters
Type	$\theta_{\mathbb{K}} > \cdots > \theta_j > \cdots > \theta_1$
Effort	$e_{\mathbb{K}} > \cdots > e_j > \cdots > e_1$
Reciprocal of effort	$e_{\mathbb{K}}^{-1} < \cdots < e_j^{-1} < \cdots < e_1^{-1}$
Performance (time)	$\Delta t_1 < \cdots < \Delta t_{\mathbb{K}+1-j} < \cdots < \Delta t_{\mathbb{K}}$

Reprinted with permission from the paper "Contract-theoretic pricing for security deposits in sharded blockchain with Internet of Things (IoT)" published in *IEEE Internet of Things Journal*.

Table 8.6 Main notations (2).

Symbol	Definition
$\mathbb{K}$	The total number of types
Δt_i	The predefined threshold time interval of completing task
$\mathbb{R}_1$	The reward determined in tournament model
$P(\text{rank} = j)$	The probability of certain effort level is in the jth order of all levels
A	The coefficient of absolute risk aversion
$\mathbb{E}$	The optimal effort that maximizes the validator's utility
p, d, γ	The coefficients evaluating the observed performance

Reprinted with permission from the paper "Contract-theoretic pricing for security deposits in sharded blockchain with Internet of Things (IoT)" published in *IEEE Internet of Things Journal*.

expected ranking only by maintaining the ex-ante optimal effort level. This assumption can assist with simplifying the model design and calculation. In the following subsections, we present the tournament model design, the optimal solution of tournament, the adverse selection model design, and the optimal solution of adverse selection model, respectively.

8.2.5.1 Tournament Model Design

As we analyze in Table 8.5, the observed performance order and the type order are opposite. That is, a validator with longer completion time of task will obtain a lower reward. Besides, by introducing the adverse selection concept, we first classify the observable time into different ranks, which simplifies the design of tournament. According to the utility function in equation (8.5) described in the system model, we redefine this function for the validator:

$$\omega(\mathbb{R}_1) = \frac{(\mathbb{R}_1)^p}{p}, \tag{8.49}$$

where p is the power coefficient and $0 < p < 1$, and $\mathbb{R}_1$ is the reward determined in the tournament model. In this model, we assume that the reward is a convex function of effort e. For simplicity, we replace e with the observed performance (time) t, then we define $\mathbb{R}_1 = (d/t)^\gamma$, where d is a predefined parameter and $\gamma > 1$. So we have

$$\omega\left(\frac{1}{t}\right) = \frac{\gamma d^{\gamma p}(\frac{1}{t})^{\gamma p}}{\gamma p}. \tag{8.50}$$

Then we have the coefficient of absolute risk aversion for the validators

$$A\left(\frac{1}{t}\right) = -\frac{\omega''}{\omega'} = \frac{1 - \gamma p}{1/t}. \tag{8.51}$$

When we set $\gamma p < 1$, as the increase of performance, the risk aversion coefficient decreases.

In this pure model, the virtual cost of stake and the penalty factor is omitted, that is, $\xi(s) = 0$ and $\varphi(\theta, \mathbb{R}, e) = 0$. Finally, we derive the expected utility function U'_V in the tournament model as follows:

$$U'_V = \sum_{j=1}^{K} \{\omega(\mathbb{R}_{1,j})P(rank = j) - \psi(e_j)\}, \tag{8.52}$$

where $P(rank = j)$ represents the probability that a certain effort level is in the jth order of all the levels. It also represents the $(\mathbb{K}+1-j)$th order of all the time intervals. Thus, we have the probability distribution function as follows:

$$P(rank = j) = P\{(\mathbb{K} - j)\Delta t \le t \le (\mathbb{K} + 1 - j)\Delta t\}$$
$$= \int_{(\mathbb{K}-j)\Delta t}^{(\mathbb{K}+1-j)\Delta t} f(t; e^{-1})dt, \tag{8.53}$$

where $f(t; e^{-1})$ is the probability density function of time, and e^{-1} is the expected value of the distribution.

According to the system model, we set $\pi(\cdot) = ge = g/\int tf(t; e^{-1})dt$ and $\mu(\mathbb{R}) = \mathbb{R}_1$, where g is a predefined evaluation coefficient. Then the optimization problem is defined as follows:

$$\max_{(\mathbb{R}_1, \mathbb{E})} U'_{BC} = \frac{g}{\int tf(t; e^{-1})dt} - \mathbb{R}_1, \tag{8.54}$$

s.t.

(a) $\mathbb{E} = \arg\max_e \int v(\mathbb{B})f(t; e^{-1})dt - \psi(e),$

(b) $\omega(\mathbb{R}_1)\int_{\Delta t} f(t; \mathbb{E}^{-1})dt - \psi(\mathbb{E}) \ge \bar{u}.$

where $\bar{u}$ is the minimal and acceptable utility of a validator node.

8.2.5.2 Optimal Solution of Tournament

From the rational standpoint, all the validator nodes try to achieve a certain rank order in their power, in order to obtain the maximum utilities. In general, we assume the distribution of the number of task completions per unit of time by validators is in conformity with the exponential distribution, that is, $F(t; e^{-1}) \sim E(e^{-1})$, and set $\psi(e) = \frac{c}{2}(e^2)$. Therefore, we can get the optimal effort choice for different rank order by taking the first derivative of the validators' utility function:

$$\sum_{j=1}^{K} \left\{ \frac{\partial\omega(\mathbb{R}_{1,j})P(rank = j)}{\partial e_j} - \psi'(e_j) \right\} = 0. \tag{8.55}$$

Owing to the design of the joint model, the validators that belong to the same type will share the same reward, so we set a step function $W(\mathbb{R}_{1,j}) = \frac{h_1(\frac{1}{t_{\mathbb{K}-j+1}})^{h_2}}{h_2}$ to replace the evaluation reward function, where $h_1 = \gamma d^{\gamma p}$, $h_2 = \gamma p$, and $t_{\mathbb{K}-j}$ denotes the starting point value of time interval $\Delta t_{\mathbb{K}-j+1}$. Equation (8.55) can be rewritten as follows:

$$\frac{h_1(\frac{1}{t_{\mathbb{K}-j+1}})^{h_2}}{h_2} \frac{\partial P(rank = j)}{\partial e_j} - ce_j = 0. \tag{8.56}$$

Then we will get all the optimal effort choice e_j^* for the different performance of validator nodes by utilizing a mathematical tool, such as MATLAB.

8.2.5.3   Problem of Adverse Selection

Since the different time intervals correspond to the different optimal efforts, suppose there are $\mathbb{K}$ time intervals. The type θ is defined as follows:

$$\theta_i = ae_i, \quad \forall i \in \{1, \ldots, \mathbb{K}\}, \tag{8.57}$$

where a is a predefined parameter, and e_i is the same as e_i^*.

With the system model under consideration, we present the type-i validator node's utility function under the adverse selection model as follows:

$$U_{V(i)} = \theta_i \omega(\mathbb{R}_i) - \eta s_i - \rho(\mathbb{R}_i) P_i(t_i \geq T_{max}), \tag{8.58}$$

where $\mathbb{R}_i = \mathbb{R}_{1,i} + \mathbb{R}_{2,i}$, $\mathbb{R}_{1,i}$ is determined by the tournament model, $\mathbb{R}_{2,i}$ is the reward determined by the adverse model, η is the virtual unit cost of stake value, s_i denotes the average stake value threshold of type-i validator nodes, $\rho(\cdot)$ denotes the penalty according to the reward, and $P_i(t \geq T_{max}) = 1 - F(T_{max}; e_i^{-1})$, which is the probability of submission delay.

Based on the contract theory, for $\forall i, j \in \{1, \ldots, \mathbb{K}\}$ and $i \neq j$, the **IR** constraint is $U_{V(i)}(\mathbb{R}_i, s_i) \geq 0$, and the **IC** constraint is: $U_{V(i)}(\mathbb{R}_i, s_i) \geq U_{V(i)}(\mathbb{R}_j, s_j)$.

8.2.5.4   Utility Function of Beacon Chain

Let λ_i denote the prior distribution probability of type-i. According to all types of validator nodes, $\forall i \in \{1, \ldots, \mathbb{K}\}$, the objective of the beacon chain is to maximize the expected utility function. This means higher ranked validator nodes with higher-stake value are more desired. According to the system model, we set $\pi(\cdot) = g_1(\theta_i)^{z_1} + g_2(s_i)^{z_2}$. With the **IR**, **IC** constraints and the monotonicity condition, the optimization problem is expressed as

$$\max_{(\mathbb{R}_j, s_i)} U_{BC} = \sum_{i=1}^{N} \lambda_i \left(g_1(\theta_i)^{z_1} + g_2(s_i)^{z_2} - \mu \mathbb{R}_i \right), \tag{8.59}$$

s.t.

$$(a) \quad U_{V(i)}(\mathbb{R}_i, s_i) \geq 0,$$

$$(b) \quad U_{V(i)}(\mathbb{R}_i, s_i) \geq U_{V(i)}(\mathbb{R}_j, s_j)$$

$$(c) \quad \theta_1 < \cdots < \theta_i < \cdots < \theta_{\mathbb{K}},$$

where g_1, g_2, z_1, z_2 and μ are pre-defined parameters.

8.2.5.5   Optimal Solution of Adverse Selection

In order to solve the problem in equation (8.59), as formulated in Section 8.2.5.4, we first prove the monotonicity condition, and then reduce the number of the constraints by showing the proofs of IC and IR constraints. The details are listed in the following steps.

Lemma 2 (Monotonicity) *For any contract $(\mathbb{R}_i, s_i)$, given $\theta_i \geq \theta_j$ and $\mathbb{R}_i \geq \mathbb{R}_j$, s_i and s_j will also satisfy the monotonic relation, that is $s_i \geq s_j$.*

Proof According to the IC constraints of different types of validator nodes, we can obtain

$$U_{V(j)}(\mathbb{R}_j, s_j) \geq U_{V(j)}(\mathbb{R}_i, s_i). \tag{8.60}$$

After transforming the inequation (8.60), we have

$$\eta(s_i - s_j) \geq (\theta_j \omega(\mathbb{R}_i) - \rho(\mathbb{R}_i)P_i) \\ - (\theta_j \omega(\mathbb{R}_j) - \rho(\mathbb{R}_j)P_j). \tag{8.61}$$

Set a new function $h(\mathbb{R}_i) = (\theta_j \omega(\mathbb{R}_i) - \rho(\mathbb{R}_i)P_i)$, and take the first derivative of $h(\mathbb{B}_i)$:

$$h'(\mathbb{R}_i) = \theta_j \omega'(\mathbb{R}_i) - \rho'(\mathbb{R}_i)P_i. \tag{8.62}$$

If $h'(\mathbb{R}_i) > 0$, we have $\theta_j v'(\mathbb{R}_i) > \rho'(\mathbb{R}_i)P_i$. Note that the minimum value of θ_j is θ_1, that is, $j = 1$, and the maximum value of P_i is 1. So we set the slope of function $\omega(\cdot)$ and $\rho(\cdot)$ as $\theta_1 \omega' > \rho'$.

Now equation (8.61) is rewritten as

$$\eta(s_i - s_j) \geq h(\mathbb{R}_i) - h(\mathbb{R}_j). \tag{8.63}$$

It is clear that when $\theta_1 \omega' > \rho'$, we have $h'(\mathbb{R}_i) > 0$. For given $\mathbb{R}_i > \mathbb{R}_j$, we have $h(\mathbb{R}_i) - h(\mathbb{R}_j) > 0$; that means $s_i > s_j$ exists when $w_2 \neq 0$. Therefore, we complete the proof of monotonic relation. $\square$

- **Reduction of IR Constraints**

The monotonicity condition already holds due to the solutions of tournament. Here the proof is omitted. Since we have previously proved the reduction of IR and IC constraints, we give only a brief description toward the proofs in the following.

The IR constraints of all types will hold if the IR constraint of type 1 can be satisfied. According to the IC constraints in equation (8.59), for type $\forall i \in \{1, \dots, \mathbb{K}\}$, we first have

$$U_{V(i)}(\mathbb{R}_i, s_i) \geq U_{V(i)}(\mathbb{R}_1, s_1). \tag{8.64}$$

Then based on the monotonicity conditions, we have the inequation defined as follows:

$$U_{V(i)}(\mathbb{R}_1, s_1) \geq U_{V(1)}(\mathbb{R}_1, s_1), \tag{8.65}$$

$$U_{V(i+1)}(\mathbb{R}_i, s_i) \geq U_{V(i+1)}(\mathbb{R}_{i-1}, s_{i-1}). \tag{8.66}$$

By combing with in equation (8.64), we have

$$U_{V(i)}(\mathbb{R}_i, s_i) \geq U_{V(1)}(\mathbb{R}_1, s_1). \tag{8.67}$$

- **Reduction of IC Constraints**

Consider three adjacent types, i.e., type $i - 1$, type i and type $i + 1$, which follow $\forall i \in \{2, \dots, \mathbb{K} - 1\}$. According to the IC constraints, then we have the following two inequations:

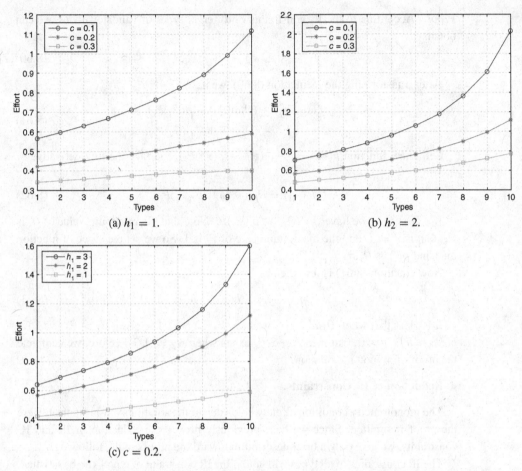

(a) $h_1 = 1$.

(b) $h_2 = 2$.

(c) $c = 0.2$.

Figure 8.11 The impact of cost c and evaluation parameter h_1 on the optimal effort choice e_i^*. Reprinted with permission from the paper "Contract-theoretic pricing for security deposits in sharded blockchain with Internet of Things (IoT)" published in *IEEE Internet of Things Journal*.

$$U_{V(i+1)}(\mathbb{R}_{i+1}, s_{i+1}) \geq U_{V(i+1)}(\mathbb{R}_i, s_i), \tag{8.68}$$

$$U_{V(i)}(\mathbb{R}_i, s_i) \geq U_{V(i)}(\mathbb{R}_{i-1}, s_{i-1}). \tag{8.69}$$

We can easily get $(\theta_{i+1} - \theta_i)\omega(\mathbb{R}_i) \geq (\theta_{i+1} - \theta_i)v(\mathbb{R}_{i-1})$ by virtue of the monotonic conditions and add it to (8.69), and then we have a new inequation.

Based on expressions (8.66) and (8.68), we have

$$U_{V(i+1)}(\mathbb{R}_{i+1}, s_{i+1}) \geq U_{V(i+1)}(\mathbb{R}_{i-1}, s_{i-1}). \tag{8.70}$$

The rest of the details are all the same as that of Section 8.2.4.2.

With the reduced constraints, the optimization problem can be redefined as follows:

$$\max_{(\mathbb{R}_j, s_i)} \quad U_{BC} = \sum_{i=1}^{\mathbb{N}} \lambda_i \left(g_1(\theta_i)^{z_1} + g_2(S_i)^{z_2} - \mu \mathbb{R}_i \right). \tag{8.71}$$

s.t.

$(a)\quad U_{V(1)}(\mathbb{R}_1, s_1) = 0,$

$(b)\quad U_{V(i)}(\mathbb{R}_i, s_i) = U_{V(i)}(\mathbb{R}_{i-1}, s_{i-1})$

$(c)\quad \theta_1 < \cdots < \theta_i < \cdots < \theta_K.$

Based on the $\mathbb{K}$ IC constraints of equation (8.71), we add all the equations that are numbered from 1 to i together and get

$$U_{V(i)} = \sum_{j=1}^{i-1} \Delta_j + \rho(\mathbb{R}_1)P_1, \tag{8.72}$$

where

$$\Delta_j = \omega(\mathbb{R}_j)(\theta_{j+1} - \theta_j). \tag{8.73}$$

For simplicity, we set

$$\omega(\mathbb{R}_j) = \mathbb{R}_j = \mathbb{R}_{1,j} + \mathbb{R}_{2,j}. \tag{8.74}$$

According to equation (8.58), we derive an expression for s_i:

$$\mathbb{R}_{2,i} = \frac{\eta s_i + \sum_{j=1}^{i-1}}{\theta_i} - \mathbb{R}_{1,j}, \tag{8.75}$$

$$\mathbb{R}_{2,1} = \frac{\eta s_1 + 2\mathbb{R}_{1,1}P_1 - \theta_1 \mathbb{R}_{1,1}}{\theta_1 - 2P_1}. \tag{8.76}$$

After substituting equation (8.75) into (8.71), (8.71) will be converted into a new problem; we differentiate U_{BC} with respect to S_i and then get

$$\frac{\partial U_{BC}}{\partial s_i} = g_2 z_2 (s_i)^{z_2-1} - \frac{\eta}{\theta_i}. \tag{8.77}$$

Next, by differentiating $\frac{\partial U_{BC}}{\partial \mathbb{B}_i}$ with respect to $\mathbb{B}_i$, we have

$$\frac{\partial^2 U_{BC}}{\partial (s_i)^2} = g_2 z_2 (z_2 - 1)(s_i)^{z_2-2}. \tag{8.78}$$

When we set $0 < z_2 < 1$, we have $\frac{\partial^2 U_{BC}}{\partial (s_i)^2} < 0$. Obviously, we can conclude that the problem is a convex problem. Therefore, we can get the optimal solution $(\mathbb{R}_i^*, s_i^*)$ by setting the first derivative to zero, we have

$$s_i^* = \left(\frac{\eta}{g_2 z_2 \theta_1}\right)^{\frac{1}{z_2-1}}. \tag{8.79}$$

Then the following optimal results can be obtained by standard optimization solvers.

8.2.5.6   Simulation Results and Numerical Analysis

In this section, we present the simulation results to prove our optimal solutions, and describe the effect of different parameters on these solutions. According to the optimal solution of Section 8.2.5.2, two important parameters h_1 and c will affect the reward $\mathbb{R}_1$ and effort. So we first set h_1 as a fixed value and set $h_2 = 0.8$, and then from Figs. 8.11a and 8.11b, we see the optimal effort choice e_i^* decreases as the cost c increases. Next, set c as a fixed value (e.g., $c = 0.2$); from Fig. 8.11c, we conclude that the optimal effort choice e_i^* increases with the parameter h_1. For the three figures, it is clear that the optimal effort choices for different types meet the monotonicity condition.

For the following simulations, we focus on the minimum threshold of stake for different types, the total rewards, and the utility of different contracts. The optimal results in the adverse model are obtained based on the tournament model. We first set $a = 30$, and compare the result with the optimal effort curve (i.e., $h_1 = 2$) as shown in Fig. 8.11c. So we have the optimal stake results for different types. From Fig. 8.12, the greater the type, the more stake is required. Figure 8.13 shows the variation of the two kinds of rewards that are determined by the proposed joint model. Both of them, as well as their sum, are consistent with the monotonicity condition. In order to simplify Fig. 8.14, we set all the utility values that are lower than zero to be zero. We can observe that the validators have the maximum utilities only when choosing the contract designed for their own, which proves the IC constraint. Besides, all these maximum incentives are positive, which explains the IR constraint.

Finally, Fig. 8.15 represents the comparison of the proposed scheme and the fixed-deposit scheme (e.g., Ethereum 2.0). We adopt the stake curve presented in Fig. 8.12 and the reward curve presented in Fig. 8.13. Without loss of generality, we scale down

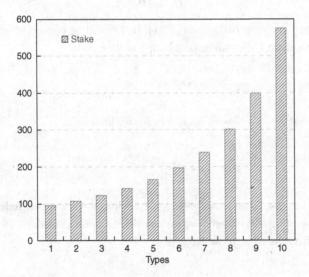

Figure 8.12 The minimum thresholds of stake for all the types. Reprinted with permission from the paper "Contract-theoretic pricing for security deposits in sharded blockchain with Internet of Things (IoT)" published in *IEEE Internet of Things Journal*.

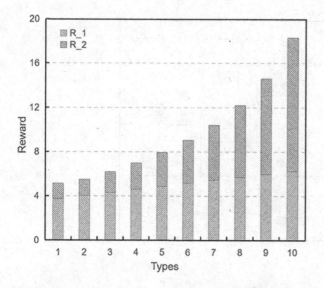

Figure 8.13 Two kinds of reward for all the types. Reprinted with permission from the paper "Contract-theoretic pricing for security deposits in sharded blockchain with Internet of Things (IoT)" published in *IEEE Internet of Things Journal.*

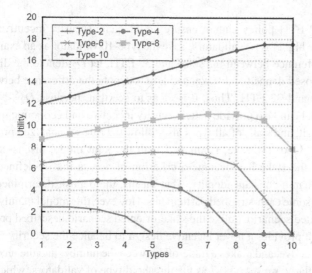

Figure 8.14 Utilities of validators when signing the different contracts. Reprinted with permission from the paper "Contract-theoretic pricing for security deposits in sharded blockchain with Internet of Things (IoT)" published in *IEEE Internet of Things Journal.*

the stake to make it accommodate the reward in the joint model. In Ethereum 2.0, only the validators whose stakes are greater than 32 ETH can afford it and are eligible for operation and maintenance within a blockchain. Just like the assumption that we made previously in Section 8.2.4, 32 ETH blocks out those validators whose types are less than 7 and leads to their disqualification from the participation of a blockchain.

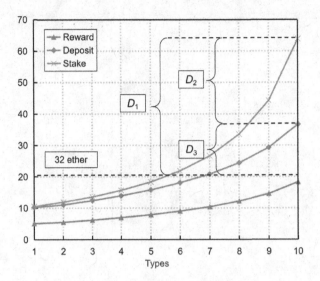

Figure 8.15 Comparison of reward, deposit, stake, and the fixed deposit (e.g., 32 ETH). Reprinted with permission from the paper "Contract-theoretic pricing for security deposits in sharded blockchain with Internet of Things (IoT)" published in *IEEE Internet of Things Journal.*

Not only that, 32 ETH policy cannot ensure an adequate security incentive for the system against the higher type validators. Take the type-10 validator as an example, let D_1 denote the difference between the stake and 32 ETH, let D_2 denote the difference between the proposed deposit and stake, and let D_3 denote the difference between the proposed deposit and 32 ETH. Thus, it is clear to see that, because $D_2 < D_1$ and $D_3 > 0$, this model can also provide better security incentive and economic incentive. The reward, deposit, and stake of all types also follow the rule we analyzed previously, namely, reward < deposit < stake. Compared with the joint model discussed earlier in Section 8.2.4, the stake has become a criterion of access that is defined by the contracts rather than a constant identity. That means, the deposit determined in this model may block some cash-strapped participants. However, this model mainly focuses on an effort-oriented scenario, unlike the stake-oriented scenario described previously in Section 8.2.4, it provides a novel incentive design to balance the security incentive and economic incentive, and makes a trade-off between the number and the incentive of participants. Similarly, we set type-7 as the threshold type of validators, which means only the validators marked with the types higher than 7 can afford the fixed deposit in Ethereum 2.0. However, the proposed model allows a wide range of validators to participate in the PoS blockchain. For the higher-type ($i \geq 7$) validators, they need to submit a higher deposit than Ethereum 2.0. The lower-type ($i < 7$) validators can contribute a minor amount of deposits while they are prohibited from participating in Ethereum 2.0. Finally, we can reach the same conclusion as in Section 8.2.4.3, that is, the security of this model is not decreased compared with Ethereum 2.0.

Analogously, there also exists an extreme case of this joint scheme. Through the calculation, if none of the required stakes is greater than 32 ETH but $\sum_{i=1}^{N} n\lambda_i s_i \geq \mathbb{D}$

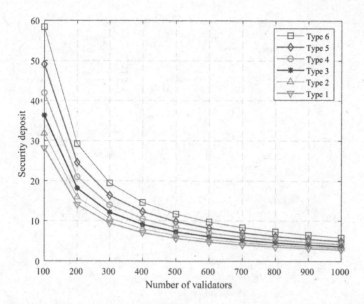

Figure 8.16 Security deposit pricing when the total number of validators varies. Reprinted with permission from the paper "Contract-theoretic pricing for security deposits in sharded blockchain with Internet of Things (IoT)" published in *IEEE Internet of Things Journal*.

exists, we can price the security deposit according to the assignment algorithm 4. All the validators' locked stake is less than 32 ETH, which can be mapped into type-i ($i \in \{1, \ldots, 6\}$) of the proposed scheme. We set an exchange rate to simplify the calculation, which is type-7 validators' stake to 32 ETH. With the assumption of uniform distribution of validators, we will first examine the total number of validators' impact on security deposit pricing. According to the security incentive in inequality (8.46) and the assignment in equation (8.47), we have the security deposit for all types of validators in Fig. 8.16. However, some pricing points are invalid due to the constraint $d_i \leq s_i$. Given the prior probability and stake of validators, we can obtain the minimum number of validators through equations (8.46) and (8.48). From Fig. 8.16, we can intuitively conclude that all validators' deposits are decreasing in the total number of validators. More validators participating can lead to a smaller share for an individual. Figure 8.16 also shows that the security deposit pricing is increasing in the validators' types, which indicates that the assignment is consistent with the monotonicity condition. We also explore how the probability of a specific type will impact security deposit pricing. Take type-6 validators as an example. From Fig. 8.17, we can observe that the security deposits are decreasing in the probability of validators (except for $\lambda_6 = 0$). The idea behind these two figures is similar: The more validators there are, the smaller share there is. Nevertheless, sometimes there may exist some unfeasible pricing points. We can easily filter out these points by using the inequality in (8.46). Consequently, given any stake value, we can determine the minimum number and feasible probability of validators based on Figs. 8.16 and 8.17.

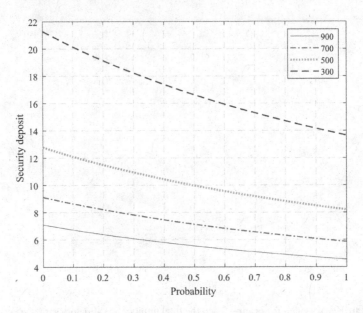

Figure 8.17 Security deposit pricing when the probability of type-6 validators varies. Reprinted with permission from the paper "Contract-theoretic pricing for security deposits in sharded blockchain with Internet of Things (IoT)" published in *IEEE Internet of Things Journal*.

8.3   Conclusion

This chapter provided the fundamental concepts of contract theory and introduced the primary type of contract theory and the necessary constraints for the problem formulations: individual rationality and incentive compatibility. In particular, we investigated the design of rewards and the pricing strategy of deposits. The proposed scheme can be applied in any blockchain network with an administrative party, where the "deposit" can represent any proof or token in the circulation of such a scenario. We can consider the following steps to implement the proposed models in a practical blockchain system. First, as the administrator in the blockchain network, the beacon chain can obtain the distribution of potential validators' stakes and performance without any private information and classify them into different types. The administrator can determine which joint model is more satisfactory based on the practical scenario. Second, the administrator starts to design the contract with the historical data and apply the empirical data to the proposed model, adjusting the system parameters and coefficients to test the optimal results until they are consistent with practice. Then he can obtain the feasible system parameters. Next, the beacon chain will broadcast the contract set to all the potential validators. They will evaluate the utilities provided by all the contracts by using their specific private information and decide whether to accept a particular contract or not. Last, the validators will exert efforts to fulfill their contractual obligations. The beacon chain will evaluate the efforts by observing the performances and pay the validators with stipulated rewards. The corresponding validator's deposit will be slashed entirely if any violation occurs. Overall, this chapter explained security and economic incentives, then analyzed the relationship of the features (i.e., stake, performance, and effort), reward, and deposit of a participant. With two complicated scenarios that we discussed before, we proposed two joint models under the contract theory framework to balance the security incentive and economic incentive. As a result, both the economic incentive and the security incentive are kept at the same time. Compared with the mainly emphasized security incentive in Ethereum 2.0, the simulation results show that the proposed optimal contract-based approach can achieve a better balance between the security incentive and economic incentive.

9 Equilibrium Problem with Equilibrium Constraints

The Stackelberg game is a strategic game that defines the sequential decision-making process, in which the leader can make a decision first and the followers act according to the decisions sequentially. Because of these characteristics, the Stackelberg game can be used for dealing with some certain problems in blockchain-based ecosystems, such as those involving different parties with varying priorities in the context of industry. The Stackelberg equilibrium, which may be derived through the backward induction approach, characterizes the solution of the Stackelberg game. However, the traditional method may fail if there does not exist a closed-form solution to the follower's problem. The game will get much more complicated if there are multiple leaders and followers.

To address such issues, mathematical programming with equilibrium constraints (MPEC) and equilibrium programming with equilibrium constraints (EPEC) have been established. The MPEC, in instance, relates to the scenario with a single leader, whereas the EPEC corresponds to the more general case with numerous leaders. The MEPC and EPEC models do not require a closed-form solution to the followers' problem, extending the coverage of the traditional Stackelberg game to address a broader range of situations. We start from variational inequality (VI) since it is vitally important for MPEC and EPEC formulation and analysis.

9.1 Variational Inequality Basics

Variational inequality theory is mainly used for studying the equilibrium of nonlinear analysis [327], which is particularly useful in formulating and analyzing the optimization problems in terms of convergence, existence, and uniqueness of solutions. It has been widely applied to broad areas, such as economics, optimization, and game theory.

9.1.1 Variational Inequalities Problem

The variational inequality (VI) problem, $\mathsf{VI}\,(\mathcal{X}, F)$, is defined on the set $\mathcal{X}$, a subset of a n-dimensional Euclidean space with a mapping $F\colon \mathcal{X} \mapsto \mathbb{R}^n$ in order to obtain a vector $x^\star \in \mathcal{X}$ that satisfies

$$\left(x - x^\star\right)^T F\left(x^\star\right) \geq 0, \quad \forall x \in \mathcal{X}. \tag{9.1}$$

For $\mathsf{VI}\,(\mathcal{X}, F)$ defined in (9.1), we have following result regarding its solution.

Theorem 15 (Existence of solution to VI problems [328]) *The VI problem VI $(\mathcal{X}, F)$ admits a solution if the set $\mathcal{X}$ is compact, nonempty, and convex, and mapping F is continuous.*

For VI problems, we are particularly interested in a class of problems that feature monotone properties.

Definition 31 (Monotone [328]) Problem VI $(\mathcal{X}, F)$ in (9.1) is

- monotone on $\mathcal{X}$ if

$$\left(x - x'\right)^T \left(F(x) - F(x')\right) \geq 0, \quad \forall x, x' \in \mathcal{X}; \tag{9.2}$$

- strictly monotone on $\mathcal{X}$ if

$$\left(x - x'\right)^T \left(F(x) - F(x')\right) > 0, \quad \forall x, x' \in \mathcal{X}, \quad x \neq x'; \tag{9.3}$$

- strongly monotone on $\mathcal{X}$ if $\exists c > 0$ s.t.

$$\left(x - x'\right)^T \left(F(x) - F(x')\right) > \left\| x - x' \right\|^2, \quad \forall x, x' \in \mathcal{X}. \tag{9.4}$$

Monotone qualities are extremely helpful in the understanding of VI issues, we can resort to the Jacobian matrix of the mapping F to assist the analysis. In particular, denote the Jacobian as J_F, we have the following theorem.

Theorem 16 *If F is continuously differentiable on $\mathcal{X}$,*

- *F is monotone if and only if J_F is positive semidefinite $\forall x \in \mathcal{X}$;*
- *F is strictly monotone if and only if J_F is positive definite $\forall x \in \mathcal{X}$;*
- *F is strongly monotone if and only if J_F is uniformly positive definite $\forall x \in \mathcal{X}$, that is, $\exists c > 0$ s.t.*

$$y^T J_F(x) y \geq c \|y\|^2, \quad \forall y \in \mathbb{R}^n. \tag{9.5}$$

The solution to the VI issues may be deduced from the following theorem due to monotonicity properties.

Theorem 17 *Suppose $\mathcal{X} \subseteq \mathbb{R}^n$ is closed and convex and $F \colon \mathcal{X} \to \mathbb{R}^n$ is continuous. Then, for the VI problem VI $(\mathcal{X}, F)$,*

- *if F is strictly monotone on $\mathcal{X}$, VI $(\mathcal{X}, F)$ admits at most one solution;*
- *if F is strongly monotone on $\mathcal{X}$, VI $(\mathcal{X}, F)$ has a unique solution.*

9.1.2 Connections with Optimization and Games

The term VI defines a broad class of problems that are closely related to convex optimization [329] and game theory [330]. To elaborate, consider a constrained optimization given as

$$\min \quad f(x) \tag{9.6a}$$

$$\text{s.t.} \quad x \in \mathcal{X}, \tag{9.6b}$$

where objective function f is continuously differentiable on a closed and compact set $\mathcal{X}$ as an n-dimensional subset of $\mathbb{R}^n$. Then, if $\mathcal{X}$ is convex, according to the minimum principle in nonlinear programming, any local minimizer of f, denoted by x^*, satisfies [329]

$$\left(x - x^*\right)^T \nabla_x f \left(x^*\right) \geq 0, \quad \forall x \in \mathcal{X}. \tag{9.7}$$

The point that satisfies the condition above is also called a stationary point. Further, if f is convex in x, then the stationary point is the global minimizer of f.

Further consider the cases that the feasible region $\mathcal{X}$ is explicitly defined by finitely many differentiable inequalities and equations

$$\mathcal{X} = \left\{x \in \mathbb{R}^n \,|\, G\left(x\right) \leq 0, H\left(x\right) = 0\right\}, \tag{9.8}$$

where $G\colon \mathbb{R}^n \to \mathbb{R}^{n'}$, $H\colon \mathbb{R}^n \to \mathbb{R}^{n''}$ are vector-valued continuously differentiable functions. Suppose the constraints satisfy certain constraint qualification [331]; then, the stationary point of (9.6a,b) satisfies the Karush–Kuhn–Tucker (KKT) condition specified as

$$\nabla_x f \left(x\right) + \sum_{\ell=1}^{n'} \mu_\ell \nabla_x G_\ell \left(x\right) + \sum_{\ell=1}^{n''} \nu_\ell \nabla_x H_\ell \left(x\right) = 0 \tag{9.9a}$$

$$H\left(x\right) = 0 \tag{9.9b}$$

$$0 \leq \mu \perp G\left(x\right) \leq 0, \tag{9.9c}$$

where $0 \leq a \perp b \geq 0$ indicates that $a, b \geq 0$ and $a \cdot b = 0$, and μ and ν are the Lagrange multipliers related with the constraints.

By revisiting the previous discussions on VI and optimization, solving the expressions (9.6a,b) is equivalent to solving the VI problem in equation (9.1), on the condition that mapping F is defined as $\nabla_x f\left(x\right)$. If $\mathcal{X}$ is convex, the equivalence is obtained in the sense that the VI problem solution corresponds to the stationary point of the optimization. Further, if f is convex, then the VI problem solution corresponds to the global minimizer of the optimization.

Let us now consider the game model defined as

$$\mathcal{G} = \left\{\mathcal{J}, \left\{\mathcal{X}_j\right\}_{j \in \mathcal{J}}, \left\{f_j\right\}_{j \in \mathcal{J}}\right\}, \tag{9.10}$$

where there are $J = |\mathcal{J}|$ agents each solving the individual optimization

$$\min \quad f_j\left(x_j; x_{-j}\right) \tag{9.11a}$$

$$\text{s.t.} \quad x_j \in \mathcal{X}_j, \tag{9.11b}$$

where the subscript j stands for all agents in $\mathcal{J}$ other than agent-j. Consider the case of a convex game where for each agent j, the problem in expressions (9.11a,b) is a convex problem; then we know that the individual problem in (9.11a,b) is equivalent to the VI problem $\mathsf{VI}_j\left(\mathcal{X}_j, F_j\right)$, which solves for x_j^* satisfying

$$\left(x_j - x_j^*\right)^T F_j\left(x^*\right) \geq 0, \quad \forall x_j \in \mathcal{X}_j, \tag{9.12}$$

with $F_j = \nabla_{x_j} f_j(x_j)$. Then, the game $\mathcal{G}$ can be represented as the form of a VI problem $VI(\mathcal{X}, F)$ with

$$\mathcal{X} = \prod_{j \in \mathcal{J}} \mathcal{X}_j, \tag{9.13}$$

and

$$F = [F_j]_{j \in \mathcal{J}}. \tag{9.14}$$

Now that we've described the game model as a VI issue, the VI problem solution corresponds to the game's Nash equilibrium, just as in the case of optimization. As a result, we may turn optimization issues or game models into VI problems and then use the VI theory to aid in the study of the original optimization or game problems.

9.2   Stackelberg Game Basics

9.2.1   Concepts and Definitions

A Stackelberg game refers to a class of strategic game models that incorporate the hierarchical decision-making process. Consider two players, denoted as A and B in a Stackelberg game who, respectively, solve the following problems

$$\min \quad f_A(x_A; x_B) \tag{9.15a}$$
$$\text{s.t.} \quad x_A \in \mathcal{X}_A, \tag{9.15b}$$

and x_B is determined as a function of x_A, by solving

$$\min \quad f_B(x_B; x_A) \tag{9.16a}$$
$$\text{s.t.} \quad x_B \in \mathcal{X}_B, \tag{9.16b}$$

where the strategy x_A is determined by A, while x_B is determined by B, while their utilities depend on the strategies of both players. In a Stackelberg game, the players operate sequentially, with the player who makes the initial move designated as the leader and the other as the follower. We choose A as the leader and B as the follower for the game described in expressions (9.15a,b) and (9.16a,b). Because of their sequential decision making, they join the game asymmetrically, which influences how they approach their optimization problems. In particular, in the first stage, the leader analyzes its own goal while also considering the reasonable reaction of the follower, which we refer to as the upper-layer problem. The lower-layer problem is solved by the follower in the second stage, which takes the leader's behavior in the first stage as a given. Because the leader's upper problem-solving takes the reaction of the followers into consideration, the leader has an advantage in the game. In contrast, the follower can only respond to the leader's actions, putting him at a disadvantage in the game. The "first-mover advantage" is a distinctive feature of Stackelberg games.

9.2.2   Stackelberg Equilibrium

The Stackelberg equilibrium is the equilibrium of a Stackelberg game. Assume that the Stackelberg equilibrium occurs for the one-leader one-follower Stackelberg game described by expressions (9.15a,b) and (9.16a,b). Then, we solve the follower's problem first by assuming a set strategy for the leader, that is, the game's lower-layer problem. In this respect, we can denote the lower optimality condition as

$$x_B^\star = \mathsf{BR}_B(x_A) = \arg \min_{x_B \in \mathcal{X}_B} f_B(x_B; x_A), \tag{9.17}$$

where BR_B is the best-response function of B, that is, the follower's optimal strategy is obtained in the form of a function that has parameters of the fixed leader's strategy. Assume that the follower's response is one-of-a-kind and that $mathsf BR_B$ appears explicitly as a closed-form function. This answer may then be applied to the leader's problem, which leads to the upper-layer problem. For the game between A and B, the upper problem can be formulated as

$$\min \quad f_A(x_A, \mathsf{BR}_B(x_A)) \tag{9.18a}$$
$$\text{s.t.} \quad x_A \in \mathcal{X}_A. \tag{9.18b}$$

By solving the upper-layer problem, the leader obtain its optimal strategy, denoted as $x_A^\star$. Then, the leader's action is substituted into the follower's response to arrive at the actual strategy for the follower as $\mathsf{BR}_B(x_A^\star)$. Finally, the optimal strategies of the leader and follower constitute the Stackelberg equilibrium. In view of this discussion, the Stackelberg equilibrium $\{x_A^\star, x_B^\star\}$ satisfies

$$\begin{cases} f_A(x_A^\star, \mathsf{BR}_B(x_A^\star)) \leq f_A(x_A, \mathsf{BR}_B(x_A)), & \forall x_A \in \mathcal{X}_A, \\ f_B(x_B^\star, x_A^\star) \leq f_B(x_B, x_A^\star), & \forall x_B \in \mathcal{X}_B. \end{cases} \tag{9.19}$$

The preceding stages are based on the implicit assumption that the follower's best-response function accepts a closed-form expression. However, this is not always the case with actual issues. When this characteristic does not hold, we cannot typically apply the preceding process directly. To address this problem, we can instead use the MPEC formulation.

9.3   Mathematical Programming with Equilibrium Constraints (MPEC)

When the rational response of the follower does not allow for a closed-form expression, we present mathematical programming with equilibrium constraints (MPEC), which provides an effective tool for dealing with such cases [332].

Generally, an MPEC problem appears in the form of

$$\min \quad f(x, y) \tag{9.20a}$$
$$\text{s.t.} \quad x \in \mathcal{X}, \tag{9.20b}$$
$$y \in \mathcal{S}(x), \tag{9.20c}$$

where f is an $(n+m)$-dimensional continuously differentiable function, $\mathcal{X} \subseteq \mathbb{R}^n$, and $S(x)$ is the solution set of the VI problem defined as $\text{VI}(C(x), F(x, \cdot))$, indicating that $y \in S(x)$, if and only if $y \in C(x)$ and

$$(y' - y)^T F(x,y) \geq 0, \quad \forall y' \in C(x). \tag{9.21}$$

Suppose $C(x)$ is defined as

$$C(x) = \left\{ y \in \mathbb{R}^m \,|\, g_i(x,y) \geq 0, \quad i = 1, 2, \ldots, I \right\}, \tag{9.22}$$

with the fact that g is twice continuous differentiable and concave in the second variable. For the MPEC specified in expressions (9.20a–c), we make the following assumptions:

- $\mathcal{X}$ is compact;
- $C(x)$ is not empty, $\forall x \in \mathcal{A}$, where $\mathcal{A}$ is an open set containing $\mathcal{X}$;
- $C(x)$ is uniformly compact on $\mathcal{A}$;
- problem $\text{VI}(C(x), F(x, \cdot))$ is strongly monotone;
- the constraints defined by g are all active while satisfying the constraint qualification.

The VI problem as MPEC constraints leads to a unique solution (due to strong monotonicity), and the unique solution is characterized by the KKT requirements (as constraint qualification holds). In particular, the KKT conditions can be specified as

$$F(x,y) - \nabla_y g(x,y) \lambda = 0, \tag{9.23a}$$

$$0 \leq \lambda \perp g(x,y) \geq 0, \tag{9.23b}$$

where λ is the multiplier related with the constraint of $C(x)$. As such, we can see that $\forall x$, there exists a unique y within the set $S(x)$. Also, this unique VI problem solution as the constraints of MPEC can by fully characterized by the KKT conditions. With the KKT conditions replacing the VI as the constraints, the original optimization problem can be rewritten as

$$\min \quad f(x,y) \tag{9.24a}$$

$$\text{s.t.} \quad x \in \mathcal{X}, \tag{9.24b}$$

$$F(x,y) - \nabla_y g(x,y) \lambda = 0, \tag{9.24c}$$

$$0 \leq \lambda \perp g(x,y) \geq 0. \tag{9.24d}$$

As a result, the MPEC issue is reformulated as a single-layer optimization problem. The optimization in equations (9.24a–d) does not, however, satisfy the constraint qualification condition. Actually, the failure of constraint qualification is a common problem when converting the MPEC to a single-layer optimization. Moreover, the constraint in (9.24d) appears in the form of complementarity, which is generally difficult to handle [332].

Consolidated research efforts have been directed to this topic since the restriction in the converted complementarity form poses a major difficulty in tackling the MPEC as a conventional optimization problem. Here we introduce an effective method proposed in [333].

For the problem in equations (9.24a–d), which appears in the smooth form, we can reformulate it in a nonsmooth form as

$$\min \quad f(x,y) \tag{9.25a}$$
$$\text{s.t.} \quad x \in \mathcal{X}, \tag{9.25b}$$
$$F(x,y) - \nabla_y g(x,y) \lambda = 0, \tag{9.25c}$$
$$g(x,y) - z = 0, \tag{9.25d}$$
$$-2\min(\lambda, z) = 0, \tag{9.25e}$$

where z is the newly introduced variable such that the optimization in equations (9.25a–e) satisfies the constraint qualification. For the problems in equations (9.20a–c) (also (9.24a–d)) and (9.25a–e), we have the following theorem.

Theorem 18 ([333])   *We say $\{x^\star, y^\star\}$ is a global (local) solution to the MPEC in the expressions (9.20a–c) if and only if there exists a pair $\{\lambda^\star, z^\star\}$ so that the quadruple $\{x^\star, y^\star, \lambda^\star, z^\star\}$ is a global (local) solution to the optimization in equations (9.25a–e).*

With the equivalence between MPEC problem and nonsmooth optimization thus established, we can resort to the problem in equations (9.25a–e) with optimization techniques to solve the original problem. For problem (9.25a–e), the main challenge lies in the nonsmooth constraint in equation (9.25e). To overcome this difficulty, the following smoothing technique was introduced [333]. Specifically, define the function ϕ_η with the parameter η as

$$\phi_\eta(a,b) = \sqrt{(a-b)^2 + 4\eta^2} - (a+b). \tag{9.26}$$

For the function ϕ_η, $\forall \eta$,

$$\phi_\eta(a,b) = 0 \Leftrightarrow a \geq 0, \ b \geq 0, \ ab = \eta^2. \tag{9.27}$$

Also, when $\eta = 0$, $\phi_\eta(a,b) = -2\min(a,b)$, and for any $\eta > 0$, $\phi_\eta(a,b)$ is continuously differentiable. Moreover, for any (a,b), $\lim_{\mu \to 0} \phi_\eta(a,b) = -2\min(a,b)$. Based on these observations, it should be clear that we can use the function ϕ_η as the smoothed version to approximate the nonsmooth constraint in equations (9.25a–e). In particular, define the function

$$\Phi_\eta(\lambda, z) = \left[\phi_\eta(\lambda_\ell, z_\ell)\right]_{\ell=1,2,\dots,m}. \tag{9.28}$$

Then, we arrive the η-parameterized version of the optimization in equations (9.25a–e) as

$$\min \quad f(x,y) \tag{9.29a}$$
$$\text{s.t.} \quad x \in \mathcal{X}, \tag{9.29b}$$
$$F(x,y) - \nabla_y g(x,y) \lambda = 0, \tag{9.29c}$$
$$g(x,y) - z = 0, \tag{9.29d}$$
$$\Phi_\eta(\lambda, z) = 0, \tag{9.29e}$$

which is a smooth problem with proper constraint qualification. The problem in equations (9.29a–e) can be regarded as an approximated version of the optimization in equations (9.25a–e). We can see that, when η is sufficiently close to zero, the problem in equations (9.29a–e) can provide a solution that is sufficiently close to the solution to the nonsmooth problem (9.25a–e), which further solves the original MPEC problem (9.20a–c). We have shown in Section 9.1.1 that the VI problem may be seen as a variant of the optimization problem or the game model. By examining the MPEC issue in equations (9.20a–c), we can see that the VI problem as a constraint may be recast as a single optimization or game. In the first instance, if the constraint in the form of VI is genuinely an optimization, the MPEC is mathematically similar to the Stackelberg game described in Section 9.2. Specifically, the VI as a constraint relates to the follower's problem, but the MPEC as a whole refers to the leader's higher problem. In specifically, for the MPEC (9.20a–c), the VI constraint for y is parameterized by the other optimization variable bmx. Similarly, in the Stackelberg game, the best strategy of the follower contains characteristics of the leader's strategy. Furthermore, the MPEC solves the VI issue as a constraint to its optimum, whereas the Stackelberg game leader must predict the follower's reaction to reach its best strategy. The second scenario, in which the VI problem is the constraint in the MPEC and corresponds to the game model, may be justified in the same way as the first, except that the optimum in the first instance is substituted with the game's equilibrium. Because the game model frequently involves more than one agent, the MPEC can result in a one-leader multi-follower game. When comparing the MPEC to a Stackelberg game, we observed in Section 9.2 that using the sequential approach to solve a Stackelberg game often necessitates a closed-form solution by the follower. The discussions here in Section 9.3 for the MPEC, on the other hand, were based on the assumption that the VI issue as the constraint permits the unique solution to provide a correct KKT representation. As a result, the MPEC issue, while more difficult, needs fewer criteria. The MPEC model broadens the Stackelberg game to more generic settings, allowing for broader applications.

9.4   Equilibrium Programming with Equilibrium Constraint (EPEC)

Equilibrium programming with equilibrium constraints (EPEC) is a natural extension of the MPEC models, incorporating multiple MPEC problems in a competitive manner [334]. Specifically, the EPEC problem concerns a set of competitive agents in $\mathcal{J} = \{1, 2, \cdots, J\}$, where each $j \in \mathcal{J}$ solves the following problem

$$\min \quad f_j\left(x_j, y; x_{-j}\right) \tag{9.30a}$$

$$\text{s.t.} \quad x_j \in \mathcal{X}_j, \tag{9.30b}$$

$$y \in \mathcal{S}(x), \tag{9.30c}$$

where $x = \left[x_j\right]_{j \in \mathcal{J}}$ and the constraint in equation (9.30c) is defined as in equation (9.20c) as a VI problem and shared among all agents in $\mathcal{J}$.

As can be seen, all agents must solve the individual problem in equations (9.30a–c) as MPEC, where all MPECs are coupled in two ways. On the one hand, each agent influences the others by finding their unique optimum in terms of x_j. On the other hand, all agents must address a common constraint in terms of y through a VI issue parameterized by x. Technically, various agents might have acquired distinct y through the shared restriction on condition of identical x, as the VI problem admits numerous solutions. As a result, optimistic and pessimistic agents are proposed, which correspond to agents who predict the most advantageous and antagonistic solution in terms of their own objective functions as the actual solution to the VI issue as constraints. We confine the study here to the scenario when the VI issue as a constraint leads to a unique solution for every fixed x due to the inherent difficulty of solution selection for the VI problem.

Denote the solution to the MPEC problem for agent-j with respect to the strategies of other agents as $\mathsf{SOL}\left(\mathsf{MPEC}\left(x_{-j}\right)\right)$, where $\mathsf{MPEC}\left(x_{-j}\right)$ corresponds to the problem in equations (9.30a–c) which is parameterized by the strategies of all other agents. Then, the equilibrium to the EPEC, denoted by $\{x^\star, y^\star\}$, satisfies

$$\left\{x_j^\star, y^\star\right\} \in \mathsf{SOL}\left(\mathsf{MPEC}\left(x_{-j}^\star\right)\right), \quad \forall j \in \mathcal{J}. \tag{9.31}$$

Note, in expression (9.31), all the agents share the common anticipation of $y^\star$ as it uniquely exists with respect to $x^\star$. Also, we use "$\in$" rather than "$=$" in (9.31) as the MPEC problem for each agent may admit multiple solutions.

The condition (9.31) has motivated employment of *diagonalization methods* to solve EPEC problems [334]. We may solve individual MPEC issues in the form of equations (9.30a–c) using the methods mentioned in Section 9.3. The issues for each agent are then solved cyclically in the Jacobi or Gauss–Seidel approach. If there is convergence, it corresponds to a solution of the EPEC problem.

As can be expected, diagonalization methods are generally complicated while the convergence cannot be guaranteed. As the constraint in equation (9.30c) admits a unique solution for each fixed x, the constraint can be handled as at a single agent. Assume that the constraint in (9.30c) is undertaken at agent-j, then the EPEC problem is decomposed as

$$\left\{x_j^\star, y^\star\right\} \in \mathsf{SOL}\left(\mathsf{MPEC}\left(x_{-j}\right)\right), \tag{9.32}$$

at agent-j and solved for

$$\left\{x_i^\star\right\} \in \left\{ \begin{array}{l} \arg\min \quad f_i\left(x_i, y^\star; x_{-i}\right) \\ \text{s.t.} \quad x_i \in \mathcal{X}_i \end{array} \right\}, \tag{9.33}$$

at all agents-$i \in \mathcal{J} \backslash \{j\}$. Note that, for the problems in expression (9.33), the parameter $y^\star$ is obtained from equation (9.32). In this respect, the original J parallel MPEC problems are reduced to one MPEC problem and $J - 1$ single-layer optimizations. This can be regarded as a subproblem by each distinguishing agent-j, denoted as sEPEC-j. For the subproblem, we have the following result regarding their solution sets.

Theorem 19 ([335]) *Denote by $\mathcal{S}$ the set of solutions for the original EPEC problem, and by $\mathcal{S}_j$ the set of solutions for the subproblem sEPEC-j. Then,*

$$S = \bigcap_{j \in \mathcal{J}} S_j. \tag{9.34}$$

In view of Theorem 19, we may treat the EPEC issue, which was initially a collection of coupled MPECs, as a single MPEC and a series of optimization problems in the conventional form. As we can see, the decomposition has the advantage of no longer overlapping optimization variables in the subproblems, which differs from the original EPEC, which shares the common variable y at all MPECs. In this regard, the inherent challenges of EPEC can be addressed to some extent using MPEC and optimization theories and methodologies.

It has been proposed that EPEC issues could be reformulated as nonlinear complementarity problems or nonlinear programming problems, with the key being to manage the VI-form constraint with alternative relaxation approaches. For details on such techniques, the interested readers can refer to [334].

As an extension of MPEC, EPEC may be considered as a multi-leader multi-follower game in which the leaders confront the MPEC issue in the form of (9.30) and the followers face the VI problem in equations (9.30a–c) as EPEC constraints. Following any of the leaders' strategies x, the followers are required to create their strategies. In this aspect, y is the lowest equilibrium among the followers since they compete with one another. Meanwhile, leaders are expected to optimize the MPEC issue, where anticipating the lower equilibrium is essential to aid upper-layer decision-making. When we compare EPEC to the classic Stackelberg game, we can see that EPEC expands it by allowing for many leaders and various followers. More crucially, EPEC presents a mathematical model for dealing with the situation in which the follower's optimum (or followers' equilibrium) does not accept a closed-form solution. As a result, EPEC expands the Stackelberg game and MPEC to address a broader range of issues with hierarchical structures.

9.5 Example: Multi-leader Multi-follower Game for Resource Pricing in Blockchain Networks

The mining process in public blockchains with the Nakamoto consensus protocol requires solving a computational puzzle, that is, Proof of Work (PoW), which is resource expensive to implement in lightweight devices with limited computing resources and energy. Thus, renting mining services from cloud providers becomes a reasonable solution; this is called cloud mining. This enables users who want to mine, namely, miners, to purchase and lease an amount of hashing power from the cloud–edge providers without any hassle of managing the infrastructure. In this section, we study the interactions among the cloud–edge providers and miners in blockchain using a multi-leader multi-follower game-theoretic approach, in order to support PoW-based blockchains application. Owing to the inherent complexity of the formulated game, we employ the Alternating Direction Method of Multipliers (ADMM) algorithm to investigate the optimum solution. Utilizing the decomposition characteristics and fast convergence of ADMM, we obtain the optimum results in a distributed manner. Simulation results demonstrate that with the proposed solutions, the optimization of the utilities of miners and the profits of providers can be jointly achieved.

9.5.1   Introduction and Contribution

Electronic trading with digital transactions is growing in popularity for e-commerce applications, where the consensus is reached through trusted centralized authorities. The introduction of centralized authorities incurs additional cost, that is, nominal fees which become more excessive when the number of digital transactions grows. In 2008, a new P2P electronic payment system called *"Bitcoin"* was introduced that avoids this additional cost caused by digital transactions [1]. As a popular digital cryptocurrency, Bitcoin can record and store all digital transactions in a decentralized append-only public ledger called *"blockchain."* The Bitcoin is the first application of blockchain technologies with the Nakamoto consensus protocol. Subsequently, the blockchain has attracted remarkable public interests via a decentralized network with independence from central authorities. With blockchain, a transaction can take place in a decentralized fashion, which greatly saves the cost and improves the efficiency. Since its launch in 2009, the Bitcoin economy has experienced an exponential growth, and its capital market now has reached over 70 billion dollars [336]. After the success of Bitcoin, blockchain has been applied in many applications, such as vehicular networks [313], smart grid systems [209, 337], and Internet of Things (IoT) [338].

The core component of the public blockchain with the Nakamoto consensus protocol is a computational process called *mining*, where the transaction records are added into the blockchain via the solution of computationally difficult puzzle, that is, the PoW. Confirming and securing the integrity and validity of transactions are processed by a set of peer nodes called *"miners."* The security of blockchain directly relies on the distributed consensus protocol maintained by these miners [339, 340]. The typical Nakamoto consensus protocol works as follows. First, the miners choose and bundle a number of transactions that are processed to form a single *"block."* Each miner broadcasts its mined block to the rest of the blockchain network as soon as it solves the puzzle in order to claim the mining reward. Then, this block is verified by the majority of miners in this network, that is, to reach consensus. After the broadcast block reaches the consensus, it is successfully added into the globally accessible distributed public ledger, namely, blockchain. The miner which mines a block receives the mining reward when its mined block is the first one to be successfully added to the blockchain. This consensus protocol guarantees the security of the PoW-based blockchain applications [14, 86].

However, the mining in blockchain applications involving PoW is confined to dedicated mining equipment. The reason is that mining in blockchains with the Nakamoto consensus protocol incurs solving a PoW puzzle (i.e., a series of hashing computations), which is a resource-expensive process. As such, cloud mining becomes a promising and viable option where the miners purchase hashing capacity from the cloud provider's mining hardware already installed in data centers. In this case, the miners with only lightweight devices are enabled to participate in the PoW-based blockchain mining without involving the issues related to installing mining hardware, managing electricity consumption, etc. Such service exists in practice and some popular providers, such as Genesis Mining, CloudHashing, BootCloudChain, and MineOnCloud, offer hashing capabilities in exchange of a fee. A similar emerging concept named EthereumFog that integrates blockchain mining and edge computing has been recently realized [341]. In EthereumFog, the miners are allowed to offload the mining task to nearby edge servers or devices. By integrating cloud–edge computing into the framework of blockchain, more miners with lightweight devices are encouraged to participate in mining, which is beneficial in terms of improving the robustness of the blockchain. However, as compensation to the cloud–edge providers providing the cloud–edge computing service, the miners need to pay for the service cost. Accordingly, the resource management among the cloud–edge providers and miners is needed.

In this subsection, we mainly study the interactions among cloud–edge providers and miners to support the optimal allocation of the computational resources. Therein, the cloud–edge providers competitively sell computing service and in turn receive revenue from miners. In particular, we formulate a multi-leader multi-follower Stackelberg game. In the first stage, the cloud–edge providers set the price competitively and obtain the revenue from charging the miners for offloading the mining task. In the second stage, the miners decide on the service demand to purchase from different cloud–edge providers. Specifically, we consider the discriminatory pricing scheme for the providers, in which different unit prices are assigned to different miners.[1] To the best of our knowledge, this is the first work to study the interactions among multiple competitive cloud–edge providers and a group of miners in PoW based blockchain networks using multi-leader multi-follower game-theoretic approach. One key challenge in characterizing the game lies in the high dimensionality of each miner's strategy space, which impedes us from employing a conventional backward induction method. To tackle this challenge, we adopt the ADMM algorithm to obtain the optimum results in a distributed manner. The main contributions of this work are summarized as follows.

1. We formulate the interactions among cloud–edge providers and miners as an EPEC, since there exist equilibrium criteria at both the level of the providers and the level of miners due to the conflicts among themselves.
2. Taking advantage of its decomposition and fast convergence properties, we employ the ADMM algorithm to achieve the optimum results in a distributed manner for such EPEC scenario, where centralized optimization solutions are highly difficult and require great complexity.
3. We conduct extensive numerical simulations to evaluate the performance of blockchain networks. The results show that with the proposed algorithm, the

---

[1] The uniform pricing where a unit price is applied to all miners is a special case of the discriminatory pricing, and hence the techniques developed in the subsection can be applied similarly and directly for uniform pricing.

optimization of the utilities of miners and the profits of providers can be jointly achieved. Our work helps to achieve the PoW puzzle offloading and guide the cloud–edge provider to strategically extract the surplus through charging miners while competing with other providers.

The rest of the chapter is arranged as follows. Section 9.5.2 presents a review of the related work. Section 9.5.3 describes the system model and Section 9.5.4 formulates the multi-leader multi-follower Stackelberg game. In Section 9.5.5, we investigate the game equilibrium solutions using ADMM. We present the performance evaluations in Section 9.5.6. Section 9.6 concludes the chapter.

9.5.2   Related Work

There have been many excellent works studying computation offloading problems in the context of cloud–edge computing [342–346]. For example, the authors in [342] designed an optimization scheme for energy-efficient application execution in a cloud-empowered mobile application platform. The authors in [343] presented a mobile edge computing offloading framework and proposed a predictive computation mode transfer scheme to achieve low-latency communication. However, the above studies merely focused on the cases of a single user or single cloud–edge provider. As such, the authors in [345] formulated a multi-leader multi-follower Stackelberg game model to solve the two-tier mobile edge computing offloading problem. The computation offloading mechanisms in [345] are centralized without considering the interactions among multiple self-organizing users [346]. The authors in [344] solved the energy-efficient workload offloading in vehicular edge networks by using a distributed consensus algorithm. Unlike the aforementioned studies, our work proposed the cloud–edge computing offloading model in PoW-based public blockchain networks. Furthermore, most of the existing work on resource management in cloud–edge computing formulated the computation offloading problems by using constrained optimization and traditional game techniques. Instead, we utilize the advanced ADMM algorithm to efficiently solve the formulated game model with reasonable complexity in a distributed manner. Further, a group of literature related to our work is the mining schemes management for blockchain networks with the Nakamoto consensus protocol. In [213], the author developed a noncooperative game among the miners. The miner's strategy is to select the number of transactions to be included in a block. In the model, solving the PoW puzzle for mining is modeled as a Poisson process. The solution of the game is the Nash equilibrium which was derived only for two miners in [213]. Then, the authors in [214] modeled the mining process as a sequential game where the miners compete for mining reward sequentially. Therein, the miners are assumed to be rational, and they have to choose whether or not to broadcast their solution, that is, the mined block. It is proved in [214] that there exists a multiplicity of Nash equilibrium. Furthermore, it is found that not propagating is an optimal strategy under certain conditions. Similar to that in [214], the authors in [215] formulated the stochastic game for modeling the mining process, where miners decide on which blocks to extend and whether to broadcast the mined block. In particular, two game models where miners play a complete information stochastic game are studied. In the first model, each miner broadcasts immediately its mined block. The strategy of each miner is to select an appropriate block to mine. In the second model, the miner selects which block to mine, but it may not broadcast its mined block immediately. For both models, it is proved in [215] that when the number of miners is sufficiently small, the Nash equilibrium with respect to mining behaviors exists.

Another research area that relates to our work is the incentive mechanisms in crowdsensing [210, 347]. In crowdsensing, the crowdsensing service provider typically provides an incentive reward to encourage the crowdsensing users' participation. In one of the pioneering works [210], the authors formulated the Stackelberg game to model the interaction among the provider and users, where the provider determines the incentive reward and the users decide on the sensing contribution level. Based on the same game model, the authors in [347] proposed the socially aware incentive mechanisms for crowdsensing with the consideration of social network effects that exist on the user side. The social network effects indicate that the participants may derive more benefit when more participants join and contribute their sensing information to the services. It is proved that the social network effects strongly promote the sensing contribution of participants as well as the profit of the platform. Previous studies mainly work on dedicated devices for mining in general blockchain networks with the Nakamoto consensus protocol. However, the application of blockchain in wireless mobile networks is constrained by the challenge brought by the PoW puzzle during the mining process. To satisfy the requirement demand for the computing capacity and storage availability in resource-limited devices, for example, mobile and IoT terminals, offloading the computing tasks to cloud–edge provider is treated as a promising solution [348–350]. In particular, some recent work investigated the exploitation of cloud/edge computing for blockchain [220, 294, 351–356]. In [220], we, for the first time, considered that users running blockchain applications on their mobile terminals, can offload their PoW puzzle computations to the cloud or nearby edge server operated by the cloud–edge provider. In [294, 351], we formulated the interactions among the single cloud–edge provider and a group of miners using a Stackelberg game to maximize the profit of cloud–edge provider and the utilities of miners. The authors in [352] presented an auction-based market model to study the social welfare optimization of the cloud–edge provider and miners. The authors in [353] proposed employing deep learning methods to solve the profit maximization issue in [294]. In [354], the author proposed a novel resource trading architecture in blockchain-based industrial IoT with incomplete information, and applied a multi-agent reinforcement learning algorithm for effectively searching the near-optimal resource management policy. Reinforcement learning [357, 358] is a promising tool to deal with the problem of information uncertainty. The authors in [355, 356] studied the computation offloading in wireless blockchain networks supported by cloud–edge computing for secure data trading.

Nevertheless, all the existing works made an unrealistic assumption that there only exists a single cloud–edge provider, which hardly captures the real-world scenarios where there are multiple cloud–edge providers. Taking cloud mining for example, CloudHashing, Genesis Mining, and MineOnCloud can all act as cloud–edge providers to offer computing service in exchange of the service fee. The interactions among cloud–edge providers further complicate the corresponding mining management and computing resource allocation. Nevertheless, the competition among cloud–edge providers and its impacts on the interactions on miners has not been explored yet. In order to achieve the optimal resource management, modeling and analyzing the competition among cloud–edge providers is practical and necessary, and this is the focus of our work.

9.5.3   System Description

In this section, we first propose the system model of cloud–edge computing enabled blockchain networks. We then present the problem formulation for the cloud–edge computing resource management.

9.5.3.1   Blockchain Basics

Blockchain with the Nakamoto consensus protocol can be employed to support P2P secure data service, for example, P2P file transfer [95, 96]. To create a chain of blocks, the mining needs to be performed. The mining process is used to confirm and secure transactions to be stored in a block. This mining process is organized as a speed game among the miners with different computing powers. The problem is a PoW puzzle, which is expensive to solve and takes high computing power, time, and energy. In brief, this PoW puzzle includes considering a set of transactions that are present in the network, solving a mathematical problem[2] that depends on this set and propagating the result to the blockchain network for this solution to be checked and reach consensus. Once all these steps are done successfully, the set of transactions proposed by the miner forms a block that is appended to the blockchain. The first miner which successfully obtains the solution of the puzzle and reaches the consensus is considered to be the winner to which a certain reward is given. This is referred to as the speed game among the miners under the Nakamoto consensus protocol. The earlier studies, for example, in [14], have found that the puzzle cannot be handled efficiently using lightweight devices, for example, mobile terminals. In the following, we introduce the use of the cloud–edge computing concept for assisting to offload computational task, namely, the mining process. More details of blockchain networks and the mining process can be found in [14].

9.5.3.2   System Model

Following [220, 294, 352–354, 359], we consider a public blockchain supported by cloud–edge computing under the PoW-based Nakamoto consensus protocol (see Fig. 9.1). In the blockchain network, a set of N nodes with local limited computing

---

[2] Solving the problem needs hashing the blockchain information by the miners, and thus we use the hash power and computing power interchangeably throughout the present book.

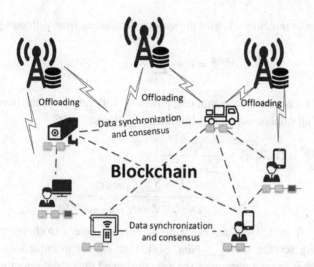

Figure 9.1 Blockchain supported by cloud–edge computing under the PoW-based Nakamoto consensus protocol. Reprinted with permission from the paper "Cloud/edge computing service management in blockchain networks: Multi- leader multi-follower game-based ADMM for pricing" published in *IEEE Transactions on Services Computing*.

power wants to participate in the consensus process as miners and make extra profit through block mining, and this is denoted as $\mathcal{N} = \{1, \dots, N\}$. To participate in the consensus process, these miners purchase the necessary computing service from cloud–edge providers[3] (e.g., Amazon EC2) without the hassle of managing the infrastructure such as seeking extra electricity sources. As such, the aforementioned PoW puzzle can be offloaded to the providers, and the offered computing service is priced by the providers. We can consider the proposed scenario as a specific DApp where blockchain works as the dedicated backbone. From the perspective of data processing, a DApp is a collection of smart contracts and transaction data in blockchain. With public blockchain, the realization of a DApp does not require a centralized infrastructure. Instead, the DApp users are allowed freely to enable their functionalities among transaction propagation and consensus participation [14].

In particular, we consider a cloud–edge computing enabled blockchain network with M providers and N miners. A group of miners denoted as $\mathcal{N} = \{1, 2, \dots, N\}$ access and consume the computing service from a group of providers which is denoted as $\mathcal{M} = \{1, 2, \dots, M\}$. Let x_{ij} denote the service demand of miner $i \in \mathcal{N}$ from provider $j \in \mathcal{M}$. Each miner i decides on its service demand from different providers, denoted by $x_i = \{x_{i1}, x_{i2}, \dots, x_{iM}\}$.

Then, let $X \overset{\Delta}{=} (x_1, \dots, x_N)$ and X_{-i} represent the service demand profiles of all the miners and of all other miners except miner i, respectively. In addition, we consider that each miner i has its initial computing power, denoted as l_i. The service demand can be treated as the computing power obtained from the providers. As such, the total

---

[3] We use the provider to denote the cloud–edge provider in the following discussion for brevity.

computing power of miner $i \in \mathcal{N}$ with the service demand x_{ij} from different providers is given by

$$x_i^{\text{total}} = l_i + \sum_{j \in \mathcal{M}} \omega_{ij} x_{ij}. \tag{9.35}$$

Thus, the miner i has a relative computing power α_i with respect to the overall computing power of all miners, which is formulated as follows:

$$\alpha_i(\boldsymbol{x}_i, \boldsymbol{X}_{-i}) = \frac{x_i^{\text{total}}}{\sum_{k \in \mathcal{N}} x_k^{\text{total}}}$$

$$= \frac{l_i + \sum_{j \in \mathcal{M}} \omega_{ij} x_{ij}}{\sum_{k \in \mathcal{N}} l_k + \sum_{i \in \mathcal{N}} \sum_{j \in \mathcal{M}} \omega_{ij} x_{ij}}, \tag{9.36}$$

such that $\sum_{k \in \mathcal{N}} \alpha_k = 1$. Here, ω_{ij} is the probability of miner i to choose provider j for the computing service, and $\sum_{j=1}^{M} \omega_{ij} = 1$, $i \in \mathcal{N}$. For example, $\omega_{ij} = 1$ (or $\omega_{ij} = 0$) means that miner i consumes (or not consumes) only the computing service from provider j.

Miners compete against each other in the mining game to be the first one to solve the PoW puzzle and receive the consequent mining reward. Following our previous works [220, 294, 352, 353], we model the successful probability of miner i to win the mining game, that is, miner i wins the mining reward, as follows:

$$P_i(\alpha_i, t_i) = \alpha_i(1 - \mathbb{P}_{\text{orphan}}(t_i)), \tag{9.37}$$

where t_i denotes the size of the block mined by miner i, that is, the number of transactions included in that block [213]. The meaning of function $\mathbb{P}_{\text{orphan}}(t_i)$ is explained as follows. After successfully solving the puzzle, the miner needs to broadcast its results to other miners for reaching consensus. However, the broadcast of the mining results in blockchain suffers from a certain delay. Thus, it is possible that the miner fails to be the first one whose mining results reach the consensus because of long latency (even though this miner finds the first valid block), which is called orphaning. The function $\mathbb{P}_{\text{orphan}}(t_i)$ quantifies the above orphaning probability.

As in [220, 294, 352–354, 359], we consider that block mining times follow the Poisson distribution, and the orphaning probability is approximated as:

$$\mathbb{P}_{\text{orphan}}(t_i) = 1 - e^{-\lambda t_i}, \tag{9.38}$$

in which the parameter λ denotes the inter arrival rate of the Poisson distribution.[4] Intuitively, the bigger the block is, the more time is needed to broadcast the block to the whole blockchain network [120].

The mining reward is composed of a fixed reward denoted by R, and a variable reward defined by rt_i, which linearly increases with the size of block [213]. Meanwhile, the miners need to pay the cloud–edge providers for the service cost. Let p_{ij} denote the

---

[4] The occurrence of solving the puzzle can be modeled as a random variable following a Poisson process with mean $\lambda = \frac{1}{600 \text{ s}}$ [213]. Generally, the complexity of finding a block is dynamically adjusted so that this operation takes $T = \lambda^{-1} = 600$ s in expectation. This is because blocks are created at a rate of 1 every 10 minutes. Then, the mining Poisson process has a fixed parameter λ for the whole network of miners.

marginal price of provider $j \in \mathcal{M}$ for offering computing service to miner $i \in \mathcal{N}$. Then, the pricing profile for provider j is denoted by $\boldsymbol{p}_j = \{p_{1j}, p_{2j}, \ldots, p_{Nj}\}, j \in \mathcal{M}$. Each miner i aims for maximizing its expected utility, which is given as follows:

$$
\begin{aligned}
u_i &= \sum_{j \in \mathcal{M}} \left((R + rt_i) P_i(\alpha_i, t_i) - \sum_{j \in \mathcal{M}} p_{ij} \omega_{ij} x_{ij} \right) \\
&= \sum_{j \in \mathcal{M}} \left((R + rt_i) \frac{l_i + \sum_{j \in \mathcal{M}} \omega_{ij} x_{ij}}{\sum_{k \in \mathcal{N}} l_k + \sum_{i \in \mathcal{N}} \sum_{j \in \mathcal{M}} \omega_{ij} x_{ij}} e^{-\lambda t_i} - \sum_{j \in \mathcal{M}} p_{ij} \omega_{ij} x_{ij} \right). \quad (9.39)
\end{aligned}
$$

Note that the resource may also include communication resource besides CPU time and energy. In this regard, we can consider that the communication cost is part of the price charged by the providers. In other words, each provider offers the service as a bundle which is composed of computing and wireless or wired communication resources. The energy consumption for the computing and communication is naturally accounted in the bundle.

In addition to the revenue from charging the miners for computing service, the providers have the service cost for operation and maintenance. The cost is related to the electricity consumption or hardware loss denoted by cx_i, where c represents the cost coefficient. Therefore, each provider j determines the pricing within the strategy space[5] $\{\boldsymbol{p}_j = [p_{ij}]_{i \in \mathcal{N}} : 0 \le p_{ij} \le \bar{p}\}$ to maximize its profit, which is formulated as follows:

$$
\begin{aligned}
\Pi_j &= \sum_{i \in \mathcal{N}} \omega_{ij} \left(\sum_{i \in \mathcal{N}} p_{ij} x_{ij} - \sum_{i \in \mathcal{N}} cx_{ij} \right) \\
&= \left(\sum_{i \in \mathcal{N}} p_{ij} \omega_{ij} x_{ij} - \sum_{i \in \mathcal{N}} c \omega_{ij} x_{ij} \right). \quad (9.40)
\end{aligned}
$$

Here, we adopt the incentive mechanism method proposed in [360], and accordingly set the probability for each miner i to choose provider j as

$$
\omega_{ij} = \frac{b_{ij}}{\sum_{k \in \mathcal{M}} b_{ik}}, \quad (9.41)
$$

where b_{ij} is the difference value between the largest price $\bar{p}$ and the marginal price p_{ij}; similarly, b_{ik} is the motivation of unit price reduction on computing service, that is,

$$
b_{ik} = \bar{p} - p_{ik}, \quad i \in \mathcal{N}, k \in \mathcal{M}. \quad (9.42)
$$

In light of equations (9.41) and (9.42), the value of ω_{ij} becomes larger, provided that miner i accesses the service from provider j with the lower price p_{ij} given the fixed pricing profiles of other providers. As such, in order to encourage more miners, each provider $j \in \{1, 2, \ldots, M\}$, inclines to offer the lower price to miners. The reason is that miners are more likely to consume the computing service from provider j when ω_{ij} increases. Hence, this results in pricing competition among providers. We provide the summary of notations in Table 9.1.

---

[5] Note that practically the price is bounded by the maximum price constraint denoted by $\bar{p}$.

Table 9.1 Summary of main notations.

Notation	Definition
x_{ij}	The service demand of miner i from provider j
x_i	The service demand of miner i from different providers, $x_i = \{x_{i1}, x_{i2}, \ldots, x_{iM}\}$
X, X_{-i}	The service demand profiles of all the miners, and the service demand profiles of all other miners except miner i
l_i	The initial computing power of miner i
ω_{ij}	The probability of miner i to choose provider j for the computing service
α_i	The relative computing power α_i with respect to the overall computing power of all miners
P_i	The successful probability of mining game for miner i
t_i	The size of the block mined by miner i
λ	The interarrival rate of the Poisson distribution
$\mathbb{P}_{\text{orphan}}(t_i)$	The orphaning probability of a block for miner i
p_{ij}	The marginal price of provider j for miner i
b_{ik}	The motivation of unit price reduction on computing service
q, t	The iteration index of the ADMM algorithm in the outer loop and the inner loop
p_j	The pricing profile p_j of provider j

Reprinted with permission from the paper "Cloud/edge computing service management in blockchain networks: Multi- leader multi-follower game-based ADMM for pricing" published in *IEEE Transactions on Services Computing*.

9.5.4   Multi-leader Multi-follower Stackelberg Game Formulation

Game theory has been regarded as a promising tool for resource management to study the interactions among the strategic agents. For example, in [202], the authors employed game theory to formulate the resource management problem in fog computing, and studied the pricing strategies for the computing service provider. The authors in [361] investigated the spectrum resource allocation issues in the unlicensed spectrum to mitigate the interference among multiple cellular operators. The noncooperative game was then developed to model the interactions among the operators and users in an unlicensed system. In this section, we model the interactions among providers and miners as a multi-leader multi-follower Stackelberg game with complete information,[6] in which we formulate the mathematical model of two sides. The Stackelberg game has been widely adopted to capture the sequential interactions among strategic agents, such as [347, 362]. The providers act as the leaders to set the price in Stage I. The miners act as the followers to determine the service demand for offloading in Stage II.

---

[6] The complete information scenario can be achieved through a broker in the resource market [337]. The broker acting as the resource market regulator can collect and manage the trading-related events, for example, service demand from miners and price information from service providers. The game model with incomplete information is worth being explored in future work.

9.5.4.1 Miners' Service Demand in Stage II

Given the pricing profiles of all providers (i.e., $P = \{p_1, p_2, \ldots, p_M\}$) and other miners' service demand (i.e., X_{-i}), the miner i decides on its computing service demand by solving the following maximization problem:

$$u_i(x_i, X_{-i}, P) = \sum_{j \in M} \left((R + rt_i) \frac{l_i + \sum_{j \in M} \omega_{ij} x_{ij}}{\sum_{k \in N} l_k + \sum_{i \in N} \sum_{j \in M} \omega_{ij} x_{ij}} \right.$$

$$\left. \times e^{-\lambda t_i} - \sum_{j \in M} p_{ij} \omega_{ij} x_{ij} \right). \tag{9.43}$$

The miner subgame problem can be written as follows.

Miner i subgame:

$$\underset{x_i}{\text{maximize}} \quad u_i(x_i, X_{-i}, P)$$

$$\text{subject to} \quad x_{ij} \geq 0$$

$$\sum_{j \in M} x_{ij} \leq D_{\max}. \tag{9.44}$$

$D_{\max}$ in the second constraint denotes the maximum service demand of one miner due to its limited total budget. Note that each miner has no incentive to unboundedly increase its service demand due to its financial burden.

9.5.4.2 Providers' Pricing in Stage I

Considering the pricing profiles of other providers (i.e., P_{-j}) as well as the service demand of all miners (i.e., X), each provider $j \in M$ determines its pricing profile p_j with the objective to maximize the expected profit. Therefore, the optimization problem for each provider is defined as follows:

$$\Pi_j(p_j, P_{-j}, X) = \sum_{i \in N} \omega_{ij} \left(\sum_{i \in N} p_{ij} x_{ij} - \sum_{i \in N} c x_{ij} \right). \tag{9.45}$$

Then, the profit maximization problem of provider j is formulated as follows.

Provider j subgame:

$$\underset{p_j}{\text{maximize}} \quad \Pi_j(p_j, P_{-j}, X)$$

$$\text{subject to} \quad 0 \leq p_{ij} \leq \bar{p}. \tag{9.46}$$

The key challenge in solving the formulated multi-leader multi-follower game lies in the high dimensionality of each miner's strategy space, which impedes us from employing conventional backward induction method. This exactly motivates us to employ the ADMM algorithm to reach the hierarchical social optimum point.

9.5.5 Stackelberg-Based ADMM Algorithm Analysis

In the framework of game theory, the miners and the providers are all assumed to be rational agents, which aim to maximize their individual payoff. However, the maximization of Π_j for provider j influences the profits of other providers and utilities of all miners. Likewise, the maximization of u_i for miner i influences the utilities of other miners and the profits of all providers. Moreover, when the number of providers and miners is large, the centralized optimization solution that simultaneously maximizes all the payoff is practically impossible. Therefore, there are no applicable existing strategies yet to address the above problem.

Following [363–366], we can treat the price p_{ij} as the incentive factor offered by provider j to miner i, since the provider can influence the service demand of miner x_{ij} by controlling the price level. Therefore, we can formulate the multi-leader multi-follower game problem in Section 9.5.3 as an incentive mechanism design, which can lead to an optimum result for the profits of providers in equation (9.45), while simultaneously considering the utilities of miners in equation (9.43). By adjusting the incentive factor p_{ij}, provider $j \in \mathcal{M}$ can indirectly enable miner $i \in \mathcal{N}$ to choose the service demand x_{ij} such that the provider's profit, Π_j is maximized. Specifically, the incentive mechanism problem is formulated as follows:

$$\underset{p_j}{\text{maximize}} \quad \Pi_j = \sum_{i \in \mathcal{N}} \omega_{ij} \left(\sum_{i \in \mathcal{N}} p_{ij} x_{ij} - \sum_{i \in \mathcal{N}} c x_{ij} \right)$$

$$\text{subject to} \quad \begin{cases} 0 \leq p_{ij} \leq \bar{p} \\ x_i = \arg\max u_i(x_i, X_{-i}, P) \\ \quad \text{subject to} \begin{cases} x_{ij} \geq 0 \\ \sum_{j \in M} x_{ij} \leq D_{\max} \end{cases} \end{cases}, \quad (9.47)$$

for all $i \in \mathcal{N}$ and $j \in \mathcal{M}$.

The hierarchical optimization problem in equation (9.47) that contains equilibrium problems at both the upper and lower stages is a standard EPEC. In such an EPEC scenario, the coordination of multiple conflicting interests, that is, the utilities of miners and the profits of providers, inevitably demand greater complexity to address. To obtain the solution that can optimize the profits of providers while simultaneously taking the utilities of miners into account, we resort to the ADMM algorithm. This is known as a parallel optimization tool with decomposition and fast convergence properties, which is especially suitable for large-scale optimization problems.

9.5.5.1   ADMM Basics

We first briefly present the basic implementation of ADMM. For ease of illustration, we consider a simple network with one service provider and N users, in which the provider aims to solve the following optimization problem

$$\underset{y}{\text{minimize}} \quad H(y) = \sum_{i=1}^{N} h_i(y_i)$$

$$\text{subject to} \quad \sum_{i=1}^{N} C_i y_i - D_i = 0, \quad (9.48)$$

where $h_i(y_i)$ is the cost for service provider j when it sells service y_i to user i. Specifically, $h_i(y_i)$ is convex on y_i, y_i is a real and scalar variable, and C_i and D_i are real, scalar constants.

Iteratively, the value of y is updated by the provider such that

$$y(t+1) = \arg\min(H(y)) - \sum_{i=1}^{N} \lambda_i(t)C_iy_i + \Psi, \qquad (9.49)$$

where

$$\Psi = \frac{\rho}{2} \sum_{i=1}^{N} \|C_iy_i - D_i\|_2^2. \qquad (9.50)$$

Here, $\|\ \|_2^2$ represents the Frobenius norm, $\rho > 0$ is a damping factor, t denotes the index of iteration step, and λ is the dual variable, which is updated as

$$\lambda_i(t+1) = \lambda_i(t) - \rho \left(\sum_{i=1}^{N} C_iy_i(t+1) - D_i \right). \qquad (9.51)$$

Algorithm 5 Multi-leader multi-follower game-based ADMM algorithm.

1: **Initialization:**
   Select initial input $p_{ij} \in [0, \overline{p}], \forall i \in N, \forall j \in \mathcal{M}$, precision threshold ϵ, $q = 1$;

2: **repeat**

3:    (Inner Loop) Utility optimization for miners through ADMM: Miners observe the set prices p_{ij}, to determine their computing service demand $x_{ij}^{(q)}$ by evaluating their resulting utilities, $u_i(x_i)$;

4:    (Outer Loop) Profit optimization for providers through ADMM: Providers predict the miner behaviors x_{ij}, employ ADMM to perform maximization for their individual profit Π_j. The optimal price $p_{ij}^{(q)}$ is obtained such that their profits are maximized;

5:    $q = q + 1$;

6: **until** $\left\| \sum_{j \in \mathcal{M}} \Pi_j \left(p_j^{(q)} \right) - \sum_{j \in \mathcal{M}} \Pi_j \left(p_j^{(q-1)} \right) \right\| \leq \epsilon$

   Output: The optimal computing service demand $x_i^* = x_i^{(q)}, \forall i \in \mathcal{N}$, and the optimal pricing profile $p_j^* = p_j^q, \forall j \in \mathcal{M}$.

It has been proved that the ADMM is guaranteed to converge to the set of stationary solutions when $h_i(y_i)$ is separable and convex [363–366]. Note that for the case of nonconvex objective functions, the convergence of ADMM can still be guaranteed under certain conditions [367].

9.5.5.2 ADMM-Based Algorithm for Multi-leader Multi-follower Game

In the following, we explain the iterated process of the ADMM-based algorithm that is utilized to optimize the profits of providers and utilities of miners in cloud–edge computing-enabled blockchain. Each iteration consists of a two-stage optimization problem as follows.

(1) **Utility optimization of miners:** In this stage, each miner $i \in \mathcal{N}$ is able to observe the announced prices $p_{ij}^{(q)}$ at the beginning of each iteration q, and decide on the computing service purchased from each provider j x_{ij}, to maximize its utility $u_i(x_i)$. Note that the superscript (q) denotes the qth iteration of the ADMM in outer loop. Each miner i aims to maximize its individual utility $u_i(x_i)$ to obtain the resulting values of x_i, and this forms the inner loop of the ADMM. Specifically, each miner i updates the value of x_i at each iteration of the inner loop as follows:

$$x_i^{(q)}(t+1) = \arg\max \left(u_i \left(x_i^{(q)} \right) \right) + \sum_{j=1}^{M} \lambda_i^{(q)}(t) x_{ij} + \Psi, \tag{9.52}$$

where

$$\Psi = \frac{\rho}{2} \sum_{j=1}^{M} \left\| \sum_{m=1, m \neq i} x_{mj}^{(q)}(\tau) + x_{ij} - D_{\max} \right\|_2^2, \tag{9.53}$$

and $\tau = t + 1$ if $m < i$, $\tau = t$ if $m > i$. Here, t is the iteration step index of the inner loop. As mentioned previously, $\rho > 0$ denotes the damping factor, and λ is the dual variable which will be updated as

$$\lambda_i^{(q)}(t+1) = \lambda_i^{(q)}(t) + \rho \left(\sum_{j=1}^{M} x_{ij}^{(q)}(t+1) - D_{\max} \right). \tag{9.54}$$

In each iteration of the outer loop q, the miners obtain a set of values of service demand, $x_{ij}^{(q)}$, which maximize their utilities at the end of the inner loop. In the meantime, such a set of values can be predicted by the providers, which will be utilized to update the values of p_{ij} in the next stage.

(2) **Profit optimization of providers:** In this stage, the providers are aware of the behaviors of miners and hence can predict the value of x_{ij}. Each provider $j \in \mathcal{M}$ adjusts the values of p_j within the strategy space that maximizes its profit by invoking ADMM as

$$p_j^{(q)}(t+1) = \arg\max \left(\Pi_j \left(p_j^{(q)} \right) \right). \tag{9.55}$$

The updated pricing profile $p_{ij}^{(q+1)}$ are then announced to the miners for next iteration, that is, the $(q + 1)$th iteration. This forms the outer loop of the algorithm.

The outer loop ends when the condition

$$\left\| \sum_{j \in \mathcal{M}} \Pi_j \left(\mathbf{p}_j^{(q)} \right) - \sum_{j \in \mathcal{M}} \Pi_j \left(\mathbf{p}_j^{(q-1)} \right) \right\| \leq \epsilon \tag{9.56}$$

is satisfied, where ϵ is the predefined threshold.

The basic framework of the above ADMM algorithm is shown in Algorithm 5. Essentially, after checking the utility function and profit function of miner and provider, respectively, we can conclude with the following proposition.

Proposition 8 *The utility function of each miner $i \in \mathcal{N}$ in equation (9.43), and the profit function of each provider $j \in \mathcal{M}$ in equation (9.45) are strictly concave.*

Proof First, we take the first-order and second-order derivatives of equation (9.43) with respect to x_{ij}, which can be written as follows:

$$\frac{\partial u_i}{\partial x_{ij}} = \sum_{j \in \mathcal{M}} \left((R + rt_i)e^{-\lambda t_i} \frac{\partial \alpha_i}{\partial x_{ij}} - p_{ij} \right), \tag{9.57}$$

$$\frac{\partial^2 u_i}{\partial x_{ij}^2} = \sum_{j \in \mathcal{M}} \left((R + rt_i)e^{-\lambda t_i} \frac{\partial^2 \alpha_i}{\partial x_{ij}^2} \right), \tag{9.58}$$

where

$$\alpha_i = \frac{l_i + \sum_{j \in \mathcal{M}} \omega_{ij} x_{ij}}{\sum_{k \in \mathcal{N}} l_k + \sum_{i \in \mathcal{N}} \sum_{j \in \mathcal{M}} \omega_{ij} x_{ij}}. \tag{9.59}$$

Specifically,

$$\frac{\partial \alpha_i}{\partial x_{ij}} = \frac{\partial \left(\frac{l_i + \sum_{j \in \mathcal{M}} \omega_{ij} x_{ij}}{\sum_{k \in \mathcal{N}} l_k + \sum_{i \in \mathcal{N}} \sum_{j \in \mathcal{M}} \omega_{ij} x_{ij}} \right)}{\partial x_{ij}}$$

$$= \omega_{ij} \frac{\sum_{k \in \mathcal{N}} l_k + \sum_{i \in \mathcal{N}} \sum_{j \in \mathcal{M}} \omega_{ij} x_{ij} - (l_i + \sum_{j \in \mathcal{M}} \omega_{ij} x_{ij})}{\left(\sum_{k \in \mathcal{N}} l_k + \sum_{i \in \mathcal{N}} \sum_{j \in \mathcal{M}} \omega_{ij} x_{ij} \right)^2}$$

$$= \omega_{ij} \frac{\sum_{k \in \mathcal{N}, k \neq i} l_k + \sum_{n \in \mathcal{N}, n \neq i} \sum_{m \in \mathcal{M}} \omega_{nm} x_{nm}}{\left(\sum_{k \in \mathcal{N}} l_k + \sum_{i \in \mathcal{N}} \sum_{j \in \mathcal{M}} \omega_{ij} x_{ij} \right)^2}, \tag{9.60}$$

and we conclude with the negativity of equation (9.58) from (9.61) accordingly.

$$\frac{\partial^2 \alpha_i}{\partial x_{ij}^2} = \frac{\partial \left(\frac{\partial \alpha_i}{\partial x_{ij}} \right)}{\partial x_{ij}}$$

$$= \omega_{ij} \frac{-\left(\sum_{k\in\mathcal{N}, k\neq i} l_k + \sum_{n\in\mathcal{N}, n\neq i} \sum_{m\in\mathcal{M}} \omega_{nm} x_{nm} \right) \left(2\omega_{ij} \sum_{k\in\mathcal{N}} l_k + 2\sum_{i\in\mathcal{N}} \sum_{j\in\mathcal{M}} \omega_{ij}^2 x_{ij} \right)}{\left(\sum_{k\in\mathcal{N}} l_k + \sum_{i\in\mathcal{N}} \sum_{j\in\mathcal{M}} \omega_{ij} x_{ij} \right)^4}$$

$$= -2\omega_{ij}^2 \frac{\sum_{k\in\mathcal{N}, k\neq i} l_k + \sum_{n\in\mathcal{N}, n\neq i} \sum_{m\in\mathcal{M}} \omega_{nm} x_{nm}}{\left(\sum_{k\in\mathcal{N}} l_k + \sum_{i\in\mathcal{N}} \sum_{j\in\mathcal{M}} \omega_{ij} x_{ij} \right)^3} < 0. \tag{9.61}$$

Recall that, from Section 9.5.3, we have

$$\Pi_j = \sum_{i\in\mathcal{N}} \omega_{ij} \left(\sum_{i\in\mathcal{N}} p_{ij} x_{ij} - \sum_{i\in\mathcal{N}} c x_{ij} \right)$$

$$= \sum_{i\in\mathcal{N}} \frac{\bar{p} - p_{ij}}{\sum_{k\in\mathcal{M}} (\bar{p} - p_{ik})} \left(\sum_{i\in\mathcal{N}} p_{ij} x_{ij} - \sum_{i\in\mathcal{N}} c x_{ij} \right)$$

$$= \sum_{i\in\mathcal{N}} \left(\frac{\bar{p} - p_{ij}}{\sum_{k\in\mathcal{M}} (\bar{p} - p_{ik})} \left(p_{ij} x_{ij} - c x_{ij} \right) \right). \tag{9.62}$$

To demonstrate the negativity of $\frac{\partial^2 \Pi_j}{\partial p_{ij}^2}$, we only need to prove the concavity of $\frac{p_{ij}(\bar{p} - p_{ij})}{\sum_{k\in\mathcal{M}} (\bar{p} - p_{ik})}$, which is shown as follows.

For ease of illustration, we denote $\bar{p}$ as A, and $\sum_{k\in\mathcal{M}, k\neq j} (\bar{p} - p_{ik}) + \bar{p}$ as B. Since $\bar{p} - p_{ik} \geq 0, \forall k \in M$, we know $\sum_{k\in\mathcal{M}, k\neq j} (\bar{p} - p_{ik}) + \bar{p} \geq \bar{p}$, that is, $B \geq A$. Then, we have

$$\frac{\partial \left(\frac{p_{ij}(\bar{p} - p_{ij})}{\sum_{k\in\mathcal{M}} (\bar{p} - p_{ik})} \right)}{\partial p_{ij}} = \frac{\partial \left(\frac{p_{ij}(\bar{p} - p_{ij})}{\sum_{k\in\mathcal{M}, k\neq j} (\bar{p} - p_{ik}) + \bar{p} - p_{ij}} \right)}{\partial p_{ij}}$$

$$= \frac{\partial \left(\frac{p_{ij}(A - p_{ij})}{B - p_{ij}} \right)}{\partial p_{ij}}, \tag{9.63}$$

where $0 \leq p_{ij} \leq A$. We then take the first-order and second-order derivatives of $\frac{p_{ij}(A - p_{ij})}{B - p_{ij}}$ with respect to p_{ij}, which can be expressed by equations (9.64) and (9.65).

$$\frac{\partial \left(\frac{p_{ij}(A - p_{ij})}{B - p_{ij}} \right)}{\partial p_{ij}} = \frac{(A - 2p_{ij})(B - p_{ij}) + (Ap_{ij} - p_{ij}^2)}{(B - p_{ij})^2} = \frac{AB - 2Bp_{ij} + p_{ij}^2}{(B - p_{ij})^2}. \tag{9.64}$$

$$\frac{\partial^2 \left(\frac{p_{ij}(A - p_{ij})}{B - p_{ij}} \right)}{\partial p_{ij}^2} = \frac{\partial \left(\frac{AB - 2Bp_{ij} + p_{ij}^2}{(B - p_{ij})^2} \right)}{\partial p_{ij}}$$

$$= \frac{(-2B + 2p_{ij})\left(B^2 - 2Bp_{ij} + p_{ij}^2 \right) - (-2B + 2p_{ij})\left(AB - 2Bp_{ij} + p_{ij}^2 \right)}{(B - p_{ij})^4}$$

$$= \frac{-6B^2 p_{ij} + 2B p_{ij}{}^2 - 2AB p_{ij} + \left(2AB^2 - 2B^3\right)}{\left(B - p_{ij}\right)^4}$$

$$\leq \frac{-6B^2 p_{ij} + 2B p_{ij}{}^2 - 2AB p_{ij}}{\left(B - p_{ij}\right)^4}. \tag{9.65}$$

From equations (9.65), we know that the upper bound of $\dfrac{\partial^2 \left(\frac{p_{ij}(A - p_{ij})}{B - p_{ij}}\right)}{\partial p_{ij}{}^2}$ is $\dfrac{2B p_{ij}{}^2 - 6B^2 p_{ij} - 2AB p_{ij}}{(B - p_{ij})^4}$. We next resort to proving the negativity of $2B p_{ij}{}^2 - 6B^2 p_{ij} - 2AB p_{ij}$, where $0 \leq p_{ij} \leq A$, and $A \leq B$. We define the following function $g(p_{ij}) = 2B p_{ij}{}^2 + \left(-6B^2 - 2AB\right) p_{ij}$. Clearly, the graph of function $g(\cdot)$ is a parabola curve, and we observe that $g(0) = 0$. As we have $g(A) = 2A^2 B - 6AB^2 - 2A^2 B = -6AB^2 < 0$, the negativity of $g(p_{ij})$ within $[0, A]$ is satisfied, from which the concavity of Π_j follows.   □

As per [365, 366], if the optimization problems faced by miners and providers are both convex, the ADMM can converge to the optimum results, that is, $x_i^*, i \in \mathcal{N}$ and $p_j^*, j \in \mathcal{M}$ in a distributed manner.

9.5.6   Numerical Results

In this section, we show the simulation results to validate the convergence performance of the ADMM algorithm to solve the multi-leader multi-follower game. Moreover, by performing simulation with different parameters, we evaluate the payoff as well as the strategies of providers and miners in cloud–edge computing-enabled blockchain. Specifically, we consider a group of N miners in the blockchain assisted by M cloud–edge computing service providers under PoW-based Nakamoto consensus protocol. We assume the size of a block to be mined by miners t_i follows the normal distribution $\mathcal{N}(\mu_t, \sigma_t^2)$. Likewise, the initial computing power of miners l_i also follows the normal distribution $\mathcal{N}(\mu_l, \sigma_l^2)$. Unless otherwise specified, the following simulation parameters are used by default [220, 294]: $M = 3$, $N = 60$, $\epsilon = 10^{-2}$, $\bar{p} = 100$, $\mu_l = 10$, $\mu_t = 200$, $\sigma_l^2 = \sigma_t^2 = 5$, $R = 10^4$, $r = 20$, $D_{\max} = 10^3$, and $c = 10^{-1}$.

9.5.6.1   Convergence

We first show the convergence of ADMM-based iterative algorithm in Fig. 9.2, for which we consider that there are three providers and three miners. For different miners, we consider that their initial computing power are 0, 10, and 20. For different providers,

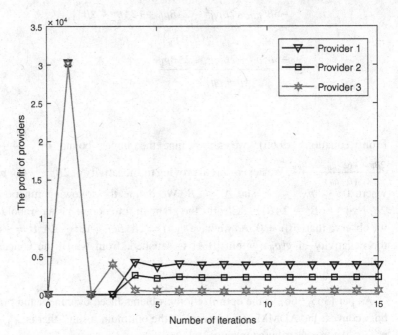

(a) The profit of different providers vs. number of iteration.

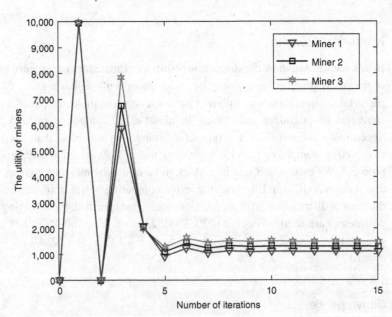

(b) The utility of different miners vs. number of iteration.

Figure 9.2 The convergence among providers and miners to reach the optimum results. Reprinted with permission from the paper "Cloud/edge computing service management in blockchain networks: Multi- leader multi-follower game-based ADMM for pricing" published in *IEEE Transactions on Services Computing*.

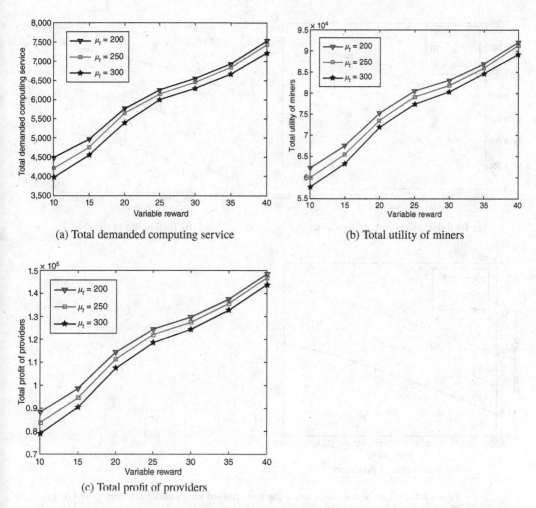

(a) Total demanded computing service

(b) Total utility of miners

(c) Total profit of providers

Figure 9.3 System performance when the variable reward varies under different values of μ_t. Reprinted with permission from the paper "Cloud/edge computing service management in blockchain networks: Multi- leader multi-follower game-based ADMM for pricing" published in *IEEE Transactions on Services Computing*.

we consider that the cost coefficients of them are 0, 0.1, and 0.2. From Fig. 9.2, we first observe that the profit of providers as well as the utility of miner all converge quickly, where only a few iterations are required. Moreover, we validate that the profit of Provider 1 after the convergence is the highest as it has the lowest service cost compared with other providers. We also observe that the utility of miner is larger when its initial computing power is higher from Fig. 9.2b. The reason is that the miner with local computing power is able to save the cost of purchasing more computing service for mining. As the initial computing power is higher, the cost savings is greater. (See also Figs. 9.3 and 9.4.)

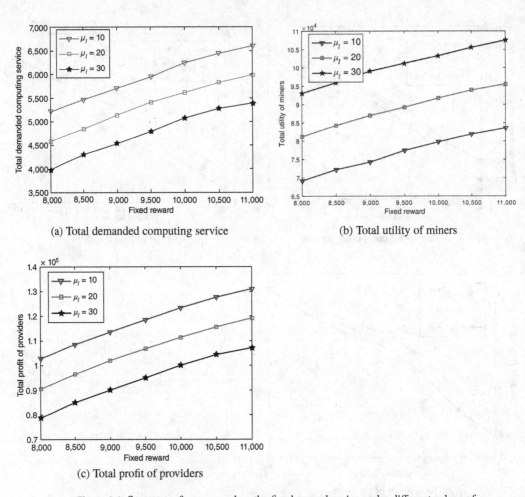

(a) Total demanded computing service

(b) Total utility of miners

(c) Total profit of providers

Figure 9.4 System performance when the fixed reward varies under different values of μ_l. Reprinted with permission from the paper "Cloud/edge computing service management in blockchain networks: Multi-leader multi-follower game-based ADMM for pricing" published in *IEEE Transactions on Services Computing*.

Figure 9.5 illustrates the relation between the precision threshold ϵ versus the number of iterations required for convergence when the number of miners and providers vary. From Fig. 9.5, we observe that the relation between the required number of iterations and $\lg(1/\epsilon)$ is approximately linear even when the number of miners or providers increases, which confirms the linear convergence as indicated in [363, 366]. This indicates that the ADMM algorithm can be easily applicable to large-scale optimization problems.

9.5.6.2   Performance Evaluation

We then evaluate the system performance for miners and providers under the proposed ADMM algorithm, as illustrated in Figs. 9.3 and 9.4. In Fig. 9.3, we observe that with

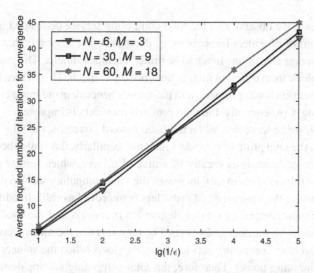

Figure 9.5 The relation between the precision threshold ϵ and the number of required iterations for convergence. Reprinted with permission from the paper "Cloud/edge computing service management in blockchain networks: Multi- leader multi-follower game-based ADMM for pricing" published in *IEEE Transactions on Services Computing*.

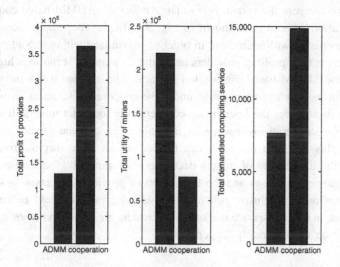

Figure 9.6 Performance comparison under ADMM-based competition and cooperation scenarios. Reprinted with permission from the paper "Cloud/edge computing service management in blockchain networks: Multi- leader multi-follower game-based ADMM for pricing" published in *IEEE Transactions on Services Computing*.

the increase of variable reward, both the total computing service demanded by miners and the total profit of providers increase. The reason is that the increasing variable reward motivates the miners to demand more computing service to win the mining, and hence the total service demand increases. As a result, the providers achieve greater profit. Furthermore, we observe that the total computing service demanded by miners and the total profit of providers increase as μ_t decreases. The reason is that when μ_t decreases, the average size of one block to be mined becomes smaller. The propagation delay of mined block from different miners does not differ much. This in turn increases the mining competition among miners, and the miners hence demand more computing service for mining. Consequently, the total profit of providers is improved.

From Fig. 9.4, we observe that when the fixed reward increases, the total utility of miners as well as the total profit of providers increase. Similarly, this is also because the increased fixed reward enhances greater incentive of miners, which further increases the total utility of miners. This in turn increases the total computing service demanded by miners, and hence the total profit of providers is improved as well. In addition, we observe that the total computing service demanded by miners and the total profit of providers increases with the decreases of μ_l. The reason is that the miners have greater motivation to purchase computing service from providers when the miners have the limited local computing power. Therefore, the total computing service demanded by miners increases, and this improves the total profit of providers. Moreover, when the local computing power of miners is higher (higher μ_l), the miners are able to save the cost of purchasing the computing service, which further increases the total utility of miners.

Lastly, we compare the system performance under the ADMM-based competition and cooperation scenarios, as shown in Fig. 9.6. In the cooperation scenario, the providers cooperate with each other in order to maximize their aggregate profit. We observe that the total profit of providers under the cooperation scenario is higher than that under the ADMM-based competition scenario. The intuition is that the providers jointly optimize their aggregate profit under the cooperation scenario, in which the providers will not offer the lower price competitively to attract miners. Instead, the providers can cooperatively encourage the miners to demand greater computing service. In this case, the providers can further extract more surplus from miners and hence the total utility of miners decreases. Consequently, the total computing service demanded increases and the total profit of providers increases as well. The future studies on the collusive pricing of cloud–edge providers can be conducted. Nevertheless, in the real service market, the providers are selfish in nature, and hence the cooperation scenario rarely happens.

9.6   Conclusion

In this chapter, we examined the concepts of variational inequality (VI), Stackelberg game, mathematical programming with equilibrium constraints, and equilibrium programming with equilibrium constraints, as well as their characteristics and solutions. Moreover, we illustrated the application of these concepts in the context of resource pricing in blockchain networks. We investigated the interactions among the cloud–edge providers and miners in PoW-based public blockchain networks, using a multi-leader multi-follower game-theoretic approach. In particular, we have employed the

ADMM algorithm to achieve the optimum results for both the miners and the providers in a distributed manner. Finally, we have conducted the numerical simulations to validate the convergence as well as evaluate the network performance. The results have shown that with the proposed solutions, the optimization for the utilities of miners, as well as the profits of providers are achieved jointly. This work has some potential future directions. One is that we can make the model more realistic by considering the mobility of users as well as the characteristics of wireless channels between different miners and their associated service providers. Nevertheless, we will further improve the practical implementation of the ADMM algorithm in future work. For example, the ADMM algorithm cannot be applied easily without the accurate modeling parameters, for example, utility formulation. As such, we will explore how to predict such values of parameters in a dynamic blockchain-empowered computing service market, for example, by using machine leaning methods [368].

Part IV

Open Questions of Cryptoeconomics

10 Open Questions about Mechanism Design in Cryptoeconomics

Satoshi Nakamoto utilized a range of scientific and economic models to develop the world's first digital currency. While many of these technologies already existed, it was Nakamoto's combination of this knowledge – in conjunction with the developed distributed ledger technology (DLT) – that ushered in a new age of decentralized digital currencies.

Based on Satoshi's invention, Ethereum founders have abstracted a new concept called "cryptoeconomics." It is the application of economics and cryptography to achieve information security goals. There is a saying from Vitalik Buterin [27], "You just cannot reason about security of the blockchain consensus protocols without reasoning about economics." Generally speaking, securing with cryptography is a conventional practice. However, it is not the same case in cryptoeconomics since security is also highly associated with the incentive mechanism. Incentives can drive the rational participants' behavior, thus promoting security when combined with cryptography. This chapter outlines the common security issues in cryptoeconomics, and highlights some key points when designing the incentive mechanisms.

10.1 Security Issues in Cryptoeconomics

Cryptography can ensure the security through the mathematical proof regardless of the actions the participants will take. As the blockchain ecosystem evolves, the system become more and more sophisticated. There are an increasing number of attacks that are implicit and long-lasting. However, this kind of behavior is always beyond the scope of known attacks. It is a great challenge for the system to detect such attacks, let alone resist the attacks using the existing cryptography. A discouragement attack is a representative example [369]. A discouragement attack occurs when an attacker acts intentionally inside a consensus mechanism in order to reduce the revenue of other validators, even at their own expense, and attempt to induce the victims to quit the network. This attack can be the first step of a long-term attack plan, with the ultimate goal being to launch the double-spending attack. This kind of attack is characterized as the economic attack, which cryptography can hardly resist. Below are two substantial malicious behaviors in cryptoeconomics: selfish mining and miner extractable value.

10.1.1   Selfish Mining and Exploitation

Is it possible for a rational miner to exploit the vulnerability of the Nakamoto proto-cols and find a strategy leading to a reward proportionally greater than the devoted resources? The answer is "Yes." This is an economic attack called "selfish mining," where dishonest miners can make a profit that is greater than their fair share. What are the risks associated with this exploitation? This section first examines the various selfish mining strategies.

The study in [100] shows that selfish miners may get higher payoffs by violating the information propagation protocols and postponing their mined blocks. Specifically, a selfish miner may hold its newly discovered block and continue mining on this block secretly. Thereby, the selfish miner exploits the inherent block forking phenomenon of the Nakamoto protocols. In this case, honest miners in the network continue their mining based on the publicly known view of the blockchain, while the selfish miners mine on their private branches. If a selfish miner discovers more blocks in the same time interval, it will develop a private longer branch of the blockchain. When the length of the public chain known by honest miners approaches that of the selfish miner's private chain, the selfish miner will reveal its private chain to the network. According to the longest-chain rule, the honest nodes will discard the public chain immediately when they learn about the longer view of the chain from the selfish miner. Such a strategy of intentionally forking results in the situation of wasted computation by the honest miners, while the revenue of the selfish miner can be significantly higher than strictly following the block-revealing protocol. More seriously, if selfish miners collude and form a selfish mining pool with a sufficiently large amount of computational power, other rational miners will be forced to join the selfish mining pool, which can devastate the blockchain network [100].

Decker et al. [177] introduce an approach based on the Markov chain model to analyze the behavior as well as the performance of a selfish mining pool. Figure 10.1 illustrates the progress of the blockchain as a state machine. The states of the system, that is, the numbers in the circles, represent the lead of the selfish pool in terms of the difference in block number between the private branch and the public branch. In Fig. 10.1, state 0 is the original state when the selfish pool has the same view as the public chain. State $0'$ indicates that two branches of the same length are published in

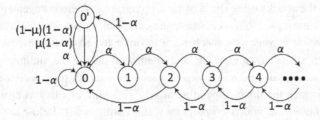

Figure 10.1 Blockchain state transition in the presence of a selfish pool (adapted from [100]). Reprinted with permission from the paper "A survey on consensus mechanisms and mining strategy management in blockchain networks" published in *IEEE Access*.

the network by the selfish pool and by the honest miners. The transitions in Fig. 10.1 correspond to the mining event, that is, a new block is mined either by the selfish pool or the honest miners. In Fig. 10.1, α represents the computational power of the selfish mining pool. Note that the transition from state 0 to state $0'$ depends not only on the computational power of the selfish pool, but also on the fraction, that is, μ, of honest miners that mine on the selfish pool's branch. In [100], the analysis on the steady-state probability of the Markov chain leads to the following two important observations.

1. For a given μ, a selfish pool of size α obtains a revenue larger than its relative size in the range of $\frac{1-\mu}{3-2\mu} < \alpha < \frac{1}{2}$.
2. A threshold on the selfish-pool size exists such that each pool member's revenue increases with the pool size.

Furthermore, there have been various studies proposed based on [100]. A new mining strategy known as the stubborn mining strategy, which is supposed to outperform the typical selfish mining strategy, was introduced [370]. The key idea behind the stubborn mining strategy is that the selfish miner is stubborn and may publish only part of the private blocks even when it loses the lead to the honest nodes.

Carlsten [371] studied the impact of transaction fees on selfish mining strategies in the Bitcoin network. Note that because of the inherent design of the token issuing scheme in Bitcoin, the constant mining reward of each block halves every time a fixed interval of blocks, that is, every 210,000 blocks, is generated. Then, it is natural to increase the transaction fee to compensate for the mining cost of the consensus nodes. The arbitrary levels of transaction fees lead to a situation where some hidden blocks may have very high values. As a result, selfish miners want to publish immediately due to the risk of orphaning. Hence, in the revised Markov chain model for selfish mining in Fig. 10.2, the author introduces a new state $0''$. State $0''$ is almost identical to state 0, except that, if the selfish miner mines on the next block in state $0''$, it will immediately publish that block instead of holding it. Compared with the original selfish mining model in Fig. 10.1, state 0 transits to state 1 with probability $\alpha(1 - e^{-\beta})$ and to state $0''$ with probability $\alpha e^{-\beta}$, where β is the size of the mining block. The new factor β is introduced to model the impact of transaction fees on the miner's decisions. With the

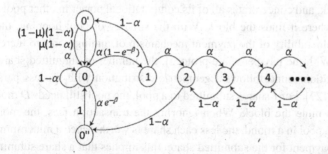

Figure 10.2 Improved Markov model for selfish mining with transaction fees (adapted from [371]). Reprinted with permission from the paper "A survey on consensus mechanisms and mining strategy management in blockchain networks" published in *IEEE Access*.

revised transition probability, if the selfish miner finds a block of high value in state 0, it may publish the block (i.e., transiting to state $0''$) instead of holding it (i.e., transiting to state 1). The analysis in [371] shows that this improved selfish mining strategy leads to positive profit for all miners regardless of their hashrates.

From the aforementioned Markov models, we note that the selfish miner may adopt various policies by choosing to release an arbitrary number of block in each state. In [372, 373], a Markov Decision Process (MDP) model is proposed to generalize such a process of policy derivation. As an example, the study in [372] considers the honest miners as nonadaptive players following the Nakamoto protocol. A similar mining competition is considered in [214] between a selfish mining pool and the honest nodes. The study in [374] extends the model of selfish mining by considering the propagation delay between the selfish mining pool and the honest community. The delay is assumed to be exponentially distributed with rate μ. The block-mining Markov model in [374] adopts a two-dimensional state of (k, l), which denotes the length of blocks built by the pool and the community upon the common prefix blocks, respectively.

The other mining strategies also include block withholding (BWH), lie-in-wait, and pool hopping. Block withholding (BWH) is a mining strategy used by selfish miners to increase their revenues through diminishing the winning probability of honest miners in mining pools [219, 224]. The impact of BWH on the Bitcoin network was studied in [375]. It is assumed that a selfish miner is able to split the computational power into different mining pools. It may spend most of its computational power to honestly mine on one pool, and use the remaining computational power to perform BWH on the other pools. To alleviate the impact of BWH attacks, modifications to the Nakamoto protocol and the pool-mining protocols are suggested in the literature. Rosenfeld [127] proposes that the pool operator should insert mining tasks for which the solutions are known in advance, and tag the miners that do not submit the results. Since it is difficult to find puzzles with expected solutions, the author suggests that some new data fields should be added to the conventional block data structure. Lie-in-wait (LIW) is a strategic attack where a selfish miner postpones submitting the block that it finds to a mining pool, and uses all of its computational power to mine on that pool [127]. In this case, an attacker first splits its computational power to mine in different pools. Then, if it finds a block in a pool, instead of submitting the block to get the reward from the pool, the attacker holds the block, and concentrates all of its computational power in other pools to mine on the pool where it finds the block. With the strategy of pool hopping, the miners exploit the vulnerability of the payment mechanism of mining pools to increase their own profits. With the pay-per-share protocol, the number of submitted shares in one block competition round follows a geometric distribution with success parameter δ and mean D [127]. For I shares submitted to a pool, the pool still needs D more shares on average to mine the block. When ignoring the transaction fees, the more shares submitted to a pool in a round, the less each share is worth. Since a miner immediately receives the payment for the submitted share, this implies that a share submitted early may have a higher reward. Therefore, a selfish miner can benefit by mining only at the early stage of a round, and then hop to other pools to increase his revenue. The study in [127] shows that there exists a critical point measured in the number of submitted shares. The best strategy of a selfish miner is to mine on a pool until this point is reached, then hop to another pool or mine by itself.

10.1.2 Miner or Maximal Extractable Value (MEV)

The abbreviation MEV first stands for miner extractable value in the context of PoW, which indicates that miners can make an extra profit by manipulating the transaction orders. Specifically, MEV measures how much money a miner may make by arbitrarily including, omitting, or rearranging transactions in the blocks they produce [376]. What makes the MEV attack possible? Below are brief introductions for the background.

In a PoW-based blockchain network, a miner is responsible for collecting and packing transactions into its mined block. Each transaction will be attached with a certain amount of fees by the transaction senders. The miner manipulates the transaction order for the following two main reasons. (1) Mining consumes a lot of electricity, which costs the miners a lot of money. (2) Each block has a finite amount of storage and can hold only a certain number of transactions. In such cases, the miner will take full advantage of the block storage and prefer to select the transactions with the higher fees to offset the cost of mining and increase their profits. Moreover, all the waiting transactions are public and can be viewed by anyone, making the transaction value extraction problem more severe. Frontrunning, backrunning, and sandwiching transactions are all opportunities for miners to take advantage of and make money. As the scalability issues arise, the mainstream of consensus protocols is experiencing the transition from PoW to non-PoW (e.g., PoS). Mining will no longer exist in the non-PoW blockchain system and using "miner" to describe the block creator may not be accurate. Maximal extractable value has so far been the most widely known interpretation for MEV.

The term MEV was first officially coined by Daian et al. in "Flash boys 2.0" [377]. However, the MEV issue was initially explored by a senior analyst called Pmcgoohan even before the release of Ethereum in 2014. He discovered the critical flaw when he saw the Ethereum draft documents. Pmcgoohan was the first to recognize that the miners had complete control over ordering and packing transactions, indicating that they could take advantage of the privilege to extract value from users without any regulation and punishment.

Most of the research literature discusses the MEV problem in the context of Ethereum. Is MEV unique to Ethereum? According to the overview of MEV, we can infer that MEV may occur on other chains, because there are so many alternative blockchain projects having the same architectures and similar consensus layers. However, in practice, MEV is less likely to occur in the Bitcoin network or other blockchain ecosystems. The answer has been given in [378]. "Complexity" and "statefulness" are two uppermost reasons for this phenomenon. Ethereum aims to serve as a globally decentralized world computer. Thus Ethereum's application layer has been designed to be more flexible and sophisticated than others. Robinson [379] describes Ethereum as a Dark Forest due to the potential vulnerabilities of smart contracts and the pending transactions in mempool. Again, he highlights that the MEV problem is still one of the most challenging issues for the research community today.

More broadly, two entities are able to extract profit from transactions: miners and searchers [380]. Miners have full autonomy to determine which transaction will be packed into the mined blocks. Unlike miners selecting and reordering transactions to get more transaction fees, the searchers always detect and identify profitable opportunities from the pending transactions in the mempool. Through sophisticated algorithms and mechanisms, searchers are able to submit a transaction with a higher transaction fee at the first sign of a lucrative opportunity from other pending transactions. By doing this, the miners will definitely select the transaction with the higher fee. Consequently, the searcher's trade will be confirmed even if the trade order was submitted much later.

The transaction senders are constantly suffering from various types of MEV hazards. Here we list two major types of MEV: (1) Frontrunning: Frontrunning is the most typical MEV problem. The searchers search all the pending transactions in the mempool for highly profitable opportunities and submit competing transactions with higher transaction fees to get faster confirmations than the victim transactions. (2) Sandwich attack: The sandwich attack is a variant of frontrunning. Searchers typically launch a sandwich attack to extract MEV from traders on decentralized exchanges by manipulating the cryptoasset prices. For example, searchers will place two orders if they have identified a trader who wants to buy a specified cryptoasset. The first order is a buy-order, which indicates that the searchers will buy the same cryptoasset at the current market price P. Generally, this trade will increase the market price of the cryptoasset. When the traders want to purchase this cryptoasset, they must pay a higher price, such as P^+. At this time, searchers will place a sell-order to sell the cryptoasset. As a result, searchers will obtain $P^+ - P$ from this attack. Especially when the trading pool is congested, searchers can easily achieve frontrunning by raising the transaction fees.

So far, the total extracted MEV has been near 700 million [381]. The existence of MEV is a result of the inherent characteristics of the Ethereum system design. There is nothing the transaction senders can do. How does the development team prevent such an exploit? An oracle network to design the fair sequencing service (FSS) based on the arrival time has been adopted [382]. An auction mechanism to separate the ordering rights from the miners, aiming to lower the extracted value by weakening the autonomy of miners has been proposed [383, 384]. The current automated market maker (AMM) model was upgraded [385] to an automated arbitrage market maker (A2MM), which is able to identify the optimal transaction routing among multiple AMMs.

However, any effort to restrict miners' ordering rights or reduce miners' revenue could easily lead to miners' illegal behaviors. If all the transaction fees are the same, the miners may collude with some of the traders to obtain an extra off-chain profit. No matter how the blockchain system is upgraded, the miners' revenue must be guaranteed to promote their ethical behaviors. As a result, it is still unclear how to resist MEV and foster market prosperity.

10.1.3   Other Emerging Security Issues

Cryptoeconomics is the great invention of Satoshi Nakamoto, and can prove things with minimal assumptions about participants and their behaviors [34]. Generally, the minimal assumption refers to the rational or honest majority, and the ultimate goal is that correct execution of the protocol must be a robust equilibrium. Assuming that the majority of rational or honest players adhere to the protocols, the system can maximize profit while minimizing losses incurred by potential attacks. The spirits behind cryptoeconomics work in two ways: (1) Ensure that the majority of rational participants following the protocols are acting in the system's best interests; and (2) increase the attack's financial cost. However, these two parts are always much questioned. How can we prove that most of the participants are rational? What if an attack has a massive budget (i.e., much higher than the attack cost)?

To begin with, cryptoeconomics provides a new study paradigm and analysis viewpoint for large-scale permissionless distributed systems, having much in common with mechanism design, which is not a "hard-core" technology, just like cryptography. It is improbable that entire mathematical proofs can be provided without any assumptions. As a result, several basic assumptions are required in cryptoeconomics. Assumptions are not unrealistic; they are frequently founded on reality and prior knowledge. We assume, for example, that the majority of participants are rational. Because the players in a permissionless distributed system are typically geographically distant, there are many difficulties with a large number of dispersed users collaborating or taking bribes. Moreover, the consensus mechanism can efficiently prevent the participants from forging multiple identities (i.e., Sybil attack). In practice, while constructing most incentive schemes, we frequently need to learn the distribution of participants based on prior knowledge. We normally assume that the participants fit into some probability distribution while calculating and analyzing the solutions. In response to the second point, Buterin stated that the attack cost is increased to reduce the risk caused by an attacker with enough resources. It implies that we can only lower the probability of such attacks, but that there is no way to eliminate them.

According to Buterin's talk [34], there is another common critique, "Whatever the cost of breaking a chain, you can just make a corresponding hedge on financial markets and get the money back by profiting from making the token price drop." This attack would occur. "But there is some maximum amount that the attack can earn by breaking the chain, and any attacker is motivated to already have taken this maximum trade." Briefly, the core idea of cryptoeconomics is to raise the cost of an attack to the point where the attacker cannot earn enough to cover the expense.

Aside from the concerns mentioned above, some other security issues in cryptoeconomics are also of great importance. These include, but are not limited to, the following.

1. **How do the different technique components achieve the Nash equilibrium of the cryptoeconomics ecosystem?** There are no suitable methods to evaluate the different technologies within the game-theory framework at the current stage.
2. **Quantify and evaluate the security incentive:** Is using the amount of security deposit the best way to calculate the security incentive?
3. **Collusion or cooperation:** Under what conditions will users choose to collude or cooperate?
4. **Impacts on forks:** How do we reduce the forks with easy and efficient incentive mechanisms?

The permissionless blockchain is a complex and sophisticated system. It is pretty challenging to design a simple and efficient incentive mechanism that motivates the participant's behaviors at each step of the consensus process. Unpredictable behaviors and attack patterns can occur anywhere and at any time. It is difficult to guarantee that the currently effective mechanisms will not induce any subsequent unexpected behavior. The next section will introduce the general process and major considerations for incentive design in cryptoeconomics.

10.2   Designing Mechanisms: Optimal versus Suboptimal

From the cryptoeconomics perspective, incentives are the foundation of any permissionless distributed system. In order to ensure the best security and stability of the system, a straightforward incentive assignment principal was proposed in [24]. (1) Maximum penalty upon conviction: If attacks or faults can be located accurately, then slash all the deposits. (2) If it is difficult to determine the scope of attack/faults, then penalize anyone suspicious. (3) Pay for performance: Rewards should be increased when the "protocol quality" improves. The advantage is that no faulty one can escape punishment, while the disadvantage is that the honest or rational actors may gradually exit the system. So far, the relevant research on the incentive design is still in its infancy. In fact, there is a branch of economics dedicated to figuring out how to design incentives that motivate the rational actors to behave in desired ways, and this is called mechanism design. How can we design an incentive mechanism in cryptoeconomics? Here are some tips.

1. Accumulate prior knowledge: As the emerging computer technologies, such as machine learning, evolve, we can take advantage of the powerful technologies to process the historical statistics data, obtaining a better understanding of the participants.
2. Outline the basic assumptions: The mathematical proofs can only be completed with some minimal assumptions.
3. Determine the upper bound of budget: This will be a critical constraint in the model.
4. Set up a specific goal: What do we want to achieve? Who will obtain the maximized profit? Who will stay on the reserved utility level? Is that possible to motivate more entries?
5. Understand the system and participants' interests: If the system's interest is prioritized, the mechanism may provide more revenues. If the interests of the participants are a high priority, the system can encourage additional entries.
6. Pick the appropriate game models: The selection of the models directly determines the qualities of outcomes.
7. Analyze the background and participant's behavior: Figure out what will happen in every step of consensus and where the participant's bad behavior will occur.
8. Test the outcomes in real world: There may be some unnoticed constraints in reality that can affect the outcomes of mechanism.

9. Sharing and updating: Sharing the results with others can promote the research of incentives in cryptoeconomics, and the feedback can be used to update the new models.

As for the model selection, there are generally two confusing questions. (1) Should we use a simple or complicated model? (2) Is one model sufficient for incentive design? Using a model that is too basic may lead us to overlook other possible events or behaviors, which can cause financial loss once they occur. Using an overly sophisticated model may impede the research by involving redundant details and obscuring the fundamental issues. When a permissionless blockchain is studied as a whole, it usually involves several parties with varying levels of rationality and other incentive evaluation metrics. Some people prefer monetary rewards, while others prefer honorary ones. Blockchain is not a stand-alone system; it has spawned a slew of complicated, hierarchical systems. In general, the mechanisms or fundamental models of these mechanisms can be helpful in understanding only certain market participants. Using a single model will become considerably more problematic whenever there are numerous parties with various utility functions. This is why the last two steps in the above process are of vital importance to the incentive design of cryptoeconomics. Even if the mathematical proof is perfect, it is difficult to demonstrate whether the outcome is achievable in practice.

When the incentives are obtained, we come up with the following question: Why it is necessary to release the design to the public and share the results with others? The answer is that this is to prevent the incentive designer from dominating the system. Incentives and decentralization are interdependent. Without incentives, there must exist a centralized entity enforcing and monitoring the actors. The system must verify and track the actors' identities and actions in order to guarantee that the protocol is strictly implemented. To build and maintain all of the processes, the system necessitates a large amount of computational resources as well as significant development expenditures. For the participants, exposing individual privacy and a strict enforcement system may reduce the engagement. In the long run, neither side gets a lasting benefit.

Therefore, providing sufficient incentives is the first step to eliminate the domination. Especially in the permissionless distributed systems, incentives can promote the rational participants to accomplish a common goal, that is, to reach consensus. It is worth mentioning that because these anonymous players are rational and driven by profit, they interact in a noncooperative manner. Even though they do not know each other, they have a same purpose since they are motivated by similar interests. Especially for the large-scale permissionless distributed system, incentives can lower the participation barriers. More entries can facilitate the consensus protocol to increase the proportion of rational or honest participants. "Show me the incentives and I will show you the outcome." This is a remark from Charlie Munger regarding how incentives drive almost everything. Cryptoeconomics applies incentives to drive the participant's desired behavior. Then the following problems arise: How can we evaluate the incentives and determine whether the outcomes are good or not? A general criterion is presented in [27]. The good outcomes may be expressed as follows.

1. Trusted execution: The protocol can be executed correctly.
2. Open access: No entry and exit restrictions.

3. Fast finality: Participants are more willing to devote more effort to complete tasks.
4. Decentralized control: System monitoring is replaced by mutual supervision among users. The majority of system transactions can be done by ballot.
5. Low cost: More equitable and reasonable income distribution. Selfish mining and frontrunning attack can be efficiently resisted.

The bad outcomes can be referred the following.

1. Safety failure: Difficult to reach consensus.
2. Censorship: Participants can be unknowingly censored.
3. Slow finality: More forks are generated. More transactions are stuck in the mempool.
4. Centralized control: Some participants collude together to extract more profit.
5. High cost: Rich gets richer and poor gets poorer. More computational resource consumption.

10.3   Summary

This chapter began with a quick overview of two new economic attacks: selfish mining and miner frontrunning, with detailed descriptions of the fundamental principles and current research. Following that, this chapter covered some unanswered questions about cryptoeconomics' security issues by explaining the fundamental concepts of cryptoeconomics, emphasizing the importance of making minimal assumptions, and restating the functional differences between cryptography and cryptoeconomics. Finally, this chapter discussed the major considerations for the incentive design in cryptoeconomics, such as the concept of incentive assignment, design techniques, model selection, and the unique nature of incentives in cryptoeconomics.

References

[1] S. Nakamoto, "Bitcoin: A peer-to-peer electronic cash system," Self-published paper, 2008. [Online] Available: https://bitcoin.org/bitcoin.pdf.

[2] V. Zamfir, "Bip001: 'Unlimited edition'," 2017. [Online] Available: www.youtube.com/watch?v=u6VSPD5TrP4&t=371s.

[3] S. Haber and W. S. Stornetta, "How to time-stamp a digital document," in *Conference on the Theory and Application of Cryptography*. Berlin/Heidelberg: Springer, 1990, pp. 437–455.

[4] A. Back, "Hashcash – a denial of service counter-measure," 2002. [Online] Available: www.cs.miami.edu/home/burt/learning/csc686.211/docs/hashcash.pdf.

[5] R. C. Merkle, "Protocols for public key cryptosystems," in *1980 IEEE Symposium on Security and Privacy*. Washington, DC: IEEE Computer Society, 1980, pp. 122–122.

[6] D. Johnson, A. Menezes, and S. Vanstone, "The elliptic curve digital signature algorithm (ECDSA)," *International Journal of Information Security*, **1**(1), 36–63, 2001.

[7] Google, "LevelDB," 2011. [Online] Available: https://opensource.googleblog.com/2011/07/leveldb-fast-persistent-key-value-store.html.

[8] E. Foundation, "Ethereum," 2013. [Online] Available: https://ethereum.org/en/.

[9] A. M. Antonopoulos, *Mastering Bitcoin: Unlocking Digital Cryptocurrencies*. Newton, MA: .O'Reilly Media, Inc., 2014.

[10] A. Demers, D. Greene, C. Hauser, et al., "Epidemic algorithms for replicated database maintenance," in *Proceedings of the Sixth Annual ACM Symposium on Principles of Distributed Computing*, 1987, pp. 1–12.

[11] H. Qureshi, "Bitcoin's P2P network," Dec. 29, 2019. [Online] Available: https://nakamoto.com/bitcoins-p2p-network/.

[12] P. Maymounkov and D. Mazieres, "Kademlia: A peer-to-peer information system based on the XOR metric," in *International Workshop on Peer-to-Peer Systems*. Berlin/Heidelberg: Springer, 2002, pp. 53–65.

[13] E. Rohrer and F. Tschorsch, "Kadcast: A structured approach to broadcast in blockchain networks," in *Proceedings of the 1st ACM Conference on Advances in Financial Technologies*, 2019, pp. 199–213.

[14] W. Wang, D. T. Hoang, P. Hu, et al., "A survey on consensus mechanisms and mining strategy management in blockchain networks," *IEEE Access*, **7**, 22 328–22 370, 2019.

[15] Wackerow, "Proof-of-stake (PoS)." [Online] Available: https://ethereum.org/en/developers/docs/consensus-mechanisms/pos/.

[16] V. Foundation, "Vechain white paper 2.0." [Online] Available: www.vechain.org/whitepaper/#bit_v48i3.

[17] B. Chase and E. MacBrough, "Analysis of the XRP ledger consensus protocol," arXiv preprint arXiv:1802.07242, 2018.

[18] V. Buterin and V. Griffith, "Casper the friendly finality gadget," arXiv preprint arXiv:1710.09437, 2017.

[19] E. Foundation, "How to stake your eth," 2022. [Online] Available: https://ethereum.org/en/staking/#stake.

[20] S. Leonardos, D. Reijsbergen, and G. Piliouras, "Weighted voting on the blockchain: Improving consensus in proof of stake protocols," *International Journal of Network Management*, **30**(5), e2093, 2020.

[21] E. Community, "Ethereum virtual machine," 2022. [Online] Available: https://ethereum.org/en/developers/docs/evm/.

[22] E. Foundation, "Introduction to smart contracts," 2022. [Online] Available: https://ethereum.org/en/developers/docs/smart-contracts/.

[23] V. Zamfir, "What is cryptoeconomics?" 2015. [Online] Available: www.youtube.com/watch?v=9lw3s7iGUXQ.

[24] V. Buterin, "Introduction to cryptoeconomics," 2017. [Online] Available: www.youtube.com/watch?v=pKqdjaH1dRo&t=413s.

[25] J. Stark, "Making sense of cryptoeconomics," 2017. [Online] Available: https://medium.com/l4-media/making-sense-of-cryptoeconomics-5edea77e4e8d.

[26] medvedev1088, "Cryptoeconomics cheat sheet." [Online] Available: https://github.com/cheat-sheets/cryptoeconomics-cheat-sheet#concepts.

[27] E. Foundation, "Programmable incentives: Intro to cryptoeconomics," 2017. [Online] Available: www.youtube.com/watch?v=9lw3s7iGUXQ.

[28] T. C. Schelling, "The strategy of conflict. Prospectus for a reorientation of game theory," *Journal of Conflict Resolution*, **2**(3), 203–264, 1958.

[29] V. Buterin, "Schellingcoin: A minimal-trust universal data feed," 2014. [Online] Available: https://blog.ethereum.org/2014/03/28/schellingcoin-a-minimal-trust-universal-data-feed/.

[30] O. Lab, "Inside arbitrum," 2018. [Online] Available: https://developer.offchainlabs.com/docs/inside_arbitrum.

[31] C. Lab, "Introduction to chainlink keepers." [Online] Available: https://docs.chain.link/docs/chainlink-keepers/introduction/.

[32] T. Bean, "bZx integrates chainlink keepers," 2021. [Online] Available: https://bzx.network/blog/bzx-integrates-chainlink-keepers.

[33] B. M. Musser, "xToken lending, powered by chainlink," 2021. [Online] Available: https://medium.com/xtoken/xlend-powered-by-chainlink-12f6c7ff21e7.

[34] V. Buterin, "Cryptoeconomics in 30 minutes by Vitalik Buterin (devcon5)," 2019. [Online] Available: www.youtube.com/watch?v=GQR1xjQn5Pg

[35] Consensys, "Quorum blockchain service enterprise blockchain simplified," 2022. [Online] Available: https://consensys.net/quorum/qbs/.

[36] R3, "Corda 4.8 tutorials," 2022. [Online] Available: https://docs.r3.com/en/tutorials/corda/4.8/os/overview.html.

[37] Shobha1617, "Active and passive attacks in information security," www.geeksforgeeks.org / active-and-passive-attacks-in-information-security/, last accessed: December 31, 2021.

[38] S. K. Das, K. Kant, and N. Zhang, *Handbook on Securing Cyber-Physical Critical Infrastructure*. Amsterdam: Elsevier, 2012.

[39] IBM, "Basic blockchain security," 2022. [Online] Available: www.ibm.com/topics/blockchain-security.

[40] V. Y. P. Michael Nieles, Kelley Dempsey, "An introduction to information security," https://nvlpubs.nist.gov/nistpubs/SpecialPublications/NIST.SP.800-12r1.pdf, last accessed: May 1, 2022.

[41] C. 4009-2015, "Committee on national security systems (CNSS) glossary," 2022. [Online]. Available: www.cnss.gov/CNSS/openDoc.cfm?9Ph8rog47/ELwKRSmFBThA==.

[42] I. Shparlinski, *Finite Fields: Theory and Computation: The Meeting Point of Number Theory, Computer Science, Coding Theory and Cryptography*. Berlin/Heidelberg: Springer Science & Business Media, vol. 477, 2013.

[43] A. J. Menezes, P. C. Van Oorschot, and S. A. Vanstone, *Handbook of Applied Cryptography*. Boca Raton: CRC Press, 2018.

[44] M.-L. Akkar and C. Giraud, "An implementation of DES and AES, secure against some attacks," in *International Workshop on Cryptographic Hardware and Embedded Systems*. Berlin/Heidelberg: Springer, 2001, pp. 309–318.

[45] W. Diffie and M. Hellman, "New directions in cryptography," *IEEE Transactions on Information Theory*, **22**(6), 644–654, 1976.

[46] K. S. McCurley, "The discrete logarithm problem," in *Proceedings of Symposium in Applied Math*, vol. 42. Providence, RI: American Mathematical Society, 1990, pp. 49–74.

[47] R. L. Rivest, A. Shamir, and L. Adleman, "A method for obtaining digital signatures and public-key cryptosystems," *Communications of the ACM*, **21**(2), 120–126, 1978.

[48] A. K. Lenstra and M. S. Manasse, "Factoring with two large primes," *Mathematics of Computation*, **63**(208), 785–798, 1994.

[49] P. D. G. Cameron F. Kerry, "Digital signature standard (DSS)," https://nvlpubs.nist.gov/nistpubs/FIPS/NIST.FIPS.186-4.pdf, last accessed: March, 2022.

[50] D. R. L. Brown, "Sec 2: Recommended elliptic curve domain parameters," 2010. [Online] Available: www.secg.org/sec2-v2.pdf.

[51] B. Wiki, "Secp256k1," 2022. [Online] Available: https://en.bitcoin.it/wiki/Secp256k1.

[52] H. Mayer, "ECDSA security in bitcoin and ethereum: a research survey," *CoinFaabrik*, June, **28**(126), 50, 2016.

[53] N. Jansma and B. Arrendondo, "Performance comparison of elliptic curve and RSA digital signatures," *nicj.net/files*, 2004.

[54] D. Boneh, B. Lynn, and H. Shacham, "Short signatures from the Weil pairing," in *International Conference on the Theory and Application of Cryptology and Information Security*. Berlin/Heidelberg: Springer, 2001, pp. 514–532.

[55] M. Wang, M. Duan, and J. Zhu, "Research on the security criteria of hash functions in the blockchain," in *Proceedings of the 2nd ACM Workshop on Blockchains, Cryptocurrencies, and Contracts*, 2018, pp. 47–55.

[56] X. Wang, A. C. Yao, and F. Yao, "Cryptanalysis on SHA-1," in *Cryptographic Hash Workshop hosted by NIST*, 2005.

[57] P. Ciaian, d'A. Kancs, and M. Rajcaniova, "Interdependencies between mining costs, mining rewards and blockchain security," arXiv preprint arXiv:2102.08107, 2021.

[58] Tarunbatra,"Transaction,"https://ethereum.org/en/developers/docs/transactions/, last accessed: May 11, 2022.

[59] Minimalsm, "Gas and fees," https://ethereum.org/en/developers/docs/gas/, last accessed: May 11, 2022.

[60] V. E. R. M. I. Abdelhamid Bakhta, "Fee market change for Eth 1.0 chain," 2022. [Online] Available: https://github.com/ethereum/EIPs/blob/master/EIPS/eip-1559.md.

[61] C. O. Community, "Recommended priority fee in Gwei," https://ethgasstation .info/, last accessed: Feburary, 2022.

[62] H. Foundation, "An introduction to Hyperledger," 2021. [Online] Available: www.hyperledger.org/wp-content/uploads/2018/07/HL_Whitepaper_Introduct iontoHyperledger.pdf.

[63] E. Hong, "How does bitcoin mining work?" www.investopedia.com/tech/how-does-bitcoin-mining-work/, last accessed: May 11, 2022.

[64] Statista, "Number of bitcoins in circulation worldwide from October 2009 to April 4, 2022," 2022. [Online] Available: www.statista.com/statistics/247280/number-of-bitcoins-in-circulation/.

[65] J. BeckMarch, "Rewards and penalties on Ethereum 2.0 [phase 0]," https:// consensys.net/blog/codefi/rewards-and-penalties-on-ethereum-20-phase-0/, last accessed: June, 2022.

[66] Moralis Academy, "Byzantine generals' problem – an introduction," https:// academy.moralis.io/blog/byzantine-generals-problem-an-introduction, last accessed: May 10, 2022.

[67] M. Van Steen and A. Tanenbaum, "Distributed systems principles and paradigms," *Network*, **2**, 28, 2002.

[68] "Bitcoin cloud mining," https://ilyasergey.net/CS6213/week-01-intro.html# what-can-be-specified-about-distributed-systems.

[69] "Notes on theory of distributed systems," https://arxiv.org/pdf/2001.04235.pdf.

[70] P. Jalote, *Fault Tolerance in Distributed Systems*. Hoboken, NJ: Prentice-Hall, Inc., 1994.

[71] G. F. Coulouris, J. Dollimore, and T. Kindberg, *Distributed Systems: Concepts and Design*. London: Pearson Education, 2005.

[72] P. Urbán and A. Schiper, "Comparing distributed consensus algorithms," in *Proceedings of IASTED International Conference on Applied Simulation and Modelling (ASM)*, no. CONF, 2004.

[73] M. J. Fischer, N. A. Lynch, and M. S. Paterson, "Impossibility of distributed consensus with one faulty process," *Journal of the ACM (JACM)*, **32**(2), 374–382, 1985.

[74] M. J. Fischer, "The consensus problem in unreliable distributed systems (a brief survey)," in *International Conference on Fundamentals of Computation Theory*. Berlin/Heidelberg: Springer, 1983, pp. 127–140.

[75] "Distributed system consensus," https://medium.com/rahasak/consensus-made-simple-76cbb6955123.

[76] E. Brewer, "CAP twelve years later: How the 'rules' have changed," *Computer*, **45**(2), 23–29, 2012.

[77] Hazelcast, "What is the CAP theorem?" https://hazelcast.com/glossary/cap-theorem/, last accessed: May, 2022.

[78] "Bitcoin cloud mining," https://lamport.azurewebsites.net/pubs/paxos-simple.pdf.

[79] "In search of an understandable consensus algorithm (extended version)," https://raft.github.io/raft.pdf.

[80] "Raft consensus algorithm," www.geeksforgeeks.org/raft-consensus-algorithm/?ref=lbp.

[81] K. Driscoll, B. Hall, H. Sivencrona, and P. Zumsteg, "Byzantine fault tolerance, from theory to reality," in *International Conference on Computer Safety, Reliability, and Security*. Berlin/Heidelberg: Springer, 2003, pp. 235–248.

[82] L. Lamport, R. Shostak, and M. Pease, "The Byzantine Generals Problem," *ACM Transactions on Programming Languages and Systems*, pp. 382–401, July 1982. [Online] Available: www.microsoft.com/en-us/research/uploads/prod/2016/12/The-Byzantine-Generals-Problem.pdf.

[83] "Introduction to distributed system design," www.hpcs.cs.tsukuba.ac.jp/~tatebe/lecture/h23/dsys/dsd-tutorial.html#Design.

[84] F. B. Schneider, "Implementing fault-tolerant services using the state machine approach: A tutorial," *ACM Computing Surveys (CSUR)*, **22**(4), 299–319, 1990.

[85] J. R. Douceur, "The Sybil attack," in *International Workshop on Peer-to-Peer Systems*. Berlin/Heidelberg: Springer, 2002, pp. 251–260.

[86] M. Conti, E. S. Kumar, C. Lal, and S. Ruj, "A survey on security and privacy issues of Bitcoin," *IEEE Communications Surveys & Tutorials*, **20**(4), 3416–3452, 2018.

[87] V. Buterin, "Bitcoin network shaken by blockchain fork," 2013. [Online] Available: https://bitcoinmagazine.com/articles/bitcoin-network-shaken-by-blockchain-fork-1363144448/.

[88] Y. Xiao, N. Zhang, W. Lou, and Y. T. Hou, "A survey of distributed consensus protocols for blockchain networks," *IEEE Communications Surveys Tutorials*, **22**(2), 1432–1465, 2020.

[89] M. Castro and B. Liskov, "Practical Byzantine fault tolerance and proactive recovery," *ACM Transactions on Computer Systems (TOCS)*, **20**(4), 398–461, 2002.

[90] C. Cachin et al., "Architecture of the hyperledger blockchain fabric," in *Workshop on Distributed Cryptocurrencies and Consensus Ledgers*, vol. 310, no. 4. Chicago, IL, 2016, pp. 1–4.

[91] M. Vukolić, "The quest for scalable blockchain fabric: Proof-of-work vs. BFT replication," in *International workshop on open problems in network security*. Springer, 2015, pp. 112–125.

[92] D. Schwartz, N. Youngs, A. Britto, et al., "The Ripple protocol consensus algorithm," *Ripple Labs Inc White Paper*, **5**(8), 151, 2014.

[93] O. Goldreich, "Zero-knowledge twenty years after its invention." *IACR Cryptol. ePrint Arch.*, **2022**, 186, 2002.

[94] F. Baldimtsi, A. Kiayias, T. Zacharias, and B. Zhang, "Indistinguishable proofs of work or knowledge," in *International Conference on the Theory and Application of Cryptology and Information Security*. Berlin/Heidelberg: Springer, 2016, pp. 902–933.

[95] T. T. A. Dinh, R. Liu, M. Zhang, et al., "Untangling blockchain: A data processing view of blockchain systems," *IEEE Transactions on Knowledge and Data Engineering*, **30**(7), 1366–1385, 2018.

[96] F. Tschorsch and B. Scheuermann, "Bitcoin and beyond: A technical survey on decentralized digital currencies," *IEEE Communications Surveys & Tutorials*, **18**(3), 2084–2123, 2016.

[97] J. Garay, A. Kiayias, and N. Leonardos, "The Bitcoin backbone protocol: Analysis and applications," in *Annual International Conference on the Theory and Applications of Cryptographic Techniques*. Berlin/Heidelberg: Springer, 2015, pp. 281–310.

[98] T. Roughgarden, "Algorithmic game theory," *Communications of the ACM*, **53**(7), 78–86, 2010.

[99] M. Babaioff, S. Dobzinski, S. Oren, and A. Zohar, "On Bitcoin and red balloons," in *Proceedings of the 13th ACM Conference on Electronic Commerce*, 2012, pp. 56–73.

[100] I. Eyal and E. G. Sirer, "Majority is not enough: Bitcoin mining is vulnerable," in *International Conference on Financial Cryptography and Data Security*. Berlin/Heidelberg: Springer, 2014, pp. 436–454.

[101] S. Athey, I. Parashkevov, V. Sarukkai, and J. Xia, "Bitcoin pricing, adoption, and usage: Theory and evidence," https://faculty.fuqua.duke.edu/~charvey/ Teaching/897_2018/Course_Materials/Athey_Bitcoin_pricing.pdf, last accessed: May, 2020.

[102] J. Wu, S. Guo, H. Huang, W. Liu, and Y. Xiang, "Information and communications technologies for sustainable development goals: state-of-the-art, needs and

perspectives," *IEEE Communications Surveys & Tutorials*, **20**(3), 2389–2406, 2018.

[103] J. A. Kroll, I. C. Davey, and E. W. Felten, "The economics of Bitcoin mining, or Bitcoin in the presence of adversaries," in *Proceedings of WEIS*, vol. 2013, no. 11. Washington, DC, 2013.

[104] M. Babaioff, S. Dobzinski, S. Oren, and A. Zohar, "On Bitcoin and red balloons," in *Proceedings of the 13th ACM Conference on Electronic Commerce*, ser. EC '12. New York, NY: ACM, June 2012, pp. 56–73.

[105] C. Cachin and M. Vukolic, "Blockchain consensus protocols in the wild (keynote talk)," in *31st International Symposium on Distributed Computing (DISC 2017)*, ser. Leibniz International Proceedings in Informatics (LIPIcs), vol. 91, Vienna, Austria, 2017, pp. 1:1–1:16.

[106] D. Hopwood, S. Bowe, T. Hornby, and N. Wilcox, "Zcash protocol specification," *GitHub: San Francisco, CA, USA*, vol. 86, 2016.

[107] H. Kopp, C. Bösch, and F. Kargl, "Koppercoin – a distributed file storage with financial incentives," in *International Conference on Information Security Practice and Experience*. Berlin/Heidelberg: Springer, 2016, pp. 79–93.

[108] A. Miller and J. J. LaViola Jr., "Anonymous byzantine consensus from moderately-hard puzzles: A model for Bitcoin," 2014. [Online] Available: http://nakamotoinstitute.org/research/anonymous-byzantine-consensus.

[109] S. Al-Kuwari, J. H. Davenport, and R. J. Bradford, "Cryptographic hash functions: Recent design trends and security notions," *Cryptology ePrint Archive*, 2011.

[110] J. A. Garay, A. Kiayias, and G. Panagiotakos, "Proofs of work for blockchain protocols". *IACR Cryptol. ePrint Arch.*, **2017**, p. 775, 2017.

[111] J. Debus, "Consensus methods in blockchain systems," *Frankfurt School of Finance & Management, Blockchain Center, Tech. Rep*, 2017.

[112] D. Kraft, "Difficulty control for blockchain-based consensus systems," *Peer-to-Peer Networking and Applications*, **9**(2), 397–413, 2016.

[113] K. Saito and H. Yamada, "What's so different about blockchain? – Blockchain is a probabilistic state machine," in *2016 IEEE 36th International Conference on Distributed Computing Systems Workshops (ICDCSW)*. Washington, DC: IEEE, 2016, pp. 168–175.

[114] J. Garay, A. Kiayias, and N. Leonardos, "The Bitcoin backbone protocol with chains of variable difficulty," in *Annual International Cryptology Conference*. Berlin/Heidelberg: Springer, 2017, pp. 291–323.

[115] L. Fan and H.-S. Zhou, "A scalable proof-of-stake blockchain in the open setting (or, how to mimic nakamoto's design via proof-of-stake)," *Cryptology ePrint Archive*, 2017.

[116] A. Kiayias, A. Russell, B. David, and R. Oliynykov, "Ouroboros: A provably secure proof-of-stake blockchain protocol," in *Annual International Cryptology Conference*. Berlin/Heidelberg: Springer, 2017, pp. 357–388.

[117] M. B. Taylor, "The evolution of Bitcoin hardware," *Computer*, **50**(9), 58–66, 2017.

[118] A. Kiayias and G. Panagiotakos, "Speed-security tradeoffs in blockchain protocols," *Cryptology ePrint Archive*, 2015.

[119] R. Pass, L. Seeman, and A. Shelat, "Analysis of the blockchain protocol in asynchronous networks," in *Annual International Conference on the Theory and Applications of Cryptographic Techniques*. Berlin/Heidelberg: Springer, 2017, pp. 643–673.

[120] C. Decker and R. Wattenhofer, "Information propagation in the Bitcoin network," in *IEEE P2P 2013 Proceedings*. Washington, DC: IEEE, 2013, pp. 1–10.

[121] K. Croman, C. Decker, I. Eyal, et al., "On scaling decentralized blockchains," in *International Conference on Financial Cryptography and Data security*. Berlin/Heidelberg: Springer, 2016, pp. 106–125.

[122] X. Liu, W. Wang, D. Niyato, N. Zhao, and P. Wang, "Evolutionary game for mining pool selection in blockchain networks," *IEEE Wireless Communications Letters*, 7(5), 760–763, 2018.

[123] P. R. Rizun, "A transaction fee market exists without a block size limit," *Block Size Limit Debate Working Paper*, pp. 2327–4697, 2015.

[124] P. R. Rizun, "Subchains: A technique to scale Bitcoin and improve the user experience," *Ledger*, 1, 38–52, 2016.

[125] A. Gervais, G. O. Karame, V. Capkun, and S. Capkun, "Is Bitcoin a decentralized currency?" *IEEE Security & Privacy*, 12(3), 54–60, 2014.

[126] N. T. Courtois, "On the longest chain rule and programmed self-destruction of crypto currencies," arXiv preprint arXiv:1405.0534, 2014.

[127] M. Rosenfeld, "Analysis of Bitcoin pooled mining reward systems," arXiv preprint arXiv:1112.4980, 2011.

[128] J. Bonneau, A. Miller, J. Clark, et al., "Sok: Research perspectives and challenges for Bitcoin and cryptocurrencies," in *2015 IEEE Symposium on Security and Privacy*. Washington, DC: IEEE, 2015, pp. 104–121.

[129] A. Laszka, B. Johnson, and J. Grossklags, "When Bitcoin mining pools run dry," in *International Conference on Financial Cryptography and Data Security*. Berlin.Heidelberg: Springer, 2015, pp. 63–77.

[130] G. Owen, *Game Theory*. Bingley, UK: Emerald Group Publishing, 2013.

[131] A. Stone, "An examination of single transaction blocks and their effect on network throughput and block size," Self-published paper, 2015.

[132] O. Ersoy, Z. Ren, Z. Erkin, and R. L. Lagendijk, "Transaction propagation on permissionless blockchains: Incentive and routing mechanisms," in *2018 Crypto Valley Conference on Blockchain Technology (CVCBT)*. Washington, DC: IEEE, 2018, pp. 20–30.

[133] I. Abraham, D. Malkhi, K. Nayak, L. Ren, and A. Spiegelman, "Solida: A blockchain protocol based on reconfigurable byzantine consensus," arXiv preprint arXiv:1612.02916, 2016.

[134] K. Baqer, D. Y. Huang, D. McCoy, and N. Weaver, "Stressing out: Bitcoin 'stress testing'," in *International Conference on Financial Cryptography and Data Security*. Berlin/Heidelberg: Springer, 2016, pp. 3–18.

[135] M. Möser and R. Böhme, "Trends, tips, tolls: A longitudinal study of Bitcoin transaction fees," in *International Conference on Financial Cryptography and Data Security*. Berlin/Heidelberg: Springer, 2015, pp. 19–33.

[136] N. Houy, "The economics of Bitcoin transaction fees," *GATE WP*, **1407**, 2014.

[137] G. Pappalardo, T. Di Matteo, G. Caldarelli, and T. Aste, "Blockchain inefficiency in the Bitcoin peers network," *EPJ Data Science*, **7**, pp. 1–13, 2018.

[138] S. Feng, W. Wang, Z. Xiong, et al., "On cyber risk management of blockchain networks: A game theoretic approach," *IEEE Transactions on Services Computing*, **14**(5), 1492–1504, 2018.

[139] P. Lab, "Filecoin: A decentralized storage network," https://filecoin.io/filecoin.pdf.

[140] M. Ball, A. Rosen, M. Sabin, and P. N. Vasudevan, "Proofs of useful work," *Cryptology ePrint Archive*, 2017.

[141] M. Ghosh, M. Richardson, B. Ford, and R. Jansen, "A torpath to torcoin: Proof-of-bandwidth altcoins for compensating relays," Naval Research Lab Washington, DC, Tech. Rep., 2014.

[142] F. Zhang, I. Eyal, R. Escriva, A. Juels, and R. Van Renesse, "{REM}: Resource-efficient mining for blockchains," in *26th {USENIX} Security Symposium ({USENIX} Security 17)*, 2017, pp. 1427–1444.

[143] T. Moran and I. Orlov, "Simple proofs of space-time and rational proofs of storage," in *Annual International Cryptology Conference*. Berlin/Heidelberg: Springer, 2019, pp. 381–409.

[144] S. Park, A. Kwon, G. Fuchsbauer, P. Gaži, J. Alwen, and K. Pietrzak, "Spacemint: A cryptocurrency based on proofs of space," in *International Conference on Financial Cryptography and Data Security*. Berlin/Heidelberg: Springer, 2018, pp. 480–499.

[145] J. Blocki and H.-S. Zhou, "Designing proof of human-work puzzles for cryptocurrency and beyond," in *Theory of Cryptography Conference*. Berlin/Heidelberg: Springer, 2016, pp. 517–546.

[146] S. King, "Primecoin: Cryptocurrency with prime number proof-of-work," *July 7th*, **1**(6), 2013.

[147] J. Andersen and E. Weisstein, "Cunningham chain. from mathworld – a wolfram web resource," https://mathworld.wolfram.com/CunninghamChain.html, last accessed: June 14, 2020.

[148] A. Shoker, "Sustainable blockchain through proof of exercise," in *2017 IEEE 16th International Symposium on Network Computing and Applications (NCA)*. Washington, DC: IEEE, 2017, pp. 1–9.

[149] M. Ball, A. Rosen, M. Sabin, and P. N. Vasudevan, "Average-case fine-grained hardness," in *Proceedings of the 49th Annual ACM SIGACT Symposium on Theory of Computing*, 2017, pp. 483–496.

[150] S. Johnson, V. Scarlata, C. Rozas, E. Brickell, and F. Mckeen, "Intel software guard extensions: Epid provisioning and attestation services," *White Paper*, **1**(1-10), 119, 2016.

[151] A. Miller, A. Juels, E. Shi, B. Parno, and J. Katz, "Permacoin: Repurposing Bitcoin work for data preservation," in *2014 IEEE Symposium on Security and Privacy*. Washington, DC: IEEE, 2014, pp. 475–490.

[152] A. Juels and B. S. Kaliski Jr., "PoRs: Proofs of retrievability for large files," in *Proceedings of the 14th ACM Conference on Computer and Communications Security*, 2007, pp. 584–597.

[153] S. Wilkinson, T. Boshevski, J. Brandoff, and V. Buterin, "Storj a peer-to-peer cloud storage network," www.storj.io/storj2014.pdf, last accessed: June, 2022.

[154] D. Vorick and L. Champine, *Sia: Simple Decentralized Storage*. Boston, MA: Nebulous Inc., 2014.

[155] A. Fiat and A. Shamir, "How to prove yourself: Practical solutions to identification and signature problems," in *Conference on the Theory and Application of Cryptographic Techniques*. Berlin/Heidelberg: Springer, 1986, pp. 186–194.

[156] V. Buterin et al., "Ethereum: A next-generation smart contract and decentralized application platform," *White Paper* 2014.

[157] A. Biryukov and D. Khovratovich, "Equihash: Asymmetric proof-of-work based on the generalized birthday problem," *Ledger*, **2**, 1–30, 2017.

[158] D. Wagner, "A generalized birthday problem," in *Annual International Cryptology Conference*. Berlin/Heidelberg: Springer, 2002, pp. 288–304.

[159] G. Wood et al., "Ethereum: A secure decentralised generalised transaction ledger," *Ethereum Project Yellow Paper*, **151**(2014), 1–32, 2014.

[160] A. Miller, A. Kosba, J. Katz, and E. Shi, "Nonoutsourceable scratch-off puzzles to discourage Bitcoin mining coalitions," in *Proceedings of the 22nd ACM SIGSAC Conference on Computer and Communications Security*, 2015, pp. 680–691.

[161] P. Daian, I. Eyal, A. Juels, and E. G. Sirer, "(Short paper) Piecework: Generalized outsourcing control for proofs of work," in *International Conference on Financial Cryptography and Data Security*. Berlin/Heidelberg: Springer, 2017, pp. 182–190.

[162] S. Dziembowski, S. Faust, V. Kolmogorov, and K. Pietrzak, "Proofs of space," in *Annual Cryptology Conference*. Berlin/Heidelberg: Springer, 2015, pp. 585–605.

[163] L. v. Ahn, M. Blum, N. J. Hopper, and J. Langford, "Captcha: Using hard AI problems for security," in *International Conference on the Theory and Applications of Cryptographic Techniques*. Berlin/Heidelberg: Springer, 2003, pp. 294–311.

[164] D. Hofheinz, T. Jager, D. Khurana, et al., "How to generate and use universal samplers," in *International Conference on the Theory and Application of Cryptology and Information Security*. Berlin/Heidelberg: Springer, 2016, pp. 715–744.

[165] S. King and S. Nadal, "Ppcoin: Peer-to-peer crypto-currency with proof-of-stake," Self-published paper, August, 19, 2012.

[166] M. Milutinovic, W. He, H. Wu, and M. Kanwal, "Proof of luck: An efficient blockchain consensus protocol," in *Proceedings of the 1st Workshop on System Software for Trusted Execution*, 2016, pp. 1–6.

[167] L. Chen, L. Xu, N. Shah, et al., "On security analysis of proof-of-elapsed-time (poet)," in *International Symposium on Stabilization, Safety, and Security of Distributed Systems*. Berlin/Heidelberg: Springer, 2017, pp. 282–297.

[168] I. Bentov, C. Lee, A. Mizrahi, and M. Rosenfeld, "Proof of activity: Extending Bitcoin's proof of work via proof of stake [extended abstract] y," *ACM SIGMETRICS Performance Evaluation Review*, **42**(3), 34–37, 2014.

[169] I. Bentov, A. Gabizon, and A. Mizrahi, "Cryptocurrencies without proof of work," in *International Conference on Financial Cryptography and Data Security*. Berlin/Heidelberg: Springer, 2016, pp. 142–157.

[170] L. Ren, "Proof of stake velocity: Building the social currency of the digital age," Self-published white paper, 2014.

[171] B. David, P. Gaži, A. Kiayias, and A. Russell, "Ouroboros praos: An adaptively-secure, semi-synchronous proof-of-stake blockchain," in *Annual International Conference on the Theory and Applications of Cryptographic Techniques*. Berlin/Heidelberg: Springer, 2018, pp. 66–98.

[172] I. Bentov, R. Pass, and E. Shi, "Snow white: Provably secure proofs of stake." *IACR Cryptology ePrint Archive*, **2016**, 919, 2016.

[173] W. Li, S. Andreina, J.-M. Bohli, and G. Karame, "Securing proof-of-stake blockchain protocols," in *Data Privacy Management, Cryptocurrencies and Blockchain Technology*. Berlin/Heidelberg: Springer, 2017, pp. 297–315.

[174] A. Poelstra et al., "Distributed consensus from proof of stake is impossible," Self-published paper, 2014.

[175] N. Houy, "It will cost you nothing to 'kill' a proof-of-stake crypto-currency," Available at SSRN 2393940, 2014.

[176] I. Eyal, A. E. Gencer, E. G. Sirer, and R. Van Renesse, "Bitcoin-NG: A scalable blockchain protocol," in *13th USENIX Symposium on Networked Systems Design and Implementation (NSDI 16)*, 2016, pp. 45–59.

[177] R. Pass and E. Shi, "Hybrid consensus: Efficient consensus in the permissionless model," Cryptology ePrint Archive, 2016.

[178] M. K. Reiter, "A secure group membership protocol," *IEEE Transactions on Software Engineering*, **22**(1), 31–42, 1996.

[179] C. Decker, J. Seidel, and R. Wattenhofer, "Bitcoin meets strong consistency," in *Proceedings of the 17th International Conference on Distributed Computing and Networking*, 2016, pp. 1–10.

[180] E. K. Kogias, P. Jovanovic, N. Gailly, I. Khoffi, L. Gasser, and B. Ford, "Enhancing Bitcoin security and performance with strong consistency via collective signing," in *25th Usenix Security Symposium (Usenix Security 16)*, 2016, pp. 279–296.

[181] J. Kwon, "Tendermint: Consensus without mining," https://tendermint.com/static/docs/tendermint.pdf, last accessed: March 5, 2021.

[182] OpenEthereum, "Proof-of-authority chains," https://openethereum.github.io/ Proof-of-Authority-Chains#: :text=Proof%2Dof%2DAuthority%20is%20a,blo cks%20and%20secure%20the%20blockchain., last accessed: April 28, 2022.

[183] B. Foundation, "Delegated proof of stake (DPoS)," https://how.bitshares.works/ en/master/technology/dpos.html, last Accessed: March 26, 2021.

[184] Y. Gilad, R. Hemo, S. Micali, G. Vlachos, and N. Zeldovich, "Algorand: Scaling byzantine agreements for cryptocurrencies," in *Proceedings of the 26th Symposium on Operating Systems Principles*, 2017, pp. 51–68.

[185] J. Green and J. J. Laffont, "On coalition incentive compatibility," *The Review of Economic Studies*, **46**(2), 243–254, 1979.

[186] T. Groves, "Incentives in teams," *Econometrica*, **45**, 617–631, 1973.

[187] A. Gibbard, "Manipulation of voting schemes: a general result," *Econometrica*, **41**(4), 587–601, 1973.

[188] M. A. Satterthwaite, "Strategy-proofness and arrow's conditions: Existence and correspondence theorems for voting procedures and social welfare functions," *Journal of Economic Theory*, **10**, 187–217, 1975.

[189] L. Hurwicz, "On informationally decentralized systems," in C. B. McGuire and R. Radner (eds.), *Decision and Organization*. Mineapolis, MN: University of Minnesota Press, 1972 (Amsterdam: North-Holland, 2nd ed., 1986).

[190] R. B. Myerson and M. A. Satterthwaite, "Efficient mechanisms for bilateral trading," *Journal of Economic Theory*, **29**, 265–281, 1983.

[191] K. J. Arrow, *Economics and Human Welfare: The Property Rights Doctrine and Demand Revelation under Incomplete Information*. New York: Academic Press, 1979.

[192] C. d'Aspremont and L. Gerard-Varet, "Incentives and incomplete information," *Journal of Public Economics*, **29**(45), 11–25, 1979.

[193] W. Wang, D. T. Hoang, Z. Xiong, et al., "A survey on consensus mechanisms and mining management in blockchain networks," arXiv preprint arXiv:1805.02707, pp. 1–33, 2018.

[194] M. Castro et al., "Practical byzantine fault tolerance," in *Proceedings of the Third Symposium on Operating Systems Design and Implementation*, vol. 99, New Orleans, LA, 1999, pp. 173–186.

[195] D. Ongaro and J. K. Ousterhout, "In search of an understandable consensus algorithm," in *USENIX Annual Technical Conference*, Philadelphia, PA, 2014, pp. 305–319.

[196] M. Vukolić, "The quest for scalable blockchain fabric: Proof-of-work vs. bft replication," in *Open Problems in Network Security: IFIP WG 11.4 International Workshop*, Zurich, Switzerland, 2015, pp. 112–125.

[197] D. D. F. Maesa, P. Mori, and L. Ricci, "Blockchain based access control," in *IFIP International Conference on Distributed Applications and Interoperable Systems*, Neuchatel, Switzerland, 2017.

[198] W. Wang, D. Niyato, P. Wang, and A. Leshem, "Decentralized caching for content delivery based on blockchain: A game theoretic perspective," in *IEEE ICC*

2018 Next Generation Networking and Internet Symposium (ICC'18 NGNI), Kansas City, MO, 2018.

[199] X. Chen, S. Chen, X. Zeng, X. Zheng, Y. Zhang, and C. Rong, "Framework for context-aware computation offloading in mobile cloud computing," *Journal of Cloud Computing*, **6**(1), 1, 2017.

[200] C. Huang, R. Lu, and K.-K. R. Choo, "Vehicular fog computing: architecture, use case, and security and forensic challenges," *IEEE Communications Magazine*, **55**(11), 105–111, 2017.

[201] R. Recabarren and B. Carbunar, "Hardening Stratum, the Bitcoin pool mining protocol," arXiv preprint arXiv:1703.06545, 2017.

[202] H. Zhang, Y. Zhang, Y. Gu, D. Niyato, and Z. Han, "A hierarchical game framework for resource management in fog computing," *IEEE Communications Magazine*, **55**(8), 52–57, 2017.

[203] Y. Zhang, N. H. Tran, D. Niyato, and Z. Han, "Multi-dimensional payment plan in fog computing with moral hazard," in *2016 IEEE International Conference on Communication Systems (ICCS)*. Washington, DC: IEEE, 2016, pp. 1–6.

[204] C. Jiang, Y. Chen, K. R. Liu, and Y. Ren, "Optimal pricing strategy for operators in cognitive femtocell networks," *IEEE Transactions on Wireless Communications*, **13**(9), 5288–5301, 2014.

[205] J.-J. Laffont, P. Rey, and J. Tirole, "Network competition: II. price discrimination," *The RAND Journal of Economics*, pp. 38–56, 1998.

[206] D. Chatzopoulos, M. Ahmadi, S. Kosta, and P. Hui, "Flopcoin: A cryptocurrency for computation offloading," *IEEE Transactions on Mobile Computing*, **17**(5), 1062–1075, 2018.

[207] H. Kopp, D. Mödinger, F. Hauck, F. Kargl, and C. Bösch, "Design of a privacy-preserving decentralized file storage with financial incentives," in *2017 IEEE European Symposium on Security and Privacy Workshops (EuroS PW)*, Paris, France, 2017, pp. 14–22.

[208] J. Backman, S. Yrjölä, K. Valtanen, and O. Mämmelä, "Blockchain network slice broker in 5g: Slice leasing in factory of the future use case," in *2017 Internet of Things Business Models, Users, and Networks*, Copenhagen, Denmark, 2017, pp. 1–8.

[209] J. Kang, R. Yu, X. Huang, et al., "Enabling localized peer-to-peer electricity trading among plug-in hybrid electric vehicles using consortium blockchains," *IEEE Transactions on Industrial Informatics*, **13**(6), 3154–3164, 2017.

[210] D. Yang, G. Xue, X. Fang, and J. Tang, "Crowdsourcing to smartphones: incentive mechanism design for mobile phone sensing," in *Proceedings of the 18th Annual International Conference on Mobile Computing and Networking*. New York: ACM, 2012, pp. 173–184.

[211] A. Chakeri and L. Jaimes, "An incentive mechanism for crowdsensing markets with multiple crowdsourcers," *IEEE Internet of Things Journal*, **5**, 708–715, 2018.

[212] A, Chakeri and L. Jaimes, "An iterative incentive mechanism design for crowd sensing using best response dynamics," in *Proceedings of IEEE ICC*, Paris, France, 2017.

[213] N. Houy, "The Bitcoin mining game," *Ledger Journal*, **1**(13), 53–68, 2016.

[214] J. Beccuti et al., "The Bitcoin mining game: On the optimality of honesty in proof-of-work consensus mechanism," *Swiss Economics Working Paper 0060*, 2017.

[215] A. Kiayias, E. Koutsoupias, M. Kyropoulou, and Y. Tselekounis, "Blockchain mining games," in *Proceedings of the ACM Conference on Economics and Computation (EC)*, Maastricht, Netherlands, 2016.

[216] Y. Lewenberg, Y. Bachrach, Y. Sompolinsky, A. Zohar, and J. S. Rosenschein, "Bitcoin mining pools: A cooperative game theoretic analysis," in *Proceedings of the ACM AAMAS*, Istanbul, Turkey, 2015.

[217] B. A. Fisch, R. Pass, and A. Shelat, "Socially optimal mining pools," arXiv preprint arXiv:1703.03846, 2017.

[218] S. Kim, "Group bargaining based bitcoin mining scheme using incentive payment process," *Transactions on Emerging Telecommunications Technologies*, **27**(11), 1486–1495, 2016.

[219] L. Luu, R. Saha, I. Parameshwaran, P. Saxena, and A. Hobor, "On power splitting games in distributed computation: The case of Bitcoin pooled mining," in *Proceedings of IEEE CSF*, Verona, Italy, 2015.

[220] Z. Xiong, Y. Zhang, D. Niyato, P. Wang, and Z. Han, "When mobile blockchain meets edge computing," *IEEE Communications Magazine*, **56**(8), 33–39, 2018.

[221] Z. Xiong, S. Feng, D. Niyato, P. Wang, and Z. Han, "Optimal pricing-based edge computing resource management in mobile blockchain," in *Proceedings of IEEE ICC*, Kansas City, MO, 2018.

[222] N. C. Luong, Z. Xiong, P. Wang, and D. Niyato, "Optimal auction for edge computing resource management in mobile blockchain networks: A deep learning approach," in *Proceedings of IEEE ICC*, Kansas City, MO, 2018.

[223] Y. Jiao, P. Wang, D. Niyato, and Z. Xiong, "Social welfare maximization auction in edge computing resource allocation for mobile blockchain," in *Proceedings of IEEE ICC*, Kansas City, MO, 2018.

[224] D. K. Tosh, S. Shetty, X. Liang, et al., "Security implications of blockchain cloud with analysis of block withholding attack," in *Proceedings of IEEE/ACM CCGrid*, 2017, pp. 458–467.

[225] N. Wang, B. Varghese, M. Matthaiou, and D. S. Nikolopoulos, "ENORM: A framework for edge node resource management," *IEEE Transactions on Services Computing*, **13**(6), 1086–1099, 2020.

[226] "Orphan probablity approximation," https://gist.github.com/gavinandres\en/5044482.

[227] E. Senmarti Robla, "Analysis of reward strategy and transaction selection in bitcoin block generation," Ph.D. dissertation, University of Washington, 2015.

[228] Z. Han, D. Niyato, W. Saad, T. Baar, and A. Hjrungnes, *Game Theory in Wireless and Communication Networks: Theory, Models, and Applications*. Cambridge: Cambridge University Press, 2012.

[229] G. Scutari, D. P. Palomar, F. Facchinei, and J.-s. Pang, "Convex optimization, game theory, and variational inequality theory," *IEEE Signal Processing Magazine*, **27**(3), 35–49, 2010.

[230] K. Suankaewmanee, D. T. Hoang, D. Niyato, S. Sawadsitang, P. Wang, and Z. Han, "Performance analysis and application of mobile blockchain," in *2018 International Conference on Computing, Networking and Communications (ICNC)*. Washington, DC: IEEE, 2018, pp. 642–646.

[231] "Docker," www.docker.com/community-edition.

[232] "Go-ethereum," https://ethereum.github.io/go-ethereum/.

[233] C. Jiang, Y. Chen, Q. Wang, and K. R. Liu, "Data-driven auction mechanism design in IaaS cloud computing," *IEEE Transactions on Services Computing*, early access, 2018.

[234] V. Krishna, *Auction Theory* (2nd ed.). Cambridge, MA: Academic Press, 2009.

[235] R. Wilson, "Auctions of shares," *Quarterly Journal of Economics*, **93**, 675–698, 1979.

[236] L. Ausubel and P. Cramton, "Demand reduction and inefficiency in multi-unit auctions," University of Maryland, Tech. Rep., 1998.

[237] C. Maxwell, "Auctioning divisible commodities: A study of price determination," Harvard University, Tech. Rep., 1983.

[238] K. Back and J. F. Zender, "Auctions of divisible goods: On the rationale for the treasury experiment," *Review of Financial Studies*, **6**, 733–764, 1993.

[239] J. J. D. Wang and J. F. Zender, "Auctioning divisible goods," *Economic Theory*, **19**, 673–705, 2002.

[240] A. Hortacsu, "Mechanism choice and strategic bidding in divisible good auctions: an empirical analysis of the turkish treasury auction market," Stanford University, Tech. Rep., 2000.

[241] K. J. Sunnevag, "Auction design for the allocation of emission permits," Working paper, Tech. Rep., 2001.

[242] G. Federico and D. Rahman, "Bidding in an electricity pay-as-bid auction," *Journal of Regulatory Economics*, **24**, 175–211, 2003.

[243] R. Johari and J. N. Tsitsiklis, "Efficiency loss in a network resource allocation game," *Mathematics of Operations Research*, **29**(3), 407–435, August 2004.

[244] S. Yang and B. Hajek, "An efficient mechanism for allocation of a divisible good," UIUC submitted to: Math Operation Research, Tech. Rep., 2005.

[245] S. Sanghavi and B. Hajek, "Optimal allocation of a divisible good to strategic buyers," UIUC, Tech. Rep., 2004.

[246] R. Maheswaran and T. Basar, "Nash equilibrium and decentralized negotiation in auctioning divisible resources," *Group Decision and Negotiation*, **12**(5), 361–395, 2003.

[247] R. T. Maheswaran and T. Basar, "Coalition formation in proportionally fair divisible auctions," *Autonomous Agents and Multi-Agent Systems*, pp. 25–32, 2003.

[248] R. T. Maheswaran and T. Basar, "Decentralized network resource allocation as a repeated noncooperative market game," in *Proceedings of the 40th IEEE Conference on Decision and Control*, 2001, pp. 4565–4570.

[249] P. Milgrom, *Putting Auction Theory to Work*. Cambridge: Cambridge University Press, 2004.

[250] D. Friedman, D. P. Friedman, and J. Rust, *The Double Auction Market: Institutions, Theories, and Evidence*. Boulder, CO: Westview Press, 1993.

[251] Y. Guo and C. Liang, "Blockchain application and outlook in the banking industry," *Financial Innovation*, **2**(1), 24, 2016.

[252] K. Christidis and M. Devetsikiotis, "Blockchains and smart contracts for the internet of things," *IEEE Access*, **4**, 2292–2303, 2016.

[253] D. Chatzopoulos, M. Ahmadi, S. Kosta, and P. Hui, "Flopcoin: A cryptocurrency for computation offloading," *IEEE Transactions on Mobile Computing*, **PP**(99), 1–1, 2017.

[254] [GreatWaves:1], "Blockchain for enterprise applications," Tractica, Tech. Rep., 2016. [Online] Available: www.tractica.com/research/blockchain-for-enterprise-applications/.

[255] H. Shafagh, L. Burkhalter, A. Hithnawi, and S. Duquennoy, "Towards blockchain-based auditable storage and sharing of IoT data," in *Proceedings of the 2017 on Cloud Computing Security Workshop*. New York: ACM, 2017, pp. 45–50.

[256] J. Kang, R. Yu, X. Huang, et al., "Enabling localized peer-to-peer electricity trading among plug-in hybrid electric vehicles using consortium blockchains," *IEEE Transactions on Industrial Informatics*, **13**(6), 3154–3164, 2017.

[257] G. Zyskind, et al., "Decentralizing privacy: Using blockchain to protect personal data," in *Proceedings of Security and Privacy Workshops (SPW), 2015 IEEE*. Washington, DC: IEEE, 2015, pp. 180–184.

[258] Z. Xiong, Y. Zhang, D. Niyato, P. Wang, and Z. Han, "When mobile blockchain meets edge computing," *IEEE Communications Magazine*, **56**(8), 33–39, 2018.

[259] X. Zhang, Z. Huang, C. Wu, Z. Li, and F. C. Lau, "Online auctions in iaas clouds: Welfare and profit maximization with server costs," *IEEE/ACM Transactions on Networking*, **25**(2), 1034–1047, 2017.

[260] A. Kiayias, E. Koutsoupias, M. Kyropoulou, and Y. Tselekounis, "Blockchain mining games," in *Proceedings of the 2016 ACM Conference on Economics and Computation*, ser. EC '16. New York: ACM, 2016, pp. 365–382. [Online] Available: http://doi.acm.org/10.1145/2940716.2940773

[261] C. Catalini and J. S. Gans, "Some simple economics of the blockchain," National Bureau of Economic Research, Tech. Rep., 2016.

[262] Y. Jiao, P. Wang, D. Niyato, and Z. Xiong, "Social welfare maximization auction in edge computing resource allocation for mobile blockchain," in *IEEE ICC*

2018 Next Generation Networking and Internet Symposium (ICC'18 NGNI), Kansas City, USA, May 2018.

[263] H. Kopp, D. Mödinger, F. Hauck, F. Kargl, and C. Bösch, "Design of a privacy-preserving decentralized file storage with financial incentives," in *Proceedings of IEEE European Symposium on Security and Privacy Workshops (EuroS&PW), 2017.* Washington, DC: IEEE, 2017, pp. 14–22.

[264] J. Backman, S. Yrjölä, K. Valtanen, and O. Mämmelä, "Blockchain network slice broker in 5g: Slice leasing in factory of the future use case," in *Proceedings of Internet of Things Business Models, Users, and Networks,* Nov. 2017, pp. 1–8.

[265] Y. Lewenberg, Y. Bachrach, Y. Sompolinsky, A. Zohar, and J. S. Rosenschein, "Bitcoin mining pools: A cooperative game theoretic analysis," in *Proceedings of the 2015 International Conference on Autonomous Agents and Multiagent Systems,* ser. AAMAS '15, 2015, pp. 919–927. [Online] Available: http://dl.acm.org/citation.cfm?id=2772879.2773270.

[266] Y. Zhang, L. Liu, Y. Gu, et al., "Offloading in software defined network at edge with information asymmetry: A contract theoretical approach," *Journal of Signal Processing Systems,* vol. 83, no. 2, pp. 241–253, May 2016. [Online]. Available: https://doi.org/10.1007/s11265-015-1038-9

[267] D. Yang, G. Xue, X. Fang, and J. Tang, "Incentive mechanisms for crowdsensing: Crowdsourcing with smartphones," *IEEE/ACM Transactions on Networking,* 2(3), 1732–1744, 2016.

[268] H. Jin, L. Su, D. Chen, K. Nahrstedt, and J. Xu, "Quality of information aware incentive mechanisms for mobile crowd sensing systems," in *Proceedings of the 16th ACM International Symposium on Mobile Ad Hoc Networking and Computing,* ser. MobiHoc '15. New York: ACM, 2015, pp. 167–176. [Online] Available: http://doi.acm.org/10.1145/2746285.2746310.

[269] L. Mashayekhy, M. M. Nejad, and D. Grosu, "Physical machine resource management in clouds: A mechanism design approach," *IEEE Transactions on Cloud Computing,* 3(3), 247–260, 2015.

[270] A. Kiani and N. Ansari, "Toward hierarchical mobile edge computing: An auction-based profit maximization approach," *IEEE Internet of Things Journal,* 4(6), 2082–2091, 2017.

[271] Z. Zheng, F. Wu, and G. Chen, "A strategy-proof combinatorial heterogeneous channel auction framework in noncooperative wireless networks," *IEEE Transactions on Mobile Computing,* 14(6), 1123–1137, 2015.

[272] M. Salek and D. Kempe, "Auctions for share-averse bidders," *Internet and Network Economics,* pp. 609–620, 2008.

[273] P. Jehiel and B. Moldovanu, "Efficient design with interdependent valuations," *Econometrica,* 69(5), 2001. [Online] Available: http://dx.doi.org/10.1111/1468-0262.00240

[274] D. Zhao, X.-Y. Li, and H. Ma, "How to crowdsource tasks truthfully without sacrificing utility: Online incentive mechanisms with budget constraint," in *Proceedings of IEEE Conference on Computer Communications (Infocom).* Washington, DC: IEEE, 2014.

[275] N. C. Luong, D. Niyato, P. Wang, and Z. Xiong, "Optimal auction for edge computing resource management in mobile blockchain networks: A deep learning approach," in *Proceedings of IEEE International Conference on Communications (ICC)*, May 2018.

[276] N. Nisan, T. Roughgarden, E. Tardos, and V. V. Vazirani, *Algorithmic Game Theory*. Cambridge: Cambridge University Press Cambridge, 2007.

[277] A. Narayanan, J. Bonneau, E. Felten, A. Miller, and S. Goldfeder, *Bitcoin and Cryptocurrency Technologies: A Comprehensive Introduction*. Princeton: Princeton University Press, 2016.

[278] N. Z. Aitzhan and D. Svetinovic, "Security and privacy in decentralized energy trading through multi-signatures, blockchain and anonymous messaging streams," *IEEE Transactions on Dependable and Secure Computing*, **15**(5), 840–852, 2018.

[279] M. Li, J. Weng, A. Yang, W. Lu, et al., "CrowdBC: A blockchain-based decentralized framework for crowdsourcing," *IEEE Transactions on Distributed and Parallel Systems*, pp. 1–1, 2018.

[280] R. B. Myerson, "Optimal auction design," *Mathematics of Operations Research*, **6**(1), 58–73, 1981.

[281] J. C. Lagarias and A. M. Odlyzko, "Solving low-density subset sum problems," *Journal of the ACM (JACM)*, **32**(1), 229–246, 1985.

[282] L. Lovász, "Submodular functions and convexity," in *Mathematical Programming The State of the Art*. Berlin/Heidelberg: Springer, 1983, pp. 235–257.

[283] J. Lee, V. S. Mirrokni, V. Nagarajan, and M. Sviridenko, "Non-monotone submodular maximization under matroid and knapsack constraints," in *Proceedings of the Forty-First Annual ACM Symposium on Theory of Computing*. New York: ACM, 2009, pp. 323–332.

[284] N. Nisan, "Algorithmic mechanism design: Through the lens of multiunit auctions," in *Handbook of Game Theory with Economic Applications*. Amsterdam: Elsevier, 2015, vol. 4, pp. 477–515.

[285] K. Suankaewmanee, D. T. Hoang, D. Niyato, et al., "Performance analysis and application of mobile blockchain," in *Proceedings of International Conference on Computing, Networking and Communications (ICNC)*, Maui, Hawaii, USA, 2018.

[286] P. Bolton and M. Dewatripont, *Contract Theory*. Cambridge, MA: MIT Press, 2005.

[287] L. Atzori, A. Iera, and G. Morabito, "The internet of things: A survey," *Computer Networks*, **54**(15), 2787–2805, 2010.

[288] I. Industries, "What is industry 4.0?" www.ibm.com/industries/industrial/industry-4-0?p1=Search&p4=43700052366136168&p5=e&cm_mmc=Search_Google-_-1S_1S-_-WW_NA-_-industrial, Oct. 2020.

[289] E. Industries, "Unlock the value of industry 4.0," www.ericsson.com/en/internet-of-things/industry4-0?gclid=CjwKCAjw7e_0BRB7EiwAlH-goLZi Xr7G3osA_J5S8nIWUpveCfwo6iA7YBYz3surpMLgT_tUxsViUxoC52IQAv D_BwE&gclsrc=aw.ds, Oct. 2020.

[290] L. A. Members, "Libra white paper," https://libra.org/en-US/white-paper/, April 2020.

[291] S. Inc., "Shiftmobility liberates vehicle data with world's first secure automotive blockchain platform," http://shiftmobility.com/press-releases/shiftmobility-liberates-vehicle-data-worlds-first-secure-automotive-blockchain-platform/, May 2018.

[292] S. Feng, W. Wang, D. Niyato, D. I. Kim, and P. Wang, "Competitive data trading in wireless-powered internet of things (iot) crowdsensing systems with blockchain," in *2018 IEEE International Conference on Communication Systems (ICCS)*. Washington, DC: IEEE, 2018, pp. 289–394.

[293] A. Asheralieva and D. Niyato, "Distributed dynamic resource management and pricing in the iot systems with blockchain-as-a-service and uav-enabled mobile edge computing," *IEEE Internet of Things Journal*, **7**(3), 1974–1993, 2020.

[294] Z. Xiong, S. Feng, W. Wang, et al., "Cloud/fog computing resource management and pricing for blockchain networks," *IEEE Internet of Things Journal*, **6**(3), 4585–4600, 2018.

[295] O. Novo, "Scalable access management in IoT using blockchain: a performance evaluation," *IEEE Internet of Things Journal*, **6**(3), 4694–4701, 2018.

[296] C. Xu, K. Wang, P. Li, et al., "Making big data open in edges: A resource-efficient blockchain-based approach," *IEEE Transactions on Parallel and Distributed Systems*, **30**(4), 870–882, 2018.

[297] Y. Zhao, J. Zhao, L. Jiang, R. Tan, and D. Niyato, "Mobile edge computing, blockchain and reputation-based crowdsourcing iot federated learning: A secure, decentralized and privacy-preserving system," arXiv preprint arXiv:1906.10893, 2019.

[298] K. Gai, Y. Wu, L. Zhu, Z. Zhang, and M. Qiu, "Differential privacy-based blockchain for industrial internet of things," *IEEE Transactions on Industrial Informatics*, **16**(6), 4156–4165, 2020.

[299] S. Popov, "The tangle," https://assets.ctfassets.net/r1dr6vzfxhev/2t4uxvsIqk0E Uau6g2sw0g/45eae33637ca92f85dd9f4a3a218e1ec/iota1_4_3.pdf, April 30, 2018.

[300] I. authors, "IoT chain," https://iotchain.io/static/wp_full_en.pdf, Nov. 2019.

[301] Atonomi, "Atonomi – the secure ledger of things," https://atonomi.io/, 2017.

[302] C. Lab, "Chain of things," https://www.chainofthings.com/, Oct. 2020.

[303] QuantumMechanic, "Proof of stake instead of proof of work," https://bitcointalk.org/index.php?topic=27787.0, June 11, 2011.

[304] V. Buterin and V. Griffith, "Casper the friendly finality gadget," https://arxiv.org/pdf/1710.09437v4.pdf, 2017.

[305] QuantumMechanic, "Proof of stake instead of proof of work," www.blockchain.com/charts/transactions-per-second?daysAverageString=7, June 11, 2011.

[306] J. Ray, "Sharding introduction r&d compendium," https://github.com/ethereum/wiki/wiki/Sharding-introduction-R&D-compendium, Oct. 17, 2018.

[307] V. Inc., "Visa inc. to announce fiscal second quarter 2019 financial results on april 24, 2019," https://usa.visa.com/about-visa/newsroom/press-releases .releaseId.16301.html, April 4, 2019.

[308] L. Luu, V. Narayanan, C. Zheng, et al., "A secure sharding protocol for open blockchains," in *Proceedings of the 2016 ACM SIGSAC Conference on Computer and Communications Security*. New York: ACM, 2016, pp. 17–30.

[309] E. Kokoris-Kogias, P. Jovanovic, L. Gasser, et al., "Omniledger: A secure, scale-out, decentralized ledger via sharding," *2018 IEEE Symposium on Security and Privacy (SP)*, pp. 583–598, 2018.

[310] V. Zamfir, "A cbc casper tutorial," https://vitalik.ca/general/2018/12/05/cbc_ casper.html, Dec. 5, 2018.

[311] E. Foundation, "Ethereum 2.0 phase 0 – the beacon chain," https://github.com/ ethereum/eth2.0-specs/blob/dev/specs/phase0/beacon-chain.md, Jan. 2021.

[312] T. Liu, J. Li, F. Shu, et al., "Incentive mechanism design for two-layer wireless edge caching networks using contract theory," *IEEE Transactions on Services Computing*, **14**(5), 1426–1438, 2021.

[313] J. Kang, Z. Xiong, D. Niyato, et al., "Towards secure blockchain-enabled internet of vehicles: Optimizing consensus management using reputation and contract theory," *IEEE Transactions on Vehicular Technology*, **68**(3), 2906–2920, 2019.

[314] J. Li, T. Liu, D. Niyato, P. Wang, J. Li, and Z. Han, "Contract-based approach for security deposit in blockchain networks with shards," in *2019 IEEE International Conference on Blockchain (Blockchain)*. Washington, DC: IEEE, 2019, pp. 75–82.

[315] Y. Zhang, L. Song, M. Pan, Z. Dawy, and Z. Han, "Non-cash auction for spectrum trading in cognitive radio networks: Contract theoretical model with joint adverse selection and moral hazard," *IEEE Journal on Selected Areas in Communications*, **35**(3), 643–653, 2017.

[316] Y. Zhang, C. Jiang, L. Song, et al., "Incentive mechanism for mobile crowd-sourcing using an optimized tournament model," *IEEE Journal on Selected Areas in Communications*, **35**(4), 880–892, 2017.

[317] E. Foundation, "Ethereum 2.0 phase 0 – deposit contract," https://github .com/ethereum/eth2.0-specs/blob/dev/specs/phase0/deposit-contract.md, Dec. 6, 2020.

[318] V. Buterin, "Highlighting a problem: stability of the equilibrium of minimum timestamp enforcement," https://ethresear.ch/t/highlighting-a-problem-stability-of-the-equilibrium-of-minimum-timestamp-enforcement/2257, June 15, 2018.

[319] E. Foundation, "Ethereum 2.0 (eth2)," https://ethereum.org/en/eth2/, Oct. 8, 2020.

[320] S. Athey, "Single crossing properties and the existence of pure strategy equilibria in games of incomplete information," *Econometrica*, **69**(4), 861–889, 2001.

[321] E. Foundation, "Get involved in eth2," https://ethereum.org/en/eth2/get-involved, 2020.

[322] Q. T. Zhong and Z. Cole, "Analyzing the effects of network latency on blockchain performance and security using the whiteblock testing platform," last accessed, vol. 29, 2019. [Online] Available: https://whiteblock.io/wp-content/uploads/2019/07/analyzing-effects-network.pdf.

[323] W. Bi, H. Yang, and M. Zheng, "An accelerated method for message propagation in blockchain networks," arXiv preprint arXiv:1809.00455, 2018.

[324] J.-J. Laffont and J. Tirole, "Using cost observation to regulate firms," *Journal of Political Economy*, **94**(3), part 1, 614–641, 1986.

[325] C. Beekhuizen, "Validated, staking on eth2: #3 – sharding consensus," https://blog.ethereum.org/2020/03/27/sharding-consensus/, 2020.

[326] M. M. Khalili, P. Naghizadeh, and M. Liu, "Designing cyber insurance policies: The role of pre-screening and security interdependence," *IEEE Transactions on Information Forensics and Security*, **13**(9), 2226–2239, 2018.

[327] D. Kinderlehrer and G. Stampacchia, *An Introduction to Variational Inequalities and their Applications*. Philadelphia, PA: SIAM, 2000.

[328] F. Facchinei and J. Pang, *Finite-Dimensional Variational Inequalities and Complementarity Problems*. New York: Springer-Verlag, 2003.

[329] S. Boyd and L. Vandenberghe, *Convex Optimization*. New York: Cambridge University Press, 2004.

[330] Z. Han, D. Niyato, W. Saad, T. Başar, and A. Hjørungnes, *Game Theory in Wireless and Communication Networks*. Cambridge: Cambridge University Press, 2011.

[331] M. V. Solodov, "Constraint qualifications," *Wiley Encyclopedia of Operations Research and Management Science*, 2010.

[332] Z. Luo, J. Pang, and D. Ralph, *Mathematical Programs with Equilibrium Constraints*. Cambridge: Cambridge University Press, 1996.

[333] F. Facchinei, H. Jiang, and L. Qi, "A smoothing method for mathematical programs with equilibrium constraints," *Mathematical Programming*, **85**(1), 107–134, May 1999.

[334] C.-L. Su, "Equilibrium problems with equilibrium constraints: stationarities, algorithms, and applications," PhD dissertation, Stanford University, Stanford, CA, Sep. 2005.

[335] S. Leyffer and T. Munson, "Solving multi-leader–common-follower games," *Optimization Methods and Software*, **25**(4), 601–623, 2010.

[336] "Crypto-currency market capitalizations," available at: https://coinmarketcap.com, 2017.

[337] Z. Li, J. Kang, R. Yu, et al., "Consortium blockchain for secure energy trading in industrial internet of things," *IEEE Transactions on Industrial Informatics*, **14**(8), 3690–3700, 2018.

[338] Z. Xiong, Y. Zhang, N. C. Luong, et al., "The best of both worlds: A general architecture for data management in blockchain-enabled internet-of-things," *IEEE Network*, **31**(1), 166–173, 2020.

[339] N. Bozic, G. Pujolle, and S. Secci, "A tutorial on blockchain and applications to secure network control-planes," in *Smart Cloud Networks & Systems (SCNS)*, Dubai, UAE, December 2016.

[340] Z. Zheng, S. Xie, H.-N. Dai, X. Chen, and H. Wang, "Blockchain challenges and opportunities: a survey," *International Journal of Web and Grid Services*, **14**(4), 352–375, 2018.

[341] "Ethereumfog," http://ethereumfog.org/.

[342] Y. Wen, W. Zhang, and H. Luo, "Energy-optimal mobile application execution: Taming resource-poor mobile devices with cloud clones," in *Proceedings IEEE INFOCOM*. Washington, DC: IEEE, 2012, pp. 2716–2720.

[343] T. Taleb, S. Dutta, A. Ksentini, M. Iqbal, and H. Flinck, "Mobile edge computing potential in making cities smarter," *IEEE Communications Magazine*, **55**(3), 38–43, 2017.

[344] Z. Zhou, J. Feng, Z. Chang, and X. Shen, "Energy-efficient edge computing service provisioning for vehicular networks: A consensus admm approach," *IEEE Transactions on Vehicular Technology*, **68**(5), 5087–5099, 2019.

[345] J. Liu, L. Li, F. Yang, et al., "Minimization of offloading delay for two-tier uav with mobile edge computing," in *2019 15th International Wireless Communications & Mobile Computing Conference (IWCMC)*. Washington, DC: IEEE, 2019, pp. 1534–1538.

[346] J. Zheng, Y. Cai, Y. Wu, and X. Shen, "Dynamic computation offloading for mobile cloud computing: A stochastic game-theoretic approach," *IEEE Transactions on Mobile Computing*, **18**(4), 771–786, 2018.

[347] J. Nie, J. Luo, Z. Xiong, D. Niyato, and P. Wang, "A stackelberg game approach toward socially-aware incentive mechanisms for mobile crowdsensing," *IEEE Transactions on Wireless Communications*, **18**(1), 724–738, 2018.

[348] X. Zhang, L. Guo, M. Li, and Y. Fang, "Motivating human-enabled mobile participation for data offloading," *IEEE Transactions on Mobile Computing*, **17**(7), 1624–1637, 2018.

[349] Z. Hong, H. Huang, S. Guo, W. Chen, and Z. Zheng, "QoS-aware cooperative computation offloading for robot swarms in cloud robotics," *IEEE Transactions on Vehicular Technology*, early access, 2019.

[350] W. Chen, B. Liu, H. Huang, S. Guo, and Z. Zheng, "When UAV swarm meets edge–cloud computing: The QoS perspective," *IEEE Network*, **33**(2), 36–43, 2019.

[351] Z. Xiong, S. Feng, D. Niyato, P. Wang, and Z. Han, "Optimal pricing-based edge computing resource management in mobile blockchain," in *2018 IEEE International Conference on Communications (ICC)*. Washington, DC: IEEE, 2018, pp. 1–6.

[352] Y. Jiao, P. Wang, D. Niyato, and Z. Xiong, "Social welfare maximization auction in edge computing resource allocation for mobile blockchain," in *IEEE International Conference on Communications (ICC)*, Kansas City, MO, May 2018.

[353] N. C. Luong, Z. Xiong, P. Wang, and D. Niyato, "Optimal auction for edge computing resource management in mobile blockchain networks: A deep learning approach," in *IEEE International Conference on Communications (ICC)*, Kansas City, MO, May 2018.

[354] H. Yao, T. Mai, J. Wang, Z. Ji, C. Jiang, and Y. Qian, "Resource trading in blockchain-based industrial internet of things," *IEEE Transactions on Industrial Informatics*, early access, 2019.

[355] Z. Li, Z. Yang, S. Xie, W. Chen, and K. Liu, "Credit-based payments for fast computing resource trading in edge-assisted internet of things," *IEEE Internet of Things Journal*, early access, 2019.

[356] Z. Li, Z. Yang, and S. Xie, "Computing resource trading for edge–cloud-assisted internet of things," *IEEE Transactions on Industrial Informatics*, early access, 2019.

[357] Z. Xiong, Y. Zhang, D. Niyato, et al., "Deep reinforcement learning for mobile 5G and beyond: Fundamentals, applications, and challenges," *IEEE Vehicular Technology Magazine*, **14**(2), 44–52, 2019.

[358] C. Qiu, F. R. Yu, H. Yao, C. Jiang, F. Xu, and C. Zhao, "Blockchain-based software-defined industrial internet of things: A dueling deep q-learning approach," *IEEE Internet of Things Journal*, **6**(3), 4627–4639, 2019.

[359] M. Liu, F. R. Yu, Y. Teng, V. C. Leung, and M. Song, "Computation offloading and content caching in wireless blockchain networks with mobile edge computing," *IEEE Transactions on Vehicular Technology*, **76**(11), 11 008–11 021, 2018.

[360] H. Zhang, Y. Xiao, S. Bu, et al., "Distributed resource allocation for data center networks: A hierarchical game approach," *IEEE Transactions on Cloud Computing*, early acess, 2018.

[361] H. Zhang, Y. Xiao, L. X. Cai, et al., "A multi-leader multi-follower stackelberg game for resource management in lte unlicensed," *IEEE Transactions on Wireless Communications*, **16**(1), 348–361, 2017.

[362] Z. Xiong, S. Feng, D. Niyato, et al., "Joint sponsored and edge caching content service market: A game-theoretic approach," *IEEE Transactions on Wireless Communications*, **18**(2), 1166–1181, 2019.

[363] Z. Zheng, L. Song, Z. Han, G. Y. Li, and H. V. Poor, "Game theory for big data processing: Multi-leader multi-follower game-based ADMM," *IEEE Transactions on Signal Processing*, early access, 2018.

[364] Z. Zheng, L. Song, Z. Han, G. Y. Li, and H. V. Poor, "Game theoretic approaches to massive data processing in wireless networks," *IEEE Wireless Communications*, **25**(1), 98–104, 2018.

[365] N. Raveendran, H. Zhang, D. Niyato, et al., "VLC and D2D heterogeneous network optimization: A reinforcement learning approach based on equilibrium problems with equilibrium constraints," *IEEE Transactions on Wireless Communications*, **18**(2), early access, 2019.

[366] N. Raveendran, H. Zhang, Z. Zheng, L. Song, and Z. Han, "Large-scale fog computing optimization using equilibrium problem with equilibrium constraints,"

in *IEEE Global Communications Conference (Globecom)*. Singapore: IEEE, December, 2017.

[367] M. Hong, Z.-Q. Luo, and M. Razaviyayn, "Convergence analysis of alternating direction method of multipliers for a family of nonconvex problems," *SIAM Journal on Optimization*, **26**(1), 337–364, 2016.

[368] H. Yao, X. Yuan, P. Zhang, et al., "Machine learning aided load balance routing scheme considering queue utilization," *IEEE Transactions on Vehicular Technology*, early access, 2019.

[369] V. Buterin, "Discouragement attacks," *ETH Research*, 2018.

[370] K. Nayak, S. Kumar, A. Miller, and E. Shi, "Stubborn mining: Generalizing selfish mining and combining with an eclipse attack," in *IEEE European Symposium on Security and Privacy (EuroS&P)*, Saarbrücken, Germany, March 2016.

[371] M. Carlsten, "The impact of transaction fees on bitcoin mining strategies," PhD dissertation, Princeton University, 2016.

[372] A. Sapirshtein, Y. Sompolinsky, and A. Zohar, "Optimal selfish mining strategies in bitcoin," in *International Conference on Financial Cryptography and Data Security*. Berlin/Heidelberg: Springer, 2016, pp. 515–532.

[373] A. Gervais, G. O. Karame, K. Wüst, V. Glykantzis, H. Ritzdorf, and S. Capkun, "On the security and performance of proof of work blockchains," in *Proceedings of the 2016 ACM SIGSAC Conference on Computer and Communications Security*, 2016, pp. 3–16.

[374] J. Göbel, H. P. Keeler, A. E. Krzesinski, and P. G. Taylor, "Bitcoin blockchain dynamics: The selfish-mine strategy in the presence of propagation delay," *Performance Evaluation*, **104**, 23–41, 2016.

[375] I. Eyal, "The miner's dilemma," in *IEEE Symposium on Security and Privacy (SP)*, San Jose, CA, USA, May 2015.

[376] S. George, "Miner extractable value (MEV)," https://coinmarketcap.com/alexandria/glossary/miner-extractable-value-mev, last accessed: May, 2022.

[377] P. Daian, S. Goldfeder, T. Kell, et al., "Flash boys 2.0: Frontrunning in decentralized exchanges, miner extractable value, and consensus instability," in *IEEE Symposium on Security and Privacy (SP), San Francisco, CA*, May 2020, pp. 910–927.

[378] C. Noyes, "MEV and me," https://research.paradigm.xyz/MEV, last Accessed: May, 2022.

[379] G. K. Dan Robinson, "Ethereum is a dark forest," www.paradigm.xyz/2020/08/ethereum-is-a-dark-forest, last accessed: May, 2022.

[380] wackerow, "Maximal extractable value," https://ethereum.org/en/developers/docs/mev/, last accessed: June, 2022.

[381] Flashbots, "MEV explorer," https://explore.flashbots.net/, last accessed: June, 2022.

[382] A. Juels, L. Breidenbach, and F. Tramer, "Fair sequencing services: Enabling a provably fair DeFi ecosystem," *Chainlink Blog*, Sept. 2020.

[383] G. Angeris, A. Evans, and T. Chitra, "A note on bundle profit maximization," Stanford University, June 2021.

[384] M. Moosavi and J. Clark, "Lissy: Experimenting with on-chain order books," arXiv Cryptography and Security (cs.CR), pp. 7–8, Jan. 2021.

[385] L. Zhou, K. Qin, and A. Gervais, "A2MM: Mitigating Frontrunning, Transaction Reordering and Consensus Instability in Decentralized Exchanges," arXiv preprint arXiv:2106.07371, Jun. 2021.

Index

Printed in the United States
by Baker & Taylor Publisher Services

Printed in the United States
by Baker & Taylor Publisher Services